ROUTLEDGE LIBRARY EDITIONS:
ECONOMICS AND SOCIETY

Volume 10

THE ECONOMICS OF THE AUSTRALIAN SERVICE SECTOR

THE ECONOMICS OF THE AUSTRALIAN SERVICE SECTOR

Edited by
K. A. TUCKER

Routledge
Taylor & Francis Group
LONDON AND NEW YORK

First published in 1977 by Croom Helm Ltd.

This edition first published in 2026
by Routledge
4 Park Square, Milton Park, Abingdon, Oxon OX14 4RN

and by Routledge
605 Third Avenue, New York, NY 10158

Routledge is an imprint of the Taylor & Francis Group, an informa business

British Library Cataloguing in Publication Data
A catalogue record for this book is available from the British Library

ISBN: 978-1-032-97576-4 (Set)
ISBN: 978-1-041-15488-4 (Volume 10) (hbk)
ISBN: 978-1-041-15497-6 (Volume 10) (pbk)
ISBN: 978-1-003-67971-4 (Volume 10) (ebk)

DOI: 10.4324/9781003679714

Publisher's Note
The publisher has gone to great lengths to ensure the quality of this reprint but points out that some imperfections in the original copies may be apparent.

Disclaimer
The publisher has made every effort to trace copyright holders and would welcome correspondence from those they have been unable to trace.

The Economics of the Australian Service Sector

Edited by K.A. TUCKER

CROOM HELM LONDON

Croom Helm Ltd, 2-10 St John's Road, London SW11

British Library Cataloguing in Publication Data

The Economics of the Australian service sector.
1. Service industries – Australia
I. Tucker, Kenneth Arthur
338.4'0994 HD9989.A/

ISBN 0 85664 354 8 cased
ISBN 0 85664 558 3 paperback

CONTENTS

PREFACE

An investigation of the economics of the service sector is rather like being involved in a lawsuit or receiving dental treatment. The magnitude of the exercise is indeterminate and the findings are unpredictable. Even so, both personal and professional experience of the dimensions of service functions in an economy are of vital importance for individual decision-making and international resource allocation.

Economic policies affecting the service sector are often imposed by default of any direct analysis; they are merely a residual that spills over from policy initiatives in agriculture, mining or manufacturing. Yet the activities that comprise the service sector are ignored or misunderstood at the risk of incurring costs that otherwise may have been avoided or of foregoing potential benefits. By overlooking a key sector in an economy, any review of the repercussions of macro-economic policy has a limited perspective. Likewise, an attempt to develop a co-ordinated competition policy at an industry or activity level is seriously jeopardised.

This collection of studies on selected service activities has two purposes. It is designed to remedy the relative scarcity of published material in this field. Previous book-length studies of the Australian economy have neglected the role of services in contributing to gross product or absorbing the workforce. Secondly, this set of studies demonstrates an emerging awareness of, and an interest in, the role and importance of various service activities within the Australian economy.

The authors show that service activities have been of crucial and growing significance in the recent development of the Australian economy. And they provide ample evidence that these functions will strongly influence structural change, economic efficiency and consumer welfare in the future.

All contributions to the book were commissioned and written between April and November 1976. Not all of the authors are economists. In view of the geographic, sociological and demographic variables that form the basis of many of the relationships under investigation in service activities, this multi-disciplinary approach is both pertinent and welcome.

No single overriding objective has been adopted in selecting topics to be included or in deciding on methods of analysis. In most cases, data constraints determined what has been feasible, while the limitations of current theoretical constructs have often directed what was desirable.

Some obvious topics such as housing services, crime control and defence, public administration, social welfare services and recreation are not covered. This is attributable to an overall space limitation and either the existence of a substantial literature on the subject or the fact that potential contributors could not be found or were too busy. A list of further reading in some of these omitted areas has been prepared with the assistance of Owen Donald, Max Neutze, Pat Weller and Glenn Withers. It contains major overseas studies and recent publications on Australian conditions.

The sectional breakdown employed in grouping the chapters is due to convenience of presentation and is not based on any classification that has inscrutable logic or inviolate principles. It has been suggested in the opening chapter that preconceived distinctions may be of more harm than help. In any case, many readers will not wish to read the contributions in the given order because of their differing preferences.

Some of the chapters have implications for issues described in other parts of the book. This degree of interconnection has not, however, been fully explored by the contributors. Their chapters were written as independent studies. But the interested and industrious reader should be persuaded to consider these aspects. For example, in which ways do communications services facilitate the improved distribution of performing arts services? To what extent does advertising expenditure determine the profitability of retail activities? How does the provision of environmental services affect the demand for health services? Further research on these and similar questions is invited. The contributors' services will be adequately rewarded if this offer is accepted.

K.A. Tucker
1 December 1976

CONTRIBUTORS

R. Bonney, Research Officer, NSW Bureau of Crime Statistics and Research.

J.S. Deeble, Department of Health.

S.F. Harris, Professor of Resource Economics, Centre for Resource and Environmental Studies, Australian National University.

R.G. Hawkins, Research Department, Reserve Bank of Australia.

W. Hickson, Department of Environment, Housing and Community Development.

R. Homel, Lecturer in Statistics, Macquarie University.

F.L. Jones, Professor of Sociology, Research School of Social Sciences, Australian National University.

D. McL. Lamberton, Professor of Economics, University of Queensland.

M.M. Metwally, Reader in Economics, University of Queensland.

P. McDonnell, Research Fellow in Sociology, Research School of Social Sciences, Australian National University.

I.W. McLean, Lecturer in Economics, University of Adelaide.

P.J. Rimmer, Senior Fellow in Human Geography, Research School of Pacific Studies, Australian National University.

D.K. Round, Senior Lecturer in Economics, University of Adelaide.

D.J.S. Rutledge, Senior Lecturer in Economics, Macquarie University.

R.B. Scotton, Senior Research Fellow, Institute of Applied Economic and Social Research, University of Melbourne.

C.D. Throsby, Professor of Economics, Macquarie University.

C.A. Tisdell, Professor of Economics, University of Newcastle.

K.A. Tucker, Fellow in Economic History, Research School of Social Sciences, Australian National University.

A. Ulph, Research Fellow, Centre for Resource and Environmental Studies, Australian National University.

T. Vinson, Professor of Behavioural Science, University of Newcastle.

G.A. Withers, Research Fellow in Economics, Research School of Social Sciences, Australian National University.

T. Williams, Senior Research Fellow in Sociology, Research School of Social Sciences, Australian National University.

PART ONE: DETERMINANTS OF SERVICE ACTIVITIES

The need for and the use of service functions within an economy is influenced by a myriad of circumstances. Economists, since the time of Adam Smith, have debated the role of services in contributing to economic growth and social welfare. They have also attempted to measure the share of output contributed by the labour force engaged in different classes of activity and have explored the demand and supply forces determining these different shares. Many of these determinants include sociological, spatial and demographic variables and are therefore closely related to environmental conditions and social relationships.

The first chapter, by the editor, provides some historical perspective and presents an overview of the features of the Australian service sector. Some guidance is also given to previous studies of service activities in Australia and the major overseas findings.

Jones, McDonnell and Williams (chapter 2) consider the respective roles of education services and other social background conditions in advancing occupational status or in augmenting economic rewards for individuals over their schooling and employment life-time.

After considering the nature of environmental problems and their classification, Harris and Ulph (chapter 3) present information on the supply costs of environmental services and the factors making up the demand for improved environmental amenity. They conclude with suggestions for institutional arrangements and other techniques designed to manage the availability and use of these services. Hickson, in an addendum, shows how the provision of government assistance for sewerage services may be evaluated for its effects.

1 THE NATURE AND SIZE OF THE SERVICE SECTOR

K.A. Tucker

Historical Origins and Policy Perspectives

A distinction is often made between the goods and service sectors of the economy.[1] The term 'goods' is usually applied to extractive, agricultural and manufacturing activities while the term 'service' denotes the remaining activities where output is considered to be less tangible. This distinction has identifiable historical precedents. It also continues to carry with it the misleading parallel dichotomy of 'productive' and 'unproductive' labour.

Over two hundred years ago Adam Smith elaborated on the nature of 'unproductive' labour – without falling into an equally untenable class distinction based on social order – by saying that:

> The labour of a menial servant. . .adds to the value of nothing. . . The labour of some of the most respectable orders in the society is, like that of menial servants, unproductive of any value, and does not fix or realize itself in any permanent subject, or vendible commodity, which endures after that labour is past. . . Their service how honourable, how useful, or how necessary soever, produces nothing for which an equal quantity of service can afterwards be procured. . . In the same class must be ranked. . . Churchmen, lawyers, physicians, men of letters of all kinds; players, buffoons, musicians, opera-singers, opera-dancers etc.[2]

The above quotation contains three definitions of unproductive labour. Labour engaged in the provision of services may be (i) unproductive of *any* value, (ii) unproductive of *surplus* value, and (iii) engaged in providing services which are incapable of realising themselves in any *permanent subject.* Definition (i) is untenable even by reference to Adam Smith's own theory of value. He had argued that diamonds, although 'useless', had a high value in exchange. It is also conceptually difficult to defend a view of effort being expended without depending upon some economic or social *relationship* that generates costs and benefits. Definitions (ii) and (iii) both imply that services make no contribution to economic growth. In the former case there is no *behavioural* link between services supplied and the accumulation of capital, while in the latter case some services are not *technically* capable of being accumulated.

The above distinctions are capable of being misunderstood and misconstrued. This is often evident in pronouncements about priorities for economic policy and in commentary on the worth of employment functions in society. Indeed, Smith could not have foreseen the subsequent abuse made of these distinctions or the changing economic circumstances that make them less valid. Studies of economic growth acknowledge the role of service inputs like education[3] and R & D expenditure. These services augment the quality of labour or capital inputs and, in turn – in processes of production and consumption – generate corporate profit or personal savings. Similarly, the feasibility of recording and reproducing the output of some services through the media and by information transmission gives some forms of final consumption a tangible quality. Furthermore, recent interest in the nature of complex feedback relationships that Smith virtually ignored by reason of definition (i) make it possible to trace the dynamic effects of service output for both intermediate services and final services. Both components of service output determine subsequent production and consumption decisions. For example, doctors providing health services[4] may contribute to improved industrial output. This production process generates incomes in several other activities which constitute alternative levels of saving or consumption that include the demand for both current and future goods and services. If Adam Smith was merely alluding to the difficulty of measuring sèrvice output and its effects, then any criticism of the distinctions he made cannot be too harsh. These problems of quantifying the private and public benefits and costs of services, and differences in productivity among services, continue to be almost intractable until a more comprehensive dynamic and distributional framework can be developed.

John Stuart Mill distinguished several categories of service labour but also maintained the 'unproductive'/'productive' division. He nominated the productive sectors as extractive, (materials) and immediate means of production (implements and tools); and those for the protection of industry, the distribution of goods and the educational and innovative functions. By contrast,

> All labour is, in the language of political economy, unproductive, which ends in immediate employment, without any increase of the accumulated stock of permanent means of enjoyment.[5]

Mill argued that a service that terminates in a permanent benefit was unproductive. But he recognised that 'though society grows no richer by unproductive labour, the individual may'.

Despite this acceptance of an adjusted distribution of benefits, Mill retained the notion of a tangible consequence to maintain his distinction. This is evident from the following example.

> When a tailor makes a coat and sells it, there is a transfer of the price from the customer to the tailor, and a coat besides which did not previously exist; but what is gained by an actor is a mere transfer from the spectator's funds to his, leaving no article of wealth for the spectator's indemnification. Thus the community collectively gains nothing by the actor's labour.[6]

To perturb the apparent validity of the distinction it is only necessary to ask two questions: 'How did the tailor learn to make the coat? and 'Why did the spectator require to attend the performance?' The answers illustrate the interdependence of production and consumption activities and the integral role of intermediate and final services. It is possibly for these reasons that Alfred Marshall defined goods as representing 'all desirable things, or things that satisfy human wants'.[7] He also described many categories of goods including free goods, transferable goods, collective goods and material goods. Marshall, like Smith and Mill, argued that, 'Services and other goods, which pass out of existence in the same instant that they come into it are, of course, not part of the stock of wealth'.[8] But he sought to break with the traditional use of the notion of 'productive' labour and in a telling footnote pointed out that:

> The attempt to draw a hard and fast line of distinction where there is no real discontinuity in nature has often done more mischief, but has perhaps never led to more quaint results, than in the rigid definitions which have been sometimes given to this term Productive. Some of them for instance lead to the conclusion that a singer in an opera is unproductive, that the printer of the tickets of admission to the opera is productive; while the usher who shows people to their places is unproductive unless he happens to sell programmes, and then he is productive.[9]

Given that Marshall noticed how such absurdities arise in any classification, it is perhaps surprising that he continued to refer to the impotence of services in being able to add to the stock of wealth. Intermediate services to industrial processes clearly enable capital assets to be invented, accumulated and maintained. Also, the consumption and savings patterns of those providing final services such as entertainment or recreation may aid this process directly by their investment choice or indirectly by augmenting the effectiveness of the labour force or by reducing some types of social cost.

Yet despite the warnings implicit in the distinctions made by these early writers on political economy, many economists, administrators and politicians continue to formulate policy perspectives based on dubious assumptions. For example, the mechanism for economic growth is invariably related to aggregate relationships between savings, investment and fixed capital accumulation. Also fiscal and monetary policies are often based on an assumption that service sector productivity – usually naively measured by output per person employed – is lower for all service activities than for agriculture, mining or manufacturing. And it is only recently that attention has turned to the role of selected service inputs – primarily education – as a possible explanation for differences in growth rates.[10]

Alternative Theories of the Growth of Services

This section is *not* intended to be a summary of the now vast literature on determinants of the growth of the service sector and on differences in its size among countries. It merely provides guidance to the major sources. The key studies should be read in the context of the historical, institutional, and environmental conditions to which they apply. It is convenient to group these findings under three main headings: (a) theories explaining structural change, (b) policies to improve productivity, and (c) problems of measurement.

The earlier discussion of historical precedents and policy prejudices shows how definitional constructs have often obscured two important aspects of the analysis of the service sector: the nature of *interdependence* among economic activities and the likelihood of incorrect interpretation based on a high level of *aggregation.* Studies of the nature and size of the service sector in the twentieth century generally focus, with varying emphasis, on these two features. In other words, the essential framework of analysis has been (a) to explore and test relationships between those variables measuring the service sector and its supposed determinants, and (b) to establish whether or not these relationships exist with varying strength and effects for different service activities.

Theories Explaining Structural Change

Two economists with close Australasian associations, Allen G.B. Fisher and Colin Clark, are attributed with having first explored the possible relationships between income growth and structural change. Their initial work in the 1930s developed into debate, in the 1940s and 1950s, about growth and development within a wider context, including the experience of less-developed countries.[11]

The Fisher-Clark hypothesis of structural change is that a higher level of (or increases in) real income per capita will be associated with a higher proportion of the work force engaged in tertiary or service sector activities. Fisher formulated an interpretation based largely on differing demand elasticities; in effect, a generalisation of Engel's law.[12] Clark argued that high income elasticity of demand for services was part of the explanation for increasing (higher) tertiary employment shares but that a typical condition of production in this sector was the difficulty of increasing labour productivity as rapidly in the production of services as in other sectors.[13]

In the 1960s, the Fisher-Clark model was refined by Baumol who stressed the distinction between the 'progressive' and 'non-progressive' sectors.[14] In the former sector, technical progress and economies of scale are characteristic of production processes and capital accumulation, with the consequence that while – with labour mobile between sectors – incomes (i.e. wage rates) are equal for the activities, the real costs of the non-progressive sector rise and it absorbs a greater share of the labour force, especially where demand is income inelastic. In this model, the intervention of government may be necessary where price or income elasticities of demand are not expressed adequately by revealed preferences or are determined by other market imperfections.

Studies by Kuznets,[15] and Chenery and Taylor[16] elaborated on the empirical content of the Fisher-Clark model by undertaking detailed time-series and cross-sectional analysis of the productivity and per capita product patterns of many countries. The most significant feature of these studies is that (a) there is some evidence to suggest a *reversal* in tendencies for productivity and labour shares between sectors and (b) there is a great *diversity* of experience for similar service activities in different countries and between activities. These findings illustrate the need to model simultaneously, as Haig[17] has done, both demand and supply determinants as interacting forces. It also appears imperative that the example of Fuchs[18] (for the US) and the suggestions of Dowie[19] (for Australia) be given greater prominence in further analysis.

Haig's study of changes in the distribution of employment between manufacturing and service industries in Australia for the period 1960-70 concluded that:

> Differences in income elasticities of demand lead to an increase of 3.3 per cent a year in the rate of growth of employment in services compared with that in manufacturing industries, while the lower productivity of service industries is responsible for a higher relative rate of change of employment in services of 1.2 per cent a year (or 1.9 per cent before allowing for the offsetting effect of price changes). Exogenous demands raise the rate of increase of employment in manufacturing relative to that of services by 1.3 per cent a year, while input-output changes also increase the relative rate of growth of employment in service industries.

The net effect of demand was therefore found to be neutral, while the major factor leading to a faster relative growth of service employment was the slower growth of productivity in services in relation to manufacturing.

This finding in many ways serves to prove the usefulness of a disaggregated approach favoured by Fuchs and Dowie. The concern of Fuchs has been to discuss a wide range of reasons for the recent shift towards service employment in the United States and to explore the implications for a continuation of this trend. The special studies of the National Bureau of Economic Research have also: (a) extensively discussed the problems of measuring output and productivity for services, and (b) provided many detailed studies of particular service activities. Dowie, after providing a broad perspective in social accounting terms, experimentally considered some input-output relationships and made a plea for a series of studies 'in carefully delimited areas such as health, education, law enforcement, entertainment, charity and so on',[20] to overcome the problems of heterogeneity and sectoral interdependence.

Policies to Improve Productivity

Recent research in the United Kingdom has, as for the United States, been similarly related to observable structural change. But the need to obtain improved productivity, and greater public sector involvement, has resulted in research findings being based more on policy options and their subsequent effects. It is also notable that policy recommendations have more often been related to simple conceptual and theoretical distinctions at an aggregate level – in the tradition of

British scholarship – than to empirical findings for various activities.

Kaldor[21] has restated the Verdoorn Law, according to which economic growth is basically dependent on the growth of manufacturing output and export-led expansion. In advanced economies, this implies the necessity of a transfer of labour from service activities to the manufacturing sector, as the share of employment in agriculture has already been reduced to a small proportion. This policy for improved overall productivity rests on three important assumptions.

First, it is implied that the rate of growth of productivity in services is significantly lower than in manufacturing activities. Secondly, it is assumed that export earnings deriving either directly or indirectly from service output are more limited in comparison with those attributed to manufacturing output. Thirdly, the interdependence between manufacturing and service activities is thought to be of little consequence. These assumptions overlook the fact that services are an extremely heterogenerous group of activities, with greatly differing capital to labour proportions. They also ignore the role of intermediate services in facilitating the export of tradable goods and underestimate the component of invisible earnings that are contributed to by the marketing abroad or domestic sale of final services.

Attempts have been made by the Cambridge economists Cripps and Tarling[22] to test 'Kaldor's Law' over the period 1950-70. In turn, Rowthorn and Kaldor[23] have exchanged views over the validity of this simple model that essentially depends on increasing returns to scale for manufacturing and the existence of disguised unemployment in both agriculture and services. The chief limitations of their differences of opinion are largely due to a failure to adequately account for the interaction between supply and demand variables in each sector, the interdependence relationship between types of service input and industrial output and the failure to test independently for the assumptions of economies of scale, technical progress and disguised unemployment in (i.e. differences in sectoral productivity) the activities making up the aggregates under discussion.

Changes in government policy on employment in the mid-1960s provided the possibility of reviewing the effects of a new employment tax on service sector productivity, employment shares and the extent of technical progress in service activities. Reddaway's[24] studies of Selective Employment Tax, in conjunction with those by George,[25] and Deakin and Seward[26] on retailing and transport, provide a wealth of evidence on selected service activities, but from a more confined perspective by comparison with that adopted by Fuchs for the US.

Two Oxford economists, Bacon and Eltis,[27] have provided a different theoretical framework for an analysis of what has been identified as 'Britain's Economic Problem'. Their approach divides the economy into two additional sectors that cross over the traditional sectoral boundaries. The 'market' sector includes goods and services sold domestically or abroad while the 'non-market' sector includes goods and services which are paid for by taxes and the growth of the money supply. They recognise that some public services are funded by government spending (e.g. education, health, and defence) while others are required to keep their charges at market rates (e.g. electricity and postal services). The mechanism leading to a slow growth of productivity for the economy operates where the share of public spending on non-market goods and services increases substantially. Wage incomes rise to reduce the share of profits, investment is discouraged due to wage-push cost increases, extra fiscal burdens are placed on the industrial sector and price controls distort the profitability of the market sector's output. The effect on employment is that the labour force is either absorbed into the non-market sector or remains structurally unemployed. Policies to improve productivity would require a reduction in public spending, a shift in the tax burden, controls on the money supply, investment incentives to industry, adjustment of the rate of exchange and a switch in public sector borrowing sources.

The debate about appropriate policies to achieve improved productivity continues, but not without encountering measurement difficulties.

Problems of Measurement

Much of the analysis of the service sector at an aggregate level has relied upon two key constructs: a social accounting system of national income, output and employment data and simple measures of labour productivity without consideration of the quantity, composition, vintage or valuation of capital goods associated with production and distribution processes. A further difficulty with any analysis is the nature of price behaviour in both factor and goods/services markets where differing features of market structure (e.g. concentration, vertical integration and diversification) may obscure the opportunity cost relationships (i.e. relative-prices) that are necessary for any reliable analysis of changing demand and supply conditions and their interaction. In addition, because goods and services have many dimensions other than price (e.g. quality, durability, reliability), some account must be taken in comparative analysis of these differences as they are reflected in output measures.

A considerable amount of research has been devoted to some of the above measurement difficulties. Hill[28] has undertaken a study of the problems of measuring real product in the empirical analysis of growth rates for different sectors and countries. Smith's[29] study focuses on the measurement and interpretation of service output changes with reference mainly to the United Kingdom.[30] Fuchs[31] and his colleagues primarily have been concerned with adjusting changes in labour and other inputs to measure 'real' factor inputs (allowing for quality and effort differences) but assuming factor prices move at the same rate for all branches of the economy. Both Smith and Dowie[32] adopt a measure of sectoral economic output change by adjusting the sector's 'real' output index by the change in its relative price.

Work on consumer demand theory has relevance to output prices. Becker[33] has developed the notion of a consumption process, analogous to a production time sequence, while Griliches[34] has explored the usefulness of 'hedonic' price indices for durable goods. Lancaster[35] has generalised these approaches to emphasise that output comprises a mix of characteristics or attributes that are capable of being identified under certain conditions to generate relationships that measure revealed preferences.

Within the Australian context, Gregory and Tearle[36] have applied the hedonic price indices framework to a study of products in the traded goods sector. By contrast, Haig and Roche[37] have offered conflicting viewpoints on the treatment of domestic product generated in banking services. And the limitations of social accounts in presenting adequate data about the costs of environmental services are illustrated by Butlin.[38]

In view of the growing emphasis on the nature of public and private sector interrelationships and the need for improved measures of the costs and benefits associated with the supply and consumption of services, some of the literature on both the economics of industrial structure and cost-benefit analysis is relevant.[39] It is undoubtedly also pertinent to attempt to develop more meaningful classifications of the nature of supply and demand conditions affecting public services. For example, the following schema (Figure 1.1) of types of public activity and methods of determining output and prices may be suitable as one framework for further empirical analysis that would underline the limitations of current measurement methods and classification devices.[40]

Figure 1.1: Types of Public Sector Service and their Supply Conditions

Process of intervention and distribution Service type and institutions	1 Government Enterprises (ownership)	2 Regulation and Protection (a) Prices/ Outputs	 (b) Factor Markets	3 Rules of Conduct	4 Cash Transfers
1. Energy services (Electricity, coal, oil, gas)	X	X			
2. Transport services (Road, rail, sea, air)	X	X			
3. Urban amenity services (Water, sewerage, pollution control, safety)	X	X			
4. Information and communication services	X	X			
5. Marketing and industrial services (Price and quality control, entry barriers)		X		X	
6. Financial and insurance services (Banking. currency and risk)	X			X	
7. Administration services (Accounting records, transactions)			X	X	
8. Health and welfare services		X			X
9. Educational services			X		X
10. Defence and crime control services	X			X	

X = *a priori* the two most prominent forms of intervention and distribution in supplying public services.

Determinants of Service Sector Activity

The determinants of service sector activity can be conventionally partitioned into supply and demand influences. Economists usually specify for the determination of supply conditions a production or cost function while on the demand side a consumption function is depicted at the household level. As both government agencies and the corporate sector also use service inputs, their requirements (i.e. demand) also can be modelled. Government expenditure functions are estimated to describe the conditions influencing the supply of services provided by public agencies.

The list of appropriate determinants would therefore include two sets of variables: those which refer to the market conditions of the factor inputs and the methods of production used and those which depict the conditions prevailing in the service output markets and the process of consumption.

The normal candidate variables have been listed by Fuchs, essentially as determinants of differential rates of growth in employment between service and other activities. They are as follows:

1. The rate of growth of per capita real income in the total economy.
2. The difference in rates of growth of technological change.
3. The differences in the factor bias of technolgical change.
4. The capital/labour ratios in the two sectors.
5. The rate of growth of the price of labour.
6. The rate of growth of the price of capital.
7. The income elasticities of demand for goods and services.
8. The potential economies of scale in goods and services.
9. The elasticity of substitution between services and goods.
10. The elasticities of substitution between capital and labour in each sector.
11. The time intensities of goods and services.
12. The initial level of hours per man in each sector and the changes in hours.

It should be noted that both demand and supply influences are combined in this listing.[41]

Further refinements could be added to this list by specifying different types of vintages of capital and different skills and quality for labour. This approach would also require alternative prices for these distinct input types. On the demand side it would be necessary to supplement the list to account for differences in sociological or demographic features such as schooling experience, family size and age structure and the employment status of consumers. Geographic variables also may be introduced to account for the spatial nature of the transaction/consumption process. In addition, the effects of fiscal and monetary policies operating through taxation schedules and access to credit arrangements are often crucial determinants of spending patterns. Finally, in many markets the presence of legislative protection or regulation to benefit some interest groups will affect both supply arrangements and demand responses.

Mix of Services

The Australian Standard Industrial Classification (ASIC) 1969, provides a starting point for any disaggregation of the service sector. The divisional breakdown of all activities is as follows:

Division A: Agriculture, Forestry, Fishing and Hunting.
Division B: Mining.
Division C: Manufacturing.
Division D: Electricity, Gas and Water.
Division E: Construction.
Division F: Wholesale and Retail Trade.
Division G: Transport and Storage.
Division H: Communication.
Division I: Finance, Insurance, Real Estate and Business Services.
Division J: Public Administration and Defence.
Division K: Community Services.
Division L: Entertainment, Recreation, Restaurants, Hotels and Personal Services.

It is usual for the service sector to be defined as incorporating Divisions D to L, while 'intermediate services' cover D, E, G and H and 'final services' F, I, J, K and L.[42] This is a necessarily arbitrary breakdown of the complex mix of services into two major components. It also will be readily noted that many services may in fact be sold to or provided for firms (i.e. intermediate inputs) at all divisions of the classification. For example, hotel and restaurant services and electricity, gas and water services may be partitioned into those demanded by firms in other activities and those required by households or government agencies.

An input-output approach to the service sector provides some indication of these complex interrelationships. By considering the types of final demand, it is also possible to show how current usage, fixed capital formation, increases in stocks and overseas supply absorb the total flow of service output. Table 1.1. shows this breakdown for the year 1968/9 at basic values (for service flows only). Table 1.2 gives similar information but by percentage composition of each service according to the basic social accounting framework. While this format gives greater emphasis to the comparative importance of intermediate and final demand for each service, it does not indicate the absorption pattern for intermediate demand alone. It is also apparent that some items are not represented as having capital expenditure outlays or export earnings. Additional information on these figures and their methods of derivation and apportionment would show this to be a simplification of the real processes under analysis.

While an input-output schema does demonstrate the inter-sectoral relationships among service and other activities, the data for any one year cannot represent the features of *changing* interaction. Ideally, several consistent input-output tables would reveal the extent to which underlying tendencies result in adaptive structural change. As a guide to this time-varying adjustment and in the absence of consecutive comparable input-output tables, it is necessary to analyse changing shares in activity and the growth rates underlying these measures.

Share of Services

Estimates of shares of services at a given date in aggregate output or input indicators are determined by differential growth rates over time. Due to the difficulties encountered in measuring both expenditure on services (i.e. output quantities at purchaser's prices) and the quantities of inputs and factor prices comprising service costs, any percentage share data must be interpreted with care and should be related to the underlying growth trends and variations.

This section provides sectoral data for gross product shares at current and constant (1968/9) prices for a ten year period, 1962/3 to 1972/3 (Tables 1.3 to 1.5). Secondly, selected indicators of sector structure and performance are given for all sectors and for wholesale distribution as at 1968/9 (Tables 1.6 and 1.7). Thirdly, data on sectoral labour force shares and composition is provided for the dates 1971 and 1976 (Tables 1.8 to 1.10). Finally, this section concludes with estimates of growth rates and their variation from trend for gross product and gross product per person employed by sectors over the period 1962/3 to 1972/3.[43]

Unfortunately, there is no adequate information available on

Table 1.1: Service Sector Flows by Intermediate and Final Demand, 1968-9 ($ million at basic values)

Supply (commodity) / Usage (industry)	Intermediate usage	Final consumption expenditure: Households	Final consumption expenditure: Government	Gross fixed capital expenditure: Private	Gross fixed capital expenditure: Public enterprises	Gross fixed capital expenditure: General government	Increase in stocks	Exports of goods and services	Total Supply (commodity basis)
36.01 Electricity	473.7	283.4							757.1
36.02 Gas	23.4	73.4					1.2		98.0
37.01 Water, sewerage and drainage	260.4	10.6	25.1						296.2
41.01 Residential buildings				1,295.4	68.0				1,363.4
41.02 Building n.e.c., construction	927.2			997.9	905.1	757.2			3,587.5
46.01 Wholesale trade	1,472.3	990.5		384.7	0.6	2.1	5.5	209.0	3,064.8
48.01 Retail trade	179.0	2,126.0		109.3					2,414.4
48.02 Motor vehicle repairs	172.5	347.6							520.1
48.03 Other repairs	125.8	76.6							202.4
51.01 Road transport	527.8	397.7		78.0	2.6	13.5	1.4	120.4	1,141.3
52.01 Railway and other transport	367.6	149.1		28.7	0.9	5.3	0.8	110.0	662.5
53.01 Water transport	231.4	86.8		15.3	0.5	2.2	0.5	246.5	583.2
54.01 Air transport	183.0	177.8		1.7	0.3	1.1	...	126.0	489.9
55.01 Communication	446.8	149.9	13.4		171.2			9.9	791.2
61.01 Banking	568.3	47.1							615.4
61.02 Finance and Life Insurance	207.4	181.6							389.0
61.03 Other insurance	211.7	121.7		0.5			...	3.4	337.4
61.04 Investment, real estate etc.	554.1	80.5		107.7				36.7	779.0
61.05 Other business services	695.4	68.0		96.6	14.9	12.4			887.3
61.06 Ownership of dwellings		2,042.1							2,042.1
71.01 Public administration	21.6	32.8	930.6					10.8	995.8
72.01 Defence			1,014.4					33.9	1,048.3
81.01 Health	17.5	618.6	379.6						1,015.7
82.01 Education, libraries, etc.	5.7	145.0	711.0						861.6
83.01 Welfare services	76.8	85.1	148.8						310.7
91.01 Entertainment	218.1	261.3	90.3					0.4	570.2
92.01 Restaurants, hotels, clubs	106.8	812.4		...			...		919.2
93.01 Personal services	41.4	204.8	0.3						246.4
99.01 Business expenses	2,786.0								2,786.0
Intermediate usage	26,429.4	15,351.0	3,337.4	4,817.9	1,340.0	1,191.7	691.1	3,699.7	56,858.2
Wages, salaries, supplements	14,029.5								14,029.5
Gross operating surplus	10,703.5								10,703.5
Commodity taxes less subsidies	117.8	1,051.5		57.1	...	–0.1	–8.5	13.3	1,231.2
Indirect taxes n.e.c.	1,109.9								1,109.9
Sales by final buyers	94.1	7.5		–116.7	–1.5	–1.4	9.0	8.9	
Complementary imports c.i.f.	376.6	69.9					0.9	0.1	447.5
Duty on complementary imports	0.1	2.7							2.8
Competing imports c.i.f.	3,658.9						–0.1	182.4	3,841.2
Duty on competing imports	338.3								338.3
Total usage	56,858.2	16,482.7	3,337.4	4,758.3	1,338.4	1,190.3	692.5	3,904.4	88,562.2

Source: *Australian National Accounts: Input-Output Tables, 1968-69 (Preliminary)* (Australian Bureau of Statistics, Canberra, 1976) Reference No. 7.9.
... denotes less than $50,000.

Table 1.2: Percentage Composition of Service Flows, 1968-9

Usage (industry) / Supplỵ (commodity)	Intermediate usage	Final consumption expenditure		Gross fixed capital expenditure			Increase in stocks	Exports of goods and services
		Households	Government	Private	Public enterprises	General government		
36.01 Electricity	62.57	37.43						
36.02 Gas	23.88	74.90					1.22	
37.01 Water, sewerage and drainage	87.94	3.58	8.47					
41.01 Residential buildings				95.01	4.99			
41.02 Buildings n.e.c., construction	25.84			27.82	25.23	21.11		
46.01 Wholesale trade	48.04	32.32		12.55	.01	.07	.18	6.82
48.01 Retail trade	7.41	88.05		4.53				
48.02 Motor vehicle repairs	33.17	66.83						
48.03 Other repairs	62.15	37.85						
51.01 Road transport	46.25	34.85		6.83	.22	1.18	.11	10.55
52.01 Railway and other transport	55.49	22.51		4.33	.14	.80	.13	16.60
53.01 Water transport	39.68	14.88		2.62	.08	.38	.08	42.27
54.01 Air transport	37.35	36.29		.35	.07	.22		25.72
55.01 Communication	56.47	18.95	1.69		21.64			1.25
61.01 Banking	92.35	7.65						
61.02 Finance and Life insurance	53.32	6.68						
61.03 Other insurance	62.74	36.07		.18				1.01
61.04 Investment, real estate etc.	71.13	10.33		13.83				4.71
61.05 Other business services	78.37	7.66		10.89	1.68	1.40		
61.06 Ownership of dwellings		100.00						
71.01 Public administration	2.17	3.29	93.45					1.08
72.01 Defence			96.77					3.23
81.01 Health	1.72	60.90	37.37					
82.01 Education, libraries, etc.	.66	16.83	82.52					
83.01 Welfare services	24.72	27.39	47.89					
91.01 Entertainment	38.25	45.83	15.84					.08
92.01 Restaurants, hotels, clubs	11.62	88.38						
93.01 Personal services	16.80	83.12	.08					
99.01 Business expenses	100.0							
Total usage	64.20	18.61	3.77	5.37	1.51	1.34	.78	4.41

Source: *Australian National Accounts: Input-Output Tables, 1968-69 (Preliminary)* (Australian Bureau of Statistics, Canberra, 1976) Reference No. 7.9.

changing output-mix, sub-activity output prices, factor input substitution, all factor prices, capital vintage or inventory turnover for all service activities. The following information therefore provides an economy-wide perspective of the relative shares of each service activity for given aggregate variables. This data cannot, in its present form, provide any explanation of changes in these shares or of the differing structural and performance features of the range of service activities.

Gross Product Shares, 1962/3 to 1972/3

Table 1.3, showing gross product shares at current and constant (1968/9) prices for *all sectors,* indicates that all service sector activities except wholesale and retail trade, and electricity, gas and water, increased their shares in current prices over the period. The same was true for mining, while agriculture and manufacturing made a reduced contribution. In constant prices, the shift between agricultural and mining activities dominated the changing share pattern, but some service activities (i.e. electricity, gas and water, transport and storage, communication, finance and business services and entertainment and personal services) increased their shares in real terms.

A more aggregated classification, as shown in Table 1.4, by *primary secondary and tertiary groups* (with services broken into intermediate and final components), gives a clearer picture of the net changes in gross product shares over the ten year period. Tertiary activities, as defined, made up 61 per cent of gross product at constant prices in 1962/3 and almost 63 per cent at the end of the period. Most of the changing share was attributable to intermediate services, but it is to be noted that, in real terms, final services comprised almost 45 per cent of the economy's output (at constant prices) in 1972/3.

The composition of *final services* in gross product at current and constant prices is shown in Table 1.5. By far the greatest share was generated by wholesale and retail activities. However, this activity contributed a lessening share over the period, along with public administration and defence, while all other services took up a higher proportion of gross product at constant prices.

Selected Indicators of Structure and Performance, 1968/9

It is usually assumed, but seldom demonstrated, that the structure and performance of service sector activities is markedly different from other activities. Table 1.6 provides some comparative descriptive data for key features of structure and performance in mining, manufacturing and services. There are considerable differences between activities in the

Table 1.3: Gross Product Shares at Current and Constant (1968-9) Prices

	ASIC classes	1962-3 Current Prices $m	1962-3 Current Prices %	1962-3 Constant Prices $m	1962-3 Constant Prices %	1972-3 Current Prices $m	1972-3 Current Prices %	1972-3 Constant Prices $m	1972-3 Constant Prices %	% change, 1962-3-1972-3 Current Prices	% change, 1962-3-1972-3 Constant Prices
Agriculture, forestry, fishing and hunting	A	1,874	11.65	1,960	10.22	3,178	7.62	2,366	7.26	–4.03	–2.96
Mining	B	244	1.52	351	1.83	1,494	3.58	1,318	4.05	+2.06	+2.22
Manufacturing	C	4,573	28.42	5,354	27.88	10,315	24.74	8,806	27.04	–3.68	–0.84
Electricity, gas and water	D	516	3.21	543	2.83	1,252	3.00	1,159	3.56	–0.21	+0.73
Construction	E	1,139	7.08	1,296	6.76	3,122	7.49	2,188	6.72	+0.41	–0.04
Wholesale and retail trade	F	2,757	17.14	3,214	16.76	6,438	15.45	4,938	15.16	–1.69	–1.60
Transport and storage; communication	G,H	1,152	7.16	1,357	7.08	3.034	7.29	2,580	7.92	+0.13	+0.84
Finance and business services	I	1,134	7.05	1,562	8.15	3,974	9.53	2,949	9.05	+2.48	+0.90
Public administration and defence	J	500	3.11	723	3.77	1,710	4.10	1,121	3.44	+0.99	–0.33
Community services	K										
Entertainment, etc.; personal services	L	1,467	9.12	1,917	10.00	4,991	11.97	3,528	10.83	+2.85	+0.83
Ownership of dwellings		832	5.17	1,083	5.65	2.761	6.62	1,992	6.12	+1.45	+0.47
Total		16,188		19,351		42,269		32,945			
Customs duties		210	1.30	233	1.22	513	1.23	423	1.30	–0.07	+0.08
Less imputed bank service charge		–309	–1.93	–410	–2.15	–1,096	–2.62	–796	–2.45	+0.69	+0.30
Gross Domestic Product		16,089	100.00	19.174	100.00	41,686	100.00	32,572	100.00		

Source: *Australian National Accounts: Gross Product by Industry at Current and Constant Prices, 1962-63 to 1974-75* (Australian Bureau of Statistics, Canberra, 1976) Reference No. 7.12.

Table 1.4: Gross Product Shares by Sectors at Current and Constant (1968-9) Prices

	ASIC Class	1962-3 Current Prices (%)	1962-3 Constant Prices (%)	1972-3 Current Prices (%)	1972-3 Constant Prices (%)	%Δ, 1962-3-1972-3 Current Prices (%)	%Δ, 1962-3-1972-3 Constant Prices (%)
Primary Activities	A-B	13.17	12.05	11.20	11.31	−1.97	−0.74
Secondary Activities	C	28.42	27.88	24.74	27.04	−3.68	−0.84
Tertiary Activities	D-L	59.04	61.00	65.45	62.80	+6.41	+1.80
Intermediate services	D.E.G.H	17.45	16.67	17.78	18.20	+0.33	+1.53
Final services	F,I,J,K,L	41.59	44.33	47.67	44.60	+6.08	+0.27
Customs duties less imputed bank service charge		−0.63	−0.93	−1.39	−1.15	+0.76	+0.22
Gross Domestic Product		100.00	100.00	100.00	100.00	–	–

Source: *Australian National Accounts: Input-Output Tables, 1968-69 (Preliminary)* (Australian Bureau of Statistics, Canberra, 1976)

Table 1.5: Gross Product Shares in Final Services at Current and Constant (1968-9) Prices

	ASIC Class	1962-3 Current Prices (%)	1962-3 Constant Prices (%)	1972-3 Current Prices (%)	1972-3 Constant Prices (%)	%Δ, 1962-3-1972-3 Current Prices (%)	%Δ, 1962-3-1972-3 Constant Prices (%)
Wholesale and retail	F	41.21	37.81	32.41	33.99	−8.80	−3.82
Finance and business	I	16.95	18.38	19.99	20.29	+3.04	+1.91
Public administration and defence	J	7.48	8.50	8.60	7.72	+1.12	−0.78
Community services Entertainment etc. personal services	K L	21.93	22.56	25.11	24.28	+3.18	+1.72
Ownership of dwellings		12.43	12.75	13.89	13.72	+1.46	+0.97
Final Services		100.00	100.00	100.00	100.00	–	–

Source: ***Australian National Accounts:*** *Gross Product by Industry at Current and Constant Prices, 1962-63 to 1974-75* (Australian Bureau of Statistics, Canberra, 1976) Reference No. 7.12.

number of enterprises and establishments per firm, average wage per person employed, value added per person, and capital expenditure as a percentage of sales. Less variation exists in sales per person and stocks as a percentage of sales. But this information has several inherent limitations. First, it does not show the variation in structure and performance that may exist *within* these broad groups. Secondly, data on the composition of the labour force and on other factor inputs would be required to explain differences in sales or value added per person. Finally, the significant information for policy purposes is the extent to which these structural and performance features are subject to change over a period.

The nature of structural change in the Australian economy is very significantly reflected in the changing characteristics of wholesale distribution. This service function links import supply with domestic supply and monitors the information flows about pricing and quantity requirements between producers and consumers. Yet the distributional role of wholesaling is almost totally ignored by economists in applied studies or in evaluating policy effects.

Table 1.7 provides information about wholesale services in Australia for the year 1968/9. It can be seen that within this activity there is substantial variation in the average size (as measured by sales per establishment) of plants, in the number of persons employed per establishment and in the level of stocks to sales and value added as a percentage of sales. The information provided also implies considerable differences in factor input proportions and the incomes of persons employed in each sub-activity. The role of tariffs, and fiscal and monetary policies in determining changes in the structural performance of this service function is a topic to which further research should contribute.

Labour Force Shares and Composition

Service activities are invariably regarded as labour-intensive. This notion also contributes to the view that labour productivity is significantly less for service activities than for other employment areas. While this partial measure of sector 'performance' may be tautologically valid where factor proportions differ between sectors or over time, the labour market implications are that the shares of the work force in service activities are necessarily higher than the shares in output. Also, changes in employment opportunities are reflected in shifts in sectoral shares. The participation rates of part-time and female employees will therefore indicate inter-sectoral differences in realising these job demands.

Table 1.6: Selected Variables for Primary, Secondary and Tertiary Activities: 1968-9

	Enterprises No.	Establish-ments per firm No.	Persons Employed No.	Average Wage $	Sales per person $	Stocks as a % of sales %	Value added per person $	Capital Expenditure as a percentage of sales %
Mining	1,087	1.343	48,259	4,434	20,866	12.61	13,531	43.20
Manufacturing	33,063	1.193	1,254,717	3,037	14,269	17.95	6,063	4.97
Services and distribution	172,230	1.129	1,324,019	1,645	20,940	12.07	5,165	2.77
Retailing	121,060	1,107	701,543	2,065	17,057	10.53	4,101	1.32

Source: *Official Yearbook of the Commonwealth of Australia, 1974* (Australian Bureau of Statistics Canberra, 1975) p.1109.

Table 1.7: Key variables for types of wholesale distribution, 1968-9

Industry class	Number of Establish-ments No.	Persons employed No.	Sales $'000	Average stock $'000	Value added $'000	Wages & salaries $'000	Persons employed per estab-lishment No.	Sales per establish-ment $	Wages per person employed $	Sales per person employed $	Stocks to sales %	Value added to sales %
General, minerals, metals and chemicals	1,355	16,017	1,200,701	159,054	169,664	54,358	11.82	886,130	3,394	74,964	13.25	14.13
Machinery and equipment	7,057	90,861	2,891,775	589,623	695,927	279,124	13.97	409,770	3,072	31,826	20.39	24.07
Building materials and supplies	4,919	50,029	1,443,969	184,657	286,233	136,707	10.17	293,550	2,733	28,863	12.79	19.82
Household appliances, hardware and furniture	1,608	15,643	620,325	78,302	123,192	44,216	9.73	385,770	2,827	39,655	12.62	19.86
Clothing, footwear and textiles	2,901	20,773	900,282	116,036	150,345	56,393	7.16	310,330	2,715	43,339	12.89	16.70
Food, beverages and tobacco	4,679	56,526	3,480,978	224,385	414,940	154,411	12.08	743,960	2,732	61,582	6.45	11.92
Other	3,982	39,408	1,248,063	176,836	287,987	106,988	9.90	313,430	2,715	31,670	14.17	23.07
Total (Average)	33,356	358,811	15,899,132	2,144,485	2,773,008	1,045,311	10.76	476,650	2,913	44,311	13.49	17.44

Source: *Official Yearbook of the Commonwealth of Australia, 1974* (Australian Bureau of Statistics, Canberra 1975) pp.1101-2.

Table 1.8: Labour Force Size and Shares by Type of Activity, 1971-6

	1971 Persons in labour force		1976 Persons in labour force		1971-6 Percentage point change
	('000)	%	('000)	%	(%)
Agriculture	428.8	7.78	366.5	6.30	–1.48
Forestry, fishing and hunting	22.1	0.40	18.5	0.32	–0.08
Mining and quarrying	78.1	1.42	82.3	1.42	–
Manufacturing	1,473.1	26.22	1,245.3	21.43	–4.79
Building and construction	471.8	8.56	496.8	8.55	–0.01
Transport and storage	291.4	5.29	333.4	5.74	+0.45
Wholesale and retail trade	967.8	17.55	1,143.6	19.68	+2.13
Finance, insurance, real estate and business services	962.7	17.46	1,269.8	21.85	+4.39
Entertainment, recreation, restaurants and hotels and personal services	370.4	6.72	370.5	6.38	–0.34
Other industries	457.1	8.29	484.1	8.33	–0.27
No previous work experience	17.0	0.31	–	–	–
Total	5,513.0	100.0	5,810.6	100.0	–

Source: *The Labour Force,* Australian Bureau of Statistics, Reference No. 6.22.

Table 1.8 provides data on labour force size and shares by types of activity for two years, 1971 and 1976, covering a five year period. Reductions in the share of the labour force have occurred in agriculture, forestry, fishing and hunting, manufacturing, building and construction and entertainment and personal services. By aggregating these activities into primary, secondary and tertiary sectors, as shown in Table 1.9, the changing role of the labour force in supplying intermediate and final services is emphasised. All services absorbed over 70 per cent of the labour force in 1976, while over 55 per cent were engaged in final service activities. Furthermore, over a relatively short period of five years, the service sector labour force had increased its share of the total labour force by over 6 per cent.

Table 1.9: Shares of Labour Force by Sectors, 1971-6

	1971 %	1976 %	1971-6 %Δ
Primary activities	9.60	8.04	−1.56
Secondary activities	26.22	21.43	−4.79
Tertiary activities	64.18	70.53	+6.35
Intermediate services	13.85[a]	14.29[a]	+0.44
Final services	50.33[b]	56.24[b]	+5.91
Total	100.00	100.00	–

Notes: a. Excludes electricity, gas and water; communication; and public administration and defence (i.e. other industries).
b. Includes the above services and 'no previous work experience' (0.31).
Source: Table 1.8.

Persons participating in the labour force cannot be considered as homogeneous with respect to sex, skills or full-time commitment. Table 1.10 provides some disaggregation of the labour force by sex and the relationship of full-time to part-time workers. In only one activity, that of community and business services, do full-time female workers exceed the numbers of full-time male workers.

Secondly, for part-time members, the ratio of female to male workers exceeds 400 per cent in three service activities (i.e. commerce, community and business services and amusement, hotels and personal services). Finally, the ratio of part-time to full-time workers is highest in the area of amusement, hotels and personal services. Further analysis

Table 1.10: Labour Force Composition by activity, 1971

	Full-time workers ('000)				Part-time workers ('000)				
	Male	Female	Persons	Females to males (%)	Male	Female	Persons	Females to males (%)	Part-time workers to Full-time workers (%)
Agriculture	340.8	39.1	379.9	11.47	11.9	33.1	45.1	278.2	11.87
Other primary	n.a.	n.a.	21.0	n.a.	n.a.	n.a.	n.a.	n.a.	n.a.
Mining	n.a.	n.a.	76.2	n.a.	n.a.	n.a.	n.a.	n.a.	n.a.
Manufacturing	1,046.3	311.3	1,357.6	29.75	17.2	48.4	65.5	281.4	4.82
Building and construction	436.0	12.4	448.4	2.84	n.a.	n.a.	17.9	n.a.	3.99
Transport and storage	249.1	23.4	272.5	9.39	n.a.	n.a.	16.7	n.a.	6.13
Finance and property	104.3	86.4	226.8	61.58	n.a.	n.a.	17.4	n.a.	7.67
Commerce	528.4	296.4	824.9	56.09	22.6	103.2	125.8	456.6	15.25
Community and business services	255.4	297.5	552.9	116.48	24.3	129.2	153.5	531.7	27.76
Amusement, hotels, personal services	127.0	126.8	253.8	99.84	15.1	92.6	107.7	613.2	42.43
Other industries	442.3	95.1	440.2	21.50	22.8	45.4	16.2	199.1	3.68
Total	3,565.8	1,288.4	4,854.2	36.13	114.0	451.8	565.8	396.32	11.66

Note: The data relates to February 1971.
Source: *The Labour Force,* Australian Bureau of Statistics, Reference No.6.22.

of wage rate data and average hours employed would be necessary to indicate the conditions surrounding these differences in work force participation characteristics among service activities.

Growth Rates

Changing trends and year-to-year variations in gross product and gross product per person employed determine changing shares in output and the labour force. Table 1.11 provides estimates of these growth rates and yearly deviations for a ten year period, 1962-3 to 1972-3. Further analysis would be required to show whether variations in labour-output rates in service activities are due more to variations in output growth (see Figure 1.2) than changes in labour inputs. However, the ranking of the trend growth rates by sector indicates that the average rate of growth in output for all activities was largely matched by the ranked trends rates of labour productivity as shown in Figures 1.3 and 1.4. The determinants of this ordering are in the main partly attributable to differences in effective levels of protection and partly due to the conditions affecting the substitution of capital for labour inputs.

Household Consumption of Services

While services are consumed by households, firms and governments, both domestically and overseas, the most frequently analysed relationship is that of the demand for final services by households. The determinants of demand for household services are principally variables measuring income, wealth or liquidity, the allocation of time to work and leisure, the prices of available services and the effects of the taxation structure on the incentive to expend effort in employment or leisure pursuits. Where the price of services is affected by protection or regulation, either directly or indirectly by reason of repercussions through the input-output relationships of the economy, this distorting condition may enter as a sub-argument into the demand or expenditure system. In addition, elements of market power, structural differences in factor or service markets or evidence of market failure due to variable risk and uncertainty or an unequal distribution of information about relevant choices will also, in part, determine the household choice options and decision-making processes in the consumption of services.

This section draws attention to previous Australian studies of the possible determinants of household consumption patterns and presents preliminary evidence from the Australian Bureau of Statistics survey of household expenditure for the year 1974/5.

Table 1.11: Trend rates of growth (1962/3-1972/3) and percentage change from preceding year for types of activity at 1968-9 prices[a]

	Trend rate of growth	1963-4	1964-5	1965-6	1966-7	1967-8	1968-9	1969-70	1970-1	1971-2	1972-3
Agriculture, forestry, fishing and hunting	2.7 (3.7)	4.1 (6.1)	4.3 (6.5)	−12.7 (−12.2)	20.5 (22.2)	−13.6 (−15.5)	25.5 (27.4)	−3.3 (−1.5)	3.2 (4.7)	7.6 (9.5)	−9.3 (−6.7)
Mining	16.0 (10.1)	4.6 (3.7)	−1.1 (−2.1)	14.9 (10.9)	13.4 (9.0)	7.4 (2.0)	18.3 (10.6)	34.4 (21.2)	39.1 (27.0)	6.6 (6.8)	10.1 (7.7)
Manufacturing	5.4 (3.4)	3.3 (−0.6)	9.7 (4.7)	1.3 (−0.2)	4.7 (3.6)	6.5 (4.8)	8.3 (5.9)	7.3 (4.4)	2.3 (1.1)	3.3 (3.6)	4.8 (4.8)
Electricity, gas and water	7.6 (5.9)	9.0 (5.8)	9.3 (5.9)	7.3 (6.0)	7.2 (1.9)	5.0 (3.6)	10.0 (9.9)	6.8 (6.1)	8.2 (7.2)	7.0 (6.0)	9.1 (7.7)
Construction	5.4 (2.9)	12.0 (7.6)	7.4 (3.4)	5.3 (2.2)	0.4 (1.4)	11.0 (9.5)	10.1 (6.0)	5.2 (0.6)	−0.4 (−2.4)	2.5 (1.0)	1.2 (−1.0)
Wholesale and retail trade	4.3 (1.8)	7.7 (4.5)	5.9 (2.5)	2.2 (0.8)	3.7 (1.0)	4.7 (2.1)	6.3 (4.1)	5.5 (2.8)	2.9 (−0.4)	1.4 (0.0)	3.8 (1.3)
Transport and storage; communications	6.7 (4.4)	8.9 (6.7)	6.8 (4.4)	4.9 (1.7)	5.3 (3.3)	8.1 (6.1)	8.5 (6.0)	8.8 (5.5)	6.3 (3.8)	3.1 (1.8)	6.0 (5.3)
Gross Domestic Product	5.6 (2.7)	6.3 (3.0)	6.6 (3.0)	2.2 (−0.7)	6.2 (3.7)	4.7 (2.1)	9.4 (6.3)	6.4 (2.6)	4.8 (1.7)	4.0 (2.7)	3.8 (2.0)

Note: a. Calculated from indexes of gross product. Figures in brackets are gross product per person employed (i.e. labour productivity).
Source: *Australian National Accounts: Gross Product by Industry at Current and Constant Prices, 1962-63 to 1974-74*, Table 7 Australian Bureau of Statistics, Canberra Reference No.7.12.

Figure 1.2: Percentage change in gross product from preceding year for service activities at 1968/9 prices

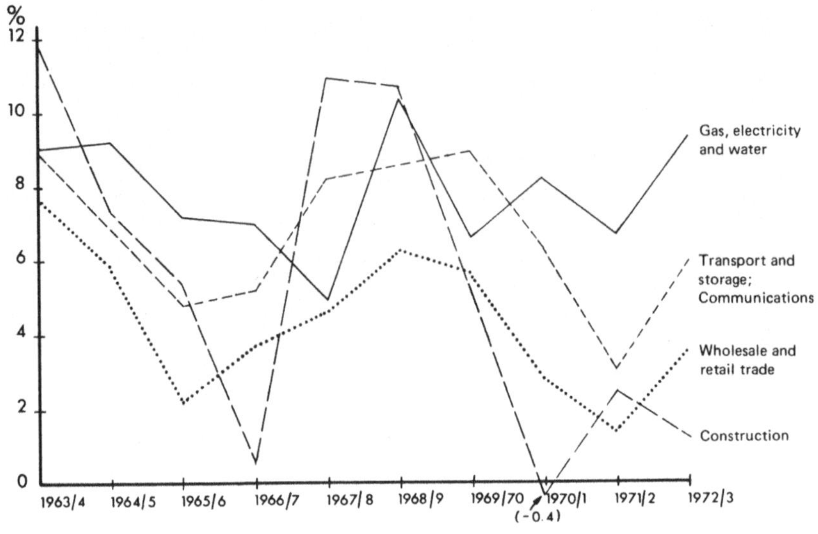

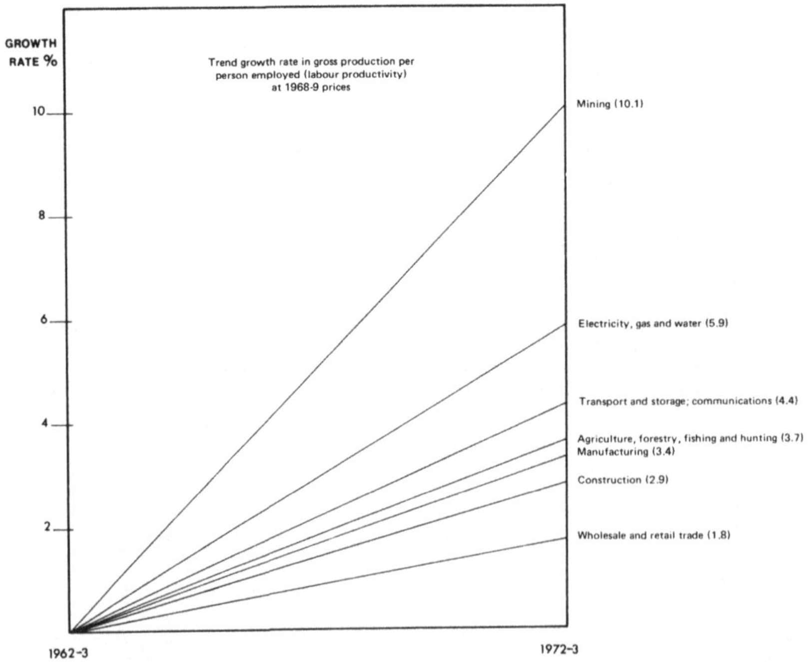

Figure 1.3

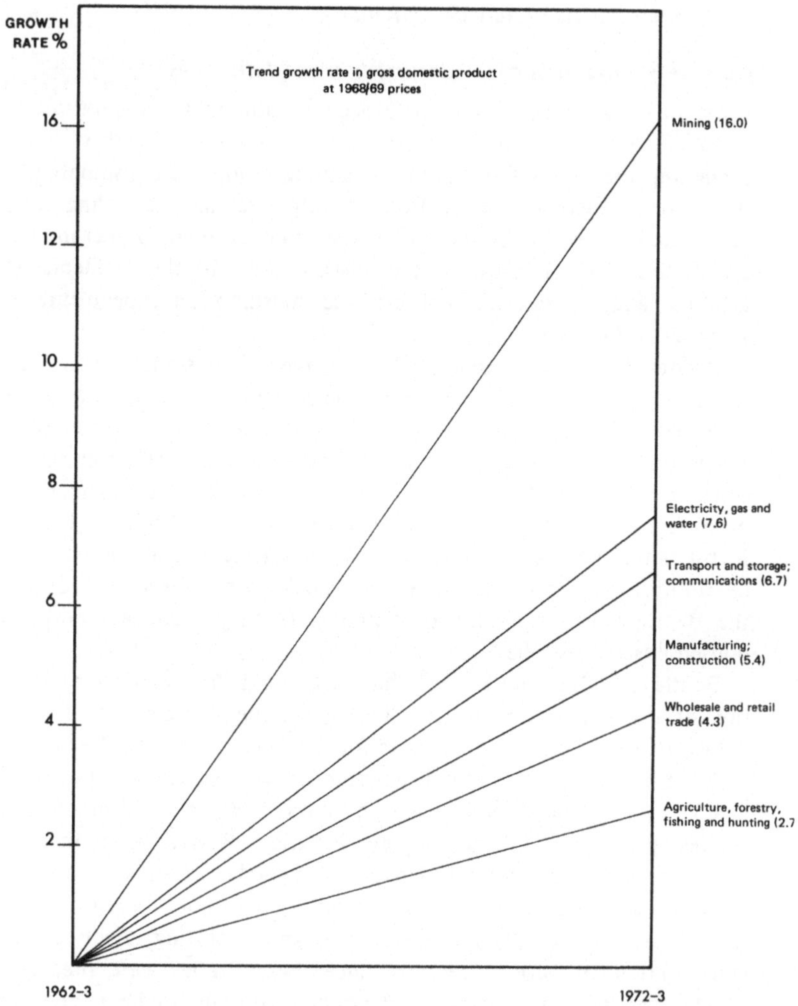

GROWTH RATE %
Trend growth rate in gross domestic product at 1968/69 prices
16
12
10
8
6
4
2
Mining (16.0)
Electricity, gas and water (7.6)
Transport and storage; communications (6.7)
Manufacturing; construction (5.4)
Wholesale and retail trade (4.3)
Agriculture, forestry, fishing and hunting (2.7
1962–3
1972–3

Figure 1.4

Previous Studies of Service Consumption and Influences

There are no available studies in Australia of household expenditure on types of *services only* that link the level of expenditure with variables explaining the level of or variations among groups of consumers (i.e. classified by incomes, occupations, family size, age, schooling etc.). There are, however, a number of studies that do focus on (a) income distribution and changes in that distribution, (b) the incidence of taxation, and (c) patterns of household consumption expenditure on *all goods and services.*[44]

Podder,[45] using data generated by a survey of consumer expenditure and finances for 1966/8, has developed measures of inequality of the income distribution of Australian families. A number of socio-economic sub-groups were also identified on the basis of family size, occupation, education and age. By contrast, Jones[46] considered the changing shape of Australian income distribution over the period 1914-15 to 1968-9. In this study, it was possible to consider differences in the changing distribution between sexes. There are no known published studies of the distribution of wealth or liquidity (money balances) only by households in Australia.[47]

Bentley, Collins and Drane[48] have estimated the incidence of taxation at the Federal, State and local government levels and of some individual direct and indirect taxes for the period 1966-7. They found that the incidence of the total tax structure was regressive in the lower income ranges. These findings have been updated and supplemented by studies prepared for the Asprey Taxation Review Committee.[49] However, recent changes in tastes, prices of goods and services, taxation schedules and deductible allowance conditions for both households and firms have undoubtedly had differential and distorting effects on the consumption of various services since these studies were prepared.

The first study in Australia of the pattern of household expenditures based on survey data is that by Podder.[50] It was based on the above-mentioned survey of consumer expenditure and finances for 1966-8. This study derived income and family size elasticities for nine groups of goods and services for the six states and Australia as a whole. These findings are summarised in Table 1.12.

If we consider the household expenditure choice framework as one in which consumers make decisions about assets that provide current and future services, money balances that facilitate future consumption expenditure and incomes generated by labour and the return on liquid assets, then it is possible to model all decisions as those of consumption or portfolio adjustment. A study by Clements[51] partitions demand

Table 1.12: Income and Family Size Elasticities for Household Expenditure, 1966-8

(log X = a+b log Y + c log Z)

Expenditure category (X)	Income (Y)	Family size (Z)	R^2
Food	.488	.386	.766
Clothing and footwear	1.489	.328	.635
Cigarettes, tobacco and liquor	1.573	.144	.398
Fuel, gas, electricity and telephone	.385	.294	.368
Fares and motor vehicle expenses	1.843	.279	.625
Medical, dental, chemist and funeral	1.379	.328	.538
Recreation and entertainment	2.091	–.571	.571
Housing services	.879	–.336	.441
Durables	2.728	–.294	.598

Source: N. Podder 'Patterns of Household Consumption Expenditures in Australia', *Economic Record,* vol.47, no.119 (1971) pp.379-98.

responses into four effects: substitution and labour income effects as well as inherited wealth and asset income effects. The period of analysis was for 1968 to 1973. A nine-good level of aggregation, with three commodities and six assets, was adopted. Only the *impact* elasticities with respect to price, interest rate and spending-power are reported, but this approach would be capable of extension in a dynamic context and also to include the effects of evolving tastes or changes in the incidence of taxation.

Pattern of Household Expenditure, 1974-5

A survey by the Australian Bureau of Statistics provided some preliminary results on the pattern of household expenditure in Australia for the year 1974-5. The distribution of expenditure according to ten broad groups of goods and services is shown in Figure 1.5 below. It can be seen that the 'basic' commodities of shelter, food and clothing make up 46.2 per cent of the total while services, including those from the use of durable assets, make up the remainder.

Of more interest than the average pattern is the way in which the proportions of total expenditure on goods and services differ for income groups or according to other socio-economic characteristics such as household composition or age of household head. Table 1.13

Figure 1.5: Household Expenditure 1974-75 Distribution Between Broad Groups of Expenditure

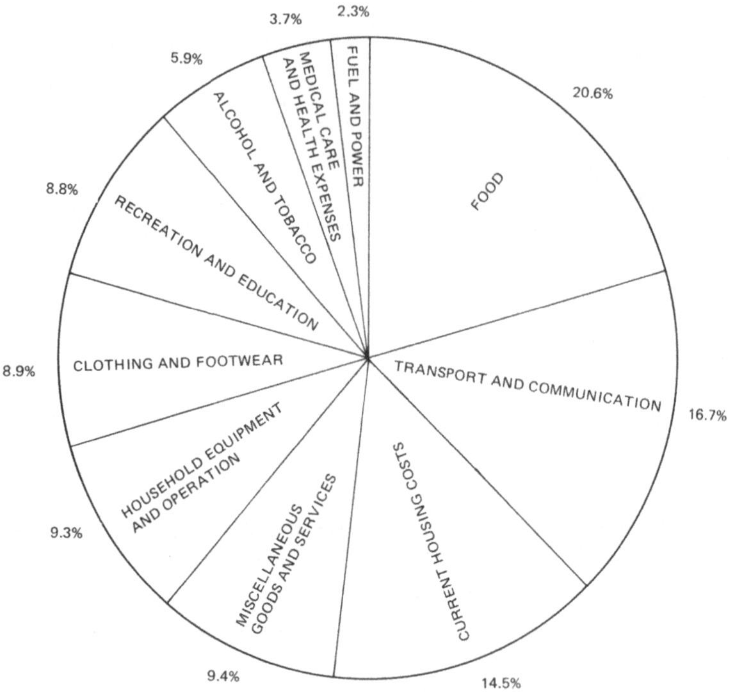

Source: ***Household Expenditure Survey 1974-75, Preliminary Results,*** **Bulletin 2 Australian Bureau of Statistics, Canberra, July 1976, Reference No. 17.20.**

shows how total expenditure is outlayed by differing percentages on the given commodity and service groups according to six average weekly income intervals.

The survey also collected data on the nature of housing occupancy, employment structure, age and sex structure and family size. It is therefore possible to calculate a number of socio-demographic variables that match the income intervals. The value of net savings can also be calculated by deducting total expenditure and other household payments from average weekly income. This information, for each

Table 1.13: Expenditure on Commodity Groups as a Percentage of Total Expenditure, by Weekly Household Income, 1974-5 (per cent)

	Average weekly household income						
Commodity group	Under $80	$80 and under $140	$140 and under $200	$200 and under $260	$260 and under $340	$340 or more	All households
Current housing costs	16.0	16.2	15.8	15.4	13.7	11.7	14.5
Fueld and power	4.0	2.7	2.4	2.1	2.1	1.7	2.3
Food	26.0	22.4	21.6	20.5	19.6	18.2	20.6
Alcohol and tobacco	5.1	5.9	5.7	6.0	6.0	6.9	5.9
Clothing and footwear	8.0	7.9	8.2	8.6	8.9	10.4	8.8
Household equipment and operation	10.0	9.0	9.5	8.8	9.3	9.7	9.3
Medical care and health expenses	3.6	4.2	4.0	3.8	3.6	3.2	3.7
Transport and communication	12.5	15.9	16.3	17.7	17.9	16.8	16.7
Recreation and education	5.8	7.5	7.8	8.2	9.4	11.3	8.8
Miscellaneous goods and services	9.0	8.3	8.6	9.0	9.6	10.9	9.4

Source: *Household Expenditure Survey 1974-75, Preliminary Results,* Bulletin 2, Australian Bureau of Statistics, Canberra July 1976, Reference No.17.20.

Table 1.14: Socio-Economic Characteristics of Households by Income Groups, 1974/5

Income Group $	Average Weekly Income $	Net Savings[a] $	Sex Ratio[b] %	Age Structure[c] %	Employment Structure[d] %	Household Occupancy[e] %
<80	47.37	−14.65	62.86	63.74	10.53	49.50
80≤140	114.30	−19.94	89.93	43.18	36.36	67.33
140≤200	168.73	−6.38	98.77	43.21	39.81	45.70
200≤260	228.32	12.77	101.16	38.82	51.47	42.65
260≤340	293.75	31.03	106.94	35.75	57.82	38.74
>340	461.71	70.18	111.98	32.76	63.05	22.06
Average	205.94	8.37	97.44	41.23	46.10	44.46

Notes: a. Defined as average weekly household income less total expenditure and other payments (includes income tax, superannuation, life insurance and purchases of dwellings and land).

b. Male persons per household as a percentage of female persons per household.

c. Persons per household under 18 years of age plus persons per household over 65 years of age as a percentage of all other persons per household.

d. Working persons per household as a percentage of all persons per household.

e. Households in rented accommodation as a proportion of households in non-rented (i.e. in process of or outright ownership) accommodation.

Source: Household Expenditure Survey 1974-75, Preliminary Results, Bulletin 2, Australian Bureau of Statistics, Canberra, July 1976, Reference No. 17.20.

income group, is shown in Table 1.14. It is apparent that considerable differences exist for these socio-economic variables across the income groups and it may therefore be hypothesised that differences in spending on goods and services may be determined by a combination of these conditions.

Elasticities of household demand with respect to average weekly income and family size are presented in Table 1.15. They are not directly comparable to those given by Podder due to classification differences for expenditure items. Also, the preliminary availability of such a small number of observations limits the analysis. Without the use of the full sample of observations, it is not possible to fully explore a constrained expenditure system, non-linear features, and the direct or indirect contribution of other socio-economic variables on differences

Table 1.15: Income and Family Size Elasticities for Household Expenditure, 1974/5

(log X = a+b log Y + c log Z,N=6)

Expenditure Category (X)	Income (Y)	Family Size (Z)	R^2
Current housing costs	.1102 (1.36)	1.1139 (5.34)	.995
Fuel and power	.4432 (3.88)	−.3885 (−1.32)	.971
Food	.4956 (6.92)	.0266 (.14)	996
Alcohol and tobacco	.6410 (4.92)	.2309 (.69)	.994
Clothing and footwear	1.1002 (6.83)	−.8773 (−2.11)	.991
Household equipment and operation	.8109 (4.61)	−.4446 (−.98)	.985
Medical and health expenses	.1438 (.97)	1.2424 (3.23)	.989
Transport and communication	.5217 (3.96)	.7426 (2.19)	.995
Recreation and education	1.1367 (5.45)	−.5356 (−1.00)	.990
Miscellaneous goods and services	1.1605 (8.27)	−1.1019 (−3.05)	.993

Note: t-statistics are shown in brackets.
Source: Household Expenditure Survey 1974-75, Preliminary Results, Bulletin 2, Australian Bureau of Statistics, Canberra, July 1976, Reference No. 17.20.

in coefficient values for different consumer groups. However, the results do indicate that income elasticity was positively greater than unity for only three types of expenditure (clothing and footwear, recreation and education, and miscellaneous goods and services), while the family size elasticity was greater than unity for two expenditure categories (current housing costs, and medical and health expenses), and was negative (suggesting diseconomies of household size in expenditure or other preference determinants) for five expenditure classes.

Household expenditure surveys omit data on non-market, illegal and self-service activities, which may, due to taxation structures or social relationships, have an important impact on the benefits or costs associated with some classes of consumption expenditure or for some consumer groups. For example, child-minding, home maintenance, gambling, dealing in prohibited goods and services, or inflicting personal injury are service functions that contribute to the welfare of individuals or groups in different ways and represent varying community gains or losses.[52]

Topics for Further Research

The foregoing description of the nature and size of the service sector and its determinants suggests that additional research could focus on a number of areas.

At a more disaggregated level, demand analysis could take into account the time-path of service use decisions and the mix of socio-economic variables that condition these observed patterns of consumption. Conditions of supply and access such as market structure, technological progress, factor input composition, and output price and quality variation require substantial research effort. The role of government agencies (e.g. Trade Practices Commission, Prices Justification Tribunal, Industries Assistance Commission), enterprises, and administrative bodies in influencing supply and demand relationships for services could also be investigated.

A number of inter-sectoral relationships and the interface of structural differences could also be evaluated for their significance and changes over time. These may be listed as follows:

1. the relationships between government (public) and private sectors in both providing and requiring services.
2. the role of intermediate services in input-output relationships between sectors and activities.
3. the nature of the costs and benefits of service activities accruing to defined groups of consumers or producers.
4. the effects of structural features and market conduct on the performance record of service activities.
5. the form of trade-offs between efficiency and equity in providing access to service functions.
6. the limitations of traditional distinctions and excessive aggregation (e.g. capital intensive/labour intensive; traded/non-traded goods and services; primary/secondary/tertiary activities) in measuring performance or in developing fiscal, monetary or other market regulation policies that affect service output, quality, prices or growth.

If any of these matters are taken up for further analysis, the results depend to a large extent on the availability of improved data sources, the use of suitable measurement techniques, recourse to realistic theories of economic relationships and considerable attention to the testing procedures adopted to verify any causative linkages.

Notes

1. See, for example, C.W. McMahon and G.D.N. Worswick, 'The Growth of Services in the Economy: I. Their Stabilising Influence' and 'The Growth of Services in the Economy: II. Do They Slow Down Overall Expansion', *District Bank Review* (December 1960 and March 1961); B.M. Deakin and K.D. George, 'Goods and Services', *London and Cambridge Economic Bulletin* (March 1965); G.D.N. Worswick and C.G. Fane, 'Goods and Services Once Again', *District Bank Review* (March 1967); and M. Hall, 'Are Goods and Services Different?' *Westminster Bank Review* (1968).
2. A. Smith, *Wealth of Nations,* Cannan edition (University Paperbacks, 1961) Book 2, Chapter 3, pp.351-2.
3. For a study that attempts to explain the technical progress 'residual' by reference to educational service inputs see E.F. Denison, *Why Growth Rates Differ* (The Brookings Institution, Washington DC, 1967).
4. While it could be said that research on the economics of education services was the dominant focus of the 1960s, research on the economics of health services achieved prominence in the 1970s.
5. J.S. Mill, *Principles of Political Economy* (Longman Green & Co, 1900) Book 1, Chapter 3, p.31.
6. Ibid, p.31.
7. A. Marshall, *Principles of Economics,* Eighth Edition (Macmillan, 1920), p.54,
8. Ibid, p.56.
9. Ibid, p.67.
10. See footnotes 3 and 4 above.
11. Some of the debate is covered in P.T. Bauer and B.S. Yamey, 'Economic Progress and Occupational Distribution', *Economic Journal,* vol.61 (1951) pp.741-55; S.G. Triantis, 'Economic Progress, Occupational Redistribution and International Terms of Trade', *Economic Journal,* vol.63 (1953) pp.627-37; Nelson N. Foote and Paul K. Hatt, 'Social Mobility and Economic Advancement', *American Economic Review,* vol.43 (1953) pp.364-78; and A.L. Minks, 'Statistical Evidence and the Concept of Tertiary Industry', *Economic Development and Cultural Change,* vol.3 (1955) pp.366-73. For a more recent contribution see M.A. Katouzian 'The Development of the Service Sector: A New Approach', *Oxford Economic Papers,* N.S. vol.22 (1970) pp.362-82.
12. Fisher's ideas and their development may be noted in 'Capital and the Growth of Knowledge', *Economic Journal,* vol.43 (1933) pp.379-89; *The Clash of Progress and Security,* (Macmillan London, 1935); 'Production: Primary, Secondary and Tertiary', *Economic Record,* vol.15 (1939) pp.24-38; *Economic Progress and Security* (Macmillan, London, 1945); 'A Note on Tertiary Production', *Economic Journal,* vol.62 (1952) pp.820-34; and 'Marketing Structure and Economic Development: Comment', *Quarterly Journal of Economics,* vol.68 (1954) pp.151-4.
13. Clark's major contributions in this field are, *National Income and Outlay* (Macmillan, London, 1938); *The Conditions of Economic Progress* (Macmillan, London, 1940); *The Economics of 1960* (Macmillan, London, 1943); and, with R.H. Fields, 'Tertiary Industries in the Economy' in C. Hartley Grattan

(ed.), *Australia* (University of California Press, 1947), pp.213-35.
14. W.J. Baumol, 'Macroeconomics of Unbalanced Growth: The Anatomy of Urban Crisis', *American Economic Review*, vol.57 (1967) pp.415-26.
15. Simon Kuznets, *Modern Economic Growth: Rate, Structure and Spread* (Yale University Press, 1966) and 'Quantitative Aspects of the Economic Growth of Nations: II. Industrial Distribution of National Product and Labor Force', *Economic Development and Cultural Change*, vol.5, (1957) Supplement.
16. Hollis B. Chenery and Lance Taylor, 'Development Patterns: Among Countries and Over Time', *Review of Economics and Statistics*, vol.50 (1968) pp.391-416.
17. B.D. Haig, 'An Analysis of Changes in the Distribution of Employment Between the Manufacturing and Service Industries, 1960-70', *Review of Economics and Statistics*, vol.57 (1975) pp.35-42.
18. Victor R. Fuchs, *Productivity Trends in the Goods and Service Sectors, 1929-61: A Preliminary Survey*, New York, NBER, Occasional Paper 89 (1964); *The Growing Importance of the Service Industries*, New York, NBER, Occasional Paper 96 (1965); *Productivity Differences Within The Service Sector* (with Jean Alexander Wilburn), New York, NBER, Occasional Paper 102 (1966); *The Service Economy* New York, NBER, General Series 87 (1968); *Production and Productivity in the Service Industries* (ed.), New York, NBER, Studies in Income and Wealth 34 (1969). Also see George J. Stigler, *Trends in Employment in the Service Industries* Princeton University Press, (1956).
19. J.A. Dowie, 'Productivity Growth in Goods and Services: Australia, USA, UK', *Economic Record*, vol.42 (1966) pp.536-54; and 'The Service Ensemble' in C. Forster (ed.), *Australian Economic Development in the Twentieth Century* (Allen and Unwin, 1970) pp.208-65;
20. Ibid, p.258.
21. N. Kaldor, *Causes of the Slow Growth of the United Kingdom*, (Cambridge University Press, 1966).
22. T.F. Cripps and R.J. Tarling, *Growth in Advanced Capitalist Economies 1950-1970* (Cambridge University Press, 1973).
23. R.E. Rowthorn, 'What remains of Kaldor's Law?', *Economic Journal*, vol.80 (1975) pp.10-19; N. Kaldor, 'Economic Growth and the Verdoorn Law – a comment on Mr. Rowthorn's Article'; and 'A reply to Lord Kaldor's Comment', *Economic Journal*, vol.80 (1975) pp.891-901.
24. W.B. Reddaway, *Effects of the Selective Employment Tax: First Report*, HMSO (1970) and *Final Report*, DAE, Occasional Paper 32, Cambridge University Press (1973).
25. K.D. George, *Productivity in Distribution*, DAE, Occasional Paper 8, Cambridge University Press (1966); and K.D. George and P.V. Hills, *Productivity and Capital Expenditure in Retailing*, DAE, Occasional Paper 16, Cambridge University Press (1968).
26. B.M. Deakin and T. Seward, *Productivity in Transport*, DAE, Occasional Paper 17, Cambridge University Press (1969).
27. Robert Bacon and Walter Eltis, *Britain's Economic Problem: Too Few Producers*, (Macmillan, 1976).
28. T.P. Hill, *The Measurement of Real Product: A theoretical and empirical analysis of the growth rates, for different industries and countries*, OECD Economic Studies Series (1971).
29. Anthony D. Smith, *The Measurement and Interpretation of Service Output Changes*, NEDO (1972).
30. Also see G. Briscoe, 'Recent Productivity Trends in the UK Service Sector', Centre for Industrial Economic and Business Research, Paper No.63 University

of Warwick (1975).

31. Victor R. Fuchs (ed.), *Production and Productivity in the Service Industries,* New York, NBER, Studies in Income and Wealth, No.34 (1969).
32. J.A. Dowie, 'Productivity Growth in Goods and Services: Australia, USA, UK', *Economic Record,* vol.42 (1966) pp.536-54.
33. G.S. Becker, 'A Theory of the Allocation of Time', *Economic Journal,* vol.75, (1968) pp.493-517.
34. Z. Griliches, 'Hedonic Price Indexes for Automobiles' in NBER, *Price Statistics of the Federal Government* (1961) and Z. Griliches and I. Adelman, 'On an index of quality change' *Journal of the American Statistical Association,* (1961) pp.535-48.
35. Kelvin Lancaster, *Consumer Demand: A new approach,* Columbia University Press (1971). Also see W.J. Baumol, 'Calculation of Optimal Product and Retailer Characteristics: the abstract product approach', *Journal of Political Economy,* vol.75 (1976) pp.674-85, and reprinted in K.A. Tucker and B.S. Yamey (eds.), *Economics of Retailing,* Penguin Modern Economics Readings (1973) pp.275-88, and D.S. Ironmonger, *New Commodities and Consumer Behaviour* Cambridge University Press (1972).
36. R.G. Gregory and D. Tearle, 'Product Differentiation and International Trade Flows: An application of the 'Hedonic' Regression Technique', *Australian Economic Papers,* vol.12 (1973) pp.79-90.
37. B.D. Haig, 'The Treatment of Banks in the Social Accounts', *Economic Record* vol.49 (1973) pp.624-8; A.W. Roche, 'The Treatment of Banks in the Social Accounts: a comment', *Economic Record,* vol.51 (1975) pp.109-15; and B.D. Haig, 'A Reply' pp.116-19. Also see B.D. Haig, 'The Measurement of Real Expenditure and Product of Goods and Services', *Economic Record,* vol.42 (1966) pp.520-35.
38. N.G. Butlin (ed.), *Sydney's Environmental Amenity 1970-1975* (Australian National University Press, 1976) Chapter 3, pp.71-92.
39. Two helpful sets of readings are P.R. Layard (ed.), *Cost-Benefit Analysis* (Penguin Modern Economics, 1974) and B.S. Yamey (ed.), *Economics of Industrial Structure* (Penguin Modern Economics, 1973).
40. Within this context, political or bureaucratic determinants of supply and demand have considerable importance. The now rapidly growing literature on the nature of public goods and the arguments of writers on 'big government', like Hayek and Friedman, should be consulted.
41. B.D. Haig, 'An Analysis of Changes in the Distribution of Employment Between the Manufacturing and Service Industries, 1960-70', *Review of Economics and Statistics,* vol.57 (1975) pp.35-42 provides an eight equation model incorporating some of these variables.
42. J.A. Dowie, 'The Service Ensemble' op cit. prefers to place intermediate services in an 'industry' group, but note that the input-output tables (Table 1.1 and 1.2) show a great deal of inter-activity variation across all services types.
43. For similar data covering the period 1890 to 1960 see J.A. Dowie, ibid, and for comments on structural and productivity change over the period, N.G. Butlin, 'Perspectives of Economic Development' in C. Forster (ed.), *Australian Economic Development in the Twentieth Century* (Allen and Unwin, 1970) pp.304-318.
44. Some time-series demand elasticities for the period 1926/7 to 1960/1 for the groups Food, Goods and Services have been estimated by Haig and Finlayson. See J.A. Dowie, 'The Service Ensemble', op.cit. p.240.
45. N. Podder, 'Distribution of Household Income in Australia', *Economic Record,* vol.48 (1972) pp.181-200.
46. F. Lancaster Jones, 'The Changing Shape of the Australian Income Distribution

1914-15 and 1968-9', *Australian Economic History Review,* vol.15 (1975) pp.21-34.

47. An aggregate short-run consumption function for Australia that includes a liquidity variable has been estimated by D.J. Smyth and P.C. Mahon, 'The Australian Short-run Consumption Function', *Economic Record,* vol.48 (1972) pp.220-31. Also see D.J.S. Rutledge and S.M. Madden, 'The Australian Short-run Consumption Function: A Comment', *Economic Record,* vol.50 (1974) pp.287-95 and D.J. Smyth and P.C. McMahon, 'A Reply', *Economic Record,* vol.51 (1975) pp.120-122. R.P. Albon and T.J. Valentine, 'Price Expectations, Partial Adjustment and the Sectoral Demand for Money in Australia, mimeo, Australian National University (1975) are undertaking research in this area.
48. P. Bentley, D.J. Collins and N.T. Drane, 'The Incidence of Australia Taxation', *Economic Record,* vol.50 (1974) pp.489-510.
49. *Taxation Review Committee: Preliminary Report* AGPS, Canberra (1974) and *Full Report,* AGPS, Canberra (1975). Also see, R.H. Wallace, 'Taxation Reform: But what is the agenda?' and A.R. Prest, 'The Australian Tax System Reviewed', *Economic Record* vol.51 (1975) pp.564-82; and P.L. Swan, 'Income Taxes, Profit Taxes and Neutrality of Optimising Decisions', *Economic Record,* vo.52 (1976) pp.166-81.
50. N. Podder, 'Patterns of Household Consumption Expenditures in Australia,' *Economic Record,* vol.47 (1971) pp.379-98.
51. Kenneth W. Clements, 'A Linear Allocation of Spending-Power System: A Consumer Demand and Portfolio Model', *Economic Record,* vol.52 (1976) pp.182-98. See also A. Powell, 'A Complete System of Consumer Demand Equations for the Australian Economy Fitted by a Model of Additive Preferences', *Econometrica,* vol.34 (1966) pp.661-75; 'Estimation of Lluch's Extended Linear Expenditure System from Cross-Sectional Data', *Australian Journal of Statistics,* vol.15 (1973) pp.111-17; and R. Williams 'Household Consumption in Australia: an examination of patterns across socio-economic classes', Preliminary Working Paper No. SP-04, Impact of Demographic Change on Industry Structure in Australia. (Mimeographed, 1976).
52. There is a growing literature on these 'unmeasured' service activities. For example, see J.A. Dowie 'Illegal Activities – as Measured and as Not', *Economic Record,* vol.46 (1920) pp.517-32; A. Gruen, 'An Enquiry into the Economics of Race-Track Gambling', *Journal of Political Economy,* vol.84 1976) pp.169-77; and R. Kidner and K. Richards, 'Compensation to the Dependents of Accident Victims', *Economic Journal,* vol.84 (1974) pp.130-42.

2 OCCUPATIONAL ACHIEVEMENT AND ECONOMIC REWARDS: SOME SOCIAL DETERMINANTS

F. Lancaster Jones, Patrick McDonnell and Trevor Williams

Introduction

The aim of this analysis is to elucidate the effects of social background and education on occupational and economic attainment, specifically the career beginnings, present job, and income of economically active men in Australia in 1973. We use previous research and new data to estimate a model of status and income attainment, giving special attention to the role of education acquired before and after beginning work, and to a wider range of indicators of social background than has usually been considered, either in Australia or other countries.

Over the last decade sociological research into the factors influencing occupational attainment has shifted from description of rates and kinds of occupational mobility between generations to the development of causal models linking social background to later achievement. Whereas earlier research addressed itself to how closely a particular society approximated the ideal of equal opportunity and how effective education was in promoting mobility, recent research has tended to concentrate on how far education serves to certify the ascribed statuses of social background, and how far the education system is a meritocratic force in later achievement. As we note below, these interests are somewhat different from those of economists concerned with resource allocation, whether public or private.

The sociological approach was exemplified in 1967 with the publication of Blau and Duncan's the *American Occupational Structure,*[1] and it is worthwhile quoting their own account of how their approach differed from earlier ones.

> The predominant emphasis in mobility research has been on the analysis of the occupational mobility matrix as a self-contained entity. Although the results of this analysis describing the mobility pattern are occasionally related to other variables, such as education or fertility, the major preoccupation is typically the internal anslysis of mobility tables, and relatively little attention is devoted to the systematic investigation of the relationships between other factors

> and occupational mobility. The tendency to conceive of mobility as a single variable and examine it largely without relating it to other variables has severely restricted the fruitfulness of mobility research. After all, the purpose of scientific enquiry is to establish and then to explain, general relationships between variables. . .[2]

These authors went on to develop a basic five-variable causal model of the process of occupational attainment, which, while using the traditional variables of mobility research (education and jobs of both fathers and sons), reconceptualised the way to study their inter-relationships. Instead of analysing mobility directly, Blau and Duncan treated the relationship of fathers' and sons' statuses causally, such that the educational and occupational experiences of sons were seen as outcomes of prior conditions, especially those relating to social background. This reconceptualisation also facilitated a switch from categoric, cross-tabular modes of analysis to more powerful methods based on continuous measures of social status.

The basic causal model introduced by Blau and Duncan is shown diagrammatically in Figure 2.1, which represents status attainment as a causal process over time: social origins influence socialisation (especially education), which influences early occupational status, which influences present status. A major hypothesis underlying such a model is that the members of industrial societies tend to make decisions as parents or as youths which serve to maintain or enhance their material and social status, a hypothesis generally supported by evidence on educational and occupational aspirations of youth.[3] To the extent that people seek other social and personal goals, models such as the one presented here will of course offer incomplete explanation. Insufficient attention has been given to date to studying the trade-off that people make between material and non-material goals.

In interpreting Figure 2.1, it is important to note that this basic five-variable model can be greatly expanded by adding other indicators of the underlying concept areas, either by generalising the content of each broad concept area or by specifying intervening social processes which link the several states of the model. Our contribution in this chapter focuses on three such extensions to the basic model. First, we consider two outcomes, rather than one, of the attainment process (occupational status and income); second, we have extended measurement of education to differentiate between education before entry to the workforce and education undertaken after beginning full-time work; and thirdly, we have broadened the conceptualisation of social

Figure 2.1: Basic model of the process of occupational achievement

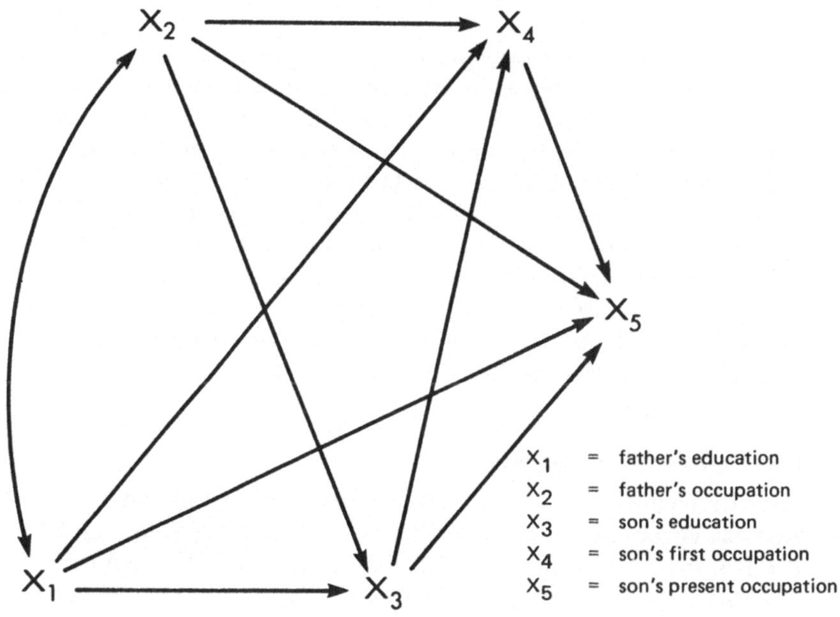

background substantially, to include not merely father's job and father's education, but also mother's education, a measure of the economic climate of the parental home, and family size. Our main reason for this third extension is that the literature is divided over how far education (and therefore later achievement) is determined by social background, an issue which bears on the question of whether education serves largely to certify social status or to provide a mechanism for social mobility between the generations. By using a wider range of background measures, we offer more scope for the identification and measurement of the effects of social background on status attainment.

Before detailing further the nature of our analysis, we should point out that the large literature in economics and sociology on the relationship between education and social inequality are somewhat independent. In economics two main concerns have been, first, whether private investment in education (or human capital) is rational, in the sense that returns exceed costs, a question generally answered in the affirmative;[4] and secondly, how far public resources should be used to encourage and to subsidise such private investment. However, in sociology the main concern has not been with resource allocation (whether private or public) but with the outcomes of the decision to stay at school and the dependence of that decision on social origins. Despite some convergence between these literatures (and one explicit attempt to rework the basic insights of both approaches into a more general framework[5]) we cannot here attempt a detailed overview of these literatures, although we later consider them in a general way in relation to our own findings. In what follows we focus on the sociological literature, if only because the data we analyse are not suitable for answering questions about decisions to invest in education rather than other forms of job-relevant activities (for example, early entry into the workforce). Our data permit us rather to address questions of the following form: given the decision to 'invest' in education, how strongly does that 'investment' influence occupational achievement and economic rewards later in life, and how dependent are such decisions on social background?

Data Sources and Measurement

The data reported in this paper are from the ANU Social Mobility in Australia Project conducted in 1973 by the Department of Sociology in the Research School of Social Sciences of the Australian National University. The 1973 survey had three major objectives: (1) to replicate a baseline study conducted in 1965; (2) to maximise the possibilities for comparison with national surveys conducted in other countries; and (3) to broaden our understanding of social mobility and stratification in contemporary Australia beyond the more restricted scope of earlier studies.

The 1973 survey was confined to persons aged between 30 to 69 years, for three reasons. First, excluding persons just entering the workforce allows true career mobility analysis for almost all persons in the sample, since by age 30 most persons have passed beyond early, transitory stages in their working life. There is some loss in not being able to examine very recent trends among young workers, and other research indicates that there are differences in the experience of younger and older workers. Second, for a given sample size a restriction of age range increases the size of included age cohorts for internal comparison and analysis of trends. Third, we wanted to embark upon the analysis of mobility among Australian women and could not do so without restricting the male sample in some way. We chose to restrict the age range rather than the sample size.

The sample was designed by the Australian Bureau of Statistics according to the principles of their Current Population Survey, resulting in a self-weighting random sample of 1 in 800 dwellings in all parts of Australia except the Northern Territory. However, our final design selected one person at random from each dwelling. Weights to compensate for the number of eligible respondents at each dwelling and for non-response have been calculated to bring the sample within population parameters. The achieved response rate was 76 per cent, which falls to 69 per cent when corrected for eligible respondents not contacted. The final achieved sample was 4,939 persons, interviewed between June 1973 and March 1974. Further details of fieldwork, sample design, and response rates are available in a volume of background papers relating to the project.[6]

This analysis focuses on occupational outcomes, the data are restricted to economically active males who reported their 1973 income. By restricting analysis to this sub-sample of 2,715 men, we reduce the problem of missing data and variable sample size for calculating correlations. When weighted and adjusted to compensate for unequal probability of selection and non-response,[7] effective sample size (equivalent to a non-weighted sample) is reduced to 2,560.

Occupation

Whenever we talk about occupations we are actually talking about occupational status scores. All occupations were coded to the three digit level of the 1971 Australian Bureau of Statistics (ABS) occupational classification.[8] Scores were then assigned to each occupation category. The development of these scores, which are uniquely calculated to reflect Australian conditions, is reported elsewhere.[9] They have been scaled to a mean of 500 and a standard deviation of 100.

Two comments about these scores need to be made. First, they are based on 45 social characteristics of members of the Australian work force. Thus they are not strictly speaking a socio-economic index in the Duncan sense,[10] but reflect a wider variety of occupational characteristics. Secondly, scores for farmers come out near the middle of the range, rather than, as with Duncan's scores, near the bottom. We believe our scale more truly reflects the social and economic status of Australian farmers.

Information on father's occupation (DADJOB) was in response to the question: 'When you were 14 years old, what kind of work did your father do?' Detailed responses were collected in the field, and, like other occupational information reported here, were coded twice. Discrepancies between first and second coding were resolved in a third and final coding of the data.

The respondent's first occupation (JOB1) is defined somewhat differently in this survey from some other mobility surveys which define first occupation as the first full-time job after finishing all full-time education. In our survey first occupation is defined as the first regular job held in a period of one year or more out of school, regardless of whether the respondent subsequently undertook further full-time education. While fewer than 5 per cent of men in our sample did undertake some further full-time education, this construction of first job allows us to elaborate the influence of education on careers. Respondent's current occupation (JOBN) is occupation at time of interview. Those not at work in 1973 have been excluded. Our basic hypothesis for the occupation variables is that the higher an earlier status (whether father's or first), the higher the later status.

Education

Father's and mother's education (DADED, MOMED) are calculated as years of education by subtracting six (the compulsory age for entering school) from the age at which the father or mother finished full-time education. Respondent's education is measured by two variables. The first includes any schooling, education or training before beginning work and any training commenced during the same year that the respondent held his first job. This last element requires explanation.

The ABS occupational classification does not in general take notice of statuses such as apprentice, trainee, probationer, and so on. In only about three categories are such beginners clearly distinguished. Many people undertake some training as part of their first job, but, for example, apprentice bricklayers and master bricklayers are coded to the same occupation category and thus have the same status score. Rather than artificially distort the relationship between education and first job status because of such coding conventions, we have included such job-related training with basic education.

Education and training received after schooling is often part-time. In the model presented here, we needed a measure of total education in terms of full-time equivalents (BASED). We obtained data on length of any courses undertaken after secondary school. In developing the present model we experimented with different weights for each year of part-time education.[11] Models estimated with five variously defined education variables (weighting part-time courses as .1, .2, .3, .5, and 1.0

to obtain a full-time equivalent) fell into two clear groups. Those with weights up to .3 formed one group, with similar patterns of relationships. Those with half and full weights formed a second group with different, and clearly illogical, patterns of relationships compared with the first group. We therefore decided to weight each year of part-time education as the equivalent of three-tenths of a year of full-time education. Since the first component of basic education was defined by a question on the age they left school, we subtracted six from the final age of finishing education to arrive at a number of years of education or training, and truncated scores of over 20 to 20.

Respondent's additional education (ADDED) is defined in a manner very like his basic education, except that it includes only education which commenced in a year later than first job. Since rather few undertook any such further education or training, the additional education variable is highly skewed, with 64 per cent with none and the rest ranging from .3 of a year to 9.4 years. In both education variables, courses lasting less than one year were not counted.

As with the occupation variables, we also hypothesise positive relationships between all education variables.

Family Size

Family size (FAMSZ) was obtained by summing the answers to two questions on (i) the number of brothers or (ii) the number of sisters, and adding one for the respondent himself. Respondents with more than eight brothers (or sisters) were coded to eight, so that maximum family size is 17. We expect family size to be negatively correlated with status (whether measured by occupation, education or income) because of the competition for family resources and the lower average resources available to any one sibling in a large family.

Income

Information on the respondent's current income (INCOME) was secured in response to the following question: 'Can you tell me the letter on this card which comes closest to your personal income, before any deductions like tax, rent or superannuation?' The card had 16 categories with weekly and yearly equivalents. The first category was under $20 a week. Categories increased by $10 a week until $120, by $20 for the next two, and by $40 for the next two. The highest category is over $240 per week. Dollar amounts representing the mid-point of each range were subsequently assigned to these categories. The first and last categories were assigned dollar amounts in terms of the average amount reported by Australians in those ranges in 1974 Current Population Survey[12] ($9 and $330 per week, respectively). Clearly, this definition of income introduces some imprecision in our estimates of dollar returns to education. Only 84 respondents who would have been eligible for this analysis were dropped because they refused to provide an income. As already implied we expect income to be a positive function of higher social background and early statuses, and to be related negatively to family size. We note that the mean weekly income of respondents in our survey was $129, a figure that can be compared with a figure of $131 from the 1974 Current Population Survey for male income recipients aged 25 to 64 years of age.[13]

Parental Income

As we mention below research elsewhere has suggested that the omission of any measure of economic well-being of a person's family of origin may downwardly bias any estimates of the effect of social background on later attainment. We were doubtful about the validity of asking respondents to estimate parental income when they were growing up and approached this general issue by asking questions about home ownership and consumer durables. Our proxy for parental income (WLTH) is an index based on the principal component of five such items: home-ownership, and the possession of a car, telephone, refrigerator, and inside toilet (these variables were initially scored as dummy variables). As analysis below shows, this variable does contribute significantly to explaining differences in later attainment.

Models and Empirical Estimates of Effects

The development and estimation of causal models in sociology unites two traditions: the structural equation models of econometricians like Fisher, Koopmans, and Wold, and the causal (path) models developed in population genetics, notably by Sewall Wright. Since their introduction into sociology about a decade ago the use of structural equation models to reflect sociological theories, and to estimate their parameters, has seen rapid growth, particularly in the application of path analysis to simple recursive models which assume independent disturbance terms and variables measured without error. In this form structural equation models are equivalent to a nested set of regression equations whose coefficients are interpreted as measures of effect.

We adopt a simple recursive formulation in this preliminary model. Thus, the system of hypothetical cause-effect relationships shown in Table 2.2. has the following characteristics: (a) it can be described by a series of five simple structural equations; (b) in each equation the variance of the effect is completely determined by specified causes and the disturbance term; (c) causation is one-way (i.e., no feedback loops); (d) all disturbance terms are assumed independent of each other and of causally prior variables; (e) all variables are assumed measured without error; and (f) the relationships among the five exogenous (social origin) variables are causally unanalysed.

The conventions of path analysis are illustrated in Figure 2.1: single-headed arrows connect postulated cause and effect, with effect at the head of the arrow; curved double-headed arrows link the two exogenous variables whose correlation remains causally unanalysed; and disturbance terms are shown as external influences on the system. Estimation of model parameters was carried out by regressing each of the five endogenous variables in the model on all causally prior variables. The standardised path and path regression (unstandardised) coefficients yielded by this procedure are shown in Table 2.2.

Before discussing our results we should say something about measurement error. As already noted the present analysis treats all variables as if they are measured without error. We know this is untrue, even for the self-reported data, not to mention the proxy information on parents. However, our survey design did not encompass multiple indicators, nor did our resources permit a remeasurement program. Our treatment of measurement error can only be informal, at least at this stage, and because we have no direct means of estimating the nature and degree of any bias introduced, we interpret the coefficients shown below, and differences between them, somewhat tentatively. We return to this point in the conclusion.

The question of specification error must also be considered. In the ten variable form shown, our model omits at least one potentially important determinant of occupational status and income, namely, a measure of the respondent's intellectual ability. To the extent that ability *directly* affects occupational status and income independently of education the model is misspecified, the parameter estimates are biased upwards from their true values, and we run the risk of overestimating the social and economic returns to education. On the other hand, if its effect on occupation and income is largely *indirect* via the educational attainment, we can have more confidence in the estimates shown.

The available evidence for another industrial country (the United States) points to a substantial effect of intellectual ability on educational attainment and thereby on occupational attainment and income.[14] Evidence for a direct effect on occupation and income –

other things equal, more intelligent individuals attain higher status and earn more – is somewhat equivocal. For example. Duncan, Jencks and Sewell and Hauser[15] demonstrate small direct effects on occupation and earnings. Alexander, Eckland and Griffin[16] find an anomalous negative effect for earnings only, while Griliches and Mason[17] suggest that the effect on earnings is marginal at best. We did not attempt to measure ability in our survey, and in this initial reporting of the data we have not yet attempted to estimate the extent of this bias, if any, by other means. However, evidence elsewhere would seem to indicate the possibility of minor bias in the direction of overestimating (but not by much) the returns to education because we have no direct measure of ability.

The omission of parental income, or a surrogate, among the occupational and educational components of the respondent's socio-economic background has sometimes been advanced as a serious misspecification affecting estimates of the economic returns to education.[18] Griffin[19] demonstrates such a bias using several US data sets, notably in samples limited to men in their early career. The possibility of such an effect being present in our data led us to include a measure of parental income indexed by household possessions, as already described.

In discussing the impact of education on occupational and economic statuses, and status attainment processes generally, we need to take some note of research in other countries. But while similar sorts of models to the one presented here have been used elsehwere (and earlier in Australia), differences in approach inhibit any sustained or detailed comparison. Although we include some comparative references, we approach direct comparisons between studies with some caution, and comparative data serve merely to provide a broader context for interpreting our results.

Correlations among the ten variables along with means, standard deviations, coefficient of variation, and number of cases are shown in Table 2.1. The estimated path coefficients (standardised partial regression coefficients) and their unstandardised analogues (path regressions) are shown in Table 2.2, together with the squared multiple correlation coefficient for each equation. In Table 2.3 the correlations among variables are decomposed into direct effects, indirect effects, and causally unanalysed components. The explanation of these terms is taken up in the following discussion.

Table 2.1 is of interest mainly because it provides an overview of the interrelationships among our data. The education variables, for example, reveal more years of education for respondents than their

Table 2.1: Correlations, Means, Standard Deviations, and Coefficients of Variation for Status Model Variables

Status Variable	Zero order correlations													
	DADED	DADJB	MOMED	WLTH	FAMSZ	BASED	JOB1	ADDED	JOBN	INCOME	X	SD	CV	No. of cases
DADED	1.000	.351	.486	.237	–.170	.361	.205	.093	.242	.181	8.45	2.98	.353	2,032
DADJOB		1.000	.193	.321	–.099	.218	.312	.005	.259	.171	515.27	111.54	.216	2,316
MOMED			1.000	.271	–.161	.372	.221	.064	.245	.171	8.21	2.02	.246	2,196
WLTH				1.000	–.182	.345	.270	.051	.327	2.86	0.00	1.00	a	2,444
FAMSZ					1.000	–.269	–.147	–.110	–.232	–.187	4.62	2.58	.558	2,547
BASED						1.000	.507	.054	.481	.363	9.57	2.28	.238	2,560
JOB1							1.000	.054	.495	.359	486.36	90.07	.185	2,558
ADDED								1.000	.254	.162	0.50	0.90	1.800	2,560
JOBN									1.000	.526	525.11	116.65	.222	2,560
INCOME										1.000	128.54	70.17	.546	2,560

a. Not calculated because the indicators forming this variable are in standardised form.

Table 2.2: Path Coefficients[a] and Path Regressions[b] for Status Attainment Model

Dependent Variables	Independent Variables: DADED	DADJOB	MOMED	WLTH	FAMSZ	BASED	JOB1	ADDED	JOBN	RSQ (Intercept)
BASED	.176 (.134)	.035[c] (.001)	.197 (.222)	.208 (.474)	−.166 (−.147)					.261 (5.595)
JOB1	−.059 (−1.777)	.213 (.172)	.026 (1.152)	.052 (4.676)	−.000 (−.015)	.454 (17.949)				.302 (224.788)
ADDED	.083 (.025)	−.052 (−.000)	.012 (.005)	.024 (.022)	−.095 (−.033)	−.024 (−.009)	.042 (.000)			.021 (.467)
JOBN	.004 (.159)	.065 (.068)	.021 (1.210)	.114 (13.305)	−.071 (−3.194)	.238 (12.165)	.296 (.384)	.210 (27.022)		.388 (169.645)
INCOME	.018 (.420)	−.018 (−.011)	−.019 (−.645)	.102 (7.124)	−.038 (−1.043)	.084 (2.587)	.094 (.073)	.047 (3.338)	.390 (.235)	.306 (−40.676)

a. Path coefficients (standardised partial regression coefficients) uppermost in each pair.
b. Path regressions (unstandardised partial regression coefficients) in parentheses.
c. An underlined coefficient is less than twice its standard error.

Table 2.3: Decomposition of Effects for Status Attainment Model

Dependent Variable	Predetermined Variable	Zero-order Correlation	Total Causal Effect	Total Direct Effect	Total Indirect Effect	Indirect Effects via BASED	JOB1	ADDED	JOBN	Causally Unanalysed Component
BASED	DADED	.361[a]	.176	.176						.185
	DADJOB	.218	.035[b]	.035						.183
	MOMED	.372	.197	.197						.175
	WLTH	.345	.208	.208						.137
	FAMSZ	–.269	–.166	–.166						–.103
JOB1	DADED	.205	.021[b]	–.059	.080	.080				.184
	DADJOB	.313	.228	.213	.015	.015				.085
	MOMED	.221	.115	.026	.089	.089				.106
	WLTH	.270	.147	.052	.095	.095				.123
	FAMSZ	–.147	–.076	–.000	–.076	–.076				–.071
	BASED	.507	.454	.454						.053
ADDED	DADED	.093	.080	.083	–.003	–.001	–.002			.013
	DADJOB	.005	–.043[b]	–.052	.009	.000	.009			.048
	MOMED	.064	.012[b]	.012	.000	.000	.000			.052
	WLTH	.051	.025[b]	.024	.001	–.001	.002			.026
	FAMSZ	–.110	–.094	–.095	.001	.001	.000			–.016
	BASED	.054	–.005[b]	–.024	.019		.019			.059
	JOB1	.054	.042[b]	.042						
JOBN	DADED	.242	.069	.004	.065	.065	–.017	.017		.173
	DADJOB	.259	.132	.065	.067	.013	.065	–.011		.127
	MOMED	.245	.104	.021	.083	.073	.008	.002		.141
	WLTH	.327	.213	.114	.099	.078	.016	.005		.114
	FAMSZ	–.232	–.152	–.071	–.081	–.061	–.001	–.019		.080
	BASED	.481	.371	.238	.133		.138	–.005		.110
	JOB1	.495	.305	.296	.009			.009		.190
	ADDED	.254	.210	.210						.044
INCOME	DADED	.181	.065	.018	.047	.048	–.013	.011	.001	.116
	DADJOB	.171	.056	–.018	.074	.009	.046	–.007	.026	.115
	MOMED	.171	.050[b]	–.019	.069	.053	.006	.001	.009	.121
	WLTH	.286	.217	.102	.115	.057	.011	.003	.044	.069
	FAMSZ	–.187	–.123	–.038	–.085	–.045	.000	–.012	–.028	–.064
	BASED	.363	.271	.084	.187		.097	–.003	.093	.092
	JOB1	.359	.215	.094	.121			.005	.116	.144
	ADDED	.162	.125	.043	.082				.082	.037
	JOBN	.526	.390	.390						.136

a. Standardised coefficients shown.

b. Coefficient < 2 s.e.

parents, and a moderately high degree of assortative mating in the parental generation (correlation of .486 between DADED and MOMED). Occupational status is highest for JOBN and lowest for JOB1, which also has lower relative dispersion. The three variables with the greatest relative dispersion are ADDED, FAMSZ and INCOME, all of which are skewed towards higher values. Only FAMSZ has a uniform negative sign with the status variables shown, indicating that the larger the number of children the lower the status of the family of origin and the lower the values of the outcome status variables. Coming from a large family constitutes a barrier to later attainment as Table 2.3 above shows. Note also that the relationship between education and jobs seems stronger for respondents than for the fathers, and cohort analysis indicates that BASED has become more important in determining career beginnings. Among men aged 30 to 39 years, the correlation between BASED and JOB1 is .589, compared with .504 for those aged 40 to 49, .358 for those aged 50 to 59.

Two other features of Table 2.1 can be noted. Firstly, looking across the first five rows of the table, we observe that on balance the social origin variables are more closely related to early statuses of the respondent (BASED and JOB1) than to later statuses (JOBN and INCOME). Secondly, the highest correlations tend to be clustered in the right hand corner of the table, representing the statuses of the respondent rather than his family of origin. These impressions are formalised and given quantitative expression in the structural equations presented in Tables 2.2 and 2.3.

Determinants of Income

Our theoretical model for the determinants of income are represented by the structural equation shown at the bottom of Table 2.2, which specifies that current income is a function of social origins, education, career beginnings, additional education, and present job. Note that all but one of the social origin variables have insignificant effects (we can therefore ignore the negative signs for DADJOB and MOMED), and only the surrogate for family income shows a significant, and positive, effective on current income. Since our income data comprise income from all sources, there are two possible lines of explanations for this effect: either more affluent parents make direct monetary contributions to their sons (including transfers of wealth which generate income streams), or better-off parents are able to channel their sons into particular kinds of occupational niches where they receive higher income net of other factors such as years of education or broad occupational category. Even though we employ a very detailed job classification there is of course residual internal variation within occupational categories (for example, the category for medical doctor includes self-employed specialists as well as salaried medical officers). Moreover, our measure of education does not distinguish kind of schooling, only amount. So there are residual elements of heterogeneity in our variables that origin measures may be picking up.

Table 2.2 shows that five variables effectively explain 31 per cent of the variation income, a figure somewhat higher than usually reported for age-comparable samples[20] and much higher than that from early career studies[21] because of the interaction between length of education and work experience.[22] The ordering of relative effects on respondent's personal income are: JOBN (.390), WLTH (.102), JOB1 (.094), BASED (.084) and ADDED (.047). If WLTH is omitted the effects of socio-economic background on income appear as entirely indirect and mediated through BASED, JOB1, JOBN and, to some extent, ADDED. The inclusion of WLTH reduces the apparent direct effect of BASED on INCOME. Even so, in this Australian sample, as in comparable US samples, income is predominantly a function of current occupational status. The effects of other significant determinants is predominantly through intervening variables. As the decomposition of the zero-order correlations in the last panel of Table 2.3 shows, WLTH has a modest direct effect on INCOME, and indirect effects of slightly greater magnitude by way of BASED and to a lesser degree JOBN. Similarly the ratio of indirect to direct effects of BASED on INCOME is two to one, the indirect effects being mediated by first and present job. The indirect effects of JOB1 and ADDED are similarly larger than their direct effects.

Determinants of Current Occupational Status

Close to 40 per cent of the variance in occupational status at time of interview can be explained by six variables with significant effects, a figure comparable to those reported by others.[23] In terms of their relative importance the determinants of current job status are: JOB1 (.296), BASED (.238), ADDED (.210), WLTH (.114) and DADJOB (.065). The sizeable effect of initial placement within the occupational structure on current status is expected, while the effect of continuing investment in education on occupational attainment (net of basic education, social background, and first job) supports the broad arguments of human capital theorists. The strength of occupational 'inheritance' (a metaphor for a complex set of unspecified relations tending to make fathers' and sons' occupational statuses similar) is indicated here to be real, but slight compared to other factors in the model. The same indeterminacy of initial occupational placement on later status seen elsewhere[24] is seen here in the almost equal effect of BASED (.238) and JOB1 (.269) on JOBN. Thus, education gained prior to entering the workforce not only effects initial placement within the occupational structure, but generates occupational status returns throughout the career.

Further Education

The R-square in Table 2.2 shows that our data cannot offer any appreciable explanation for additional educational attainments. The three determinants with statistically significant effects – FAMSZ (–.095) DADED (.083) and DADJOB (–.052) – explain only 2.0 per cent of the variance and none of the other possible effects add to the explanation. The literal interpretation is that, other things equal, (1) respondents from higher education backgrounds tend to return to school after they enter the labour force and (2) those from families in higher occupational status groups and larger families tend not to. The seemingly rational argument that low status individuals advance their initial occupation attainments through further education is not supported here though it has been elsewhere,[25] possibly because in the West German study apprenticeships were counted as further education. As noted above, the way in which the Australian census classification of occupations is constructed eliminates any similar effect in our Australian data.

Career Beginnings

The degree of explanation of variability in JOB1 is about as effective as with income. The effect of BASED (.454) on initial job status is strong, over double the direct effect of DADJOB (.213) which represents both occupational 'inheritance' and probably attitudinal variables affected by social origins, such as motivations, aspirations, and the like. The apparently anomalous and small negative effect of DADED (–.059) simply means that among individuals of similar educational level and similar occupational backgrounds, those with higher educated fathers tend to have first jobs of marginally lower status. WLTH has a modest positive effect on first job, while the other origin variables have no significant impact.

Basic Education

The variables in our model explain slightly less of the variance in BASED (26 per cent), a figure comparable to US samples.[26] However, we employ a larger set of origin variables. Note that the education and economic environments of the home, rather than job status *per se,* exercise the main effects on son's basic education, while family size has, as expected, a negative effect on years of education obtained.

Direct and Indirect Effects

To this point we have mainly examined the direct effects shown in Table 2.2 and have said little about indirect effects. In simple recursive models such as the one presented here, the correlation between any two variables (DADED and JOBN, for example) can be decomposed into three parts: that due to the direct influence of DADED on JOBN; that due to the indirect effect of DADED on JOBN via intervening variables (like BASED, for example); and a causally unanalysed component (joint effect) due to the unanalysed exogenous correlation of DADED with the origin variables.[27] The first two components (direct and indirect effects) specified by the model are termed the *total causal effect.*

Table 2.3 provides such a decomposition of the zero-order correlations in our model. Using the same example as before, the total correlation between DADED and JOBN (.242) can be decomposed into an unanalysed component (.173), an insignificant direct effect (.004), and a total indirect effect of .065 mediated by BASED, JOB1 (–.017) and ADDED (.017).

We restrict our examination of indirect effects to the two status outcomes of interest, JOBN and INCOME. For JOBN the influence of DADED is largely indirect through BASED (.065), whereas the indirect influence of DADJOB is mainly through JOB1; the indirect effect of BASED (roughly one half the size of the direct effect at .133) is also via JOB1, while that of JOB1 is negligible (.009). Since no variables intervene between ADDED and JOBN there can be no indirect effect in this case.

Social origins contribute to current job status largely through their effect on educational attainment and career beginnings. In terms of an added-variance model, social origins exert slightly less influence on current job than basic education, further education and first job: the five social origin variables explain a maximum of 18.1 per cent of the variance in current job, or about 46 per cent of the total variance explained when all the antecedent causes specified in our model are included.

The influence of social origins is slightly lower in the case of income, accounting for 11.5 per cent of the variance when the additional effects of BASED, ADDED, JOB1, and JOBN are taken into account, or 37 per cent of the total. As with current job status, the effects of social origins are largely dispersed over intervening variables, except for WLTH whose direct effect is of similar magnitude to the indirect effect. The indirect effect of BASED (about twice its direct effect, .187 and .084 respectively) is via occupational attainments, that of initial occupational placement is through current job (.116), and ADDED (.082), of necessity, via JOBN.

In many respects the structure of our basic model approximates that of similar models estimated for US samples. Social and economic statuses reflect social background largely because advantageous social origins confer an educational advantage on the individuals in question. We find, as did Blau and Duncan, that education and social origins contribute to initial occupational placement, and to subsequent occupational attainments. However, point of entry into the occupational structure does not fix subsequent attainments. Education continues to exert an impact on occupational and economic status throughout the course of a man's career. In addition, we find support for human capital arguments in the social and economic gains from increments in basic prework education which continue to accrue even after entry into the labour force.

The Social and Economic Impact of Education

Our model can be interpreted concretely to estimate gains in current status and income flowing from years of education gained before and after beginning work. The coefficients in question are the standardised coefficients and unstandardised coefficients shown in Table 2.2. Their respective interpretations are: other (specified) things equal, a *one-standard deviation* change in a cause produces an N-standard deviation change in the effect (where N is a path coefficient); and, other (specified) things equal, a one-*unit* change in a cause produces an N-unit change in the effect (where N is a path regression). The latter coefficients are sometimes called metric coefficients because they preserve the original metric of both variables.

Consider the occupational status gains from education first. Using the standard deviation values shown in Table 1 and the standardised parameters in Table 2.3, we can see that, controlling for social background, a one-standard deviation change in BASED produces a .371

standard deviation change in JOBN (total causal effect, Table 2.2). That is, a year of basic education, net of the influence of social origins, products occupational status returns of some 19 status points [(.371) (116.65) ÷ (1) (2.28)]on a scale ranging from a low of 331 to a high of 880. Such a change approximates, for example, the status difference between civil and electrical engineers, university reachers and executive CAE teachers, clergy and airline pilots, plumbers and auto mechanics. Of these 19 status points, some 14 are due to the direct effect of BASED on JOBN net of the effects of other causes of JOBN, and the remainder accrues via indirect effects, largely via JOB1 (see Table 2.3). Similarly, one year of additional education (ADDED) adds some 27 status points net of other causes of JOBN [(.21) (116.65) ÷ (1) (.90)]. Put another way, individuals alike in all other (specified) respects will differ in status by a factor of 19 times their difference in years of basic education; for a high school graduate compared with a man with a bachelor's degree such a difference amounts to some 60 to 70 status points. And individuals alike in all respects including level of basic education but differing by one year in their investment in additional education will differ by some 27 status points.

The issue of economic gains from education can be approached in similar fashion. Recall, however, that income was measured on a 16 category scale, and each category is an income range. As a result the dollar values shown are more approximate than the occupational status scores.

An increment of one year in BASED net of social background effects returns a little more than $18 per week [(70.17) x (.271) ÷ (1) (2.28)] in additional income, or about $400 a year. Of this $400, about a third is due to the direct influence of BASED on INCOME net of other influences, and the remainder to indirect effects of education via the two occupational status variables. Similarly, a year of additional education returns about $10 per week [(70.17) x (.125) ÷ (1) (.90)], or some $500 a year, one third of which is due to the direct effect of ADDED on INCOME and the remaining two-thirds to an indirect effect via JOBN. In other words, individuals alike in all (specified) respects but differing by one year in BASED will differ by some $400 a year in current income. Again, individuals alike in all respects including BASED but differing in their investment in ADDED will differ in income by a factor of $500 times the difference in years of education. But we should also note that coming from an affluent background is almost as good an 'investment' as basic education. The WLTH variable contributes about equally to current status and to current income, both directly and indirectly through BASED. Its direct effect on income is about $350 a year [(.102) (70.17) ÷ (1) (1.02)], an amount not much less than the figure estimated for a year of basic education. Affluent families provide double insurance for their sons, in that they enable them to get more basic education and then contribute directly to their current income, either by cash transfers, or by influencing aspects of education and jobs not directly measured in our model.[28]

Conclusion

In this preliminary analysis we have sought to develop a relatively straightforward extension of a by now conventional model of the process of status attainment. With cross-sectional data on Australian men aged between 30 and 69 years in paid employment in 1973, we have been successful in explaining substantial parts of the variation in job statuses and current income, with a modest number of variables. The question arises, of course, as to how far the estimates we have given will vary for different age groups and different sub-groups. We have carried out a number of preliminary analyses not reported here which identify some interesting departures from our overall estimates. Thus, if we consider only employees we find that we can explain almost 40 per cent of the variance in current income. Not only is this level of explanation higher than when all workers are included but the pattern of relative effects is somewhat different. Both BASED and ADDED have heightened effects for employees. Clearly formal education is less important for entrepreneurs, whose income is highly dispersed (and variable over time), and less readily explicable in terms of the variables in our present model. Similarly, although the level of explanation for current job status is about the same for both employee and self-employed/employer groups, father's occupation (DADJOB) is a much more significant determinant of current status for the self-employed/employer group than for employees, and BASED is of no direct importance at all. Education is obviously a more effective determinant of social and economic rewards in formalised, bureaucratic settings.

Analysis by age cohorts suggests few major changes over time, except (as mentioned above) some evidence that the link between basic education and career beginnings has become stronger. The partial regression coefficient for BASED on JOB1 is 17.949 overall, but 22.580 for the youngest cohort in our sample (men aged 30-39) and only 12.117 for men twenty years older (50-59).[29] Also, our model explains more of the variance in current income among men well along in their working lives. Thus, we can explain 37 per cent of the variance in income for the 50 to 59 year-old cohort but only 25 per cent in the 30 to 39 year-old cohort, a difference mainly attributable to a heightened effect of current job. We take this difference to be evidence of wage contours for experience and seniority within specific occupational categories.

Our model is not successful in explaining variation in education obtained after beginning work, a finding we attribute to the fact that men with the lowest educational levels are largely excluded from pursuing further education while those with the highest have little incentive to do so. Further education appears to be sought mainly by the middle mass, and thus there is no linear relationship between basic and further education. In our sample ADDED appears to be most important for men who started work in the depression of the 1930s and least important for those who first sought work afterwards.

As a final point, we confront the possible objection that our estimates of the relative importance of social origins on later statuses and rewards may be downwardly biassed because the measures of home background are retrospective and therefore less reliable. There are two responses to such an objection, one general, the other specific. The general response is that we have included several, not just one or two, measures of social origins as a means of guarding atainst attenuation due to unreliability in recollection. Thus, we would expect errors in background variable to be partially corrected by other background variables, providing reporting errors are not very highly inter-correlated.

The specific answer is that the most carefully conducted study of response errors available shows conclusively that retrospective responses about parental status are at least as consistent over time (and in that restricted sense, as 'reliable') as reports of current statuses.[30] Therefore, the effect of correcting for reliability is not radically to alter any estimate of the relative importance of social background on later attainment but rather to increase the total level of explanation provided by the model. Thus, we feel moderately confident in our conclusions about the relative impact of family background on later social and economic rewards. Parents do improve their sons' chances of higher occupational and economic rewards by enabling them to get more years of education, an opportunity which, according to our data, is more available to higher status families if only because their opportunity costs are less. A wider question is how far public resources allocated to the educational system should be used to facilitate status maintenance across the generations and how far they should be used to facilitate the mobility chances of socially disadvantaged groups, not to mention the re-training of workers whose skills have become obsolete because of changing technology or shifts in the demand for specific goods and services.

Notes

1. Peter M. Blau and Otis D. Duncan, *The American Occupation Structure* (Wiley, New York, 1967).
2. Ibid., p.8.
3. Australian youth have high occupational expectations, with large proportions expecting to enter professional jobs. Large majorities also believe that education is required for work roles. See W.F. Connell, R.E. Stroobant, K.E. Sinclair, R.W. Connell, and K.W. Rogers, *12 to 20: Studies of City Youth* (Hicks Smith and Sons, Melbourne, 1975) especially chapter 9. See also N.F. Dufty, 'Vocational Choices of 13-14 Year Old Males in Relation to Intelligence and Reasons for Job Choice', *Australian Journal of Education,* vol.4, April 1960, pp.38-56.
4. For Australian evidence, see Richard Blandy and Tony Goldsworthy, 'Private Returns to Education in South Australia', in G.S. Harman and C. Selby Smith, *Readings in the Economics and Politics of Education* (Pergamon Press, Sydney, 1976); and C. Selby Smith, 'Rates of Return to Post-Secondary Education in Australia', *Economic Record,* vol.51, December 1975, p.455-85. For overseas data, see Mark Blaug, *An Introduction to the Economics of Education* (Allen Lane The Penguin Press, London, 1970); Elchanan Cohn, *The Economics of Education* (Lexington Books, D.C. Heath and Company, Lexington, 1972); and George Psacharopoulos, *Returns to Education: An International Comparison* (Elsevier Scientific Publishing Company, Amsterdam, 1973).
5. Aage B. Sorensen, 'Growth in Occupational Achievement: Social Mobility or Investment in Human Capital', in Kenneth C. Land and Seymour Spilerman (eds.), *Social Indicator Models* (Russell Sage Foundation, New York, 1975) pp.335-65.
6. Leonard Broom, Paul Duncan-Jones, F. Lancaster Jones and Patrick McDonnell, *Investigating Social Mobility,* (Department Monograph No.1, Department of Sociology, RSSS, Australian National University 1977).
7. Ibid.
8. Australian Bureau of Statistics, *Classification and Classified List of Occupations* (Commonwealth Government Printing Office, Canberra, 1971).
9. Leonard Broom, Paul Duncan-Jones, F. Lancaster Jones and Patrick McDonnell, 'The Social Standing of Jobs: Status Scores for All Australian Occupations', in Broom *et al.,* op. cit.
10. Otis Dudley Duncan, 'A Socio-economic Index for All Occupations', in Albert J. Reiss, *Occupations and Social Status* (Free Press, New York, 1961), pp.109-38.
11. The two other studies in this area which converted part-time education to full-time equivalents do not specify the manner in which the transformation was made. See Walter Muller, 'Family Background, Education, and Career Mobility' in Walter Muller and Karl U. Mayer (eds.), *Social Stratification and Career Mobility* (Mouton, The Hague, 1973) pp.223-55; and William H. Sewell and Robert M. Hauser, *Education, Occupation, and Earnings* (Academic Press, New York, 1975) p.20.
12. Australian Bureau of Statistics, *Income Distribution 1973-74* (Australian Bureau of Statistics, Canberra, 1976). Ref. No. 17.6.

13. Ibid., Table 13.
14. Otis Dudley Duncan, 'Ability and Achievement', *Eugenics Quarterly*, vol.15, March 1968, pp.1-11; Christopher Jencks, *Inequality* (Basic Books, Inc, New York, 1972); William H. Sewell and Robert M. Hauser, *Education, Occupation and Earnings* (Academic Press, New York, 1975); Karl Alexander, Bruce. K. Eckland, and Larry J. Griffin, 'The Wisconsin Model of Socioeconomic Attainment: A Replication', *American Journal of Sociology*, vol.81, September 1975, pp.324-42.
15. Duncan, op cit., p.6; Jencks, op. cit., p.339; Sewell and Hauser, op. cit., ch.3.
16. Alexander, Eckland, and Griffin, op. cit., pp.330-5.
17. Zvi Griliches and William M. Mason, 'Education, Income and Ability' in Arthur S. Goldberger and Otis Dudley Duncan (eds.), *Structural Equation Models in the Social Sciences* (Seminar Press, New York, 1973) pp.285-316.
18. Larry Griffin, 'Specification Biases in Estimates of Socioeconomic Returns to Schooling, *Sociology of Education*, vol.49, April, 1976, pp.121-39. Samuel Bowles, 'Schooling and Inequality from Generation to Generation', *Journal of Political Economy*, vol.80, May-June 1972, pp.S.219-S.251.
19. Ibid.
20. Cf. Jencks, op. cit., p.339.
21. Alexander, Eckland, and Griffin, op. cit., p.330; Sewell and Hauser, op. cit., p.100.
22. See Jacob Mincer, *Schooling, Experience, and Earnings*, New York, National Bureau of Economic Research, 1974, p.47.
23. Blau and Duncan, op. cit., p.170; Jencks, op. cit., p.339; Alexander. Eckland, and Griffin, op. cit., pp.330-35; Sewell and Hauser, op. cit., p.100.
24. Blau and Duncan, op. cit., p.170; Walter Muller, op. cit., pp.223-55.
25. Ibid., p.234.
26. Blau and Duncan, op. cit., p.170; Jencks, op. cit., p.339.
27. Blau and Duncan, op. cit., p.170; Duane F. Alwin and Robert M. Hauser, 'The Decomposition of Effects in Path Analysis', *American Sociological Review*, vol.40, February 1975, pp.37-47.
28. The variances for both BASED and JOB1 are unequal across age cohorts, being higher for younger than older men. For this reason unstandardised coefficients provide the appropriate comparisons. See Ronald Schoenberg, 'Strategies for Meangingful Comparison', Chapter 1 in Herbert L. Costner, *Sociological Methodology, 1972* (Jossey-Bass, San Francisco, 1972).
29. We cannot compare our estimates directly with other Australian data. Selby Smith (op. cit.) presents data on post-secondary education only, and Blandy and Goldsworthy (op. cit.) focus on lifetime incomes. They therefore include earnings foregone (the indirect private costs of investing in education) in their estimates of lifetime income. Their estimates of *direct* private costs, in 1969 dollar-values, were $100 per annum for secondary school, and $500 for tertiary degree courses.
30. William T. Bielby, *Response Errors in Models of the Intergenerational Transmission of Socioeconomic Status* (Center for Demography and Economy, University of Wisconsin-Madison, 1976). Working Paper 76-26. The validity, or accuracy, or retrospective reports is a question on which there is much less information.

3 THE ECONOMICS OF ENVIRONMENTAL SERVICES

S.F. Harris and A. Ulph

Life is like a sewer. What you get out of it depends on what you put into it.

T. Lehrer

1. Introduction

Widespread public interest in the environment emerged relatively recently in Australia. It was stimulated by growing concerns about a rather narrow range of specific environmental issues: chemical residues in foodstuffs and in effluents into water courses and ocean outlets; emissions into urban atmospheres; and the loss of natural features or wildlife species through agricultural and mining operations, the building of dams or the harvesting of timber, particularly for woodchipping. It also arose out of concerns about the environment in the broad sense of the capacity of the biosphere to maintain and sustain life; this included the exhaustibility of resources and the degradation of the upper atmosphere, and extended into population control, food production and distribution, energy generation and supply, and indeed the whole question of economic growth and development.

An examination of environmental services, defined as society's actions to deal with these problems, will reflect these concerns, but it will reflect rather more the provision of traditional services such as garbage, sewerage, and other waste disposal; it will also reflect those, often of long standing, related to protection of the resource base, generally coming under the term conservation, such as soil erosion, weed and pest control and the establishment of wildlife and nature reserves.

The above definition of environmental services is too general to be operational. After discussing the nature of environmental problems in the next section, we provide a more detailed specification of environmental services in Section 3. In Section 4, we examine available evidence on services provided in Australia. The actual level of such provision will reflect demand as well as supply factors and these are examined in Sections 5 and 6. Finally, we discuss the broader issues concerning the institutional arrangements for the provision and management of environmental services.

2. The Nature of Environmental Problems

In order to understand the nature of environmental services, we need to consider more carefully the kind of problems the services are designed to address.

The Australian Government legislation defines the environment very broadly as including 'all aspects of the surroundings of man, whether affecting him as an individual or in his social groupings' [17]. In the present context, a more illustrative, if also perhaps less all embracing definition is that in the Victorian legislation which defines the environment as the physical factors of the surroundings of human beings, including 'the land, water, atmosphere, climate, sound, odours, tastes, the biological factors of animals and plants and the social factor of aesthetics' [54].

For some observers, these definitions need extending to include the social, philosophical and ethical value systems and systems of beliefs that reflect a particular form of relationship of man to nature, and of man's social environment. While recognising that these aspects of human behaviour and attitudes affect the nature of the environmental services provided, and perhaps the success they achieve, we shall look at environmental services more narrowly without, however, going to the other extreme by limiting our interest simply to pollution abatement and control.

Natural phenomena, such as earthquakes and cyclones contribute to environmental change or deterioration in a substantial way. Nevertheless, the problems of the environment stem largely from the production and consumption activities of man. In these activities, man transforms natural resources for his own use. These materials are not destroyed but are returned to the natural environment in one form or another and ultimately as waste products or residuals of man's activities.

These residuals[1], in the form of physical wastes, noise, odours, chemical deterioration, or visual unattractiveness, can create difficulties because the amounts produced are heavily concentrated, as, for example, with urban sewage or airport noise levels; because they are toxic when released, such as mercury and cadmium, or they become toxic after release, such as atmospheric reactions to motor vehicle exhaust gases or water body reactions to excessive nutrient inflows; or because they may be irreversible, such as permanent contamination of ground-water or destruction of aboriginal cave paintings.

Environmental problems of this kind have become more pronounced for four principal reasons. First, the magnitudes of these residuals have become large relative to the capacity to absorb them. Their rapid growth has been substantially a consequence of the combined growth of populations and real incomes, and increased production activities. Second, the pace of the increase, particularly in the extent and variety of toxic residuals produced, poses particular problems, and the long time lags associated with their ultimate emergence as health problems involves high levels of uncertainty in assessing their impact and the societal risks they impose. Third, environmental resources, such as land and water, into which residuals were previously deposited without undue difficulty, are increasingly required for other purposes, such as increased leisure activities, consequent upon economic growth. Fourth, over and above these specific demands for environmental resources, demand for improved, rather than diminished, environmental amenity appears to be associated with both rising real incomes and education levels. This also accounts substantially for the increased concern for the preservation of historic and aesthetically valuable monuments, wildlife species, or wilderness areas.

Before examining the institutional arrangements needed to modify the behaviour of producers and consumers which gives rise to these problems, we need to discuss two related economic concepts: externalities, and public good or common property resources.[2]

An external cost arises when the production cost of a firm or the welfare of an individual or group of individuals is affected unintentionally by the production or consumption activities of others. Thus if, with a particular production procedure, a farmer causes additional water or soil runoff from his property onto others, this is an external cost.[3] Many, if not most, of the external costs in the environmental field in fact consist of the disposal of the residuals of the production or consumption processes. This is not exclusively so however; access by an added irrigator to a stream may reduce the supply to others, thus constituting a cost to them.

An external cost problem need not be a public policy issue. Theoretical discussion by Coase and Dales among others has considered the trading of external costs [15, 18]. For example, if a factory on a geographically isolated water course releases residuals which reduce water quality, and consequently affect the production processes or recreational benefits of only a small number of others, this could possibly be resolved privately by bargaining between the parties involved. Thus, affected fishermen could, in principle, seek to purchase the property rights in the use of the river. It may become a public policy issue if the costs of organising the market and of policing these property rights are too high and the problem has to be resolved by regulation or by a system of charges.

The characteristic environmental issue involves a situation in which no one individual has an incentive, except through altruism or because of the constraints of social norms, to act on his own.[4] For a single producer to limit his residual disposal into the environment may achieve no perceptible impact; moreover, since he would be involved in additional costs, unless all take comparable action and incur similar costs, he may be disadvantaged competitively. For a recipient of the effects of others' residual disposals, the cost of taking action to limit them will commonly be far greater than his own possible gain because of the difficulties of preventing 'free riders' benefiting; only if gains to all individuals can be taken into account may the effort be warranted. Action to manage the resource has therefore to be taken collectively. This will normally require public sector involvement, though collective action by common interest groups, such as bushwalking or swimming clubs, may often be sufficient.

A second reason for public sector involvement relates to resource conservation. Concerns with issues such as soil conservation may stem from the external costs they cause in terms of silting of water courses and depositing of soil elsewhere. In part, however, they arise from the desire to conserve the physical characteristics of the soil for future generations.

If the farmer causes his soil to erode, the physical capacity of that soil is reduced over time; other things being equal, its value to future generations will be diminished. It implies that the farmer involved discounts the future quite heavily and this rate would normally be regarded as too high for society as a whole, taking into account its concern for future generations.

It could be argued that these conservation issues, which really concern rates of investment in soil or other productive resource maintenance, are not environment issues as such but questions of optimum use of productive resources, and that environmental issues really concern the competition for environmental resources with effects on final consumers.

Nevertheless, it appears common practice to consider resource conservation as part of the general range of environmental issues; in part because the rate at which resources are utilised substantially determines the quantity of residuals produced [44], and in part because it is difficult in practice to separate conservation issues from other environmental issues. For example, apart from the commercial, recreational, scientific and wildlife habitat functions of forests and fisheries, trees or species of fish are often valued for their own sake.

The implication of the public good or common property nature of environmental resources is that, left to itself, the private market mechanism provides the wrong kinds of incentives and disincentives, the wrong kinds of information signals on which consumption and production decisions are to be made. Although it is commonplace to draw the conclusion from this that public action is required, many of the causal factors, such as the high costs of information gathering, may make it equally difficult for a public authority to act optimally.[5]

3. The Classification of Environmental Services

The term, environmental service, might be defined in several ways. To clarify the distinction, and to draw attention to the nature of choice in the community's or an individual's preference for a particular level environmental amenity, we use a very simplified diagrammatical exposition.

Figure 3.1

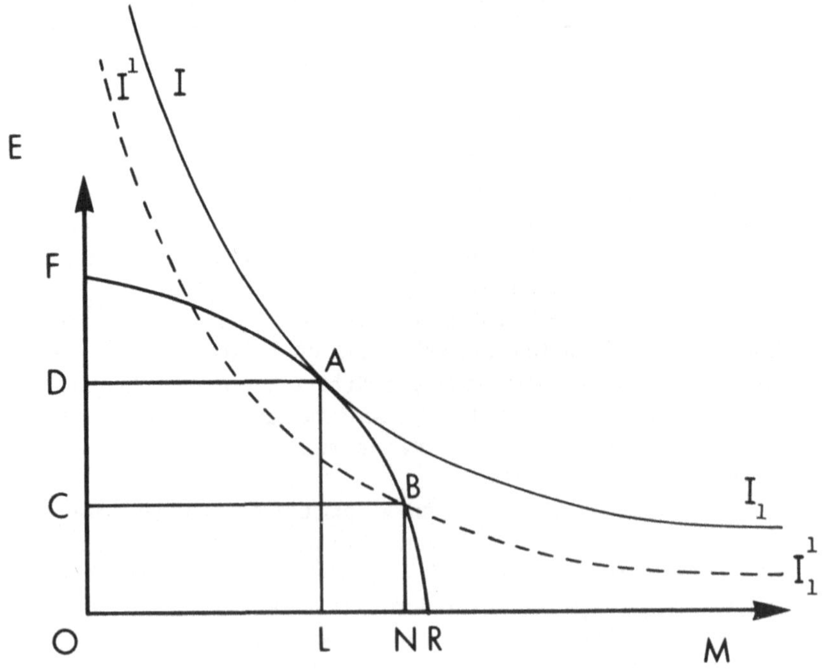

In Fig.3.1, the vertical axis measures environmental amenity (broadly defined)[6]; on the horizontal axis is measured the flow of material goods. Given its resource endowment and utilising fully the technology available to it, society can produce a totally unaffected environment and environmental amenity OF, or material goods OR, or some combination of the two along the production possibility frontier FR. II_1 is an indifference curve from the social welfare function reflecting society's willingness to substitute environmental amenity for material goods at a given level of social welfare.[7]

The point of tangency A is the social optimum showing that society is prepared to sacrifice environmental amenity FD for material goods OL. If in Australia, despite remedial steps already taken, the degree of environmental degradation is currently excessive in relation to society's balancing of costs and benefits, this could be shown in terms of the community in fact operating at point B. The loss of environmental amenity would then be FD plus CD, the latter being unwillingly borne. Point B is sub-optimal because it puts society on a lower level of total social welfare (material and non-material welfare) than it need by, given the production (material and non-material) possibilities.

We can use this framework to examine three different uses of the term environmental service and different categories of cost of providing such services. The first covers the services provided by environmental resources, land, air, and water; these range from absorption of society's residuals to various forms of recreational, visual, physical, or aesthetic amenity. They are measured along the vertical axis: for example, the point OD is the level of environmental services sought and provided at the social optimum. The problem with this definition is the difficulty of providing an operational measurement.

Secondly, we could define environmental services as the sacrifice in material welfare required to obtain a given level of environmental amenity. The costs of any set of environmental services are determined along the horizontal axis. In practice, complete environmental purity is impossible: some emissions to the atmosphere, water courses, and so on, do take place, with the consequent reduction, DF, in the total potential supply of environmental services. At A, the cost of environmental services OD are represented by the sacrifice of material welfare LR. These costs, LR, may take several forms:

> they reflect opportunity costs in terms of goods not produced because of their potential environmental impact, e.g. oil from the Barrier Reef; produced differently and at a higher cost to avoid using

heavily polluting materials, e.g. kraft instead of sulphite papers; or produced in different locations to reduce their environmental impact;

they reflect the direct, largely private, costs of specific measures to limit the environmental impact of production processes, e.g. installation of special filtering equipment;

they reflect direct, largely public sector, costs of disposing of residuals that do occur, e.g. garbage and sewage disposal expenditures, or of otherwise remedying past environmental damage.

LR represents the costs of providing environmental services OD on the assumption that the operation of the institutional arrangements required to achieve the social optimum is costless. To achieve a social optimum, however, an alternative market framework has to be provided that can supply information, exclude 'free riders' and generally manage and control environmental resources. This requires financial resources which are likely to be significant. They can be represented, as in Fig.3.2, by shifting the production frontier inwards to F_1R_1.

Figure 3.2

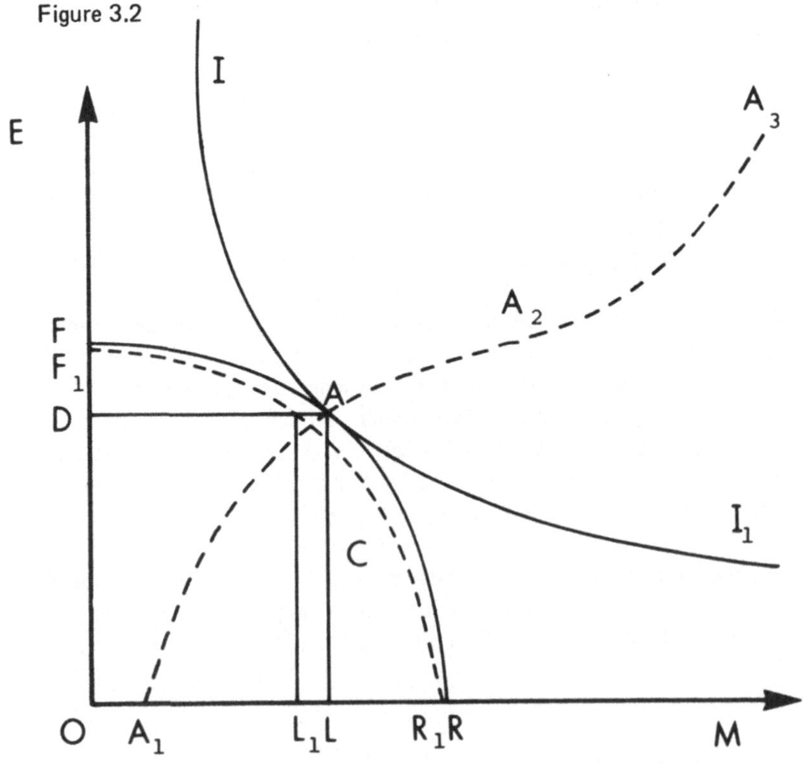

Finally, a more limited view of environmental services is concerned with the management of the residuals from human activities. These represent part of the costs LR in Fig.3.1. Although important since they represent substantial environmental expenditures, we prefer a wider definition. We shall therefore adopt the second definition of environmental services.

The supply of these services in Australia can be classified into four main groups:

(i) the provision of an alternative to the market for environmental management;
(ii) the management, for health, safety and environmental amenity reasons of the residuals that still arise;
(iii) the enlargement of the assimilative capacity of environmental resources; and
(iv) the conservation of environmental, including historical and wildlife, resources.

Though clear distinctions are not always possible,[8] the following grouping lists the main Australian services provided under each of these headings.

(1) *Provision of an Alternative Framework to the Market*

- assembly and maintenance of environmental data and its analysis
- establishment of environmental quality standards and targets
- monitoring of environmental quality such as air pollution, water quality, and noise levels, and incidence of pesticide and other chemical residues
- the public dissemination of environmental information
- environmental impact statement procedures and preparation
- research into environmental problems
- urban, regional and environmental planning

(2) *Control and Disposal of Residuals*

- garbage disposal
- sewerage, stormwater and drainage
- smoke abatement, motor vehicle emission controls
- noise and other nuisance controls
- anti-litter activities

(3) *Changing the Assimilative Capacity of the Environmental Resource*

- river flow control systems

(4) *Conservation of Environmental Resources and Restoration of Past Environmental Damage*

- soil conservation
- protection of agricultural land against noxious weeds, pests and diseases
- forestry and fisheries conservation and management
- bushfire, flood control, other disasters and natural hazards
- irrigation systems management
- conservation of aboriginal religious sites, carvings, paintings, archeological and other sites considered part of the national heritage
- preservation of wilderness areas, national parks, endangered species of flora and fauna
- preservation and restoration of historic buildings and monuments

4. The Supply of Environmental Services in Australia

In attempting to measure the supply of such services in Australia, two major data deficiencies emerge. First, although controls and regulations applied by the public sector imply substantial costs for the private sector, only fragmentary data is available on the extent of those costs. Secondly, although there has been a significant improvement in the availability of data on public sector expenditures, it is not available in sufficient detail to compare easily with our classifications.

We have presented the available data on public sector outlays in Table 3.1 for the period 1965/6 to 1975/6. A broad description of the items covered is given in the notes to the table and further detailed discussion of data sources and definitions is provided elsewhere [53]. In general terms, the tabulated data would generally cover the first two of our four classifications.

Both in absolute and relative terms, there has been a marked growth in these public sector outlays. In order to look at the changes in real terms, price and per capita quantity indexes are shown in Table 3.2. From this we can show that, of the average annual growth of total public expenditure on environmental services, 62 per cent was due to rising costs, 27 per cent to rising per capita output and 11 per cent to population growth.

The State components of the aggregate indexes showed broadly comparable patterns for sewerage services; the main exceptions were for Queensland, where the figures for output per head rose by some 68 per cent and for Western Australia, where the increase in per head output is shown as only 14 per cent. For garbage, the quantity of services stayed broadly in line with population growth overall. In Queensland and Tasmania, there appeared to be quite significant

Table 3.1: Relative Changes in Environmental Service Outlays by Public Authorities in Australia: 1965-6 to 1974-5[a]

Year	Operating Expenses[b] (i) $M	Capital Expenses[c] (ii) $M	Total (i) & (ii) (iii)[d] $M	Ratios: (ii) as a % of Public Fixed Investment (iv) %	Ratios: (ii) as a % of Total Fixed Investment (v) %	Ratios: (iii) as a % of GDP (vi) %
1965-6	98.7	121.5	222.1	5.7	2.1	1.1
1966-7	108.6	135.3	246.3	6.2	2.3	1.1
1967-8	120.1	139.4	262.5	5.9	2.1	1.1
1968-9	135.7	155.0	296.8	6.1	2.1	1.1
1969-70	150.0	183.8	338.3	6.7	2.3	1.1
1970-1	169.7	216.2	391.5	7.4	2.5	1.2
1971-2	201.0	256.4	464.1	7.8	2.7	1.3
1972-3	238.1	311.4	557.4	9.0	3.1	1.3
1973-4	277.3	356.9	643.5	9.2	3.0	1.3
1974-5[e]	339.6	464.9	817.3	8.5	3.2	1.5

Notes: a. The expenditures included in each category are those covered by the ABS Purpose Classifications 6.3, 7.5 and 7.9 set out in detail in [2, pp.91-6].

b. Operating expenses are made up of –

(i) general government final consumption expenditure on sewerage and drainage, sanitation and garbage, protection of the environment, recreational facilities and services (including parks, playgrounds, zoological gardens and beaches but also stadiums, community centres and public halls), and other recreation and related cultural service programmes including national parks and wildlife reserves, historic sites and buildings and other elements of the national estate. These are gross figures before deduction of receipts from charges for goods and services and do not include any allowance for depreciation; and

(ii) outlays of state trading enterprises for the same economic purpose. This is similarly a gross figure from which revenue has not been deducted.

These figures differ from the net figures generally presented in [2].

c. Capital outlays consist of expenditures on new fixed capital assets for the same purposes.

d. Includes in addition to the items included in clauses (i) and (ii) expenditures on soil conservation which amounted to $12.8m in 1974-5; they rose to $18.6m in 1975-6.

e. Subject to revision.

Source: Derived from special tabulations supplied by the Australian Bureau of Statistics; and information supplied by the Bureau of Environmental Studies.

Table 3.2: Provision of Environmental Services: Price and Quantity Indices for Australia: Total Expenditure

Year	Garbage	Sewerage	Other Environment Protection	Recreation	National Estate etc.	Soil Conser-	Total
			Price Indices				
1965/6	100	100	100	100	100	100	100
1966/7	103	105	104	105	105	105	105
1967/8	112	109	108	110	110	110	105
1968/9	115	118	112	115	115	117	117
1969/70	123	125	118	122	122	124	124
1970/1	143	134	126	133	134	135	135
1971/2	157	147	136	146	148	148	148
1972/3	178	160	148	159	161	161	162
1973/4	191	181	169	183	186	183	183
1974/5	230	218	212	231	235	222	222
		Per Capita Quantity Indices					
1965/6	100	100	100	100	100	100	100
1966/7	102	107	95	97	100	115	104
1967/8	102	107	83	97	134	134	104
1968/9	105	109	204	97	194	168	108
1969/70	103	121	184	96	231	171	115
1970/1	96	134	103	97	168	190	119
1971/2	97	146	133	97	172	206	127
1972/3	100	155	337	107	215	218	138
1973/4	107	158	401	98	220	226	138
1974/5	103	163	458	100	257	252	142

Notes:

Coverage

The expenditures included in the categories garbage, sewerage, other protection of the environment, recreation and national estate etc., are as detailed in the Notes to Table 3.1. As explained, these are gross expenditures including current and capital outlays. The soil conservation expenditure figures for the years 1970/1 to 1975/6 were provided by the Bureau of Environmental Studies; estimates for earlier years were made from individual State data.

Method

Except for soil conservation the indexes were formed by Divisia aggregation of capital and current expenditure series.

Current Expenditure. Price and quantity indexes were constructed for each of the six States, based on current expenditures only. For 'sanitation and garbage', a cost index was used based on State award wages for an average garbage crew. For 'sewerage and drainage', a quantity index was constructed based on the number of units connected to the sewerage system. For 'protection of the environment', recreation and the national estate etc., quantity indexes were derived by using the implicit national accounts deflator for public consumption expenditure. Australia wide indexes were constructed for each service by Divisia aggregation across States; aggregation was also carried out by service type, by Divisia indexes, for each State and for Australia.

Total Expenditure. Current and capital price and quantity indexes for sewerage and drainage, garbage and sanitation, other protection of the environment, recreation, national estate etc., in Australia were combined using Divisia aggregation. The resulting price index was used to derive a quantity index for soil conservation.

The categories, now including soil conservation, were combined again using Divisia aggregation. Finally, the quantity indexes were converted to per capita series.

reductions in output per head, and a large growth, by some 70 per cent, in South Australia. For both sewerage and garbage these differences may be explained by differences in initial levels of per capita expenditure. Since there are difficulties with the classification of expenditures both within and between States, these comparisons should be treated with considerable caution.

The costs we have discussed are essentially public sector costs dealing particularly with pollution control and abatement. Measurement difficulties in the private sector, however, are substantial conceptually as well as practically. For example, a firm can usually estimate the costs of meeting specified environmental or residual discharge standards; but the cost may be large if the standard is applied suddenly or to relatively new plant, involving retrofitting of appropriate control equipment, or be low or indeterminate if able to be absorbed in the normal plant replacement program [44, p.134].

Few data are available on private sector control costs. Gilpin estimated that some 5 to 6 per cent of the capital cost of a power station may be attributed to air pollution control measures, 5 to 10 per cent for oil refineries, and 10 to 15 per cent of the costs of plant in other process industries [25, p.56]. Murphy who suggested that capital expenditures for NSW for the 5 year period 1963-4 to 1967-8 for pollution control amounted to approximately $2 per head annually, provided generally comparable estimates for a range of industries with an average percentage cost of control of some 7.5 per cent. These estimates ranged from less than 1 per cent for gas works to over 30 per cent for scrap metal recovery [40, p.73]. The latter figure compares with rather more fragmentary evidence provided elsewhere on capital costs but which also pointed to added running costs of 5 to 10 per cent [37].

Clearly, the private costs are large; some 200 or so Australian firms now produce environmental control equipment available for export [21], and various items of equipment are imported, although the figures are not separated in official statistics. A sizeable consulting industry has also emerged [10, pp.60-1].

From these various pieces of information, allowing for costs relating to residual emissions other than those to the atmosphere described above, and for the increase in standards since the time period covered by Murphy, it appears possible that total private costs approach at least 50 to 100 per cent of the levels of public costs. Butlin *et al.* estimate that in the Sydney region, private outlays on waste management/ pollution control, net of purchases from the government sector, could be of the same order of magnitude as public sector outlays [11, Chapt.2]. In these circumstances, therefore it seems possible that, in the light of the figures in Table 3.1, total environmental expenditures in Australia could amount to at least 2 to 3 per cent of gross domestic product (GDP).

It is useful to compare the general orders of magnitude of these figures with others available here or overseas, recognising the difficult problems of comparing magnitudes often with substantial differences in what is or is not included. In comparison with the ratio of total expenditure to GDP shown in Table 3.1, the estimates of Butlin *et al.* for the Sydney region for 1971-2 showed 1.8 per cent of GDP spent by public authorities on pollution abatement and control; with estimated private expenditures, and an allowance made for subsequent real growth in outlays, an estimate of at least 3.5 per cent in 1974/5 is given [11, p.73]. Substantial magnitudes have been experienced overseas, though it is difficult to disentangle costs incurred publicly from private outlays.

In the US, where environmental problems are normally assumed to be greater than in Australia, the 1970 and 1972 legislation on air and water quality 'incontrovertibly represented a national commitment of many hundreds of billions of dollars' [32, p.70]. Annual costs of pollution abatement from 1972 to 1976 to meet US legislative requirements were estimated at some 1.5 per cent of gross national product (GNP), or an additional 1 per cent after allowing for existing expenditure levels.

Estimates for OECD countries as a whole suggested lower expenditure rates of around 0.5 to 2.0 per cent of GNP per annum, investment and operating costs, over the period 1971 to 1975 [43]. The exception was Japan, where environmental abatement since 1973 accounted for some 2 per cent of the Government budget, and in total for some 3 to 5.5 per cent of GNP [30, p.5].

It appears, then, that estimates for Australia are not substantially out of line with those for other countries when allowance is made for definitional differences and for variations in coverage of the estimates. At the same time, the data do not suggest that Australia's expenditures are on the lower end of the international scale. Why this should be is not completely evident but possibly the environmental advantages of overall geographic size in relation to population are offset, at least in part, by the costs of distance in providing environmental services, as with sewerage services, and the high degree of urbanisation and concentration of industry.

In order to explain how the provision of environmental services varies, we need to consider both demand and supply factors. In terms of our simple model in Fig.3.1, changes over time or space could affect either the indifference curves of the social welfare function or the production trade-offs between material welfare and environmental amenity.

The social welfare function can itself change, or be changed. For example, the social optimum may have moved from B to A in Fig.3.1 simply as a result of a unilateral change in preferences or because new information became available. The relative position of A on the curve may change as FR moves outwards because preferences for environmental amenities became more pronounced at higher income levels. This latter can be shown in Fig.3.2 by a locus of points (A_1, A_2 . . .A_n), for different total welfare situations; as this curve has been drawn, it shows little or no willingness to substitute environmental services for material welfare at low incomes, but as total welfare grows, a substantial proportion of each further increment is sought as environmental amenity.

The shape of the social welfare function may be influenced by advertising or persuasion. Governments would not normally seek to change attitudes beyond ensuring that accurate information was available to enable revealed preferences at A to be accurately reflected in the operation of the alternative market, unless they saw the environment as a 'merit good', one that would normally be undervalued by society. That the environment is seen as a merit good might well be concluded from the various school and educational programs seeking to draw attention to environmental complexities, however belated and limited in practice [42]. Particular interest groups, including a substantial number of voluntary organisations such as the Australian Conservation Foundation, Friends of the Earth, Keep Australia Beautiful Council and the like, seek to influence the preference system by advertising and persuasion. If simply providing accurate information, this would help to move society from B to A in Fig.3.1 rather than change the shape of II_1, but it may be that II_1 could also be changed.

Second, the production substitution relationships can change. For example, there may be a lack of information about technical relationships between inputs and outputs of environmental amenity and material goods including residuals; improved information flows may increase efficiency such that changes to different processes to reduce environmental impact may not involve losses of total productive (including environmental amenity) capacity. In other words, the economy could be operating below its production possibility frontier, e.g. at C in Fig.3.2. This may be a result of imperfect price signals external to a given economic activity, i.e. allocative inefficiency; or internal to such an activity, i.e. X-inefficiency [35]. Society may also be operating at less than its technically feasible maximum, and hence within its production frontier, in providing direct environmental services such as sewerage and garbage disposal; increased information may enable these costs to be reduced.

The internalising of the external costs of the various production processes – the provision of an alternative market system – would move society's point of operation from B towards A since production and consumption decisions would reflect more accurately the real costs and benefits to society. Investment in research may develop new technological relationships which, over time, would change the shape of the production possibility curve to increase the level of environmental amenity for a given output. Of course, research may reveal previously hidden environmental costs and so reduce environmental amenity for a given output. Data limitations make it impossible to examine many of these factors, but we shall attempt to examine some influences on environmental service supply and demand in Australia.

5. Factors Affecting the Supply of Environmental Services

The evidence in the previous section points to substantial sums, in excess of 1.5 per cent of GDP, now being spent on environmental services in the public sector. It also indicated that there had been a significant increase in the unit cost of providing such services; between 1965/6 and 1974/5, the unit cost of environmental services expenditures, current and capital, rose by about 120 per cent on the basis measured by our indexes, while consumer prices rose by 75 per cent in the same period. It was not possible to isolate qualitative factors in the analysis, but the higher rate of growth of unit costs was probably due to a mix of strong cost pressures on the supply side meeting a sustained or strongly growing demand for environmental services.

To consider some of the factors affecting such costs, we undertook a cross-section study of local government authorities in Queensland, the only State where both garbage and sewerage services are provided by such local authorities. From Australian Bureau of Statistics' data [1], we calculated total operating expenses for sewerage and garbage, averaged for each local authority over the three years to 1973-4.[9] Output proxies used were the number of sewered dwellings and population for sewerage and garbage respectively. As a measure of population density, we took population numbers divided by the local government authority area; a preferred measure would have been the density of population in the relevant urban area, but data for this was not available for the time period in question.

A regression was run of the form

$$\log C = a + b \log Q + c \log P$$

where C is total cost, Q is output, and P is population density. The use of logarithms allowed us to test for economies of scale.[10]

The results were as follows:[11]

Sewerage: $\log C = 8.32 + 0.51 \log Q + 0.16 \log P$
(23.49) (10.7) (4.04) $R^2 = 0.69$

Garbage: $\log C = 2.43 + 1.05 \log Q + 0.04 \log P$
(3.72) (13.81) (1.36) $R^2 = 0.84$

These results suggest substantial economies of scale in sewerage services but constant returns in garbage. These are confirmed by plotting average costs against output, and Fig.3.3 shows the results for sewerage services. As a check for robustness, we omitted Brisbane from the sample, and the results were virtually unaltered.[12]

The population density sign is mildly surprising, however; we had thought it possible that in more densely populated areas the amount of trunking, vehicle mileage and the like, would be less per unit of output, thus lowering costs. A possible explanation is that quality of service in highly populated areas is higher with more frequent garbage collections, larger amounts collected per head, and more sewage treatment, and that this offsets cost reductions.

In a US cross-sectional study, Hirsch found no significant economies of scale in garbage collection, although he was able to measure quality variables such as frequency of collection and pickup location, i.e. kerb-side or rear of house, which significantly affected costs [28]. In a further US cross-sectional study, Golueke and McGauhey found limited scale economies in garbage collection and disposal, which were exhausted in towns with a population size of 50,000 [27]. Our results are broadly consistent, therefore, with other findings.

A further factor affecting the costs of environmental service is the

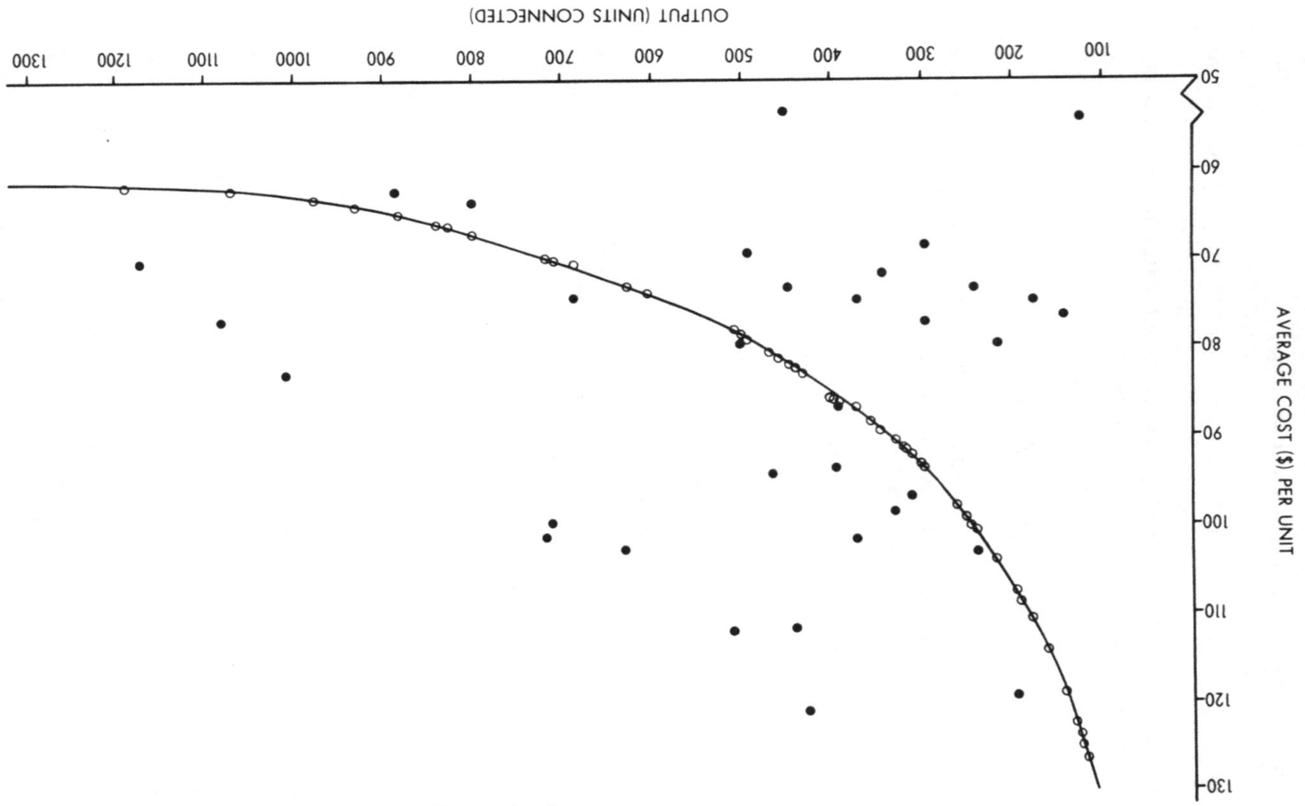

Figure 3.3: Average Cost Curve for Sewerage, Queensland

quality of environmental amenity sought. This is relevant for waste management disposal, though we have no data on which analysis could be undertaken. It is likely to be more critical for air and water quality. There is substantial overseas evidence, however, of increasing marginal costs of improving environmental quality[48]. In the US, one estimate for eliminating 85 to 90 per cent of water pollution was $61 billion; achieving a 99 per cent freedom from pollution added a further $58 billion; 100 per cent freedom would cost another $200 billion.[13]

6. The Demand for Environmental Services

In our earlier discussion of the nature of the environmental problem, we have referred to a range of factors which affected the demand for environmental services. In seeking to take further the analysis of the demands for environmental services, we face a problem that because of the public or collective good nature of an environmental resource, normal demand analyses do not apply.

One way of looking at demand, however, is to consider the damage costs that are involved in the absence of environmental services. Measurement of environmental damage costs, like environmental service costs, is critically important despite the obvious difficulties. Moreover, the use of a common standard of value such as monetary values is essential, despite its limitations, since only if there is a common measuring stick to compare material and environmental costs and benefits, can society choose efficiently how much environmental amenity it is willing to forego or to pay for in terms of material benefits gained or sacrificed. At the margin, it would be illogical to incur a social cost for environmental control greater than the social benefits expected. Consequently, management of environmental resources will require estimates of the costs of environmental damage and the costs of their avoidance or removal, though little has been done in Australia in this respect.

The costs of environmental damage are not easy to measure. Obvious difficulties arise in the social valuation of noise nuisance or abatement, visual disfigurement, a reduction in recreational facilities or amenities, or simply in the reduction of recreational options. Although most Australians would consider the fouling of beaches with human and industrial waste as involving substantial amenity loss, to estimate in monetary terms the benefits of cleaning up such beaches in, say, Sydney or Melbourne would be difficult.

While overseas experience is not completely relevant to Australian circumstances, the US is better able to provide estimates of environmental damage costs. In the US, it was estimated that a 50 per cent reduction in air pollution levels in major urban areas would save over $2 billion annually in terms of reduced morbidity and mortality, calculated on the very conservative basis of earnings foregone [33]. Other costs, beyond earnings foregone, such as medical services, laundry and cleaning costs, building maintenance, air filtering systems and the like, were also substantial quite apart from the more general costs of reduced 'quality of life'. Air pollution costs in total in the US were estimated at about $16 billion, or some $80 per head, per year. In Britain, some $750m. was estimated as the annual cost of air pollution alone [25].

Air pollution in Australia is not generally thought to have reached US, European or Japanese proportions, though for reasons given earlier the differences may not be large, and certainly substantial problems have emerged in particular locations [50]. Important water pollution problems have also emerged [51, 57], although for water even the US has been unable to provide aggregate estimates.

In Australia, the overall assimilative capacity of the environmental resource is normally considered to be greater than common overseas, because of the geographic size of the continent. Nevertheless, the magnitudes of produced mine wastes, by-products from processing ores and from heavy and chemical industries, waste paper and scrap metal, and industrial garbage are large and pose substantial environmental management problems [7]. While some of these residuals such as paper and scrap metal are largely recycled and hence not waste products, many are dumped such as most of the 2.5 million or so tonnes of fly ash produced annually by power stations [46]. In addition, large volumes of capital wastes, such as scrapped motor vehicles (some 300,000 per year) and household appliances, and agricultural and municipal wastes are produced each year. A household waste survey puts the average per head garbage volume in the Melbourne area at 3.4 kg per week [22]; a similar estimate was made earlier [51] for a Sydney suburb.[14] If extended to the whole Australian population, this would represent some 2.3 million tonnes per year. For the Greater Metropolitan Area of Melbourne alone, the total of municipal garbage and other refuse, and industrial and commercial refuse, omitting airborne emissions, for 1973/4 was estimated at almost 2 million tonnes [23], of which about one-third was municipal garbage. The Sydney Metropolitan Waste Disposal Authority has planned on the basis of 1.5 million tonnes of solid wastes for disposal in 1975, rising to 1.8 million tonnes in 1976 [39].

In some cases, demand arises from a specific technical or scientific judgement as to community needs. An illustration is the recommendation by the International Union for Conservation of Nature, that a minimum of five per cent of the national land area be set aside as national reserves [19].

Data on areas of reserves have the disadvantage that they do not necessarily reflect either the quantitative contribution of particular land areas to technical or scientific objectives, or the economic or social costs of setting aside reserve areas. Within these quite severe limitations, the available data as set out in Table 3.3 indicate that although present reserve areas fall short of the recommended level, the area in such reserves is increasing.

Table 3.3: National Park or Reserve Areas in Australia

	1971 Hectares	1974 Hectares	1974 Area as % of State Area
Australian Capital Territory	10,056	14,053	5.7
New South Wales	1,260,040	1,638,570	2.0
South Australia	3,327,232	3,592,412	3.7
Tasmania	432,827	466,761	6.8
Victoria	256,836	267,155	1.2
Queensland	829,587	1,147,237	0.7
Western Australia	1,493,170	1,770,484	0.7
Northern Territory	4,761,506	5,054,201	3.8
	12,371,257	13,950,873	1.8

Notes: These figures represent the national park, wildlife or other reserve areas controlled by the nature conservation service in each State.
Source: Information supplied by the Australian National Parks and Wildlife Service; and [55, pp.107-8].

To attempt to illustrate some of the characteristics of demand for environmental services, we have tried to look specifically at the demand in Australia for sewerage services, again through a cross-section study of Queensland data.[15] Although normal demand analysis is not easy to apply in these circumstances, to the extent that preferences for locally provided public services can be reflected both through the political process and the ability of people to move to areas providing the mix of services sought, it should be possible to relate a community's supply of services to the usual price and income variables affecting consumer choice.

As our measure of the public good aspect of sewerage services we took the proportion of houses sewered in each local authority. For a price variable, the theory of public goods suggests that a public service will be provided until the marginal cost of one more unit equals the sum of the prices each individual is prepared to contribute to its provision.[16] The appropriate price for environmental services, therefore, would be the marginal cost of that service. Because of the lack of income data on a local authority basis, retail sales per capita were used as a proxy variable. Population density is the same as measured in the section on costs. Because both the level of output of the service and the marginal cost of its provision are determined by the interaction of both supply and demand effects, we have to estimate their functions simultaneously. The complete model is

$$R = a + bM + cY + aP + u \qquad (1)$$
$$K = e + fQ + gP + v \qquad (2)$$
$$M \equiv \log f + K - Q$$
$$R \equiv Q - H$$

where

R = proportion of houses sewered
M = marginal cost of sewering one more house
Y = per capita income
P = population density
Q = number of houses sewered
K = total costs
H = total number of houses

all measures logarithmically (so that the corresponding coefficients are elasticities); u and v are error terms.

The results were as follows:

$$\underset{}{R} = \underset{(0.87)}{1.70} - \underset{(1.87)}{1.06M} + \underset{(2.09)}{1.03Y} - \underset{(1.39)}{0.05P} \qquad R^2 = 0.73$$
$$K = \underset{(16.11)}{7.17} + \underset{(10.92)}{0.67Q} + \underset{(1.80)}{0.07P} \qquad R^2 = 0.69$$

The results for the cost function are somewhat different from the single-equation estimate presented earlier, although still showing significant scale economies. The demand equation shows unit price and income elasticities, although the coefficients in the demand equation are barely significant.

Naturally, there are a number of extensions one could make to the above analysis which might improve the results. No account is taken either of public or private substitutes for sewerage services. The income variable reflects only the constraint imposed by locally available income, which could be weakened by grants from the Federal Government; this would allow an interesting analysis of the extent to which local and central government funds are complements or substitutes. An attempt at such an analysis has been made by Hickson in the addendum to this chapter. Furthermore, distribution of income may be important as could be other demographic variables such as age structure or family size. Nevertheless, the results are of some interest by themselves.

We saw earlier that the important questions in the supply of environmental services relate not simply to the achievement of particular technical environmental quality objectives, but also to the manner in which judgements on these technical objectives are made and the least cost way of achieving specified standards. Moreover, in providing environmental services, measures can also be taken to improve the ways in which society chooses between the options available to it, as well as to expand the range of its options.

A major influence in the practical implementation of these approaches is the existing legal and administrative framework for environmental management in Australia.

7. Environmental Management

Environmental management functions are principally State and local government responsibilities, though the manner of their performance varies substantially from State to State. These functions are embodied in a multitude of Acts, regulations and by-laws, with each body responsible for administering that power also enforcing environmental requirements.

Environmental provisions are included in statutes dealing with such disparate matters as: clean waters, country roads, aerial spraying, protection of animals, summary offences, local government, health, fisheries, fibres and sponges, bushfires, mining, noxious trades, and so on. Environment legislation in Queensland [3] consists of over 70 such statutes, and nearly 80 in Tasmania [4].

The Federal Government has explicitly entered the environment management field only recently [38]. Its principal functions, outside of its Territories, are concerned with environmental impacts of projects which it is financing, such as irrigation projects; where it has a direct jurisdiction, such as in offshore and continental shelf matters; in the international field, such as transnational pollution, or conservation of migratory birds or species of fish or mammals such as whales; where it exercises its international trading powers, for environmental purposes indirectly, as in the case of beach sand mining, or directly, in the control of exports of native wildlife and related products; and in research.

To many, it would also be seen as having an important role to play in developing uniformity, or at least consistency, among the states. Through the three Federal-State Councils of Ministers, the Australian Environment Council, the Council of Nature Conservation Ministers, and the Australian Water Resources Council, a number of measures have been taken to achieve consistency such as, in the case of pollution control, the adoption of the 'polluter pays' principle, i.e. that as far as possible the external costs of a process having an environmental impact should be made internal to that process, by a system of taxes or direct regulations, rather than the public sector dealing with the problems and meeting the costs through general tax revenue. However, other such Councils, such as those for Transport or Agriculture, are often involved in environmental policy issues.

Uniformity is a complex issue; although there are arguments as to why uniformity in standards in such things as motor vehicle emissions is desirable [110], there are differences in the assimilative capacity of the environment which support arguments for different standards [48]. It is possible that by applying different environmental standards, or applying common standards differently, a competitive advantage in attracting development could be achieved by one State over others. On the other hand, even accepting a common preference schedule, if an environmental resource is scarce in one State but not in another, it is incurring unnecessary costs to apply the same standards to both.

Apart from this aspect, from an economic viewpoint, interest in these arrangements lies in:

(i) how the legal and administrative framework affects the bargaining process for internalising external costs;
(ii) the extent to which the administrative framework reflects acceptance of the environment as a complex interrelated system; and
(iii) the extent to which controls have been of a price or tax nature,

rather than direct regulation, and what are the implications.

So far as the first of these issues is concerned, in some overseas countries resolution of conflicts over the environment is largely settled by private litigation in the courts, the legislative system establishing the principles under which the relative rights of individuals can be so determined. The US system of prior appropriation, and for water, the UK system of riparian rights, differ markedly from the Australian system where the government has a much larger role in the allocation of natural resources [14]. The courts' role as an agency and as a means of establishing both an understanding of the nature of conflicts, and in resolving those conflicts, is therefore much less than, for example, in the US. Governments must consequently play a larger role both in airing and resolving conflicts, and in planning and implementing environmental management.

Second, awareness of the interrelationship of environmental factors is increasing partly because of a greater understanding of the interrelatedness of residuals. One form of residual, whether a solid, gaseous or liquid material or as energy – heat or noise – can often be changed into another. Coal burned for electricity generation gives off particulates which can be released into the atmosphere, or washed out and the solid residual disposed of onto land; depositing of residues on land may, through leaching, affect water quality; again, reductions of aircraft noise by modified landing and take-off patterns may increase exhaust gas residuals generated.

Such awareness is also growing because it is increasingly recognised that the siting and extent of comprehensive planning of urban and industrial development can greatly reduce, or enlarge, environmental damage and the problems of residuals disposal according to the relationship with environmental resources which exists or is established.

Treatment of the environment as an interrelated system therefore suggests that an integrated approach would be preferable to each specific issue being treated separately. As well as the development of Federal-State consultative procedures, which has taken place, each of the States has moved towards a more co-ordinated approach, but to varying degrees. Generally, the method has been to establish a new agency or agencies to co-ordinate the activities of existing agencies; Environment Protection Agencies (EPAs) as in Victoria and Western Australia, Environment Control Councils as in Queensland, and the like.

The nature of the powers accorded these agencies varies; the Queensland Environmental Control Council, for example, has powers seemingly limited to initiating investigations [20]. In NSW, rather more powers are provided to the relevant agencies but, up to the present at least, a clear division has occurred between the State Pollution Control Commission (SPCC) and the NSW Planning and Environment Commission. Except possibly for the SPCC and the Victorian EPA [26], none of the bodies appear to have strong executive functions. Consequently, despite some movement towards coordination, there remains a large element of apparently piecemeal specialisation.

There are a number of possible reasons for this. Some may emerge from the traditional inadequacies of the administrative or political process, such as a lack of perception of the physical or economic interrelations among environmental issues; or ministerial or bureaucratic opposition to change or to new competing power bases. These difficulties are particularly hard to surmount given that in practice most government agencies have functions with environmental implications.

Furthermore, the interrelationships in the environmental field are so complex politically that governments may be keen to keep them 'on as symbolic a plane for as long as possible' [20, p.252]. Butlin *et al.* suggest that the NSW State Government limited the role of the NSW Planning and Environment Commission because it did not wish to be drawn extensively into the process of local government in its balancing of competition between development interests and local residents [11, p.52]. These various factors are, no doubt, important in particular situations.

Some explanations, however, are rather more complex. Existing organisations have, properly, their existing interests to pursue; a water supply authority will see itself judged on the purity of the water it supplies, and the imposition of new organisations with different objectives must create conflicts unless each interrelated set of objectives is appropriately modified. Some existing administrative organisations reflect particular economic constituencies, such as agriculture or industry; in a pluralistic system these interests will be pressed against the disadvantages posed by environmental policies. There is, moreover, some conflict of roles in an environmental agency which like the SPCC has an advocacy role for environmental interests as part of this pluralistic process while having, at the same time, a balancing or judgemental role. Furthermore, to coordinate a number of agencies effectively requires common and explicit objectives;[17] yet knowledge of all the physical and economic relationships between environmental quality and human, animal and plant life is still lacking, so that a common model could, in any case, be established only with difficulty.

More importantly, the lack of common objectives rationally reflects the need to achieve a political judgement based on the respective costs and benefits of the options available; there is consequently no objective, even given full information, which can exist in the abstract beforehand. The purpose of the administrative or management system is to strike a balance, not just between material and non-material goods but also between different forms of non-material goods, such as between noise and smoke emissions, or gaseous and solid residuals.[18]

The difficulty in environmental management is therefore that, because of the complex interrelationships and trade-offs between environmental issues, a degree of centralisation of management is desirable. On the other hand, the degree of technical knowledge required to handle environmental resources is large, and the environmental effects of a particular residual have to be judged in terms of their specific occurrence since they will vary according to location, wind, or stream flow, and the like. The identification of standardised units of environmental damage seems unlikely [6, p.27] and consequently, specialist groups must have a large say in the management of environmental resources.

More fundamentally, apart from the inherent complexity of environmental issues which mitigates against effective centralised management, it is necessary to recognise that the environmental management process is one of simulating the bargaining processes of the market or of political decision-making. Consequently, an overriding power for one agency would therefore be inappropriate since it would not permit an effective adjustment to be made to the views of all the interests concerned. Nevertheless, the major interrelationships among environmental resources tend to occur in geographic regions, such as a river valley or airshed; State and local government agencies only infrequently have similar boundaries. The gains from a regional approach extend from relatively simple issues such as stormwater drainage, the 'poor relation' in the water, sewerage and drainage trio [29, p.27], to much wider urban or regional planning issues such as those of the River Murray.

One means by which the information flow in the decision-making process has been improved is through State and Federal legislation requiring environmental impact statements (EIS) for major developments. The extent to which these are effective in bringing environmental issues into the decision-making process varies between the Federal Government and the States, from State to State and from time to time. The requirement for such statements has the advantage that it transfers the burden of proof away from those affected; the previous situation, according to Kneese, implicitly assumed that growth was the central public objective and that external costs would be small [31, p.161]. Such statements still suffer from two limitations. First, they are still an adjunct to the planning process rather than being an integral part from the initiation of a project, though this is increasingly less true; and second, many of the important environmental issues are not covered by EIS processes.

Judgements on how effective existing management processes are depend in part upon value judgements or qualitative assessments of whether environmental amenities have been maintained or improved to the degree society would wish to pay for. While there have been undoubted improvements, part of the difficulty is that society remains badly equipped even to make those judgements. In this sense, if in no other, environmental management must be seen as inadequate.

There may be other gaps. Part of the debate about environmental management relates to its income distribution effects, not just between present and future generations to which we referred earlier, but among the present generation. The issue is complex: action to reduce residuals may benefit those living near the source more than those more distantly located, but those on higher incomes can possibly afford to live in environmentally more congenial areas [5, 34]. Butlin *et al.* have suggested that in the Sydney metropolitan area the lower income suburbs have borne a disproportionate share of the environmental costs in Sydney [11, pp.56-7].

Given the growing pressures likely on environmental resources, it must be validly open to question whether existing arrangements will prove adequate in managing and allocating the use of environmental resources.

The earlier discussion suggested that much of the environmental problem arises from the fact that the market price is not the 'right' price for environmental services; the market price is zero, and hence producers and consumers try to use unlimited amounts of them. It is therefore the objective of environmental policy that these resources should only be used to the point where marginal costs of avoiding environmental damage equal the marginal costs of environmental damage itself. This level of environmental resource use can be achieved by the prescription of a technical standard, and most Australian environmental management is through such prescribed standards usually related to the residuals being dispersed into the atmosphere, sewers or elsewhere. Increasingly, however, financial charges are being introduced directly into the environmental management process. As an illustration, Table 3.4 shows the annual fee payable in respect of an effluent discharge point, expressed as a per unit of discharge of specific waste load levels, for industrial effluent discharged into sewers in Victoria.

Table 3.4: Calculated Per Unit Equivalent[a] of Fees payable for Industrial, Trade or Process Waste Discharges in Victoria, 1975-6

Rated Waste Load Rates – Intervals[b]	Maximum Flow Rate of Effluent Cubic Metres Per Day: Less than 50 (25)	51 to 500 (275)	501 to 5000 (2750)	5001 to 50000 (27500)	Over 50001 (75000)
			$		
Up to 1000 (0.5)	0.8	0.4	0.07	0.04	0.03
1001 to 5000 (2.5)	0.8	0.1	0.07	0.01	0.03
5001 to 10000 (7.5)	2.7	0.5	0.10	0.02	*
10001 to 20000 (15.0)	2.7	0.5	0.12	*	*
Over 20001 (25.0)	3.2	*	*	*	*

Notes:

* not stated.

a. mid points of the ranges have been taken and arbitrary figures chose as end points of open ended class intervals.

b. Per unit rate for each 1000 units.

Source: State of Victoria, Environment Protection (Licence Fees) Regulations, 1973, Statutory Rules No.24, made under the Environment Protection Act 1970, Schedules J and K.

Although the unit rate generally rises with the rated waste load of the effluent, the rate per unit declines substantially with the volume of effluent. Yet in general terms, there would appear to be little reason for charging significantly different unit rates for effluent discharges according to the quantities discharged.[19]

It is customarily argued by economists that the management of environmental resources by means of setting standards is inefficient. A major reason is that the information required to set the standards at the appropriate level are too exacting and cannot normally be met; however, how close or distant the technical standards are from an economic optimum is seldom possible to determine, given the limited information available either of damage costs or of abatement costs. A second reason is that the standards are normally set either on purely technical criteria, unrelated to their costs and benefits, or on political criteria based on the bargaining strength of those affected; we have also argued, however, that the management function includes providing a framework for political decision-making, and this criticism similarly does not appear to hold completely.

The alternative that economists tend to favour is a tax or charge per unit of residual [12] ; this is seen to have the advantages, first, that it would encourage a pattern of residual management among different producers that would minimise total costs. Some producers may find it inexpensive to reduce residuals; to others it may be costly. There is no reason why each should be required to meet identical standards if the ultimate effect is the same.

A second advantage is that charges provide a clear incentive to adopt new technology as it emerges. Reducing the environmental impact of a production or consumption process may involve producing a different, less adverse, product; using different raw materials or a different production process; moving the activity to a different location; dealing differently with the residuals; or increasing the size of the environmental resource itself. Levying a tax equal to the marginal social cost of the environmental damage would provide an effective incentive to select whichever is the economic means of reducing that damage.

A third argument has been put forward that charges are likely in practice to be more enforceable than regulations, the latter either being determined under a centralised uniform system and hence inefficient, or being very diverse to meet the diversity of the problem and consequently arbitrary and inequitable [32, p.91] .

Debate is proceeding on the practicability of applying charges of this kind in the absence of substantial data, and in situations where separate charges ideally are required according to the circumstances of the environmental resource, its location, the time of day or year, the precise location of the residuals producer, and so on. Despite the obvious practical difficulties involved, there is evidence to suggest that cost reductions using a system of charges could be substantial [32, p.90] . Debate is also proceeding on the theoretical superiority of such charges in situations of imperfect competition, and where costs of obtaining the necessary information may exceed the savings from an optimising approach [16, 52, 57] .

It would be difficult, at this early stage in the development of knowledge in this field, to suggest major changes in methods. Rather more use of economic evaluations would clearly be warranted in attempts to estimate the optimum methods, standards, or charges. As we have seen some of the local regulations are a mixture of technical standards and pricing systems in a direct sense; this is often the case indirectly when a technical requirement is backed up with penalties which take on a price mechanism characteristic, with the penalty reflecting a charge – at times apparently a very low charge.

Obviously, however, a substantial gap exists in information availability, both in terms of quantifying the benefits of environmental services and in terms of costs of providing such services.

8. Conclusion

Pressures on environmental resources in Australia will grow substantially with population and economic growth. Difficult choices will have to be made by the community in the use of those resources.

The knowledge available on physical and biological interrelationships in the use of environmental resources is very limited; it is for this reason that the desirability is frequently argued of keeping open the physical options and not doing things that may have irreversible and undesirable effects. It is even more limited in respect of the economic costs and benefits of environmental services. Yet without this knowledge, the inevitable choices between not only material welfare and environmental amenity but also different forms of environmental amenity, must be inefficiently made.

The supply of environmental services, including the overall management of the environment and the provision of a basis for making community choices in this way, is a new kind of institutional function, the optimum manner of whose performance is by no means self-evident and for which assessments of efficiency are particularly difficult. However efficient this institutional framework may be in other respects, it still falls far short of requirements in terms of the provision of a knowledge basis for community decision making.

Acknowledgements

Comments and suggestions from Frank Fenner, Ben Smith, Mark Salmon and Max Neutze in particular helped in developing this paper; comments on an earlier draft by a number of university and official colleagues have led to substantial improvement. Errors remaining are our fault. Special thanks are due to officers of the ABS for their help in providing a substantial amount of data and in helping to interpret it, to various officers of the Bureau of Environmental Studies, the National Parks and Wildlife Services and the Department of Environment, Housing and Community Development for information, comment and assistance in various forms. We also acknowledge with appreciation the co-operation of many organisations in providing information, not all of which we have yet been able to use: the Sydney Metropolitan Water Sewerage and Drainage Board, the Melbourne and Metropolitan Board of Works, the Hunter District Water Board, the Perth Metropolitan Water Supply, Sewerage and Drainage Board, the WA Public Works Department, the SA Engineering and Water Supply Department and the Victorian Environment Protection Agency.

The research assistance of Chris Findlay, Kevin Lyall, Owen Rankin and Andrew Shurman is gratefully acknowledged and our thanks are due to Elizabeth Barta who drew the diagrams.

Notes

1. The term 'residual' is used in preference to pollution or waste. Pollution is a 'vague term expressing an unspecified degree of impurity', [8, p.8] while 'waste' is accurate as a description only if in the market it has no value or a value less than the variable costs of its production and utilisation. Bower and Basta prefer the term 'non-product output' to waste defined in this way. [9]
2. There are differences in that consumption of a public good by one individual does not diminish consumption by another, and the good, such as a visual amenity, is available to all whether wanted or not; useful access to a common property resource e.g. a water course, can be reduced by its use by others. In either case, in the absence of collective action, no-one is excluded from using the resource, and no-one has an incentive to incur costs to mitigate damage since all benefit, whether contributing to these costs or not; that there will be those who do not reveal, or who understate, their preference for an environmental amenity, known as 'free riders', points to the difficulty of assessing the value of environmental services. [41, p.8]
3. More precisely, an external (technological) dis-economy.
4. Such behaviour patterns may be important at least for small scale environmental problems, such as neighbourhood rowdiness.
5. Thus, centrally planned economies are not necessarily better placed to handle environmental problems than mixed market economies.
6. The environment can be considered as a stock or as a flow concept. We are treating it here as a flow, on the simplifying assumption that the environmental 'stock' is maintained, in the same way as the flow of material goods concept assumes that the capital stock is maintained. In practice, the possibility of an irreversible running down of parts of the environmental stock is an aspect of the special nature of the environmental problem.
7. This is an oversimplification of the relationship between environmental amenity and material welfare. This relationship may at times be one of complementarity rather than of substitutability, such as where an improvement in environmental quality increases productivity though reduced mental or physical ill health or increased incentives. It is normally accepted, however, that in aggregate the relationship is principally one of substitutability.
8. For example, most public property or collective goods are, very broadly, environmental since they affect environmental health, safety, or aesthetics. Some, such as art galleries, museums, and zoological gardens are not commonly regarded as environmental services, though the preservation of national buildings and monuments and of wildlife and plant species often are.

9. For sewerage, operating expenses consist of working expenses plus debt charges, while for garbage they are revenue expenditure. Clearly they are not ideal measures of operating expenses.
10. There are increasing, constant, or decreasing returns to scale as b is less than, equal to, or greater than 1.
11. The figures in brackets are t statistics. For 102 degrees of freedom, the 5% significance level is 1.96.
12. An alternative would have been to use a cubic functional form. Although, in trying this form, a good fit was obtained, supporting the above conclusions, the associated multicolinearity led us to abandon this form. Lack of data did not permit more detailed analysis considering such factors as quality of service, age structure of capital equipment and movements in factor prices.
13. Estimates by the Environment Protection Agency, the Council on Environmental Quality and the Council of Economic Advisors given in evidence before the House of Representatives Committee on Public Works and cited in [32, pp.22-23].
14. For comparison, this is equivalent to something over 1 lb per person per day in 1974; the US generated 4.5 lb in 1965 or an estimated 5 lbs per person per day in 1974 [13]. For the UK, a comparable figure of 2 lb applied in 1970 [24].
15. A similar analysis was attempted for garbage but the data was inadequate.
16. More rigorously, the marginal rate of transformation of a public into a private good should equal the sum of the individuals' marginal rates of substitution.
17. Lindblom has argued that a dominant common purpose is not necessary, and that mutual adjustment of differing interests may itself be an important coordinating factor. [36, partic. Chapt.1] Even then, a common system is still required by which such mutual adjustment is made effective. Moreover, the argument here holds where coordination though centralised direction is the objective.
18. In any administrative system involving group decision taking, voting rules are important in determining the trade-offs required to achieve these balances.
19. These fees are understood to be currently under review.

References

1. Australian Bureau of Statistics, Australian Municipal Information Service File.
2. Australian Bureau of Statistics, *Public Authority Finance: State and Local Authorities*, 1973-4 (Ref. No.5.43) (Canberra, 1976).
3. Australian Conservation Council, *Environmental Protection Legislation* (Canberra, 1975, mimeo).
4. Australian Mining Industry Council, *Australian Environmental Legislation and Policy: A Summary* (Canberra, 1972, mimeo).
5. William Baumol, 'Environmental Protection and the Distribution of Incomes', in OECD, *Problems of Environmental Economics*, (Paris, 1972).
6. W. Beckerman, 'Environmental Policy Issues: Real and Ficticious', in *Problems of Environmental Economics*, op.cit.
7. J. Beretka, 'Industrial Wastes and By-Products Generated in Australia: The Results of a Survey', *Proceedings of the Royal Australian Chemical Institute*, vol.40, (1973).
8. Blair T. Bower *et al.*, *Waste Management: Generation and Disposal of Solid, Liquid and Gaseous Wastes in the New York Region*, A Report of the Second Regional Plan (Regional Plan Association, NY, March 1968).
9. Blair T. Bower and Daniel J. Basta, *Residuals – Environmental Quality Management: Applying the Concept* (Johns Hopkins University Centre for Metropolitan

Planning and Research, October, 1973).
10. *Bulletin,* 7 August, 1976.
11. N.G. Butlin (ed.), *Sydney's Environmental Amenity,* 1970-1975, Botany Bay Project, Report No.1 (ANU Press, Canberra, 1976).
12. Tony Chisholm, Cliff Walsh and Geoffrey Brennan, 'Pollution and Resource Exhaustion', *Australian Journal of Agricultural Economics,* vol.18, No.1 (April 1974).
13. R.M. Clark *et al.,* 'Cost of Residential Solid Waste Collections', *Journal of Sanitary Engineering Division,* ASCE, 1971.
14. Sandford D. Clark, 'Conservation and Government: Towards an Understanding of Roles', *Search,* vol.5, No.4 (June 1974).
15. R. Coase, 'The Problem of Social Costs', *Journal of Law and Economics,* vol.3 (October 1960).
16. A Coddington, 'Notes on Information and Administrative Costs in the Theory of Externalities', in *Problems of Environmental Economics* (OECD, Pàris, 1972).
17. Commonwealth of Australia, *Environment Protection (Impact of Proposals) Act, 1974.*
18. J.H. Dales, 'Land, Water and Ownership', *Canadian Journal of Economics,* November 1968.
19. R.F. Dasmann, 'Classification and Use of Protected Natural and Cultural Areas', *IUCN Occasional Paper,* No.4, International Union for the Conservation of Nature, Morges, 1973.
20. Robert Dempsey and John Power, 'The Politics of the Environment' in Amos Rapoport, *Australia as Human Setting: Approaches to the Desired Environment* (Angus and Robertson, Sydney, 1972).
21. Department of Overseas Trade, information supplied to the authors.
22. Environment Protection Authority, *Municipal Waste Services in the Greater Melbourne Area and Provincial Centres,* EPA, Victoria, August 1975, Report No. LW3.
23. Environment Protection Authority, *Garbage Analysis Programme,* Stage One, EPA, Victoria, Report No. LW4.
24. S.L. Feldman, 'Waste Collection Services; A Survey of Costs and Prices', in S. Mushkin, *Public Prices for Public Products* (The Urban Institute, Washington, 1972).
25. Alan Gilpin, *Air Pollution,* (University of Queensland Press, Brisbane, 1971).
26. Graeme A. Golden, 'The Environment Protection Act 1970 – How Does It Affect You?', *Australian Business Law Review,* vols.1-2, 1973-4, pp.18.31.
27. C.G. Golueke and P.H. McGauhey, *Comprehensive Studies of Solid Waste Management,* Third Annual Report, (UCLA, Berkeley, 1971).
28. W.Z. Hirsch, 'Cost Functions of an Urban Government Service: Refuse Collection', *Review of Economics and Statistics,* February 1965.
29. Hunter District Water Board, *Annual Report,* 1974-5.
30. Japan External Trade Organisation, *Environmental Control in Japan,* JETRO Marketing Series No.15.
31. Allan V. Kneese, 'Environmental Pollution: Economics and Policy', *American Economic Review,* vol.61, (May 1971).
32. Allan V. Kneese and Charles L. Schultze, *Pollution, Prices and Public Policy* (The Brookings Institution, Washington, 1975).
33. Lester B. Lave and Eugene P. Seskin, 'Air Pollution and Human Health', in Robert Dorfman and Nancy S. Dorfman (eds.) *Economics of the Environment* (W.W. Norton, NY, 1972).
34. Richard Lecomber, *Economic Growth versus the Environment* (Macmillan, London, 1975) Chapter 6.

35. H. Liebenstein, 'Allocative Efficiency versus X-Efficiency', *American Economic Review*, vol.55 (June 1966).
36. Charles E. Lindblom, *The Intelligence of Democracy* (The Free Press, New York, 1965).
37. L.J. Lyons and C.S. Tonkin, 'Recycling of Metal from Scrapped Automobiles in Australia', *The 1974 Waste Management and Control Conference (University of NSW, July* 1974).
38. D.F. McMichael, 'Environmental Management in Australia – A Challenge for Cooperative Federalism', talk given to Royal Institute of Public Administration, NSW Regional Group, Sydney, June 1975.
39. Metropolitan Waste Disposal Authority, *Sydney Regional Solid Waste Management Plan*, Phase 1, Sydney, June 1974.
40. R.P. Murphy, 'Air Pollution and Urban Development', *Royal Australian Planning Institute Journal*, vol.8, No.3, (July 1970).
41. R.A. Musgrave, *The Theory of Public Finance* (McGraw Hill Kogakusha, Tokyo, 1959).
42. Beverley O'Neill, 'Environmental Education in Australian Schools', in *Education and the Environmental Crisis*, Australian Academy of Science, Report No.13 (Canberra, 1970).
43. OECD, *Survey of Pollution Control Estimates* (Paris, 1972).
44. D.W. Pearce, *Environmental Economics* (Longmans, London, 1976).
45. State of Queensland, *State and Regional Planning and Development, Public Works Organisation and Environment Control Act*, 1971-3.
46. Ronald S. Rosich, 'Resource Recovery in Waste Management', *The 1974 Australian Waste Management and Control Conference*, University of NSW, July 1974.
47. Clifford S. Russell, *Residuals Management in Industry: A Case Study of Petroleum Refining* (Johns Hopkins University Press for Resources for the Future, Baltimore, 1973).
48. Peter Samuel, 'The Economics of Pollution', in Bob Dempsey (ed.), *The Politics of Finding Out: Environmental Problems in Australia* (Cheshire, 1974).
49. Senate Select Committee on Air Pollution, *Report*, Parts I and II, Parliament of the Commonwealth of Australia, Parliamentary Paper No.91A (Government Printing Office, Canberra, 1970).
50. Senate Select Committee on Water Pollution, *Report*, Parliament of the Commonwealth of Australia, Parliamentary Paper No.98 (Government Printing Office, Canberra, 1970).
51. H.K. Toner, cited in A.E. Barton, *Problem of Waste Disposal in the Metropolital Area of Sydney* (Parliament of NSW, May 1970).
52. Ralph Turvey, 'On Divergences Between Social Cost and Private Cost', *Economica*, August 1963.
53. Alistair Ulph, Chris Findley and Stuart Harris, 'Analysis of Public Costs of Environmental Services in Australia', *CRES Working Paper No. R/WP6* (Australian National University, Canberra, November 1976).
54. State of Victoria, *Environment Protection Act, 1970.*
55. *Wildlife in Australia*, vol.13, No.3 (September 1976).
56. Gavin Wood, *An Assessment of Eutrophication in Australian Inland Waters*, Australian Water Resources Council Technical Paper, No.15 (Department of Environment, AGPS, Canberra, 1975).
57. Lord Zuckerman and W. Beckerman, 'Minority Report', Royal Commission on Environmental Pollution, *Third Report*, HMSO, Cmnd 5054, September 1972.

ADDENDUM: THE IMPACT OF COMMONWEALTH FINANCIAL ASSISTANCE FOR SEWERAGE FACILITIES

W. Hickson*

Introduction

The rapid growth in specific-purpose Commonwealth programmes that require costs subsidies for capital works has highlighted the need to develop suitable techniques for evaluating their effectiveness. This note contains a study of the impact of one Commonwealth Government Programme (The National Sewerage Programme) upon the level of capital expenditures on sewerage in two states, Queensland and Tasmania. The approach adopted in this study can be applied to other areas of public funding or assistance for a wide range of urban and environmental services. More specifically, it could be employed to evaluate alternative Federal financing arrangements. For example, it would be possible to investigate the effects that differing formal conditions attached to the payment of Federal funds can have upon levels of programme output and state effort.

Background

In 1973 the Commonwealth Government initiated a programme of loan (and later 30 per cent grant) assistance for sewerage works.[1] The stated objectives of the National Sewerage Programme were to remove the 'backlog' of unsewered dwellings by 1982 and to upgrade standards of sewerage treatment to accommodate the resultant increase in waste loads. Therefore, the provision of ear-marked Commonwealth funds was intended to promote a higher level of service output (i.e. connections) and to accelerate an improvement in the quality of that service (i.e. treatment). The reticulation backlog was defined as the number of residential buildings and vacant lots which were not provided with a piped sewerage service as at June 1973.[2]

During the period 1973/74-1975/76 the Commonwealth Government allocated funds totalling $259 million to sewerage authorities in over 60 urban centres. This Commonwealth assistance was intended to cover the deficiency in funding needed to enable state and local authorities to undertake an accelerated works programme that would remove the existing backlog by 1982.

Specification Difficulties

Cross sectional data is used to analyse the determinants of sewerage outlays, with attention focused on the role of Federal funding as a supply influence. Given that the observations actually used relate only to the first three years of a ten year programme, some comment is warranted on the reliability of the results as a guide to programme design and evaluation.

Decision-making and implementation lags have been largely ignored in this analysis. However, it is clear that an observed law response to Federal allocations during the first few years of a programme's operation may be quite different to the behaviour pattern that emerges over a longer time period. Factors such as physical resource constraints, commitments to projects already under construction and more immediate priorities than sewerage reticulation (e.g. treatment) may contribute to delays both in achieving a higher profile of expenditures and in reducing the unsewered backlog. Moreover, delays in the recording of financial and works information may lead to estimates of response parameters that are atypical and misleading during the early period of the programme.

For the purpose of predicting the effects of alternative levels of Federal funding, time series analysis of individual governments clearly would be preferable. Until data is available for additional years of the Programme's operation, therefore, the findings of this regression analysis cannot be generalised, although a comparison can be made of the size and stability of the coefficients for each explanatory variable in the two years studied. It would be expected that a large part of any lagged response to Federal allocations in the first year would be incorporated in data relating to the second year.

A further difficulty involves a high degree of collinearity among the independent variables (especially Federal assistance) which prevents inferences being made about the relative strength of particular determinants (see Morss, 1966). Since no explicit matching conditions were attached to payments made un the National Sewerage Programme, the analysis of this programme is not limited to the same extent as the study of some U.S. Government programmes in which the amount of Federal aid provided was an explicit function of expenditures actually undertaken. Thus, expenditure variables were, in effect, being regressed on their components. In contrast, allocations made under the National Sewerage Programme represent, in effect, a form of income supplementation, and, therefore, can be properly treated as an independent variable in the analysis.

Measuring the Response to Federal Assistant Programmes

Most of the early studies dealing with the impact of Federal assistance programmes in the US attempted to isolate their 'price' and 'income' effects. In general, it was assumed that the expenditure response to a Federal ear-marked grant is a function of the 'price' elasticity of demand by the local community for that particular activity. In addition to lowering the effective 'price' (or charge) of a good or service, the provision of specific-purpose assistance has an income effect by augmenting the budgetary revenue of the local authority.

Although externalities of consumption make it impossible to quantify either a 'unit' or a 'price' of a public good, some insight into the relative valuation of public goods by local communities can be obtained by calculating the elasticity of total expenditures in response to the Federal subventions. If, for example, the demand for a particular function is inelastic, the introduction of Federal assistance will lead to a less than proportionate increase in expenditures on that function. In this case, the income effect is dominant and the specific-purpose Federal assistance releases funds for expenditures on non-assisted activities (see Smith, 1968, p.351).

Cross-sectional studies conducted in the US and Canada by Sacks and Harris (1964), Michas (1969), and Fisher (1964) conclude that three factors – population density, per cent of population urbanised and per capita income – are the main determinants of the functional outlays (current and capital) of state and local governments. Osman (1966) and Smith (1968) included Federal financial aid as an additional independent variable in their regression equations. Their findings suggest that Federal aid, *at the margin,* stimulated rather than replaced all major functional expenditures *financed from internal sources* (i.e. the regression coefficients of Federal aid were significantly greater than zero). However, Smith's estimates of the (average) 'price' elasticity of demand for selected spending functions are less than unity, implying that some Federal funds were used to increase expenditures on other functions and/or to lower rates and charges for the aided activity. This study adopts Smith's approach for estimating the response to Federal programs.

In the case of the National Sewerage Programme it was recognised that the provision of Commonwealth funds could result in a reduction in the relative level of agreed state effort. In an attempt to control the possible 'leakage' of Commonwealth funds into other areas, a 'gentleman's agreement' was used to ensure that the states maintained their share of the accelerated works programme that was necessary to achieve the Programme's objectives. Although the Commonwealth undertook to finance the shortfall in funding between the costs of a 'normal' and an 'accelerated' works programme, no explicit matching formula was devised. This was partly because it was appreciated that most sewerage authorities are multi-purpose organisations each with quite different expenditure priorities. In the event, not only did most states fail to maintain their agreed real levels of capital expenditure on sewerage, but the Commonwealth Government also reduced its own level of funding below that originally promised.

In the light of the Programme's objectives, it is useful to estimate the extent to which state-local authorities increased their expenditures in response to the provision of the Commonwealth assistance. As the gentleman's agreement was satisfied so long as the states maintained their agreed share of the accelerated works programme, it is also necessary to consider the impact made by the Commonwealth's financial contribution upon the target backlog itself. In the following analysis, therefore, two related hypotheses are tested:

1. that state-local capital expenditures on sewerage increased by more than the proportionate increase in Commonwealth assistance
2. that a large part of the observed reduction in the number of unsewered dwellings within each authority's jurisdiction can be attributed to the provision of Commonwealth funds for backlog sewerage works.

Data Sources

Data for this study has been obtained from information held by the Commonwealth Department of Environment, Housing and Community Development. This information covers the capital expenditures on sewerage system works and treatment facilities and the principal sources of funds of authorities participating in the Program.

Data for Queensland were adequate for only 14 out of the 20 eligible local authorities, while data for all 9 local authorities in Tasmania were included.[3] These two states were chosen primarily because the provision of sewerage services in their metropolitan areas is the responsibility of local government rather than state departments (e.g. in Adelaide) or semi-government authorities (e.g. in Sydney, Melbourne and Perth). Allocations to the 23 authorities in Queensland and Tasmania accounted for 10 per cent of total Commonwealth assistance for sewerage works during the two year study period. Whereas the test of the first hypothesis remains confined to Queensland and Tasmania, sufficient information was available for an additional 11 authorities in Victoria (9), South Australia (1) and Western Australia (1) to allow a more generalised conclusion concerning the backlog objective.

The Model

Estimates of the expenditure response of state and local governments to Commonwealth sewerage payments are obtained by means of a log linear equation of the form:

$$y = a + \sum_i b_i x_i + b_{i+1} A + u \qquad .....(1)$$

The dependent variable (y) represents annual per capita capital outlays on sewerage (including treatment) by each state and local authority. The variable y includes expenditures financed from own (state-local) sources and Commonwealth assistance (A).[4] The explanatory variables $x_1 \ldots x_i$ represent demand influences. Given that an increase in the number of sewered dwellings would tend to be associated with 'A' (see later), this source of funds variable would also reflect a large part of variations in sewerage 'output'.

Three types of response to Commonwealth assistance are possible. First, if the estimated coefficient of Commonwealth Government assistance (b_{i+1}) is positive but less than unity, it can be postulated that such assistance is associated with a less than proportionate increase in state-local expenditures on that function (i.e. some substitution of Commonwealth for state-local effort has taken place). in this case there is some 'leakage' of Commonwealth assistance. Second, if $b_{1+1} > 1$, then an increase in Commonwealth funding per capita (CAP) of 'x' per cent increases total sewerage expenditure per capita (STP) by more than 'x' per cent. In this second case the effect is stimulative in the sense that the programme induces state and local authorities to spend a greater amount from their own resources. Third, if $b_{i+1} > 0$, then complete substitution occurs.

The remaining (i) independent variables can be classified into economic and demographic categories, although some of these demographic factors influence not only the local community's demand for sewerage services but also its ability to finance the supply of those services. The ability to finance sewage disposal is a function mainly of the income of the state or local government authority and its borrowing capacity. On the demand side, retail sales per capita (SSP) for 1973/74 are taken to be a proxy for income levels in each area for each year of the period. Finally, the demographic variables include a measure of differences in inter-area servicing costs as well as a measure of the degree to which new demand must be met:

PG represents the rate of population growth over the period 1970/71 to 1974/75
PD represents gross population density at the 1971 Census
PU represents per cent of the population urbanised at the 1971 Census.

Since the variable PD provied to be insignificant and in any case, highly correlated with PU, it was omitted from the equations. A priori, one would expect the signs of the coefficients of retail sales per capita and population growth to be positive. In the case of PU, though, one would expect a negative coefficient indicating that lower levels of expenditure per capita are required with the more intensive use of sewerage facilities in those local government areas which are relatively more highly urbanised.

Empirical Results

Table 3A.1 provides the correlation matrix of the variables for the two sub-periods and as an average for the whole period. The results of ordinary least squares regressions are presented in Table 3A.2. Separate equations were run for the two years in which large Commonwealth allocations were made (namely, 1974/75 and 1975/76) and for both years taken together (i.e. STTP and CATP). The last equation might be expected to reflect the average influence of changes in Commonwealth assistance that are spread over a period longer than a single year.

The elasticities of response to the Commonwealth assistance provided in each year are of a similar magnitude and less than unity, implying an increase in overall expenditures but some degree of substitution of Commonwealth assistance for state-local effort. The coefficient for the two-year period is 0.37, indicating that total expenditures on sewerage works are relatively inelastic with respect to Commonwealth assistance.[5] However, data for a greater number of the elapsed years up to the target date is needed to confirm that this pattern persisted and could not easily be redressed in later years.

All three demand variables have significant coefficients in the aggregated estimate. In particular, the coefficient of PU lends support to the expectation of lower per capita costs of service provision in the more highly urbanised localities.

Although the elasticity of total spending with respect to Commonwealth assistance is less than unity, the aggregate amount of Common-

Table 3A.1: Simple Correlation Coefficients (n = 23)

Sub-periods, 1974/5 and 1975/76[1]

	STP_{75}	CAP_{75}	PG	PU	SSP	Mean	Standard Deviation
STP_{75}	1.00	0.45 (0.53)	0.67 (0.42)	–0.62 (–0.55)	–0.34 (–0.12)	0.03 (0.04)	0.03 (0.03)
CAP_{75}		1.00	0.18 (0.46)	–0.13 (–0.49)	–0.13 (–0.27)	0.01 (0.01)	0.01 (0.01)
PG			1.00	–0.70 (–0.70)	–0.54 (–0.54)	4.27 (4.27)	4.76 (4.76)
PU				1.00	0.44 (0.44)	77.96 (77.96)	25.42 (25.42)
SSP					1.00	0.001 (0.001)	0.001 (0.001)

Total over period, 1974/75-1975/76

	STTP	CATP	PG	PU	SSP	Mean	Standard Deviation
STTP	1.00	0.46	0.58	–0.62	–0.24	0.08	0.06
CATP		1.00	0.36	–0.34	–0.22	0.02	0.02
PG			1.00	–0.70	–0.54	4.27	4.76
PU				1.00	0.44	77.96	25.42
SSP					1.00	0.001	0.001

Note: 1. Correlation coefficients for 1975/76 are shown in brackets.

Table 3A.2: Regression Coefficients Explaining Variations in Capital Expenditure on Sewage Disposal Per Capita, 1975/75 and 1975/76 (23 local government areas in Queensland and Tasmania only)

		Independent Variables						
Dependent Variable	Constant	CAP_{75}	CAP_{76}	CAT	PG	PU	SSP	R^2
STP_{75}	5.07 (1.76)	0.32* (2.45)			0.28* (2.11)	–1.03* (–2.70)	0.44 (1.64)	0.53
STP_{76}	4.65 (2.07)		0.35* (3.00)		0.15 (1.60)	–0.66* (–2.24)	0.53* (2.51)	0.50
STT	5.04 (2.23)			0.37* (2.83)	0.19* (1.91)	–0.72* (–2.51)	0.50* (2.35)	0.53

Notes: 1. t-statistics are shown in brackets beneath regression coefficients.
2. * indicates coefficient is significant at 5 per cent level (one-tail test).

wealth funding (CAS) may have contributed to an increase in the number of dwellings connected to the service over the three year period (RSD). To test this second hypothesis concerning the 'output' objective of the Programme, the Spearman rank correlation coefficient between log RSD and log CAS was calculated. For urban centres in five states the correlation value was 0.61, indicating a significant degree of association. There was virtually no association, however, between the change in the number of *unsewered* dwellings and total Commonwealth assistance for sewerage.

It is possible that the true relationship may be obscured. Lags in making and recording household connections to the service may explain much of this poor performance. Further, the backlog might be actually growing in size as new residential development takes place in unsewered areas.

The picture becomes a little clearer if the observations are segmented into two groups, according to whether or not the area's recent population growth rate has exceeded or fallen short of 3 per cent per annum. From Table A.3 it is evident that Commonwealth assistance is much more highly associated with changes in the number of sewered dwellings in slow growing areas than in fast growing municipalities, although the reduction in the mean proportion of dwellings unsewered is less in the case of slow growing areas. It may be concluded that allocations made under the National Sewerage Program have played a greater role in increasing the number of sewerage connections in the slower growing local government areas. Indeed, this is what one might expect from a programme of financial assistance aimed at removing a backlog which, in principle, is fixed in time.

Table 3A.3: Impact of National Sewerage Programme Upon the Backlog of Unsewered Dwellings (34 local government areas in five states, excluding NSW)

	Mean Proportion of Unsewered Dwellings 1973/74	1975/76	Partial Regression Coefficient for CAS[1]
	%	%	
Fast growing areas (n=15)[2]	56.5	43.4	0.16
Slow growing areas (n=19)	27.0	24.7	0.81

1. Obtained from regression log RSD = a + b log CAS.
2. Fast growing areas are those in which population growth has been equal to or greater than 3 per cent p.a.

Conclusions

The preliminary findings for Queensland and Tasmania provide tentative support for the hypothesis of an inelastic expenditure response to the National Sewerage Programme in the two states in these years. In other words, the direct income effect of the Program during its establishment stage appears to have outweighed any 'price' substitution effect. The evidence available to date also lends support to the hypothesis that Commonwealth assistance was associated with an increase in the number of sewered dwellings, especially in the slower growing and older settled areas in five states.

To adjust for the simultaneity that obviously exists between levels of Commonwealth assistance and aggregate expenditures on sewerage, two-stage least squares estimation could be used in association with an investigation of the overall sources of funds and expenditure priorities of each local authority. Further, to account for the size of the expenditure elasticities, additional information describing the supply response to Commonwealth assistance should be obtained.

Notes

* This research was conducted as part of a Master of Commerce Degree while the author was employed by the Department of Environment, Housing and Community Development. The views expressed in this paper are solely those of the author and do not necessarily reflect the views of the Department.

1. Commonwealth financial assistance for sewerage works in the period 1973/74 was $27.9m. For the period 1974/75 it was increased to $117.8m. (incl. carry overs) and in 1975/76 it was $113.2m. (1975/76 Budget Paper, No.9, p.41).
2. The target backlog thus excluded those dwellings which remained unconnected to a service which was already provided, as well as those additional dwellings which were built in backlog areas after 1973.
3. The mean values of the Commonwealth assistance and retail sales (income) variables were calculated for the sample of observations included in the analysis and the sub-set excluded because of data difficulties. The respective mean values were 710 ($000) and 579 for Commonwealth assistance in 1974/75 and 120.2 ($m) and 109.9 for retail sales. The differences in the mean values are not significant at the 0.05 level.
4. To avoid some of the multicollinearity problems between y and A, one can regress the amount of spending on the functions from own sources (i.e. net of Federal assistance) upon the level of assistance received. In this case the coefficient of A will be one less than the coefficient in equation (1). (See Pogue and Sgontz, 1968, p.95). Gramlich (1972) argues that for the purpose of testing the significance of the Federal assistance variable it does not make any difference whether total expenditure or expenditure from own sources is used as the dependent variable. It is quite defensible to use gross rather than net expenditures because the state or local authority does not *have* to increase its gross spending by the full amount of the Federal grant allocated (p.107).
5. This is not to deny the presence of some expenditure stimulation at the margin

(i.e. $\frac{dy}{dA} > 1$). When the equations for each year are estimated using unlogged values of the variables, the results are:

$$STP_{75} = \underset{(1.53)}{0.036} + \underset{(2.31)}{0.889}\,CAP_{75} + \underset{(1.96)}{0.003}\,PG - \underset{(-1.45)}{0.0003}\,PU + \underset{(0.41)}{2.102}\,SSP;\ R^2 = 0.52$$

$$STP_{76} = \underset{(1.71)}{0.059} + \underset{(1.61)}{1.077}\,CAP_{76} + \underset{(0.33)}{0.0006}\,PG - \underset{(-1.55)}{0.0005}\,PU + \underset{(0.91)}{6.50}\,SSP;\ R^2 = 0.29$$

While there appears to be a mild stimulatory effect in 1975/76 (but not in 1974/75) marginal responses are difficult to interpret in the case of lumpy sewerage investments.

Bibliography

1. Fisher, G.W., 'Interstate Variations in State and Local Government Expenditure', *National Tax Journal,* Vol.17, No.1 (March 1964) pp.55-74.
2. Gramlich, E.M., 'A Comment on O'Brien's "Grants-in-Aid"', *National Tax Journal,* Vol.25, No.1 (March 1972) pp.107-108.
3. Michas, N.A., 'Variations in the Level of Provincial Municipal Expenditures in Canada: An Econometric Approach', *Public Finance,* Vol.24, No.4, 1969, pp.579-613.
4. Morss, E., 'Some Thoughts on the Determinants of State and Local Expenditures, *National Tax Journal, Vol.19, No.1 (March 1966) pp.95-104.*
5. Osman, J.W., 'On the Use of Intergovernmental Aid as an Expenditure Determinant', *National Tax Journal,* Vol.21, No.3 (September 1968) pp.437-47.
6. Pogue, T.F., and L.G. Sgontz, 'The Effect of Grants-in-Aid on State-Local Spending', *National Tax Journal,* Vol.21, No.2 (June 1968), pp.190-99.
7. Sacks, S. and R. Harris, 'The Determinants of State and Local Government Expenditures and Intergovernmental Flows of Funds', *National Tax Journal,* Vol.17, No.1 (March 1964) pp.75-85.
8. Smith, D.L., 'The Response of State and Local Governments to Federal Grants', *National Tax Journal,* Vol.21, No.3 (Sept. 1968) pp.349-357.
9. Stevens, S., 'Specific Purpose Grants for Roads in Australia', Fourth Conference of Economists, Canberra, 19-23 August 1974.

PART TWO: SERVICES OF ENERGY, COMMUNICATIONS AND DISTRIBUTION

Many services are largely designed to cope with the spatial characteristics of economic development. Distance, terrain, and density of settlement require a mixture of intermediate and final services for the production and consumption of basic needs like food, clothing and accommodation. A network of communication and distribution facilities depends considerably on the physical environment and resource endowments but also quite significantly on structural features arising out of the functions of private enterprise and the public sector within a mixed economy.

Energy services, as an intermediate input in production and consumption activities, have a wide range of different uses and perform interdependent functions. Hawkins (chapter 4) considers the nature of the energy market and changing trends in the demand for these services. His main focus is a cross-sectional study of electricity demand and retail prices and the extent of cross-subsidisation implicit in the rates of levy set by supply authorities.

Lamberton's study (chapter 5) deals with the structure and growth of Australian communications services in comparison with those for the USA and the USSR. He explores the institutional and operational features of three service areas: postal, telecommunications and broadcasting.

Transport services are usually thought of as having separate modes for land, air or water. But, as Rimmer shows (chapter 6), freight forwarding services are organised on a multi-modal basis. Structural elements and their changing impact are revealed in a diversified mix of service functions which have wide-ranging implications for business conduct and measured performance.

Tucker's approach (chapter 7) for retail services is to explicitly relate performance to a number of structural features, including the level of concentration, for each type of retail activity.

4 THE MARKET FOR ENERGY SERVICES*

R.G. Hawkins

1. Introduction

As the ecologists proclaim so forcefully, energy has an importance beyond its contribution to gross domestic product. Yet its role as an intermediate service has been little studied by Australian economists. In part this may reflect the inherent technical complexities of the energy industries; partly it is due to the inadequacy of much of the published information and the secretiveness of many of the institutions; partly it is a tribute to the smooth functioning of the energy market over most of the post-war period.

But, as the events of December 1973 showed in a global context, large sections of the energy market are dominated by only a few producers, amounting in the case of gas and electricity to natural monopolies. Consumers are often unorganised, demand is inelastic in the short-run, because of the impossibility of altering existing stocks of durable goods, and governments have intervened in the market in many arbitrary ways. The energy market therefore deserves more attention than economists have paid it in the past.

This chapter provides an introduction to the economics of the Australian market for energy services. In the first two sections there is an examination of historical trends in the use of energy services and an outline of important features of the energy market, again within an historical context. There follows a relatively lengthy section, examining supply and demand in a particular market – the retail electricity market in New South Wales. The concluding section briefly reviews some policy issues.

2. Trends in the Use of Energy

In the twenty years to 1971/2 gross input of energy into the Australian economy grew at an annual rate of 4.5 per cent. During the same period gross domestic product at constant prices grew by 4.6 per cent per annum. During the decade from 1951/2 to 1961/2 the elasticity of gross input of energy with respect to gross domestic product was slightly less than one, and it was approximately equal to one in the next decade. Darmstadter *et al.*[1] have calculated similar elasticities for a number of other countries; in the United States the elasticity was 0.81 over the period from 1950 to 1965, while the average in fifteen other developed countries was slightly over one. So by international standards there was a relatively rapid increase in Australian energy consumption.

These comparisons are of energy in physical terms, measured in megajoules, without any allowance for convenience or efficiency of utilisation. This measure of the total energy dissipated by the consumption of fuels is readily comprehensible to the scientist or engineer and is useful for many engineering and environmental purposes. But it is unsatisfactory to the economist, who believes that the relative prices of different fuels equal their relative marginal social costs in production and their relative marginal utilities in consumption, and hence that values are more appropriate than physical quantities as measures of energy flows in an economy. Valuing gross input of energy at producers' prices in 1961/2 makes some difference to the growth rate over the twenty years to 1971/2; the average annual increase was 5.4 per cent, implying an elasticity of 1.16 with respect to real gross domestic product. This relatively high elasticity is due to substantial increases in the use of relatively valuable crude oil, hydroelectricity and natural gas, the last of these making its first appearance in Australia in 1961/2.

As is shown in Table 4.1, in 1951/2 black coal was the biggest input in physical terms, constituting 51 per cent of gross input. Crude oil and net imports of petroleum products were the second most important input of energy, supplying 26 per cent. Ten years later, black coal and petroleum furnished roughly equal proportions of gross input, and by 1971/2 crude oil and petroleum products occupied the dominant position held by black coal twenty years previously.

Thus far, attention has been focused on the initial inputs of each form of energy into the Australian economy. An alternative is to concentrate on energy purchased by final consumers. The difference between this measure of final consumption and gross input of energy represents, in physical terms, energy lost in conversion and distribution of energy, and, in values, the value added in conversion plus the costs of distributing energy to final consumers.

Movements in final consumption of energy are shown in Table 4.2. Considering, first, energy measured in physical terms, the most important trend was the steady decline in the share of primary (unconverted) forms of energy, particularly black coal. This decline was offset by substantial increases in the use of electricity and petroleum products, especially fuel oil. The comparable proportions valued at purchasers'

Table 4.1: Gross Input of Energy

	Megajoules x 10^9			1961/2 £ million		
	1951/2	1961/2	1971/2	1951/2	1961/2	1971/2
Black Coal	487.6	528.4	675.6	61.0	63.5	76.7
	(51.2)	(40.1)	(29.6)	(34.6)	(29.1)	(15.1)
Brown Coal	63.4	165.6	223.2	3.6	8.6	11.2
	(6.7)	(12.6)	(9.8)	(2.0)	(3.9)	(2.2)
Wood & Bagasse	145.6	79.7	82.9	18.5	8.6	8.0
	(15.3)	(6.1)	(3.6)	(10.5)	(3.9)	(1.6)
Crude Oil	38.1	563.0	1028.6	7.1	104.9	191.7
	(4.0)	(42.7)	(45.1)	(4.0)	(48.0)	(37.8)
Hydroelectricity	5.9	17.8	42.1	10.9	32.7	77.3
	(0.6)	(1.4)	(1.8)	(6.2)	(15.0)	(15.3)
Natural Gas	0.0	0.0	102.2	0.0	0.0	107.7
	(0.0)	(0.0)	(4.5)	(0.0)	(0.0)	(21.3)
Gross Input of Energy	740.7	1354.5	2145.6	101.0	218.3	472.6
	(77.7)	(102.8)	(94.4)	(57.4)	(100.0)	(93.3)
Net Imports of Petroleum Products	212.5	−37.4	126.8	75.1	0.1	34.2
	(22.3)	(−2.8)	(5.6)	(42.6)	(0.0)	(6.7)
Gross Input of Energy	953.2	1317.1	2281.4	176.1	218.4	506.8
	(100.0)	(100.0)	(100.0)	(100.0)	(100.0)	(100.0)

Note: Figures in brackets are percentages.
Source: Ch.2, R.G. Hawkins, ***The Demand for Energy in Australia,*** Ph.D. Thesis, Canberra, Australian National University, 1975.

prices in 1961/2 illustrate the dangers of measuring energy flows as gross physical quantities; electricity is elevated from a minor role to become the single most important form of emergy consumed throughout the period, while black coal diminishes in importance.

Over the two decades, the elasticities of final consumption of energy with respect to changes in gross domestic product, both valued at constant prices, were 1.23 and 1.28 respectively. A standard interpretation of this would be that energy is a superior good, whose consumption rises with the standard of living; but it should also be noted that between 1951/2 and 1971/2 the implicit deflator of gross domestic product doubled, whereas that for consumption of energy rose by only fifteen per cent. It is therefore equally likely that energy was substituted for other consumer goods and factors of production. These alternative explanations have very different long-run implications for future trends in energy consumption, and it is most important to attempt to distinguish between them through empirical research.

From Tables 4.1 and 4.2 it can be seen that in 1951/2 59 per cent of

Table 4.2: Final Consumption of Energy by Fuel

	Megajoules x 10^9			1961/2 £ million		
Primary Energy	1951/2	1961/2	1971/2	1951/2	1961/2	1971/2
Black Coal	289.8	274.6	300.8	32.9	30.0	32.0
	(39.2)	(29.6)	(18.4)	(9.4)	(4.8)	(2.3)
Brown Coal	7.0	7.9	5.8	0.9	1.0	0.7
	(0.9)	(0.9)	(0.4)	(0.3)	(0.2)	(0.1)
Wood & Bagasse	142.8	77.5	79.5	18.3	8.5	7.8
	(19.3)	(8.3)	(4.9)	(5.2)	(1.4)	(0.6)
Final Consumption of Primary Energy	439.6 (59.5)	360.0 (38.8)	386.1 (23.7)	52.1 (14.8)	39.5 (6.3)	40.6 (3.0)
Secondary Energy						
Briquettes	3.2	17.2	25.7	0.7	3.7	5.5
	(0.4)	(1.9)	(1.6)	(0.2)	(0.6)	(0.4)
Motor & Aviation Spirit	108.0 (14.6)	211.9 (22.8)	387.0 (23.7)	118.0 (35 7)	230.4 (36.8)	425.5 (31.2)
Kerosenes	20.5	31.9	85.8	15.3	23.4	60.2
	(2.8)	(3.4)	(5.3)	(4.3)	(3.7)	(4.4)
Other Petroleum Products	92.8 (12.6)	194.6 (21.0)	487.0 (29.8)	35.6 (10.1)	77.5 (12.4)	214.5 (15.7)
Electricity	36.1	77.1	183.6	95.7	212.7	510.2
	(4.9)	(8.3)	(11.2)	(27.2)	(33.9)	(37.5)
Town Gas	18.3	24.4	75.1	27.1	35.6	104.9
	(2.5)	(2.6)	(4.6)	(7.7)	(5.7)	(7.7)
Gasworks By-products	20.6	11.2	2.2	7.3	3.9	0.8
	(2.8)	(1.2)	(0.1)	(2.1)	(0.6)	(0.1)
Final Consumption of Secondary Energy	299.4 (40.5)	568.3 (61.2)	1246.3 (76.3)	299.7 (85.2)	587.2 (93.7)	1321.5 (97.0)
Total Final Consumption of Energy	739.0 (100.0)	928.3 (100.0)	1632.4 (100.0)	351.8 (100.0)	626.7 (100.0)	1362.1 (100.0)

the physical quantity primary energy was purchased directly by final consumers, while 41 per cent passed into the conversion industries. Ten years later, with the decline of black coal and the rapid growth of oil refining, only 27 per cent was purchased directly by final consumers, and in 1971/2 the proportion had sunk to 18 per cent.

In Table 4.3, final consumption of energy is disaggregated by sector. In physical terms, manufacturing industry (excluding oil refining) was the most important final consumer of energy throughout the period, accounting for about 40 per cent of the total. At the beginning and end of the period, households accounted for about 25 per cent of the total; but there were substantial shifts in the composition of consumption, away from wood and into petroleum products. Valued at purchasers'

Table 4.3: Final consumption of Energy by Sector

	Megajoules x 10⁹			1961/2 £ million		
Primary Energy	1951/2	1961/2	1971/2	1951/2	1961/2	1971/2
Mining	8.6	2.6	8.1	1.0	0.3	0.9
	(1.2)	(0.3)	(0.5)	(0.3)	(0.0)	(0.1)
Manufacturing	204.4	256.8	334.6	20.2	25.5	33.1
	(27.7)	(27.7)	(20.5)	(5.7)	(4.1)	(2.4)
Households (including private motoring)	110.6	41.9	30.7	16.3	6.2	4.6
	(15.0)	(4.5)	(1.9)	(4.6)	(1.0)	(0.3)
Transport (except road)	104.4	48.0	2.0	12.6	5.7	0.2
	(14.1)	(5.2)	(0.1)	(3.6)	(0.9)	(0.0)
Other (including road transport)	11.7	10.7	10.8	1.9	1.7	1.7
	(1.6)	(1.2)	(0.7)	(0.5)	(0.3)	(0.1)
Final consumption of Primary Energy	439.6	360.0	386.1	52.1	39.5	40.6
	(59.5)	(38.8)	(23.7)	(14.8)	(6.3)	(3.0)
Secondary Energy						
Mining	5.2	10.2	27.1	7.4	13.8	36.8
	(0.7)	(1.1)	(1.7)	(2.1)	(2.2)	(2.7)
Manufacturing	52.2	112.3	327.5	51.4	95.5	266.0
	(7.1)	(12.1)	(20.1)	(14.6)	(15.2)	(19.5)
Households (including private motoring)	74.1	144.2	360.1	96.5	206.6	521.4
	(10.0)	(15.5)	(22.1)	(27.4)	(33.0)	(38.3)
Transport (except road)	59.3	89.8	179.0	23.9	38.1	77.9
	(8.0)	(9.7)	(11.0)	(6.8)	(6.1)	(5.7)
Other (including road transport)	108.7	211.8	352.7	120.4	233.2	419.3
	(14.7)	(22.8)	(21.6)	(34.2)	(37.2)	(30.8)
Final Consumption of Secondary Energy	299.4	568.3	1246.3	299.7	587.2	1321.5
	(40.5)	(61.2)	(76.3)	(85.2)	(93.7)	(97.0)
Total Final Consumption of Energy	739.0	928.3	1632.4	351.8	626.7	1362.1
	(100.0)	(100.0)	(100.0)	(100.0)	(100.0)	(100.0)

prices in 1961/2, consumption by households becomes the most important use of energy. Their share rose from 32 per cent in 1951/2 to 39 per cent in 1971/2, while that of manufacturing was only about 20 per cent. The residual category, 'other consumers', also accounted for over 30 per cent of the value of energy consumed. This residual category comprises agriculture, commerce, construction, government and road transport, all of which have become substantial users of petroleum products. It is an indication of the weaknesses of the Australian data that the residual category necessarily comprises such a large proportion of the total.

Tables 4.1 to 4.3 reveal a number of common themes and contrasting patterns. An increasing consumption of energy was accompanied by a rise in the proportion of primary fuels passing into the energy conversion industries and by a growth in the relative importance of secondary (converted) fuels in final consumption of energy. Final consumption of petroleum products and electricity increased relative to that of black coal and wood. Apart from the general movement from primary to secondary fuels, the pattern of final consumption underwent relatively small changes. Measured at purchasers' prices in 1961/2, manufacturing industry and households marginally increased their shares, while those of transport and other consumers declined slightly. Only the residual category 'other consumers' never relied on black coal to any significant extent, and hence was unaffected by the general shift from primary to secondary fuels.

3. Features of the Energy Market

The shifts in the energy market described in the previous section reflect the interaction of supply and demand factors, both in the energy market and throughout the rest of the economy. On the demand side, the shifting level and composition of production and consumption, technological advances and the substitution of capital for labour all affected the demands for individual fuels. On the supply side, there were new discoveries of indigenous fuels. There were also developments in the energy conversion industries, responding to these discoveries, to new technology and to the changing nature of demand and competition.

Australia emerged from the Second World War with an economy dominated by coal. Rapid industrial expansion during and after the war compounded the debilitating effects of the Great Depression on the coal industry and led to a chronic coal shortage. There was also a shortage of electrical generating capacity. In 1947, the Joint Coal Board was established by the Commonwealth and New South Wales Governments in an urgent effort to improve the performance of the coal industry. The Board inaugurated programmes of modernisation and mechanisation. It rationed supplies when necessary and controlled prices, which were raised to cover rapidly increasing production costs. Meanwhile, the unreliability of coal supplies from New South Wales caused the governments of the energy-deficient states of Victoria and South Australia to invest heavily in developing indigenous sources of inferior coals.

The great coal shortage evaporated with the end of the post-war boom in 1951. In part this was due to the economic downturn and to rapidly rising production; but more important in the long term was the emergence of trends away from coal consumption, outside New South

Wales, in the railways and in industry generally. Technological advances in the supply and use of petroleum products, rising incomes, the falling global price of crude oil and the rapidly increasing price of coal all contributed to the general trend.

In transport, the introduction of the diesel-electric locomotive, commercial aviation and oil-fired shipping all increased the consumption of oil relative to coal. Rising affluence and the mass-produced passenger car caused a rapid increase in the consumption of motor spirit. Within industry, the packaged oil-fired boiler of small capacity offered savings in capital and labour costs, greater controllability and efficiency, more convenient storage of fuel and the absence of ash; so it gradually replaced coal in this field, even in New South Wales where coal remained a cheaper source of energy.

The rapid rise in consumption of petroleum products made it economical to construct oil refineries in Australia.[2] In the decade to 1961/2, refinery capacity rose from less than a million tons of crude oil per year to more than seventeen million tons. An important by-product of this was a large increase in the supply of fuel oil. Being a joint product, for which there was little demand on export markets, it was rational for the oil companies to lower the price to whatever extent was needed to displace coal from the industrial market. There were dramatic falls in the price of fuel oil in each state as the new refineries came into production, and consequent substantial increases in consumption.

Until 1954 the price of motor spirit was controlled under wartime legislation throughout Australia. After 1954 price control was gradually abandoned in all states except South Australia. In the absence of other price-fixing bodies, the Prices Commissioner in South Australia effectively set maximum wholesale prices for a wide range of petroleum products. With the development of refineries in Australia, discounts off the maximum permissable prices of the heavier products became common, hastening the displacement of coal in the industrial market.

There is controversy over the extent to which these discounts represented oligopolistic collusion on the part of the oil companies, as was suggested at the time by the Joint Coal Board.[3] By normal standards, the marketing of petroleum products is a concentrated industry, with four companies controlling 67 per cent of sales and eight companies 91 per cent. Inelastic demand in the short run for many of the lighter products would have permitted cross-subsidisation of sales of the heavier products, and vertical integration from crude oil production to retail sales would have allowed profits to be taken at any stage of the production process. The Joint Coal Board pointed to the fact that industrial fuel oil was sold cheaper than marine fuel oil as evidence of price discrimination. But in 1964 the Tariff Board found that prices has fallen in all markets as a result of competition between the oil companies, and that the lower industrial price was possible, because of economies of scale in distribution. The published evidence does not allow a definite conclusion to be drawn.

The oil companies have also attracted controversy over the retailing of motor spirit. It has often been suggested[4] that the companies were allowing a proliferation of retail outlets in an effort to increase market shares, thereby increasing the average costs of distribution. State Governments have sometimes intervened in order to achieve a reduction in the number of outlets. In addition, in 1975 the Trade Practices Commission found that the oil companies' practice of requiring retailers to stock only one brand of petrol and lubricants contravened the Trade Practices Act.

The price of coal also fell gradually during the fifties and sixties, because strong competition from oil forced producers to pass on the cost reductions achieved through mechanisation. Between 1957 and 1967 the average free-on-rail price at the colliery in New South Wales declined by 8 per cent; but this was not enough to allow coal to compete with fuel oil in many industries. It was only the growing export trade in coal and the increasing demand of a few larger users, such as the Electricity Commission of New South Wales, that kept the output of coal from declining. By 1971/2 the consumption of solid fuels was confined to a few large industries, such as steel, cement and metallurgical coke. In these industries either coal possessed particular technological advantages, or else the scale of operation was so large that costs could be reduced by integrating the operations of the colliery and the factory using its output.

During the last few years the position has altered because of the discovery of indigenous supplies of crude oil and natural gas, and more recently the substantial rise in the price of imported crude oil. The last of these is only just beginning to influence the recorded statistics, and its long-term impact is difficult to assess.

The production of indigenous crude oil began on a large scale in the Bass Strait in 1970; by 1971/2 locally produced crude oil provded two thirds of the input to Australian refineries. The price of indigenous crude oil was fixed for a period of five years from September 1970, at import parity as at October 1968, and Australian marketers were penalised if they did not absorb a proportion of local crude oil. Crude oil from the Bass Strait yielded a lesser proportion of heavier products than did imported crude oils. As a result the price of fuel oil rose quite rapidly.

In 1969 substantial production of natural gas began in South Australia and Victoria, and in 1971 in Western Australia. The production of natural gas is characterised by high capital costs and very low marginal costs of production below the capacity of existing wells. In Victoria there were drastic reductions in the price of gas, especially for large industrial users, and consumption rose dramatically. Between 1969 and 1973 industrial sales increased eleven-fold. Natural gas was fully competitive with other industrial sources of energy, and rapidly acquired a large share of the market.

Thus in recent years the petroleum industry has experienced increased costs and sharper competition in certain markets. At the same time, the Prices Justification Tribunal has monitored it to ensure that supply shortages have not been passed on in increased profit margins.[5]

4. The Retail Electricity Market in New South Wales

Up till this point there has been little discussion of the market for electricity. Unlike most other fuels, except reticulated gas, the residential and commercial sectors are major consumers of electricity, and there is generally a single monopolistic supplier. This disparity of market power and the unusual technical characteristics of the supplying industry have led economists to pay particular attention to the industry.[6] Some statistics of the electricity and gas industries are given in Table 4.4.

In the early post-war period the industrial sector was the principal consumer of electricity. However, in all states there was a vigorous subsidised expansion of distribution networks into rural areas, which increased the number of domestic customers. At the same time domestic stocks of electrically powered consumer durables rose rapidly. These partly exogenous increases in the consumption of electricity combined with the rationalisation of many small distribution networks into much larger entities to allow the realisation of substantial economies of scale. Declining unit capital costs and the generally declining cost of coal input to power stations meant that the average price of electricity rose only slightly in the twenty years to 1971/2.

In most states the bulk of the generation and distribution of electricity is concentrated in a single authority. New South Wales is exceptional in that generation and distribution are separated, the former controlled by the Electricity Commission of New South Wales,

Table 4.4: Selected Statistics of the Electricity and Gas Industries

	Electricity	Gas
Number of Enterprise Groups, June 1969	144	37
Number of Establishments,		
June 1969	171	55
June 1972	153	40
Employment, June 1972	62,480	8,707
Turnover, 1971/2, $ million	1444.4	147.7
Composition of Turnover, 1971/2, %		
Purchasers, transfers in, etc.	40.9	38.7
Wages and Salaries	23.0	28.0
Value added, less wages and salaries	36.6	33.7
Fixed Capital Expenditure as a % of Value Added, 1971/2	52.5	47.3
Concentration Ratios, 1968/9		
% accounted for by the 8 largest enterprise groups:		
Employment	68.2	87.5
Turnover	66.3	88.5
Fixed Capital Expenditure	70.0	92.9

Sources: Australian Bureau of Statistics, Electricity and Gas Establishments: Details of Operations and Industry Concentration Statistics: Details by Industry Class, 1968/9

and the latter dispersed among about 50 local authorities, under the guidance of the Electricity Authority of New South Wales. This unique structure has allowed the modelling of both the supply and the demand sides of the market, and the estimation of the parameters of the supply and demand functions. Such a model is described in this section. The method adopted is to take a cross-section of retailing authorities in New South Wales and the Australian Capital Territory in the year 1971. Equations are specified, explaining the average consumption of electricity by residential, commercial and industrial customers, and the average prices paid by them. The equations for average prices are specified in such a way that it is possible to estimate the degree of cross-subsidisation inherent in the structure of retail prices.

In 1971, over 80 per cent of the electricity consumed in New South Wales was sold by 44 retail authorities. The Australian Capital Territory was served by its own authority. There was a wide dispersion of sizes among the authorities; at one extreme lay Sydney County Council, with 565,000 customers, and, at the other, Ivanhoe franchise with 95. There were wide variations in the proportions of residential, commercial and industrial customers and in the degree of urbanisation.

The Australian Capital Territory draws the bulk of its electricity from the Snowy Mountains Authority and the remainder from the Electricity Commission of New South Wales. In New South Wales most of the retailing authorities draw the bulk of their supplies from the Electricity Commission. For these supplies they are charged according to a single schedule, irrespective of location. The schedule is in two parts, comprising a constant energy charge and a constant maximum demand charge per kilovolt-ampere (KVa), drawn during the daily period of peak demand. The maximum demand meters are reset monthly, and the demand charge is revised quarterly in line with the costs of wages and materials.[7]

Average demand per customer is highest in the industrial sector; in 1971 it varied between authorities from 30,000 to 9 million kilowatt-hours (Kwh) per annum. Average commercial demand varied from 6,000 to 40,000 Kwh, and average residential demand from 1,000 to 7,000 Kwh. Average receipts per Kwh sold ranged from one to eight cents.

The retail price of electricity is set independently by each retailing authority. Within New South Wales, the Electricity Authority encourages the Councils to set prices according to the costs of providing each service, but does not compel them to do so, although it has the statutory power. One one plane this is sensible because it allows Councils to meet local competition from other forms of energy in particular uses. But on another plane it allows the Councils, which are indirectly elected by local authorities, to bend before the pressure of local vested interests and to grant questionable cross-subsidies from one class of consumer to another.

As with other consumer goods, residential demand for electricity should depend on a consumer's real income, tastes and the relative prices of electricity and substitute fuels. However, the demand for a source of energy, such as electricity, differs in two important respects from the demand for other non-durable consumer goods. First, electricity is desired, not for its own sake, but because it enables a flow of services to be obtained from existing consumer durables. Secondly, the provision of a supply of a particular fuel to a consumer may require a considerable capital investment.

As regards the first point, the stock of electrical appliances is more or less fixed in the short run. If, as seems likely, utilisation rates are insensitive to changes in electricity prices, then the demand for electricity should be price and income inelastic in the short run. In the longer run, the stock of appliances can be varied and the consumer's choice of fuel for a particular application will depend on the prices and efficiencies of the different appliances, as well as on the prices of the various fuels. In a cross-sectional study of a relatively compact area, such as New South Wales, it seems reasonable to assume that the prices of appliances are constant and that their technology is everywhere the same. Thus the results of the study should provide a clear indication of the partial effects on the demand for electricity of variations in the price of electricity, holding the prices of appliances and their technology constant.

As regards the second point, in some areas particular fuels may be unavailable, while in others consumers may have to pay heavily to acquire a supply. Consumers may therefore be expected to behave differently, depending on whether they have connections to supplies of particular fuels. This effect must be taken into account in specifying the model.

The preferred empirical result, estimated by two-stage least squares, is as follows:

$$
\begin{aligned}
D_r = \; & \underset{(0.26)}{.41} - \underset{(-3.45)}{2.31}\, N_{eg}/N_e + \underset{(3.77)}{4.36}Y - \underset{(-3.75)}{5.37}\, A_h \\
& + \underset{(3.13)}{0.91}\, A_p - \underset{(-4.47)}{0.93}\, P_{re} - \underset{(-1.93)}{2.38}\, B
\end{aligned}
$$

$$R^2 = .988 \qquad \text{S.E.E.} = 69.3$$

D_r denotes average consumption per residential customer; N_{eg}/N_e is the proportion of electricity customers having a supply of gas; Y is average per capita expenditure on retail sales; A_h is the proportion of unoccupied holiday homes; A_p is the average number of persons per household; p_{re} is the average residential price of electricity, and B is the average residential consumption of black coal. Climate variables are found to be insignificant. Heteroskedesticity is eliminated by multiplying all variables by $\sqrt{N_{re}}$, where N_{re} is the number of residential electricity customers.

This equation implies that the price and expenditure elasticities of domestic electricity demand, calculated at the sample means, are –0.55 and 0.93 respectively. The equation also implies that demand for electricity declines as the number of gas connections and holiday homes increases. Among the particular items that can be gleaned from the equation, it appears that the Australian Capital Territory's present high consumption of electricity would be reduced by 800 Kwh per annum, or 11 per cent, if the proportion of households with a gas connection was as high as in Sydney, and by 1000 Kwh if the price rose to the sample average. Average consumption in a coastal area, such as Bega Valley, would increase by 1100 Kwh per annum, if the proportion of holiday homes fell to the sample average.

Two different models are advanced to explain commercial and industrial consumption of electricity. The first supposes that the demand for electricity (D) by a particular industry group is determined by cost minimisation subject to a production function, to the prices of factors including electricity, (P_K, P_L, P_e), and to an output target (W).

$$D = g(W, P_K, P_L, P_e)$$

In the second approach, the industry's production function is solved directly for electricity consumption.

$$D = h(W, K, L)$$

In both equations, K and L represent capital and labour respectively. Linearised forms are estimated for each of the two categories, commercial and industrial consumption of electricity. The first equation is suitable for answering the question whether the demand for electricity is influenced by the prices of electricity and other fuels, the second focuses on the elasticity of demand with respect to output.

Inadequate data reduce the usefulness of the estimated equations, and they are not reported here in detail. The estimates suggest that commercial and industrial demand for electricity is insensitive to the price of electricity and other fuels. Commercial demand for electricity varies positively with average retail sales and negatively with the average number of retail employees per electricity customer. The linear form of the estimating equation suggests that there are increasing returns to scale in retailing, but one must be hesitant in ascribing much weight to the result.

These results suggest that the retail demand for electricity is insensitive to variations in the average price, except in the residential sector. Demand is sensitive to demographic variables such as household size and the proportion of holiday homes, but not to climate variables. It is also affected by variations in personal income, and by the levels of industrial and commercial activity.

Turning to the model of price formation, it will be recalled that

Councils are financially autonomous and are free to set their own prices. However, the Electricity Authority of New South Wales recommends that tariffs should be based on costs of supply.[8] It suggests that costs for each category of consumption be divided into an energy-related cost, a maximum-demand-related cost and a fixed overhead cost. Joint costs, which occur in the last two categories, are to be allocated according to the share of each category of customer in maximum demand, or according to relative numbers in each category of consumer.

There is no guarantee that the Electricity Authority's recommendations are followed. Indeed, there is ample evidence that tariffs are often unrelated to the costs of supply. According to various reports[9] on electricity supply in New South Wales, there are a number of reasons why prices may depart from costs. These include:

(a) a general desire to subsidise rural consumers, through explicit state subsidies, through the uniform wholesale price and by internal cross-subsidisation within each Council's area;
(b) a widespread desire to match the prices charged in adjacent areas;
(c) a need to meet the demands by large industrial and commercial consumers for lower prices;
(d) a desire to increase total sales by subsidising domestic consumers at the expense of industrial consumers;
(e) an occasional desire to promote industrial development in rural areas by subsidising the industrial price of electricity, and, lastly,
(f) the need to match the prices of competing fuels, particularly for gas for domestic use.

It therefore appears that on balance domestic consumers may be subsidised at the expense of industrial and, possibly, commercial consumers.[10]

In order to derive an estimable model, the various influences on electricity prices are divided into three groups – costs, cross-subsidies and competition from other fuels. These three influences are combined in a relatively simple model, which can be used to establish the importance of each of the three influences on electricity prices, and the rough magnitude of the internal cross-subsidisation inherent in the structure of retail prices.

It is supposed that, in general, the price of electricity is based on costs and that other effects represent a departure from a norm based on costs. The Electricity Authority's standard procedure for establishing costs is used as the basis of a model explaining average retail prices in the residential, commercial and industrial categories. To this basic model further terms are added to represent cross-subsidies and the effects of competition from other fuels.

The theoretical model is of the form:

$$P_e = aC + bL + cP_t$$

where C is a vector of independent variables representing costs, L captures cross-subsidies and P_t are the prices of competing fuels. Possible influences on costs include dummy variables for individual franchise areas (F), average consumption per customer (D), the number of customers and rate of growth of consumption, the geographical dispersion of customers (A), and the load factor. This last is proxied by climatic variables and by the proportion of unoccupied holiday homes.

Cross-subsidies are represented as follows:

$$\text{Industrial:} \quad V = v_0 + v_1 (K_i/K_t) + v_2 (K_c/K_t)$$

$$\text{Commercial:} \quad S = s_0 + s_1 (K_i/K_t) + s_2 (K_c/K_t)$$

$$\text{Residential:} \quad T = -\left[s_0 + s_1\left(\frac{K_i}{K_t}\right) + s_2\left(\frac{K_c}{K_t}\right)\right]\left(\frac{K_c}{K_r}\right) - \left[v_0 + v_1\left(\frac{K_i}{K_t}\right) + v_2\left(\frac{K_c}{K_t}\right)\right]\left(\frac{K_i}{K_r}\right)$$

where V, S and T are respectively the rates of levy, in cents per Kwh, on industrial, commercial and residential sales, and K represents total consumption by residential, commercial, industrial and all consumers. The expression for the industrial levy is justified in the following way.

If there is a levy on industrial sales, it is likely that the rate of levy declines as the ratio of industrial to total sales increases, for two reasons. In the first place, a given rate of subsidy on residential sales can be achieved with smaller rates of levy on industrial sales: in the second place, it is likely that the bargaining power of industrial consumers increases along with their relative importance. This suggests that the rate of levy declines as (K_i/K_t) increases. In addition, it is possible that commercial consumers also subsidise residential sales, so that, at a given proportion of industrial sales, the industrial levy declines as residential sales decrease relative to commercial sales. This suggests that the rate of levy may decline as (K_c/K_t) increases.

The expression for the levy on commercial sales is similarly justified. The expression for the levy on residential sales T follows from the identity:

$$VK_i + SK_c + TK_r \equiv 0$$

which states that the net subsidy must be zero.

The equations are estimated jointly by two-stage least squares, maintaining the restrictions across equations on the coefficients of the cross-subsidy terms. The results indicate that variables representing the cost of supply, other than dummy variables, are significant in explaining the industrial and residential prices, but not the commercial price. Variations in the average quantity purchased have a small influence on the industrial and residential prices, the elasticity of price with respect to quantity being –.05 and –.06 respectively, when evaluated at the sample means. The proportion of the population living in urban areas also has a significant influence on the residential price, the elasticity being –0.11.

When the price of heating oil is included in the equation, the fit is improved, but other costs lose significance. It is thought that the price of heating oil captures other cost effects rather than the influences of competing fuels.

Cross-subsidy coefficients are significant, and suggest that the levy on industrial sales averages 0.86 or 0.59 cents per Kwh, depending on whether the price of heating oil is excluded or included, with corresponding subsidies to residential consumers of 0.50 and 0.62 cents per Kwh. The levy on commercial sales is –0.48 and +0.43 cents per Kwh. The results suggest that from $30 to $40 million is levied annually from industrial customers and an equivalent subsidy is paid to residential consumers. It is unclear whether commercial customers pay or receive a subsidy, though one inclines to the former view on a priori grounds.

Thus it appears that cross-subsidies lead to a thirty per cent lowering of average residential electricity prices and a similar increase in the average industrial price. There may be a smaller fourteen per cent increase in the average price paid by commercial consumers.

The estimated coefficients imply different behaviour by different retail authorities. Broadly speaking, the Councils appear to divide into three behavioural patterns. First, there appears to be a strong desire to avoid high residential prices. One group of Councils, with a heavy industrial load, is able to achieve low residential prices with only a small rate of levy on industrial sales. Examples appear to include Sydney, Illawarra, Nepean River, Shortland and Prospect. Another group of

Councils still achieves a high residential price, even with high rates of levy on industrial sales. This group apparently includes Bega Valley, Ulan, New England, Central West, Upper Hunter, Mullumbimby and South West Slopes.

Secondly, a number of councils appear to offer relatively favourable treatment to commercial consumers, without either achieving low residential prices or offering high subsidies to residential consumers. This group includes Monaro, New England, Bega Valley, Hunter Valley and Macleay River.

Thirdly, there appears to be a strong urge on the part of Councils in the Sydney region to achieve a uniform level of residential prices. Sydney, Prospect and Nepean River are apparently fortunate in having a large industrial load and can achieve low residential prices with only a moderate levy. Mackellar and St George achieve low prices, but only at the cost of high levies on commercial and perhaps industrial consumers. Blue Mountains and Brisbane Water are not so fortunate, and fail to achieve residential prices in the lowest quartile, in spite of high estimated levies on industrial and/or commercial consumers. Interestingly enough, this apparent pattern of behaviour in the Sydney region bears out the criticisms voiced by Maguire.[11]

One final comment may be ventured concerning these results. In 1974 the Energy Authority Investigation Committee suggested that a number of (unidentified) rural Councils offered low industrial electricity prices as an inducement to industrial development. In estimating the equations it was found that four Councils, Brisbane Water, Southern Tablelands, Peel-Cunningham and Macquarie had exceptionally low industrial electricity prices and exhibited larger negative residuals than any of the other Councils. It is therefore concluded that these particular Councils are indeed setting industrial electricity prices at artificially low levels.

5. Energy Policy

The pricing behaviour described in the previous section may clearly be causing substantial allocative distortion and redistribution of income. Yet it has never been the subject of public debate or scrutiny. The primary concern of energy policy in Australia has been to safeguard future supplies of (preferably indigenous) primary fuels and to determine export policies. The allocative efficiency and the redistributive aspects of energy pricing have generally passed unnoticed, although the organisation of the energy market and the study reported in the previous section suggest that they are potentially important.

There have been some exceptions to this in recent years, notably the surveillance of the petroleum industry by the Prices Justification Tribunal and the Trade Practices Commission. But, even in this case, the market is so affected by the Commonwealth Government's policies on the pricing of crude oil and the excise on motor spirit, that serious distortions may remain.

The general inelasticity of demand for each fuel and of supplies of alternative fuels in the short run encourages governments to intervene to ensure supplies, and tempts suppliers to abuse their market power. Official encouragement of indigenous supplies of energy has sometimes purchased extra security at a considerable cost in inefficiency.[12] Such costs should be fully taken into account in determining future energy policy.

Concentration in energy supply increases the market power of the supplying firms. In the case of coal, competition from oil and the technological stimulus provided by the Joint Coal Board seem to have encouraged efficient and competitive behaviour through most of the post-war period. In the case of oil, frequent surveillance by the Tariff Board, the South Australian Prices Commissioner, the Prices Justification Tribunal and the Trade Practices Commission has prevented the worst abuses of market power, but it may at times have been difficult to monitor the pricing behaviour of foreign affiliates of Australian companies. The position is aggravated by the high proportion of foreign ownership, by the degree of vertical integration of the industry and by the diversified nature of many of the companies.

Considerable questions overhang the performance of the electricity and gas industries. Both form natural monopolies, often protected by statute. Both fall under the jurisdiction of state governments and are therefore immune from the probing of bodies such as the Prices Justification Tribunal and the Trade Practices Commission. An example of their pricing behaviour has been explored in the previous section and found to exhibit considerable arbitrariness. Clearly there is a need for greater public accountability in these industries. The onus for this falls on State Governments, who should be encouraged to shoulder their responsibilities.

Notes

* This chapter reflects research done while the author was at the Department of Economics, Research School of Social Sciences, The Australian National University. The views expressed are solely those of the author.

1. J. Darmstadter, P.D. Teitelbaum and J.G. Polach, *Energy the World Economy*

(Baltimore, Johns Hopkins Press for Resources for the Future, 1971).

2. The construction of oil refineries in Australia was encouraged by several factors: increased thermal efficiency of refineries and increased economies of scale in ocean transport eliminated the advantages of transporting crude oil rather than products; the expanding Australian market allowed the achievement of economies of scale in refinery construction. Subsidiary reasons included the apparently increasing instability of Middle Eastern countries, the tariff on imported petroleum products and inducements offered by State Governments.
3. See for example p.70 of the Joint Coal Board's Annual Report for 1963/4.
4. See, for example. J. McB. Grant, 'The Petroleum Industry', Ch.8 in A. Hunter (ed.), *The Economics of Australian Industry* (Melbourne, Melbourne University Press, 1973), and D. Ferguson, *The Price of Motor Spirit in Queensland* (Canberra, Australian Automobile Association, 1973).
5. For details of the operations of the Prices Justification Tribunal, see its annual reports and also J.P. Niewenhuysen and N.R. Norman, *Australian Competition and Prices Policy* (London, Croom Helm, 1976).
6. The most recent comprehensive study of the Australian electricity industry is by G.D. McColl *The Economics of Electricity Supply in Australia.* (Melbourne University Press, 1976). The econometric model summarised in this section is described in greater detail in R.G. Hawkins, 'The Demand for Electricity: A Cross-Section Study of New South Wales and the Australian Capital Territory', *Economic Record* 51, 1975, 1-18, and in 'The Retail Price of Electricity in New South Wales', unpublished, 1976.
7. The uniform bulk-supply tariff obviously implies a subsidy to more remote consumers. This has been estimated at between $8 million and $12 million annually, and may be compared be explicit government subsidies to high-cost areas of about $4 million annually (Energy Authority and Electricity Tariffs Investigation Committee, *Report*, Sydney 1974).
8. The Electricity Authority of New South Wales, *The Selection of Tariffs by Electricity Supply Authorities*, in three parts, Sydney 1965-1973.
9. These includes the Local Government Electricity Association's *Rationalisation of Electricity/Retail Tariffs in New South Wales*, Sydney, 1971, and the Electricity Authority's *Report on the Investigation of Electricity Distribution in New South Wales*, Sydney, 1972, in addition to the report cited in a previous footnote.
10. It is ironic to note that such cross-subsidisation would appear to be illegal under section 49 of the Trade Practices Act, which prohibits most forms of price discrimination, but that the act does not apply to State Government instrumentalities.
11. F. Maguire, 'Instability in the Development of the Electricity Supply Industry in New South Wales', *Australian Quarterly*, 38, 1966, pp.9-25.
12. A prime example of this was the construction of briquetting factories in Victoria in the early 1960s, after they had been made uneconomic by the falling price of petroleum products. See B.M. McFarlane, *Economic Policy in Australia: the Case for Reform*, Melbourne, Cheshire 1968.

Bibliography

Adelman, M.A., *The World Petroleum Market* (Baltimore, Johns Hopkins Press for Resources for the Future 1972).

Anderson, K.P., *Residential Energy Use: An Econometric Analysis*, R-1297-NSF (Rand Corporation, Santa Monica, California, 1973).

Australia, Department of National Development, *Energy in Australia* (Canberra, 1967).

Australia, Industries Assistance Commission/Tariff Board, various reports on the oil industry, Canberra.

Australia, Royal Commission on Petroleum, *Reports* (Canberra, 1975-6).

Bell Journal of Economics and Management Science, *Symposium on Analytical Models of Energy Policy*, 5, 1974, pp.461-594.

Breyer, S.G., and MacAvoy, P.W., *Energy Regulation by the Federal Power Commission* (Washington, Brookings Institution, 1974).

Cochrane, S.McL., 'Protection of the Australian Crude Oil Industry', *Australian Economic Papers*, 7, 1968; pp.189-205.

The Conference Board, *Energy Consumption in Manufacturing* (Cambridge, Ballinger, 1974).

Darmstadten, J., *et al.*, *Energy in the World Economy* (Baltimore, Johns Hopkins Press for Resources for the Future 1971).

Evans, D.G., *Fuels for Electricity Generation in Australia*, paper presented at the Conference of the Institute of Fuel (Australian Membership), Brisbane, 1970.

Ferguson, D., *The Price of Motor Spirit in Queensland* (Canberra, Australian Automobile Association, 1973).

Hawkins, R.G., 'The Demand for Electricity: A Cross-Section Study of New South Wales and the Australian Capital Territory', *Economic Record*, 51, 1975, pp.1-18.

Hunter, A., (ed.), *The Economics of Australian Industry* (Melbourne, Melbourne University Press, 1963).

Hunter, A., 'Natural Gas in Australia', *Australian Economic Papers*, 6, 1967, pp.25-46.

Joint Coal Board, *Annual Reports*, Sydney.

Kalma, J.D., and Johnson, M., *Energy Use in Australia: A Survey of Recent Literature*, Technical Memorandum 76/3, CSIRO Division of Land Use Research (Canberra, 1976).

Kalma, J.D., *Sectoral Use of Energy in Australia*, Technical Memorandum 76/4, CSIRO Division of Land Use Research (Canberra, 1976).

Ling, S., *Economies of Scale in the Steam-Electric Power Generating Industry* (Amsterdam, North-Holland, 1964).

Macavoy, P.W., and Pindyck, R.S., *The Economics of the Natural Gas Shortage (1960-1980)* (Amsterdam, North-Holland, 1975).

Maguire, F., 'Instability in the Development of the Electricity Supply Industry in New South Wales, *Australian Quarterly*, 38, 1966, 9-25.

McColl, G.D., *The Economics of Electricity Supply in Australia* (Melbourne, Melbourne University Press, 1976).

Murray, R., *Fuels Rush In: Oil and Gas In Australia* (Melbourne, Sun, 1972).

New South Wales, Energy Authority and Electricity Tariffs Investigation Committee, *Report* (Sydney, 1974).

Posner, M.V., *Fuel Policy: A Study in Applied Economics* (London, Macmillan, 1973).

Turvey, R., (ed.), *Public Enterprise* (Harmondsworth, Penguin, 1968).

5 STRUCTURE AND GROWTH OF THE COMMUNICATIONS INDUSTRY

D. McL. Lamberton*

Introduction

The economics of information and knowledge is a topic of expanding interest to both economics and managerial science. 'The production, storage, dissemination, and utilisation of society's stock of information resources is an expensive business, as indicated by the huge allocation of resources to formal education, R & D, communications, consumer education, market research, and the like'.[1] Making a lot of heroic assumptions, Machlup, in 1962, estimated that knowledge production and distribution might, in an industrial society such as the United States of America, account for as much as 29 per cent of the gross national product.[2] More recent work has distinguished a *primary* information sector that sells information goods and services to both intermediate and final demand and a *secondary* information sector that includes information services that are produced and consumed without any market-place transactions. Preliminary results estimated the primary and secondary shares in value added in the US economy at 27.8 per cent and 20-24 per cent respectively.[3]

In Australia the number of persons whose occupation is primarily concerned with the production and distribution of information increased from 549,074, or 17.0 per cent of the workforce, in 1947 to 1,440,461, or 27.5 per cent of the workforce, by 1971. In 1911 the percentage of the workforce was 8.5. These workforce trends are shown in Table 5.1 and were developed in the course of a research project on the Australian information industry.[4]

Rising trends in information based activities have led Denison to conclude that investment in information and knowledge is the fundamental source of productivity growth.[5] Drucker refers to 'the knowledge economy' and asserts that: 'The systematic and purposeful acquisition of information and its systematic application, rather than 'science' or 'technology', are emerging as the new foundation for work, productivity, and effort throughout the world'.[6] Representative of more extreme views are Daniel Bell's notion of *The Post-Industrial Society* in which the major institutions '. . .will be a vast array of

Table 5.1: The Structure of the Australian Workforce 1911–1971: Occupation Approach

Sector		1911	1921	1933 Total	1933 Excluding Unemployed	1947	1961	1966	1971[a]
Primary	Total	561,777	551,338	622,665	502,823	522,113	502,823	502, 333	475,456
	% W.F.	31.0	27.0	23.2	22.3	16.5	12.0	10.5	9.1
Secondary (Manufacturing)	Total	486,769	566,939	829,886	667,465	1,006,367	1,369,410	1,572,955	1,635,222
	% W.F.	27.0	27.5	30.9	29.5	31.5	33.0	33.0	31.2
Tertiary (Service)	Total	608,805	698,071	813,834	729,328	1,118,877	1,351,145	1,489,053	1,684,459
	% W.F.	33.5	34.0	30.3	32.3	35.0	32.5	31.0	32.2
Information	Total	155,925	234,458	419,951	360,088	549,074	949,914	1,216,521	1,440,461
	% W.F.	8.5	11.5	15.6	15.9	17.0	22.5	25.5	27.5
Total workforce		1,813,276	2,050,806	2,686,336	2,259,704	3,196,431	4,173,292	4,780,862	5,235,598
Total population		4,455,005	5,435,734	6,629,839	6,629,839	7,579,358	10,508,186	11,550,562	12,755,638
% of population in workforce		40.7	37.7	40.5	34.1	42.2	39.7	41.4	41.0

a. Of 240,706 originally classed as occupation not stated in 1971 Census, 235,890 have been allotted on the basis of estimates derived from the ABS post-enumeration survey.

Note: The occupations included in the information sector are based on the 1971 Census tabulation and include the following (Code numbers refer to the minor group codes used in that Census): 1. Architects, engineers and surveyors professional. 2. Chemists, physicists and other physical scientists. 3 (Part) Biologists, agronomists, and related scientists (but excluding vetinarians). 8. Teachers. 10. Law professionals. 11. Artists, entertainers, writers and related workers. 12. (Part) Draughtsmen and tracers (but excluding technicians, technical assistants, laboratory technicians and assistants). 13. Other professional, technical and related workers (e.g. accountants, economists, advertising etc.). 14. Administrative and executive officials – Government. 15. (Part) Employers, managers, workers on own account (a) finance and property (b) community and business services. 16. Bookkeepers and cashiers. 17. Stenographers and typists. 18. Other clerical workers. 19. Insurance, real estate salesmen and valuers. 20. Commercial travellers and manufacturers' agents. 38. Telephone, telegraph, telecommunications operators. 39. Postmasters, postmen and messengers. 52. Printing trades workers. 69. Photographers and camera operators.

Source: Commonwealth Bureau of Statistics: Australian Census.

conglomerations of universities, research institutes, research corporations'[7]; and the idea of *The Knowledge Revolution.*[8] However, one need not subscribe to such emotive concepts to appreciate the importance of information in our society, and few would quarrel with Shubik's view of man as '. . .the uncertain decision maker acting under severely restricted conditions of information embedded within a communication system upon which he is becoming increasingly more dependent'.[9]

The communications industry as a part of the 'information sector', is concerned with the distribution of information and knowledge. It performs functions in the information chain which are analogous to those of transportation and retailing in the material goods chain. The precise definition of the boundaries of such an industry presents considerable conceptual difficulties. However, difficulties over boundary definitions are a commonplace in the social sciences and the limits actually chosen must be related to the purpose for which the definition is required. A degree of arbitrariness is usually unavoidable. In this presentation we shall be concerned with the structure and growth of postal, telecommunication, radio and television services in Australia. Clearly much wider definitions are possible. However, given that some selectivity is necessary, this definition may be justified as embracing major areas of investment and on the grounds of enabling some comparability with overseas 'communications industry' studies, in particular the structure of US and USSR communications output in a recent study.[10]

After a brief review of the history of the communications industry, this chapter examines the structure of the industry and makes comparisons with the structure and changes in structure of the industry in the USA and USSR. Each of the five major branches of the industry, i.e. postal service, domestic telecommunications service, overseas telecommunications service, commercial broadcasting, and the national broadcasting and television service, are then considered. Despite existing data problems, these branches of the industry emerge as significant components of the service sector; significant not only because of the share of resources they absorb but also because they may have an added role in shaping preferences and influencing income distribution.

History in Brief[11]

Australia's first postmaster, Mr Isaac Nichols was appointed in Sydney on 25 April 1809. Uniform postage rates were established in 1850, and in 1891 the Australian colonies joined the Universal Postal Union. At Federation in 1901 all postal services were placed under the control of the Federal Postmaster-General. By 1939 the number of postal articles handled per year was over one thousand million; by 1961 this total had doubled. In the next five years to 1966 the total of postal articles handled increased to over two thousand five hundred million. Since then there has been a small annual increase. However, in the period 1964-74 the number of items handled per capita of the population has declined slightly and the postal service has been losing money. Nevertheless, the postal service is still an important channel of communication particularly for social and personal information; for example, in 1975 the largest single mailing in Australia's history took place when 9.8 million individually addressed cards concerning Medibank were despatched.

Australia's first telegraph line was opened in 1854 between Williamstown and Melbourne and in 1858, Sydney, Melbourne and Adelaide were linked by telegraph. The Victoria-Tasmania submarine telegraph was opened the following year and two years later in 1861 the Sydney-Brisbane line was operational. In 1872 the Australian network was connected to London via Adelaide and Darwin and in 1877 Perth was connected to the network via Adelaide. In 1878, only two years after the invention of the telephone, the first trunk telephone calls were demonstrated in Australia and two years later in 1880, the first telephone exchanges were opened at Brisbane, Sydney and Melbourne. At Federation all telecommunication services were taken over by the Commonwealth under the control of a Federal Postmaster-General. By 1912 there were 100,000 telephone subscribers in Australia and the numbers increased by almost a 6 per cent average annual growth rate, reaching 500,000 by 1940, one million by 1953 and two million by 1965 when the STD service was introduced. By 1975 there were just over 3.5 million subscribers when Telecom Australia was created as a separate entity from Australia Post.

Early developments in radio were concerned primarily with communication with ships at sea, the first official record of experimental transmissions being in 1901. In 1905 the Wireless Telegraphy Act and Regulations were introduced, requiring all radio stations to be licensed by the Postmaster-General and to be subject to the requirements of the act. The first radio broadcasting stations, 2FC and 2BL were opened in Sydney in 1923 and the National Broadcasting Service was established in 1929. In 1934 the first overseas radio-picture service opened between Australia and Britain. By 1940 the number of civil radio communication stations, including broadcasting and amateur stations, had reached 1000, and was to reach 50,000 by 1962. In 1956 the first national and commercial television stations opened in Sydney and Melbourne. By 1960 one million television sets had been licensed and one national and two commercial television stations were operating in each state capital. Over the next ten years the system of television stations was gradually expanded to cover provincial and later remote country centres. In 1975 colour television was introduced and a system of FM radio transmitters installed. The number of TV stations increased between 1960 and 1975 from 16 to 132. While the overall annual growth rate was 15 per cent, growth in the number of TV stations tended to be concentrated before 1967 and since 1970. The number of television viewers' licences increased from 954,995 in 1960 to 3,012,833 in 1974 – a growth rate of 8.5 per cent. This represented a change in percentage of licences to population from 9.29 to 22.87.

Industry Structure

The communications industry can be divided into five branches with a number of sub-branches. The five branches are:

1. The Postal Service
2. The Telecommunications Service
3. The Overseas Telecommunications Service
4. Commercial Broadcasting (Radio & TV)
5. National Broadcasting and Television Service

There are in addition separate government networks, which, though technically interconnected are administratively separate and whose output is not fully reflected in the statistics. For example, since December 1953 the Meteorological Bureau has operated a private Commonwealth-wide teleprinter network. An estimated 10 per cent of all telegrams transmitted prior to 1952 were unpaid meteorological telegrams. Since 1955 the Meteorological Bureau has sent 80 per cent of its traffic over this private network.

The measure of output of communications services is notoriously difficult and most econometric studies have relied on revenues as an appropriate surrogate.[12] In a mixed economy this presents considerable problems. The postal service, for example, has suffered substantial trading losses in the period since 1964, the deficit being covered in part by cross-subsidisation from the profitable telecommunications service and the remainder from general government revenue. The National

Table 5.2: Australian Communications Industry Structure: Revenue

Branch	1950 $'000	%	1960 $'000	%	1965 $'000	%	1970 $'000	%	1974 $'000	%
Post										
Postage	27,893	30	79,935	25	103,032	21	149,035	17	224,246	15
Total	30,721	33	86,522	27	112,191	22	161,866	19	244,996	17
Telecom										
Telephone Rental	11,644	12	46,561	15	82,175	16	126,669	15	235,816	16
Telephone Calls	28,206	30	97,843	31	142,722	28	280,757	33	517,375	35
Telegrams	7,559	8	9,830	3	11,423	2	15,120	2	19,499	1
Leased Telegraph	494	1	3,515	1	5,846	1	9,253	1	15,155	1
Total	49,736	53	164,651	52	257,853	51	463,378	54	853,435	58
OTC										
Telephone	117	0.1	544	0.2	3,049	0.6	11,076	1.3	28,041	1.9
Telex	–	–	472	0.1	2,235	0.4	6,522	0.8	16,346	0.7
Telegraph	1,096	1.2	4,424	1.4	6,515	1.3	9,821	1.1	9,760	0.7
Leases	–	–	419	0.1	1.738	0.3	7,943	0.9	7,204	0.5
Total	1,389	1	5,979	2	14,034	3	38,231	4	66,074	4
Commercial Broadcasting										
Radio	6,357	7	20,503	6	24,550	5	37,059	4	56,587	4
TV	–	–	20,638	6	49,695	10	91,191	11	132,299	9
Total	6,357	7	41,141	13	74,245	15	128,250	15	188,886	13
National Broadcasting & TV	5,993	6	20,093	6	43,715	9	63,009	7	113,766	8
Grand Total	94,196	100	318,386	100	502,038	100	854,734	100	1,467,157	100

Notes:
a. OTC review figures for 1950 and 1960 understate its share due to changes in the accounting system.
b. National Broadcasting and TV revenue figures are not meaningful and total expenditure including capital expenditure has been used as a surrogate variable.
c. Only the main items of revenue are shown in the breakdown.
d. Discrepancies in percentage totals due to rounding error.
e. OTC figures are shown to one decimal place to illustrate comparative internal changes over time, no additional accuracy is implied.
Sources: Postmaster-General's Department Financial & Statistical Bulletin (Annual). Australian Broadcasting Control Board Annual Reports. Australia: Treasurer's Statement of Receipts and Expenditures accompanied by the Report of the Auditor General (Annual). Overseas Telecommunications Commission Annual Reports.

Table 5.3: Australian Communications Industry Structure: Operating Expenditure

	1950 $'000	%	1960 $'000	%	1965 $'000	%	1970 $'000	%	1974 $'000	%
Postal Service	33,028	35	85,066	28	114,809	24	181,834	22	299,514	22
Telecommunications	49,738	52	165,251	54	251,024	53	441,528	54	794,443	57
OTC	776	1	5,334	2	11,547	2	27,626	3	43,295	3
Commercial Radio	6,184	6	15,314	5	19,205	4	27,483	3	43,420	3
Commercial TV	–	–	17,509	6	44,050	9	74,521	9	108,306	8
National Radio and TV	5,671	6	16,197	5	34,492	7	57,616	7	98,423	7
Grand Total	95,397	100	304,671	100	475,127	100	810,508	100	1,387,201	100

Notes:
a. National Broadcasting Expenditure does not include provision for depreciation and therefore slightly understates its share.
b. Discrepancies in percentage totals due to rounding errors.
Sources: As for Table 5.3.

Broadcasting Service is not conducted on commercial principles and hence no meaningful data on revenue are available. Furthermore, as the different corporations, public, semi-public and private, use conceptually different methods of accounting, the comparisons on this basis must be considered to be extremely crude. It appears that operational expenditure is more nearly conceptually similar for all branches of the industry and therefore may offer more meaningful structural comparison ratios. Both approaches are shown in tables 5.2 and 5.3.

The two alternative approaches to industry structure produce little significant difference in results. The somewhat higher percentage share of the postal services suggested by the expenditure method reflects the substantial losses incurred by that sector. The telecommunications sector is seen to be the largest sector of the industry and the telephone as the most important service for both internal and overseas use. Domestic and overseas telecommunications accounted for 54 per cent of output (measured by revenue) in 1950. This share grew to 62 per cent by 1974. The rate of change was not uniform over time nor amongst component activities. Domestic services declined by 2 per cent between 1950 and 1965 but grew in share by 7 per cent between 1965 and 1974. In contrast, overseas services increased fourfold between 1950 and 1970 and then showed signs of stabilising. These changes in output as measured by revenue are set out in Table 5.6. Tabulation of changes using the alternative expenditure measure are presented in Table 5.7. While differences between the two measures emerge in five-year sub-periods the broad changes over the entire period are very similar. The greatest apparent difference is for overseas services. This is a result in part of rounding of figures. OTC is +3.0 on a revenue basis and +2.0 on an expenditure basis. The figures correct to first decimal place are 3.0 and 2.4 respectively.

Differential rates of change were experienced by component activities. The most marked decline was experienced by domestic telegraph services – a decline in share from 8 per cent in 1950 to one per cent in 1974. Postal services experienced a relative decline from approximately one-third to one-sixth. Commercial radio declined from 7 per cent to 4 per cent. Overseas telephone services showed the greatest relative expansion: 0.1 to 1.9 per cent. Newcomers such as overseas telex and leasing and TV also expanded relatively as Table 5.6 shows. Telegraph services have shown a marked decline. As a result of the study by J.P. Lewis some broad comparisons with the American and Soviet communications industries are possible. Tables 5.4 and 5.5 are drawn from that study, the output being calculated on a revenue basis.[13]

Table 5.4: The Structure of US Communications Output

Branch of Communications	1950		1960		1965		1970	
	10^6 Dollars	Percent	10^6 Dollars	Percent	10^6 Dollars	Percent	10^6 Dollars	Percent
Postal Service	1,677	29.6	3,277	24.8	4,483	24.3	6,473	23.3
Long Distance Telephone	1,208	21.3	3,058	23.1	4,706	25.5	8,042	29.3
Telegraph	228	4.0	349	2.6	413	2.2	402	2.1
City and Rural Telephone	1,997	35.3	4,665	35.3	6,114	33.1	8,685	31.3
Radio Broadcasting	445	7.8	598	4.5	793	4.3	1,137	4.1
Television	106	1.8	1,269	9.6	1,965	10.6	2,808	10.1
Totals	5,662	100.0	13,216	100.0	18,474	100.0	27,741	100.0

Source: Reproduced from 9, p.433. Percentages do not add to 100 presumably because of rounding. Total for 1970 adds to 27,547. Error in original may be in either total or a component item.

Table 5.5: The Structure of Soviet Communications Output

Branch of Communications	1950		1960		1965		1970	
	10^6 Rubles	Percent	10^6 Rubles	Percent	10^6 Rubles	Percent	10^6 Rubles	Percent
Postal Service	384.3	52.5	586.4	43.1	859.3	42.7	1260.4	38.3
Long Distance Telephone	85.9	11.7	170.8	12.5	288.6	14.3	555.3	16.9
Telegraph	110.8	15.1	169.3	12.4	224.7	11.2	356.0	10.8
City Telephone	55.8	7.6	117.8	8.7	171.1	8.5	344.4	10.4
Rural Telephone	32.3	4.4	100.1	7.4	148.0	7.3	267.1	8.1
Radiofication	45.5	6.2	108.6	8.0	164.3	8.2	236.0	7.2
Radio Broadcasting and Television	18.4	2.5	108.1	7.9	157.4	7.8	272.5	8.3
Totals	734.0	100.0	1361.3	100.0	2013.3	100.0	3291.9	100.0

Source: 9, p.434.

The Australian and US industries are seen to be similar in structure, with the broadcasting media having a rather larger share of the Australian industry, and the postal service rather less. This was true of broadcasting media throughout the period 1950-70. As can be seen from Table 5.4 postal services were more important in Australia than in the US in 1950. While these services have experienced a relative decline in both countries, that decline has been much greater in Australia than in the US. In the US, however, the postal service monopoly includes access to householder and business letter boxes which may account for part of the difference. However, the US postal service, unlike its Australian counterpart, has not made a profit since 1945. Telecommunications services are provided by government-regulated private enterprise in the USA and it seems likely that more aggressive marketing techniques may be partially responsible for the larger size of this sector.

In the Soviet Union the postal service has a much larger comparative share of the market. It is responsible for a much larger proportion of the delivery system for magazines and periodicals than postal services in the USA or Australia.[14] Collectively Radiofication (the system of wired broadcasting to home receivers) and ordinary radio and television are comparable to the USA and rather smaller than Australia in terms of market shares. Telegraph is seen to be rather more important in the Soviet Union although there too it is declining.

Perhaps the most obvious comparison, however, is in the size of each of the three systems measured as a proportion of their respective national products. In 1970 (the latest year for which comparisons are available), and on the assumption that gross revenues are a reasonable surrogate for output, Australian communications accounted for approximately 2.9 per cent of GNP. Lewis estimated that in the same year US communications accounted for nearly 3 per cent of GNP, whilst for the Soviet Union the industry output was of the order of one half of one per cent of GNP.[15] The growing importance of the Australian communications industry is illustrated by its increasing contribution to GNP, as shown in Table 5.8. The data does, however, suggest some decline in the rate of growth in the 1970-4 period. It should perhaps be added that in the Soviet case a significant part of communications activities are operated by defence services. The same is true of the US and, probably to a lesser extent, of Australia. Data do not permit adjustment on this account.

Table 5.6: Australian Communications Industry Structure Changes in Percentage of Revenue Shares

Branch	1950-60	1960-65	1965-70	1970-74	1950-70	1960-70	1950-74
Post							
Postage	–5	–4	–4	–2	–13	–10	–15
Total	–6	–5	–3	–2	–14	–10	–16
Telecom							
Telephone Rental	+3	+1	–1	+1	+3	+1	+4
Telephone Calls	+1	–3	+5	+2	+3	+2	+5
Telegrams	–5	–1	0	–1	–6	–1	–7
Leased Telegraph	0	0	0	0	0	0	0
Total	–2	–1	+3	+4	+1	+2	+5
OTC							
Telephone	+0.1	+0.4	+0.7	+0.6	+1.2	+1.1	+1.8
Telex	+0.1	+0.3	+0.4	–0.1	+0.8	+0.7	+0.7
Telegraph	+0.2	–0.1	–0.2	–0.4	–0.1	–0.3	–0.5
Leases	+0.1	+0.2	+0.6	–0.4	+0.9	+0.8	+0.5
Total	+1.0	+1.0	+1.0	0	+3.0	+2.0	+3.0
Commercial Broadcasting							
Radio	–1	–1	–1	0	–3	–2	–3
TV	+6	+4	+1	–2	+11	+5	+9
Total	+6	+2	0	–2	+8	+2	+6
National Broadcasting and TV	0	+3	–2	+1	+1	+1	+2

Source: Table 5.2.

Table 5.7: Australian Communications Industry Structure: Changes in Percentage of Expenditure Shares

	1950-60	1960-65	1965-70	1970-74	1950-70	1960-70	1950-74
Postal Service	–7.0	–4.0	–2.0	0	–13.0	–6.0	–13.0
Telecommunications	+2.0	–1.0	+1.0	+3.0	+2.0	0	+5.0
OTC	+1.0	0	+1.0	0	+2.0	+1.0	+2.0
Commercial Radio	–1.0	–1.0	–1.0	0	–3.0	–2.0	–3.0
Commercial TV	+6.0	+3.0	0	–1.0	+9.0	+3.0	+8.0
National Radio and TV	–1.0	+2.0	0	0	+1.0	+2.0	+1.0

Source: Table 5.3

Table 5.8: Australian Communications Industry Revenues as Percentage of GNP

	1950 %	1960 %	1965 %	1970 %	1974 %
Telecommunications (incl. OTC)	0.94	1.18	1.27	1.55	1.70
Total	1.78	2.28	2.48	2.86	2.92

Source: Table 5.2 and Australian National Accounts.

Australia Post

Until 1975 the Australian postal service was administered by a department which was also responsible for telegraphs and telephones. Australia Post was created as a separate 'public utility' in 1975 following the recommendations of the [Vernon] *Commission of Inquiry into the Australian Post Office.* The postal service has, in common with the postal services of the UK and the USA, been a prime victim of political uncertainty about the trade-off between efficiency and welfare criteria of operation. On the one hand successive governments have required that the postal service should regard itself as a commercial undertaking which should at least cover its aggregate costs, including a variously defined 'normal rate of return' on borrowings. On the other hand they have generally been unwilling to accept the economic implications of this approach and have continued to impose, explicitly or implicitly, a series of requirements to supply 'merit goods', by way of politically imposed pricing policies.

Hence a complex system of cross-subsidisation has been developed, together with an accounting system, the effect of which, whether by accident or design, is to obscure the economic realities of the situation. In its admission to the Vernon Inquiry the PMG Department stated: 'For historical reasons there are substantial cross-subsidisations of services. . . The major cross-subsidisation is to the registered newspaper and periodical category.'[16]

The department itself recognises the dubious nature of the assumptions on which its social welfare role is predicated, which, whatever their historical justification, appear to have questionable validity in the latter half of the twentieth century: 'The original social purpose of the concessional rates to encourage the dissemination of news and information and to develop greater literacy has long since lost its significance.'[17]

This statement echoes earlier sharp comment by the UK Prices and Incomes Board, who in 1968 observed on a similar situation in that country: 'We see no good reason for the subsidisation of the newspaper proprietors by the rest of the service. . .'[18]

Nevertheless, the public has been conditioned to expect cheaper tariffs for printed papers than for letters, whereas except for savings associated with bulk posting and a possible small savings from the ability to defer handling in rush periods, the unit costs of handling different classes of mail would appear to be the same. In its submission to the Vernon committee the then PMG Department included details of service costs, earnings and profitability for the year 1971-2[19] (Table 5.9). It may be seen that the imputed loss on registered publications exceeds the profit claimed for ordinary letter post, which was the only profitable service. The table also makes clear the degree of cross-subsidisation between letter-post and other classes of mail services.

We would wish at this point to examine cross-subsidisation between services more explicitly by estimating the percentage shares of costs attributable to each service and then calculating the percentage change in earnings (or price, assuming equal demand elasticities) necessary to earn an equivalent percentage surplus/deficit for all services. The cost estimations are inadequate for this purpose. For example, the Vernon Commission (vol.2, p.91) commented that 'we are not able to express a confident view regarding the operating results for individual postal services'. Referring to equipment-oriented costs in telecommunications, the Commission observed (vol.2, p.74) that 'only approximately 45 per cent of these [costs] are allowed to service programmes on bases which we considered to be satisfactory'. The inadequacies of the data appear to overwhelm the cross-subsidisation.

The postal service has generally been regarded as a statutory monopoly. However, that monopoly is restricted to the carriage or conveyance of letters for reward[20], and does not include parcels or, apparently, advertising material. Thus the department complained:

> Increasingly the Department faces competition from private enterprise. Particularly is this so in the carriage of parcels interstate, courier services within capital cities and delivery of household items such as catalogues. In almost every case competitors 'cream off' profitable segments of the business leaving the unprofitable segments to the Department.[21]

Table 5.9: Product Profitability

	Earnings $m	Expenses $m	Profit/Loss $m
Domestic Mail			
Letters	122.3	113.2	9.1
Other Articles	17.6	18.4	–0.8
Registered Publications	5.5	15.1	–9.6
Registered Articles and Parcels	6.3	10.6	–4.3
Parcels	9.0	10.9	–1.9
Special Services	2.1	2.3	–0.2
Overseas Mail	30.0	31.9	–1.9
Money Transfer	4.6	7.6	–3.0
Other	15.9	14.6	1.3
	213.3	224.6	–11.3

In this context, it is, however, interesting to note that the parcels service has been the fastest growing category of business, with a growth in terms of articles handled of 34 per cent between 1966 and 1972 compared with 7.3 per cent for letters and negative growth for all other major categories of business. It is generally conceded that public utilities, particularly those granted statutory monopoly powers, ought to behave in a non-discriminatory way. In commenting on pricing policy, the Vernon Commission affirmed that Australia Post should be required to exercise its powers in such a way that services are made available to all potential users in a non-discriminatory way.[22] Regrettably the Commission felt itself unable to define what it meant by discrimination although the context appeared to imply that it might be synonymous with differentiation.

The term 'discriminatory behaviour' is usually applied to actions by economic agents possessing some degree of monopoly power, who use that power to act (i.e. price or non-price behaviour) differentially according to the relative elasticities of demand in different segments of a *single* market. The limits to what constitutes a single market are defined in terms of cost and, *a fortiori,* markets may be differentiated on the basis of cost. For example, Section 49 of the Trade Practices Act 1974-76 is designed to prevent discrimination 'between purchasers of goods of like grade and quality' in relation to price, discounts, allowances, etc.; the provision of services or facilities; and the making of payments for services or facilities. Discrimination is, however, permitted if it 'makes only reasonable allowance for differences in the cost or likely cost of manufacture, distribution, sale or delivery resulting from the differing places to which, methods by which or quantities in which the goods are supplied to the purchasers'. Thus the standard practice by postal services of applying a common tariff regardless of cost differentials is, by definition, discriminatory. This not only tends to misallocate resources, but makes it difficult to compete in markets where close substitutes exist, since it leads to overpricing in low cost highly elastic markets. Attempts to compromise between equity and efficiency by internal cross-subsidisation are seldom successful.

However, clause 75(1) of the Postal Services Bill 1975-76 requires Australia Post to consider profitability and, in particular, to follow a policy designed to recover all expenditure properly chargeable to revenue *and* to provide for not less than half its capital expenditure. Table 5.10 shows that postal services are labour-intensive in contrast to telecommunications that are capital-intensive. Attempts to determine the price-elasticity of demand for various mail services have not been notably successful, although it is clearly a necessary prerequisite to proper tariff setting in a profit-oriented organisation. The Vernon Commission found, for example, that 'The APO has carried out a certain amount of work on the elasticity of demand for its services but interpretation of their results presents difficulties'.[23] In a recent paper, Nissen and Lago[24] commented on the unsatisfactory state of the art, which they attributed to the use of an annual data base coupled with unsatisfactory statistical techniques. Without denying the validity of this and similar criticisms, it may be contended that the problem stems from a much more fundamental cause: namely, an implicit assumption that the various services represent markets which can usefully be regarded as homogeneous.

Few people would wish to deny that important role which the postal service has played in the economic and social development of Australia. It developed into a nationwide network for the transmission of information, goods (parcels) and money, both nationally and internationally. The postal service as currently conceived is, however, highly labour-intensive. Attempts at mechanisation do not appear to have been notably successful in containing rising costs. It has had to face increasing competition from the more capital-intensive telecommunications networks in the transmission of parcels and money. In the period 1964-74 it incurred a total net operating loss of $197.25 million largely paid for by the users of the telecommunications services by cross-

Table 5.10: Comparative Figures Postal and Telecommunications Year Ended 30 June 1973

	Postal	Telecommunications	Combined
Fixed Assets (at cost less depreciation)	$125.3 m.	$2,886.9 m.	$3,012.2 m.
Working Capital	4.8	237.4	242.2
	$130.1 m.	$3,124.3 m.	$3,254.4 m.
Less provision for Long Service Leave	20.1	54.5	74.5
Net Funds	$110.0 m.	$3,069.9 m.	$3,179.9 m.
Earnings	$226.5 m.	$ 710.6 m.	$ 937.1 m.
$ Earnings/$ Net Funds Employed	$ 2.06	$ 0.23	$ 0.29
Approximate full-time employees (excluding those engaged in capital work)	31,000	58,000	89,000
Fixed Assets (depreciated) per employee	$ 4,000	$ 50,000	$ 34,000
Profit (+) or Loss (–)	–$20.9 m.	+ $62.1 m.	+ $41.2 m.
Profit or Loss as per cent Net Funds	– 19.0%	+ 2.0%	+ 1.3%
Profit or Loss as per cent Earnings	– 9.2%	+ 8.7%	+ 4.4%
Composition of Expenses			
	Per Cent	Per Cent	Per Cent
Wages and Salaries	65.5	41.8	48.4
Materials and General	18.8	10.1	12.5
Depreciation	2.2	22.9	17.2
Superannuation	5.3	3.7	4.1
Long Service Leave	1.9	1.3	1.4
Interest	6.3	20.2	16.4
	100.0	100.0	100.0

Source: 21, vol1, p.35. Calculated by Commission from data supplied bythe APO.

subsidy. In the light of this record, therefore, the postal service in its present form must, like many labour-intensive industries, be regarded as vulnerable. The Vernon Commission commented (vol.1, p.186) as follows:

> The APO has been active in seeking ways to improve the efficiency of its postal operations by mechanisation and by rationalising its post office network and all such avenues for cost saving should undoubtedly be pursued vigorously in the future; the need is very great. The problems are considerable, particularly in respect of industrial relations. . .and progress is unlikely to be rapid. However, even assuming that work in these directions continues with some success, it is clear that savings by way of rationalisation, methods improvement, mechanisation and labour productivity cannot possibly offset cost increases of the magnitude of those indicated. . . on the assumption of wage and salary rates increasing by 12½ per cent in the 1974-75 year and 10 per cent in each of the following two years.

Telecommunications

The monopoly power of the Telecommunications Commission (Telecom) is far more extensive and all embracing than that of the postal service. In particular the Act provides that, with the exception of state or national rail or road passenger authorities, unless authorised by the Commission:

> . . .a person other than the Commission –
> (a) shall not erect, maintain or operate a telecommunications installation within Australia; or
> (b) attach a line, equipment or apparatus to a telecommunications system.[25]

Furthermore, the penalty for infringement of the statutory monopoly, (imprisonment for 2 years) is extremely severe compared to the penalty, ($1000 fine) for infringement of the postal monopoly. The Act also extends the monopoly to the publication of telephone directories and to the sub-leasing of authorised services, e.g. private teleprinter networks. This latter power is of some importance to the expansion of data networks which, together with the issue of the demarcation between telecommunications and in-house computer to computer linkage, has been the subject of legal action in the United States.

The pricing policy for telecommunications has been built up from the fixed cost structure of the installed equipment. This has been split into cost for local circuits, trunk exchanges, inter-exchange circuits etc. For wire distribution, cost is some function of distance and the number of switching points through which a call must be routed. This may be contrasted with satellite distribution systems in which cost is independent of distance. Some recognition of peak and off-peak pricing is evident in the lower charges for calls outside the local area during non-business hours. The pricing policy for telecommunications and particularly telephone services is inter-related with problems of equity and equality of access to information. A recent Canadian report on telecommunications, for example, suggested that equality of access to information might require a flat rate for telephone calls regardless of distance.[26] The incorporation of this and similar social factors into pricing policy might be a significant factor in both business and population decentralisation as both commercial and social activity becomes more information intensive.

The importance of the telephone service relative to other communications media has already been suggested. On a world scale it has been estimated that between 1964 and 1974 the total number of telephones in service increased from 171 million to 336.3 million: an average annual growth rate of 7 per cent compound. In a similar period the number of telephones in service in Australia increased from 2.67 million to 5 million: an average annual growth rate of 6.5 per cent. By 1974, however, the world total per 100 population was only 8.6 telephones whilst Australia's was 37.7 compared to North America with 63.9 and Europe with 17.2.[27]

Broadcasting

The market structure of Commercial Broadcasting in Australia, is controlled by the Australian Broadcasting Control Board, a statutory body, which monitors compliance with provisions of the *Broadcasting and Television Act 1942-1973.* This Act contains provisions which are designed to control monopolisation of the radio broadcasting and television media. The problem of control of the broadcasting media has been a matter of continuing concern both in Australia and overseas and has generated a considerable body of literature.[28] This has been of particular concern where the control might be exercised by newspaper interests, in particular the national dailies.

In the case of radio broadcasting, Section 90A of the Act provides that a person shall not have a prescribed interest in licenses, nor be a director of two or more companies that between them are in a position to exercise control of licenses for:

(a) more than one metropolitan commercial broadcasting station in any one State;
(b) more than four metropolitan commercial broadcasting stations in Australia;
(c) more than four commercial broadcasting stations in one State; or
(d) more than eight commercial broadcasting stations in Australia.

The Act defines a prescribed interest, as a shareholding or voting interest in excess of 15 per cent, held *directly* or *indirectly* in a licensee company. However, where prescribed interests or directorship were held prior to 24 September 1968, the effective date of the legislation, they may be retained (but not extended).

The provisions relating to ownership and control of television stations are somewhat more restrictive. Control of a company is deemed to exist if a person has a voting or shareholding interest exceeding 15 per cent. A prescribed interest is defined broadly, as a voting, shareholding, or financial interest, *direct* or *indirect*, in excess of five per cent. The Act prescribes that a person shall not have a prescribed interest in:

(a) each of three or more licences;
(b) each of two or more licences in a state or territory; or
(c) each of two or more licenses for stations in a State and within a radius of thirty miles of the General Post office in the capital city of the State.

Interests held prior to 17 December 1964, the effective date of the legislation, are exempt. Further, a person shall not be a director of two or more companies that are, between them, in a position to exercise control of three or more licenses. Indirect holdings and interests are to be calculated on a proportional basis.

The Australian Broadcasting Control Board publishes details of shareholding interests in its annual reports. The complexity of cross-ownership of shares between companies makes it somewhat difficult to see the extent of the interests and control involved in particular cases. As previously indicated, an important issue is the extent to which newspapers are in a position to control broadcasting. Accordingly, Table 5.11 sets out the cross-ownership of shares between newspapers, for the national dailies.

On the basis of the definition in the Act, it appears that Herald and

Table 5.11: Percentage Direct and Indirect Shareholdings of Capital City Newspaper Companies in other Capital City Newspaper Companies

Shares held in → / Shares held by ↓	Advertiser	Davies Bros.	J. Fairfax	Herald & Weekly Times	News Ltd	Queensland Press Ltd
Advertiser	–			6.5		1.5
Davies Bros.		–		0.015		
J. Fairfax			–			
Herald & Weekly Times	30.9	48.15		–		39.3
News Ltd					–	
Queensland Press Ltd.	0.1	6.2		7.8		–

Note: a. Queensland Press Ltd owns 100 per cent of Queensland Newspapers Pty. Ltd and Telegraph Investment Co. Pty. Ltd.
b. The Herald and Weekly Times owns 100 per cent of West Australian Newspapers Ltd.
c. Advertiser Newspapers owns 100 per cent of Midlands Broadcasting Services Ltd.
d. Davies Bros. own 50 per cent of Commercial Broadcasters Pty. Ltd.
e. John Fairfax Ltd owns 45 per cent of Newcastle Newspapers and 30 per cent of J.C. Williamson Ltd.
f. News Ltd owns 33 per cent of Tamworth Newspapers Ltd.

Source: Australian Broadcasting Control Board 26th Annual Report for the year ended 30 June 1974.

Weekly Times Ltd controls Advertiser Newspapers (Adelaide), Davies Bros. Ltd (Hobart), and Queensland Press Ltd. Tables 5.12 and 5.13 show the interests of the capital city newspaper companies in broadcasting and television.

Again on the basis of the definition in the Act, John Fairfax Ltd controls five radio broadcasting stations and has a prescribed interest in another, and three television stations. The Herald & Weekly Times has direct control of two radio-broadcasting stations and indirect control of six others, and in addition controls one television station directly, two indirectly and has financial interests in six others. Furthermore, because of geographical and State separation the degree of competition between companies in the media is substantially less than would appear on the surface.

Table 5.12: Radio Broadcasting Interests of Capital City Newspapers: Percentage Direct and Indirect Holdings

	Advertiser	Davies Bros.	J. Fairfax	Herald & Weekly Times	News Ltd	Queensland Press Ltd
4AD Adelaide	L					
5DN Adelaide			28			
5MU Murray Bridge	6.9					
5PI Crystal Brook	L					
5SE Mt. Gambier	L					
7HO Hobart		50				
7EX Launceston		0.64				
3XY Melbourne			10			
3AW Melbourne			28			
3DB Melbourne				L		
GL Geelong				100		
2GB Sydney			28			
2CA Canberra			28			
2WL Woolongong			28			
4BH Brisbane			4			
4BK Brisbane						L
4AK Oakey						L
4AM Atherton						14.5

Note: 'L' indicates that the Newspaper Company is the licensee of the station.
Source: As for Table 5.11

Table 5.13: Commercial Television Interests of Capital City Newspapers: Percentage Direct and Indirect Holdings

	Advertiser	Davies Bros.	J. Fairfax	Herald & Weekly Times	News	Queensland Press Ltd
ADS Adelaide	40	D		D		D
ATN Sydney			94			
BTQ Brisbane	D	D		3D		28D
BTW & GSW					4	
CTC Canberra			30			
DDQ Darling Downs			0.15			
ECN & NEN					1.7	
HSV Melbourne	D	D		85D		D
NBN Newcastle			4			
NTD Darwin					4.9	
NWS Adelaide					100	
ITQ Mt. Isa					4.9	
QTQ Brisbane			59			
SAS Adelaide	D	5.4		D		D
TNT Tasmania	D	6.4		D		D
TEN Sydney				0.7		
TVT Hobart		12.8		D		
TVW Perth		5.4D		1.5D		D
VEW Kalgoorlie					4.6	

Note: 'D' indicates an additional indirect dividend interest through cross-ownership of shares between newspapers not generally significant for control.
Source: As for Table 5.8.

Conclusion

Clearly, this chapter reveals the unresearched character of this service activity and the lack of research findings. Knowledge is limited. As in all other parts of the information sector of the economy rapid change not only causes that knowledge to date rapidly but also emphasises the urgency of the need for comprehensive and sustained inquiry. Major technological changes are imminent and yet an adequate understanding of existing conditions is lacking. There are limits to what can be extracted from inadequate cost data and inadequate demand studies. Some additional information will be yielded by the satellite feasibility study, the Green report, and the inter-Departmental Committee deliberations on the ALBIS (Australian Library Based Information Service) and Public Library inquiries.

Despite this situation, we must remember that the power to control information flows is the power to control the minds of people. The important issue is that, whether or not that power is used or abused, it exists. It is a fact of life that commercial media owners are businessmen, and hence hold in common many attitudes and opinions which may not be shared by other interest groups. 'To the extent that they influence news coverage, they are likely to influence it in the same direction'.[29] Most media owners may use their power sparingly. However, a recent American study concluded that a community served by a media monopoly is, typically, substantially less knowledgeable as to current events information than one served by competing media. The study concluded that

> The crucial point is that the monopoly's adverse effects on the public – current and potential – would continue to exist regardless of the motivations and actions of the monopoly owner.[30]

The commercial broadcasting media, in addition, are peculiar in that the service sold is advertising (broadly defined). The consumer is not the customer and hence can exercise little effective control over the product particularly in monopoly situations.

The consequences of the structural features of the communications industry are far reaching. There seems to be an emerging appreciation of the profound implications of social information processing for equality. In Starrett's words,

> It is not enough that all individuals have access to the same institutions and markets; they must also have access to the same 'correct'

information. . . [T]he real advantage in 'controlling the means of production' does not necessarily depend on monopoly power (although such power may be an important factor), but can derive from having access to better information, or a better position in the institutional structure.[31]

References

* With assistance from J.M. Barnes.

1. D.M. Lamberton, 'The Necessity for a National Information Policy', *The Australian Library Journal,* 23 (July 1974) p.213.
2. F. Machlup, *The Production and Distribution of Knowledge,* (Princeton University Press, Princeton, N.J., 1962).
3. M. Porat, 'Defining The Information Sector', *Bulletin of the American Society for Information Science,* 2 (February 1976) pp.34-5.
4. D.M. Lamberton and J.M. Barnes, 'The Growth of the Australian Information Society', Sociological Association of Australia and New Zealand Conference, 1976.
5. E.F. Denison, *Why Growth Rates Differ: Postwar Experience in Nine Western Countries,* (Brookings Institution, Washington, DC, 1967), p.279.
6. P. Drucker, *The Age of Discontinuity,* (William Heineman Ltd, 1968, Pan Books Edition, 1971), pp.324-5.
7. D. Bell, 'The Post-Industrial Society', in Eli Ginzberg (ed.), *Technology and Social Change* (New York, 1964) p.44.
8. D.N. Chorafas, *The Knowledge Revolution* (Allen and Unwin, London 1968).
9. M. Shubik, 'Information, Rationality and Free Choice in a Future Democratic Society' in D.M. Lamberton (ed.), *Economics of Information and Knowledge,* Penguin, Harmondsworth, Middlesex, 1971, p.361.
10. J.P. Lewis, 'Postwar Economic Growth and Productivity in the Soviet Communications Industry' in *The Bell Journal of Economics and Management Science,* 6, 2 (Autumn 1975), pp.430-50.
11. Australian Post Office, *The Australian Post Office: History at a Glance 1809-1975* (Australian Post Office, 1975).
12. A.R. Dobell *et al.,* 'Telephone Communications in Canada: Demand, Production, and Investment Decisions', *Bell Journal of Economics and Management Science,* 3, 1 (Spring 1972), pp.176-219.
13. J.P. Lewis, op.cit., pp.433 and 434.
14. J.P. Lewis, ibid, p.435.
15. J.P. Lewis, ibid.
16. Postmaster-General's Department *Australian Post Office Commission of Inquiry: submission by the Postmaster-General's Department,* May 1973, vol.4, p.380.
17. Ibid.
18. *Post Office Charges,* NBPI Report No.58, Cmnd. 3574, HMSO 1968, p.53.
19. PMG submission, op.cit., vol.1, p.75.
20. *Postal Services Bill 1975,* Australia, House of Representatives, Clause 85, p.49.
21. *PMG submission,* op.cit., vol.4, p.346.
22. Report of the Vernon Commission of Inquiry into the Australian Post Office, vol.1, April 1974, p.232.
23. Ibid, p.186.
24. D.H. Nissen and A.M. Lago, 'Price Elasticity of the Demand for Parcel Post Mail', *Journal of Industrial Economics,* XXIII, 4 (June 1975), pp.281-99.

25. *Telecommunications Bill 1975;* Australia, House of Representatives, Clause 94, p.53.
26. *Instant World: A Report on Telecommunications in Canada,* Ottawa, Information Canada, 1971, p.34.
27. American Telephone & Telegraphy Company, *The World's Telephones: As of January 1, 1974,* American Telephone & Telegraph Company (December 1974), Table 1.
28. H. Mayer, 'What Should (and Could) We do about the Media?', G. Major (ed.), *Mass Media in Australia* (Hodder and Stroughton, Sydney, Australia, 1976) pp.164-245.
29. P.M. Sandman, D.M. Rubin and D.M. Sachsman, *Media: An Introductory Analysis of American Mass Communications* (Englewood Cliffs, N.J. Prentice-Hall, 1972).
30. American Institute for Political Communication, *The Effects of Local Media Monopoly on the Mass Mind* (The American Institute for Political Communication, Washington DC, 1971) pp.35-6.
31. D. Starrett, 'Social Institutions, Imperfect Information, and the Distribution of Income', *Quarterly Journal of Economics,* XC, 2 (May 1976), p.282.

6 FREIGHT FORWARDING: CHANGES IN STRUCTURE, CONDUCT AND PERFORMANCE

Peter J. Rimmer

> The many diverse problems facing Australian transport today encompass all modes, whether rail, road, sea or air. Nevertheless by viewing all modes together it becomes possible to recognise the most effective way in which each can contribute to improving the nation's total transport system. This philosophy, the multi-modal approach, underlies all facets of our national transport policy. . .the Government is concerned that scarce resources in Australia are used efficiently and to the best effect. It has been recognised that this depends not only on proper planning, but also on the existence of a pricing system which reflects adequately the costs of providing and operating services and facilities.
>
> Department of Transport, *Australian Transport 1973-74* (Australian Government Publishing Service, Canberra, 1973) p.2, p.18.

The Freight Forwarder's Role

Australia's domestic transport system has to be looked at in a different light from its North American and European counterparts. Bayliss has shown for Europe and Taaffe and Gauthier have demonstrated for the United States that their transport systems can be adequately described by comparing the conflicting and competing roles played by air, rail, road, water and pipeline modes.[1] Such modal comparisons in Australia would provide a misleading account of the development of the country's domestic freight transport system since the Second World War without recognition of the pivotal role played by the freight forwarders in moving goods between the states and territories of the Commonwealth.[2]

Prior to the advent of the 'freight forwarder', the methods providing the services of consignment, delivery and cargo handling in Australia's interstate trade were radically different. A common procedure was for the consignor to deliver to the line haul terminal (wharf or railway station), in whatever form of packaging was deemed appropriate, using either a company vehicle or a local carrier In some instances, the consignor employed a forwarding agent to arrange the collection of the goods for shipment and to raise the necessary documentation. On arrival at the originating terminal the line haul mode took charge of the goods and arranged for them to be loaded. At the destination terminal the line haul mode was responsible for unloading and storing the goods in terminal sheds. The shipment was then collected from the sheds by the consignee, local carrier or the forwarding agent after further documentation.[3] Thus, there was no overall responsibility for the journey as a whole and the supply of different services was only loosely co-ordinated.

The freight forwarder, as distinct from the forwarding agent, assumes responsibility for the movement of goods from door-to-door as part of a total package of transport services. This package also offers consignors a wider range of services embodying a choice of line haul modes: a feature that distinguishes the freight forwarder from the conventional air, road or rail contractor who can only offer one line haul mode. The bundle of services is available at an inclusive rate (price) and with a single invoice to cover all aspects of the movement of goods between consignor and consignee. Such a system replaced the multiple charges and varying assortment of documents that were used previously.

In fulfilling the door-to-door service specified on the single invoice the forwarder either owns or sub-contracts for the use of the following equipment and plant:

- space in line haul terminals and warehouses,
- ancillary equipment such as fork lifts and cranes,
- pick up and delivery fleets,
- conventional air, rail, road or sea line haul equipment,
- intermodal line haul equipment such as trailers, containers and pallets,
- specialised line haul equipment for the carriage of goods requiring either insulation or refrigeration, liquid and bulk cargoes and heavy haulage,
- a fleet of pull vehicles for repositioning intermodal line haul equipment.[4]

With access to such facilities and equipment the forwarder is able to offer a series of specialist door-to-door services for insulated and refrigerated freight, dry and liquid bulk items, and heavy haulage. It is also possible to provide a range of scheduled and non-scheduled services for general goods which are tailored to specific consignment features or client preferences.

Three distinct types of consignment (i.e. output types) can be identified (Figure 6.1).[5]

Full unit consignments (FCL) which may be either:
- semi-trailers (capacity 20 tonnes mass or weight and density of $68m^3$)
- jumbo road/rail containers (capacity 20 tonnes mass and density of $74m^3$)
- ISO (International Standards Organisation) type containers (20'x8'x8' with a capacity of 17 tonnes mass and density of $31m^3$).

Part loads (LCL) which usually refer to 50 per cent or more of the capacity of the carrying unit and generally signify a semi-trailer or flexi-van type container and not an ISO type container.

Small consignments which are usually less than one tonne, with the majority of very small consignments (averaging less than 35 kg) being handled by the specialist express companies.

A Sydney consignor, for example, with fifteen tonnes for pick up to go to Melbourne to three or more separate facilities is offering a full load (FCL) with three drops. However, a Sydney consignor with fifteen tonnes for pick up, five tonnes each for Melbourne, Brisbane and Adelaide is offering only part loads (LCL).

Where a consignment of ten or more tonnes of dense freight (e.g. lead ingots) is involved, but is less than the full mass (weight) capacity of the line haul unit, it will be routed back to the terminal to be topped up with high cubic freight (e.g. tennis balls). The marriage of these types of LCL consignments is the essence of the freight forwarding operation.

The biggest overlap of consignment categories (i.e. intermediate sizes) occurs with the small consignments of general freight in less than one tonne lots which are normally handled by pick up and delivery fleets. However, the vast majority of LCL consignments between one and ten tonnes (i.e. less than half the capacity of the line haul unit) may be also categorised as 'smalls', as they are again normally handled by local pick up and delivery fleets. In addition, they usually incur dock handling costs at both despatch and receiving terminals, and may be married in the consolidator's terminal with other general cargo.

As the freight forwarders have been most successful in managing

Fig.6.2: Output Characteristics and Facility requirements of Different-Sized General Cargo Consignments

Consignment size	Average mass kg	Average density[a] m^3	Other features	Pick up and delivery	Terminal activities
1. Full unit load	15,000	$62m^3$	No intermediate drops Full container load Fork lift	Pull truck and trailer	None
			Intermediate		
2. Part load	10,000	$41m^3$	Fork lift or manhandled	Table top with gates and tarpaulins when required	Consolidation using dock labour
			Intermediate		
3. Parcel	35	$0.1m^3$	Manhandled	Parcel van	Consolidation using dock labour

Note: a. Average density of general freight is $3.1m^3$ (110 cubic feet per tonne). Lead ingots, for example, are less than $1m^3$ per tonne and ping pong balls more than $50m^3$ per tonne.

these part load and parcel consignments they have been able to exert an increasingly stronger influence on the Australian domestic transport industry. There is, therefore, a pressing need to examine major changes in structure, conduct and performance of the freight forwarding industry since the Second World War.

The plan of this chapter is to first describe the key post-war changes in the structure of the transport industry and to highlight the role of freight forwarding. The focus then shifts to an examination of the growth and size of key freight forwarding firms. In the absence of suitable census data, corporate information is used to indicate the nature of vertical integration and diversification, degree of concentration, sources of absolute cost differences and scale economies and the incidence of mergers. Aspects of market conduct in price and non-price competition precede a section on performance and allocative efficiency. The chapter concludes with comment on the role of government as both regulator and competitor.

Post-War Changes in the Structure of the Transport Industry

This examination of the structure of the Australian freight forwarding industry focuses on aspects of the size and growth of firms, degree of concentration, product differentiation, barriers to entry and economies of scale. Before discussing these structural conditions it is pertinent to list the main features of the establishment and subsequent development of the industry since 1939 which stem from changes in the transport task and variations in the relative importance of rail, road, sea and air transport.

Developments Since 1939

Without a land-based transport system providing rapid transit, the Australian economy in 1939 was not highly integrated. Individual states functioned to some extent as self-sufficient regional islands. Breaks of gauge and multiple handlings hampered interconnections between the several railway systems and inadequate motor vehicles and punitive railway protection taxes severely constrained long-distance road transport. Therefore the dominant mode in interstate freight movements was coastal shipping. General cargo services, however, were costly and unreliable because of the inefficiency of bulk handling in a high wage situation and recurrent industrial unrest by seamen and waterside workers. Collapsible containers holding up to two tonnes of freight were used but damage was common and pilferage rampant. There was no overall responsibility for the movement between consignor and consignee.

The coastal shipping-dominated pattern of trade between the states in 1939 was disrupted by the Second World War and its aftermath. A marked increase in the interstate traffic task occurred after the cessation of hostilities as manufacturers, who had developed under war-time protection from overseas suppliers, endeavoured to satisfy the pent-up demand for consumer goods. Losses of shipping and the run-down of railway equipment prevented these modes capitalising on the expansion of interstate trade. Air transport was able to handle some of the urgent freight but the scope of its activities was limited by cost. However, road transport was not so inhibited in its operation.

After the abolition of petrol rationing the long-distance road transport industry expanded rapidly. It was aided by ex-servicemen investing their gratuities in war surplus trucks, including superior heavy-duty American equipment, and local carriers and miscellaneous transport operators extending their activities into interstate road transport. Despite the then existing tonne-kilometre tax on all goods carried interstate to protect the state railways, the road hauliers succeeded in demonstrating the virtues of a door-to-door service on a single invoice. The appeal of road transport was boosted by continued labour unrest on the waterfront, which reduced coastal shipping's competitiveness, and the Victorian State Railways Strike in 1949. Permits were freely available during the Strike and the road hauliers were able to display the speed, regularity and flexibility of their service to a new range of customers. Even the imposition of higher fees and the refusal of regulatory authorities to grant permits for interstate movement after the Strike could not stunt the stimulus afforded long-distance road transport.

Once railway rolling stock was rehabilitated and the conversion from steam to diesel power was affected, the several railway systems of Australia sought to contain the development of the larger road transport operators who had developed from either one truck firms, long established local carriers or passenger transport activities. The railways entered into an agreement with some of the major road transport operators that transformed them into national freight forwarders. Under an agreement in 1952, known as the Forwarding Agents' Scheme, the freight forwarders undertook the collection and delivery of commodities and to use the railway as the line haul mode in interstate movements; the client being charged an inclusive rate for the whole movement. The forwarders were conceded flat rates of so much per tonne between capital cities, with a prescribed minimum tonnage to be loaded into each of the available vans. This concession enabled freight forwarders to offer their clients a service using rail or road as the line haul mode.

The Forwarding Agents' Scheme did not prevent a loss of market share for the railways in interstate movements because the railway protection tax on interstate freight movements was declared invalid in 1954, as it contravened Section 92 of the Australian Constitution guaranteeing freedom of trade between States.[6] Although road maintenance charges to pay for the wear and tear of roads were deemed to be applicable, the long-distance road industry received an enormous boost from the tax saving and further attracted clients from the railways.

The railways responded to the renewed challenge of road transport by reducing rates and making technological improvements such as the institution of the bogie exchange, to facilitiate the transfer of wagons between the different gauged railway systems, and a rail gauge standardisation programme to link state capital cities into a single 1.43m network (Sydney-Melbourne 1962).[7] The freight forwarders sought to take advantage of these developments by introducing equipment that was interchangeable between rail and road such as flexi-vans, flexi-flats and flexi-frigs in 1962. In return for their assistance in boosting the general freight volume of the railways the freight forwarders were given a privileged locational advantage by exclusive use of a goods shed with sidings flush with a road on one or both sides of the loading docks. A new series of incentive agreements were also made with the freight forwarders offering a guaranteed annual hire contract between adjacent capitals in 1966. Volume was sufficient in 1970 for one forwarder to send a full train load six nights a week in both directions between Melbourne and Sydney. Freight forwarders were thereby encouraged to invest in container terminals replete with gantry cranes.

The partnership between the freight forwarders and the railways drove some 'bomb' road hauliers out of business but most operators responded to the intensified competition by introducing better equipment. Losses of freight to the freight forwarders' rail operations were not stemmed by these measures and some of the large road companies sought contracts with the railways to transform themselves into freight forwarders.

The competitive position of the remaining road transport companies operating between ten and twenty trucks was not improved by the Interstate Drivers Award. Several medium-sized operators were unable to afford the increases and relinquished their businesses. As a result the amount of cargo handled on a direct contractual basis declined markedly. After the Interstate Drivers Award the freight forwarders extended the practice, initiated in 1960, of selling their trucks and employing subcontractors, either on a permanent or itinerant basis, to perform the necessary line haul by road. This type of operation benefited the freight forwarders because they were able to pare their rates to a minimum without having to consider the variable costs involved in vehicle operations.

Any tendency towards stable market shares as between rail and road in interstate transport was prevented by concurrent developments in coastal shipping. After losing general cargo consistently through the 1950s to land-based transport between mainland capital cities and to air transport in the Tasmanian trade, coastal shipping made a come-back by consolidating its position in the movement of bulky goods through automation and then by recapturing general cargo through the introduction of roll-on, roll-off and container vessels.[8] These developments enabled the forwarder to gain a large share of the Tasmanian trade because all cargo had to be pre-consolidated before loading and the main carrier, the government-owned Australian National Line, was precluded by *The Australian Coastal Shipping Agreement Act 1956* from acting as a freight forwarder on its own account. After initial resistance by the shipping companies operating the terminals the freight forwarders were also able to extend their activities into general cargo services between mainland capital cities and peripheral areas of Australia, such as North Queensland, partly by agreements with shipping companies and partly by becoming shipowners on their own account. As a result, the freight forwarders were then able to offer their clients a combination of services using three different line haul modes – sea, rail and road. However, the resurgence of the coastal shipping industry against land-based transport has been blunted, particularly on mainland capital city routes by high and rising labour and shipbuilding costs.[9] Although coastal shipping services have been curtailed the freight forwarders have the inherent flexibility to shift their business to another mode where necessary.

The freight forwarders have also made repeated attempts to operate a more efficient air freight service of their own, especially between non-adjacent states, but their efforts have been thwarted by what is known as the 'two airline policy'. Under this duopoly agreement established in the *Airline Agreement Act 1952-73* only limited chartering facilities are available to freight forwarders because scheduled interstate freight services are reserved for aircraft operated by the Commonwealth

Government-owned Trans Australia Airlines (TAA) and the privately-owned subsidiary of Ansett Transport Industries, Ansett Airlines of Australia (AAA). Even if chartering was possible by freight forwarders, the acquisition of suitable freight aircraft would be prevented by the *Airlines Equipment Act 1958* which is intended to avert excess capacity in air transport and co-ordinate replacements and new acquisitions by ensuring that TAA and AAA have comparable, but not necessarily identical, fleets. In these circumstances the forwarders have had to be content with limited charters and dovetailing their pick up and delivery services with the services provided by the two main airlines.

Besides being able to add air, albeit on a limited basis, to rail, sea and road transport as line haul modes, the development of freight forwarding has also been assisted by the development of a branch network in every capital, streamlined paper work in which a single note replaced a bill of lading, and computers.[10] It has also been assisted by variations in the transport task that have stemmed from changes in the Australian economy. Of particular importance has been the continued development of Australian manufacturing industry and the increasing specialisation of activities on a single large plant geared to serve the national market. This has boosted the interstate transport task. As a result the freight forwarders have vertically integrated into warehousing and distribution so that they are in a position to handle the entire output of manufacturers by distributing such items as groceries from the point of production or storage to the individual retailer or retail organisations covering the national market.[11]

The Relative Importance of Freight Forwarding

Variations in the comparative shares of individual modes in Australia's expanded freight task since 1939 have undoubtedly benefited the freight forwarders. There are, however, no comprehensive statistics available to document the development of the freight forwarding industry. The only available time series data on transport, shown in Table 6.1, emphasise the dominance of road transport in tonnes carried, the importance of the coastal shipping industry in terms of tonne-km, the improved position of the railways and the relatively small role played by air transport in freight movement. However, such figures are woefully inadequate for gauging changes in the position of individual modes and the part played by the freight forwarders. In generating industry data there is no attempt by the public authorities to distinguish between interstate, intrastate and intrametropolitan markets.

The only statistics available that identify different spatial markets

Table 6.1: Freight Transport Shares and Growth Rates in Australia by Mode

Year ending 30 June	Public rail	Private rail[a]	Road	Sea	Air	Total
	Thousand million tonne-kilometres					
1950	10.9	0.4	8.2	16.1	0.03	35.6
1960	12.9	0.5	13.3	30.3	0.05	57.1
1965	18.0	0.6	17.4	41.5	0.06	77.6
1970	23.6	9.2	24.9	65.0	0.09	122.8
1975[b]	29.0	26.0	33.0	74.0[c]	0.10	162.1
			Percentage			
1950	30.6	1.0	23.1	45.2	0.1	100.0
1960	22.6	0.9	23.3	53.1	0.1	100.0
1965	23.1	0.8	22.4	53.6	0.1	100.0
1970	19.2	7.5	20.3	52.9	0.1	100.0
1975[b]	17.9	16.0	20.4	45.6[c]	0.1	100.0
Average annual growth rate			Percentage			
1960-65	6.8	−0.1	8.0	7.0	n.a.	6.8
1965-70	5.9	126.0	6.5	9.6	n.a.	9.6
1970-75	3.9	24.2	4.9	2.5	n.a.	5.4
			Million tonnes			
1965	59.3	4.7	440.0	23.4	0.1	527.5
1970	75.5	37.2	700.0	32.5	0.1	845.2
1975	87.0	104.4	950.0	42.0	0.1	1183.5
			Percentage			
1965	11.2[b]	0.9	83.4	4.5	0.0	100.0
1970	8.9	4.4	82.8	3.9	0.0	100.0
1975	7.4	8.8	80.2	3.6	0.0	100.0
Average annual growth rate			Percentage			
1970-75	2.9	22.9	6.3	n.a.	n.a.	7.0

Notes: a. Includes only iron ore railways in South Australia and Western Australia and the Emu Bay Railway in Tasmania.

b. Preliminary estimates.

c. New series commencing 1971-72; not strictly comparable with earlier estimates.

Sources: Commonwealth Bureau of Roads, *Report on Roads in Australia – 1973,* Commonwealth Bureau of Roads, Melbourne, 1973, p.40; Bureau of Transport Economics, *Freight Movements in Australia: Preliminary Estimates,* Transport Outlook Conference, Canberra 29-30 July 1975.

are those in Table 6.2 which show tonnes moved in 1971/2. These figures indicate that almost 936 million tonnes were moved *intrastate* and 45 million *interstate.*[12] Within these intrastate movements a distinction is made between shorter haul intra-regional flows dominated by road and the longer haul inter-regional flows in which rail had a larger share than road because of the regulations protecting the state railways against road-based competition. Although the existence of these regulations constrained or denied freight forwarders the use of road transport in movements between regions within states they obtained a foothold in movements by rail. However, the main sphere of freight forwarding activity by 1971-2 was in interstate movements.

Table 6.2: Market Shares of Intrastate and Interstate Freight 1971-72

Mode	Intrastate				Interstate		Total	
	Intra-regional		Inter-regional					
	tonnes	per cent	tonnes	per cent	tonnes	per cent	tonnes	per cent
Rail	91.9	10.7	37.6	48.5	7.3	16.2	136.8	13.9
Road	762.5	88.9	28.5	36.8	9.0	20.0	800.0	81.6
Sea	3.8	0.4	11.4	14.7	28.6	63.6	43.8	4.5
Air	–	–	0.0	0.0	0.1	0.2	0.1	0.0
Total	858.2	100.0	77.5	100.0	45.0	100.0	980.7	100.0
Percentage of totals	(87.51)		(7.90)		(4.59)		(100.00)	

Source: Bureau of Transport Economics, *Long Distance Freight Outlook,* Transport Outlook Conference, Canberra 29-30 July 1975.

The estimated share of the tonnage moved by freight forwarders (and major road operators) in 1971/2 differed from the general market share by mode, as they were responsible for 30 per cent of tonnes moved by road, 20 per cent by rail and less than 3 per cent by sea.[13] However, the freight forwarding statistics refer only to interstate movements between capitals and provincial cities. If this narrower basis of comparison is used the freight forwarders would be responsible for 60 per cent of movements by road, 40 per cent by rail and 8 per cent by sea. Such figures vary between routes as freight forwarders, for example, accounted for 53 per cent of movements by road between Melbourne and Sydney and 54 per cent of movements by rail. However, these estimates are a misleading guide to the relative importance of freight forwarders because the statistics on tonnes moved include low value, bulk goods such as iron ore and coal which are generally handled by rail and coastal shipping on a siding-to-siding or terminal-to-terminal basis. If these commodities are removed from the statistics the revised figures would show that not only was sea transport a less dominant mode but the freight forwarders were firmly entrenched in interstate general cargo movements.

Changes since 1971/2 have probably strengthened the freight forwarders' share of *intrastate* movements but there may also have been a weakening of their share of *interstate* movements. The decision to abolish regulations designed to protect the railways in South Australia and New South Wales, for example, has probably resulted in freight forwarders obtaining a greater share of road-based movements in those states. This development has been countered by the collective decision of the several railways systems of Australia and, in particular, the Public Transport Commission of New South Wales to enter into competition with established freight forwarders through their container services. While such changes are difficult to document they serve to remind us of the dynamic relationship between the different line haul modes and the freight forwarder and the public and private sectors.

Much emphasis has been placed on the technological innovations in the various modes since 1939.[14] These changes, however, have been overshadowed by the organisational change that has resulted from the diffusion of the concept of door-to-door consignments on a single invoice pioneered by the freight forwarders. It is against this background that the growth and structure of the individual companies comprising the freight forwarding industry must be considered. By focusing on the firm a more detailed examination of the *process* of change is possible.

Size and Growth of Freight Forwarding Firms

Corporate developments within the freight forwarding industry mirror the problems and opportunities created by an increase in the volume of freight, the imbalance of trade within and between states and changes in the status of air, rail, road and sea transport. An examination of the growth of individual freight forwarding companies is a necessary counterpoint to the study of developments in the Australian transport industry since 1939; particularly as the services offered by the freight forwarders have been a powerful force in generating new flows within and between states. However, the statistics available for undertaking such a task are grossly inadequate because the range of activities collectively known as freight forwarding is not recognised as an industry in terms of the Australian Standard Industrial Classification (ASIC).

The only data available on transport enterprises in Australia are derived from information on payroll tax and other returns in 1974. Such data, given in Table 6.3, highlight the varying size of transport enterprises. They range from rail, with the largest average size undertaking in terms of employment, through air, water and road to

Table 6.3: Average Size and Size Distribution of Transport Enterprises by Different Modes, 1974

	ASIC Groupings				
	510 Road	520 Rail	530 Water	540 Air	551 Other transport and storage[a]
Total enterprises	7,024	24	367	278	891
Total employment[b]	96,873	90,414	30,552	35,301	10,815
Average employment per enterprise	13.8	3767.3	83.3	127.0	12.1
Employment groups					
Legitimate zeros[c]	0.43		2.18		
Over 1000	0.11	25.00	1.91		
500–999	0.07		1.63	5.04	2.24
200–499	0.20		4.09		
100–199	0.44		3.81		
50–99	1.77		5.99	4.32	2.69
20–49	6.31	75.00	10.35	9.35	9.54
10–19	13.38		13.90	10.79	15.94
5–9	23.09		19.36	24.86	26.86
1–4	49.86		31.06	43.17	33.22
Not available	4.34		5.72	2.52	9.54
Total	100.00		100.00	100.00	100.00

Notes:

a. Although freight forwarding is included in ASIC 551 it could end up in other categories from being associated with conglomerate activity.

b. Employment is for 1973 and is to be used as a guide only.

c. Components which do not employ labour in their own right. They operate using the labour resources of another company (usually parent or subsidiary companies but not always).

Source: Unpublished data from Australian Bureau of Statistics.

other transport and storage with the smallest. As freight forwarding is part of the other transport and storage group, the averages could be misleading and the data on transport enterprises are therefore also disaggregated into groups of different employment sizes. It should also be noted that a single input (i.e. persons employed) measure of size is inadequate where the capital intensity of activities differs between modes and across scale and part-time employment may also bias the measure.

The size interval breakdown shows that most enterprises in other transport and storage and all modes except rail employ less than ten employees. These figures are also understated because many firms employing 1-5 persons go unreported if they do not meet the $40,000 wage threshold for paying the payroll tax. Even taking such considerations into account, the figures for other transport and storage underestimates the strength of freight forwarding companies because groups of companies are variously allocated to road, sea and air categories and the subcontracted activities of owner-driver are not recorded. This claim cannot be checked, however, because data from the freight forwarding component of ASIC 551 are not separately available.

Vertical Integration and Diversification

Given such data limitations recourse has to be made to annual company reports to try and establish the size and growth of freight forwarding firms. Such information is generally only available for public companies. But here there are problems of determining the freight forwarding component where the company may be vertically integrated with line haul modes. As indicated by Figure 6.2, Thomas Nationwide Transport, for example, has vertically integrated into coastal shipping through the bulk and general cargo carrier and container terminal owner, Bulkships Ltd. In turn, Bulkships established a consortium with New Zealand interests to acquire the sole trans-Tasman shipping operator, the Union Steam Ship Co. Ltd of New Zealand, from its United Kingdom-based owner, Peninsular and Oriental Steam Navigation Company (P&O) of Great Britain (which had a 20 per cent share in the freight forwarder Mayne Nickless Ltd). Thomas Nationwide Transport was invited to manage the shipping company. Only an amendment of the Companies Act by the State Government of Victoria prevented Thomas Nationwide Transport's bid to integrate with Australia's major private airline operated by Ansett Airlines of Australia; it has, however, retained a large minority

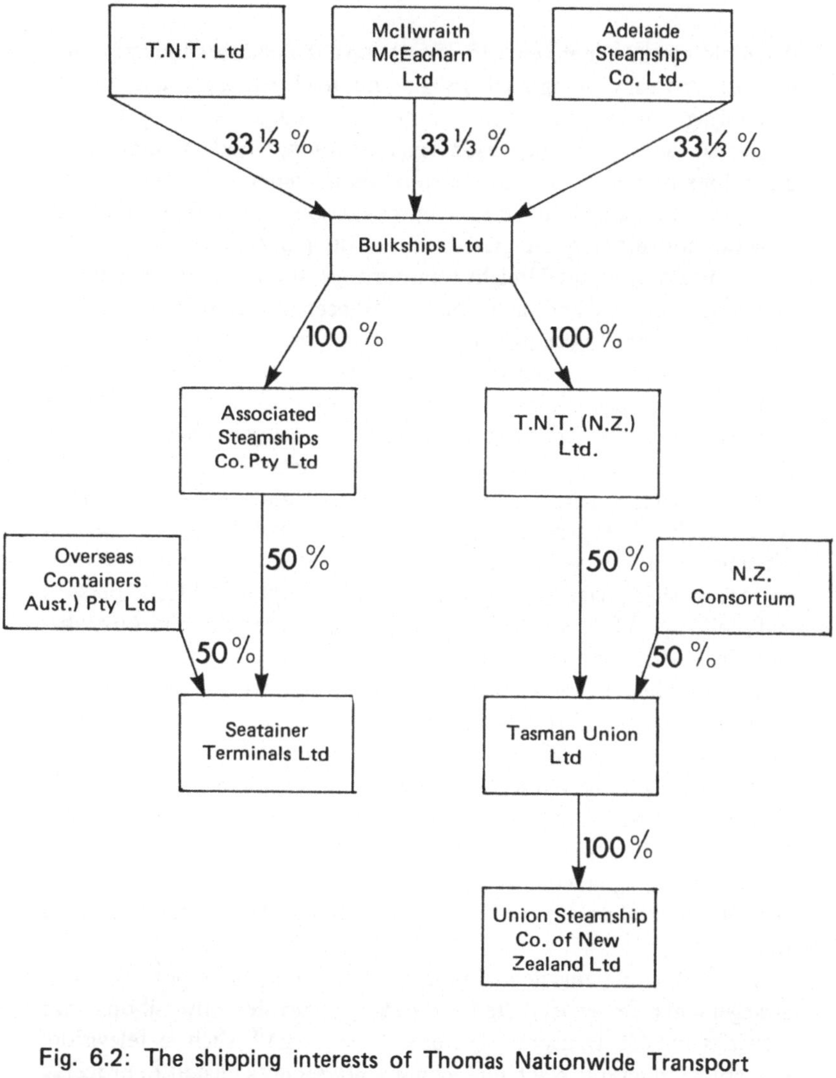

Fig. 6.2: The shipping interests of Thomas Nationwide Transport (TNT) Ltd, 1972.

Notes: Since this date further changes in ownership have taken place. TNT's share in Bulkships is now (1976) 50 per cent (McIlwraith McEacharn and Adelaide Steamship have 25 per cent each).

Source. Commonwealth of Australia *Senate Standing Committee on Industry and Trade (Reference: Proposed takeover of Ansett Transport Industries by Thomas Nationwide Transport Ltd) Canberra, Thursday, 27 April 1972 (Official Hansard Report),* Government Printer of the Commonwealth of Australia, Canberra, 1972.

shareholding (23.4 per cent) in Ansett. Ansett Transport Industries has in turn vertically integrated its air and road passenger and freight forwarding services with hotel, motel, and tourist resort operations, insurance and transport-based manufacturing and trading. The difficulties of untangling such companies is compounded by 'narrow-spectrum diversification' involving expansion into other transport activities not vertically integrated to its existing operations.[15]

The diversification of freight transport operations into such activities as courier services and taxi trucks has been undertaken by freight forwarders either by acquiring an existing firm or establishing a new division. These new activities are initiated to counter risk and uncertainty, induce growth and either initiate or promote competition with existing rivals. Another diversification strategy has been to export the freight forwarding concept to overseas countries such as the United States, Canada, Brazil, Singapore, Papua New Guinea and New Zealand. As a result of expansion by diversification and integration within Australia and overseas, the Thomas Nationwide Transport Group owned, in 1975, over 100 subsidiaries which employed 11,000 persons and used over 4,000 vehicles and more than 120 terminals in Australia, New Zealand and North America.

The problem of using annual company reports as a gauge of the number and size of freight forwarding companies is aggravated even further by contractual agreements (i.e. a substitute for ownership) between freight forwarders and other organisations to engage in passenger services and leisure travel activities. For example, Mayne Nickless and Trans Australia Airlines have established a passenger coach service and an agreement exists between Thomas Nationwide Transport and the Australian Council of Trade Unions (ACTU) to establish a travel service.

The difficulties engendered in interpreting company reports by these arrangements are exacerbated by freight forwarders diversifying into activities outside transport (i.e. broad spectrum)[16] such as television, primary production, plant hire, community services related to property maintenance and civil engineering. Such a multiplicity of interests by conglomerate organisations makes it difficult to isolate the freight forwarding activities in a conglomerate. As it is not possible to obtain the number and size of firms, reliance has to be placed on a survey undertaken by Rimmer in 1967 to gain an indication of the level of concentration at that time.[17] When the survey was undertaken it was believed that the top eight freight forwarding firms handled almost 68 per cent of interstate freight whether it went by rail, road or sea.[18] In the December quarter 1975 the top four forwarders and road operators accounted for 45 per cent of interstate movements between state capitals and provincial cities, the top eight, 61 per cent and the top twenty, 78 per cent.[19]

Concentration

The survey indicated that freight forwarders can be divided into two broad categories:

- *national freight forwarders* distributing goods on an Australia-wide network (i.e. national concentration),
- *area specialists* concentrating in moving goods on specific routes such as between Melbourne and Adelaide (i.e. regional concentration).

In its *Inquiry into Transport to and from Tasmania,* the Nimmo Report indicated that there were approximately thirty firms engaged in freight forwarding between Tasmania and the mainland of which twenty-six were area specialists.[20] The national freight forwarders are dominated by public companies with varying degrees of overseas financial support while the area specialists are largely private operators financed from Australian capital sources. Attention is focused on the national freight forwarders, most of whom are members of the National Freight Forwarders Association established in 1962, because they dominate the volume of goods handled by the freight forwarding industry. In particular, interest is centred on four major firms comprising Thomas Nationwide Transport Ltd, Brambles Industries Ltd, Ansett Freight Express Pty Ltd, a subsidiary of Ansett Transport Industries Ltd, and Mayne Nickless Ltd. Fleetways (Holdings) Ltd is also included in the group, but this organisation is much smaller than the four major firms which all feature in the list of Australia's hundred biggest companies. Comparable information is not available for such firms as Ipec (Interstate Parcel Express Company Pty Ltd), Tradex Transport, United Transport Holdings Australia Pty Ltd (formerly AUT Holdings Ltd) and Youngs Transport Agency. Although the collective strength of the major firms indicated in Table 6.4 cannot be documented with precision it behoves us to explain why the industry has this particular structure.

Economies of Scale and Entry Barriers

As entry into the freight forwarding industry is unfettered by legal

Table 6.4: Financial Characteristics of the Major National Freight Forwarding Companies 1975

	Ansett	Thomas Nation-wide Trans-port	Mayne Nick-less	Brambles	Fleet-ways
Revenue ($A million)					
Total	327	288	168	158	n.a.
Australia only	n.a.	143	n.a.	n.a.	n.a.
Freight forwarding	32	n.a.	n.a.	n.a.	n.a.
Assets ($A million)					
Total	239	153	84	97	17
Freight forwarding	17	n.a.	n.a.	n.a.	n.a.
Net profit ($A million)					
After tax	8.2	9.0	6.1	8.5	n.a.
Employment (numbers)	13,375	20,000	n.a.	4,600	n.a.
Ratios:					
Profit/revenue (per cent)	2.5	3.1	3.6	5.3	n.a.
Profit/assets (per cent)	3.4	5.9	7.3	8.7	n.a.
Assets/employment ($A per head)	17,794	7,650	n.a.	21,087	n.a.
Assets/revenue (capital output ratio)	0.73	0.53	0.50	0.61	n.a.

Source: Annual company reports for 1975.

restriction and unconstrained by associations of freight forwarders, its distinctive structure is largely attributable to economies of scale and diversification. Such barriers impede but do not prevent the small firm entering the industry. Except for specialist services requiring a tanker, pantechnicon or refrigerated equipment the supply cost of services is not capital-intensive and leasing and hire purchasing arrangements are available. In general, the small volume operators are more profitable than the large forwarder averaging 6 per cent after tax as against 3.5 to 4 per cent.[21] However, the advantage is not sustained once a threshold is reached where the volume carried is of sufficient magnitude to warrant centralised administration and large terminal operations (i.e. organisational scale economies rather than plant economies). These capital-intensive facilities are not profitable until the administrative machinery ensures over a long period that a large volume is flowing through the terminal. The labour component in the industry's cost structure forces firms to obtain as much volume as quickly as possible to maintain a reasonable rate structure. Smaller companies have, therefore, merged to use the same facilities and lower throughput costs on a quantum basis. In this way it is possible for the enlarged company to obtain greater revenue per unit of capital by avoiding the duplication of facilities and excess capacity. Only a few companies have secured sufficient volume to be both more profitable than small firms at a large scale and provide an efficient range of services to clients.[22] This strength of large firms may arise as much from pecuniary economies (i.e. lower cost of rail space) as from real economies of operation.

Mergers and Internal Growth

Economies of scale are not the only factor determining high levels of the industry's concentration. At least 200 transport companies have been acquired by or merged with the major national freight forwarders between 1960 and 1975 – a process that has resulted in fewer national freight forwarders (see Figure 6.3). To a degree some excess capacity in the freight forwarding industry contributed to this trend. Also, as the freight forwarders grew in size there was a pressing need to obtain backloadings to reduce excess capacity through peak loads so that movements from the companies' home base would be a profitable undertaking. Balanced loadings were obtained either by acquiring an agent in a centre and hoping for an increase in trade to warrant the establishment of a depot or by purchasing the terminal operations and good will of a local carrier.

The initial method of attracting trade on the basis of competitive rates and service sufficed as a means of promoting much of the expansion of individual freight forwarders during the 1950s. However, the need for the national freight forwarders to obtain the necessary volume to cover their contracts with the railways, promote the efficient utilisation of their own rail, sea and road equipment and to provide customers with an Australia-wide service, resulted in them acquiring, as indicated in Table 6.5, a series of companies in all Australian states for either cash or shares. Mayne Nickless, for example, extended its activities to forty centres in Australia and Thomas Nationwide Transport to sixty-two centres, at locations claimed to serve about 86 per cent of the population. The essential purpose of these takeovers however, was to increase turnover as a means of maximising sales (not profits), acquiring management, cheaper assets (i.e. undervalued) and

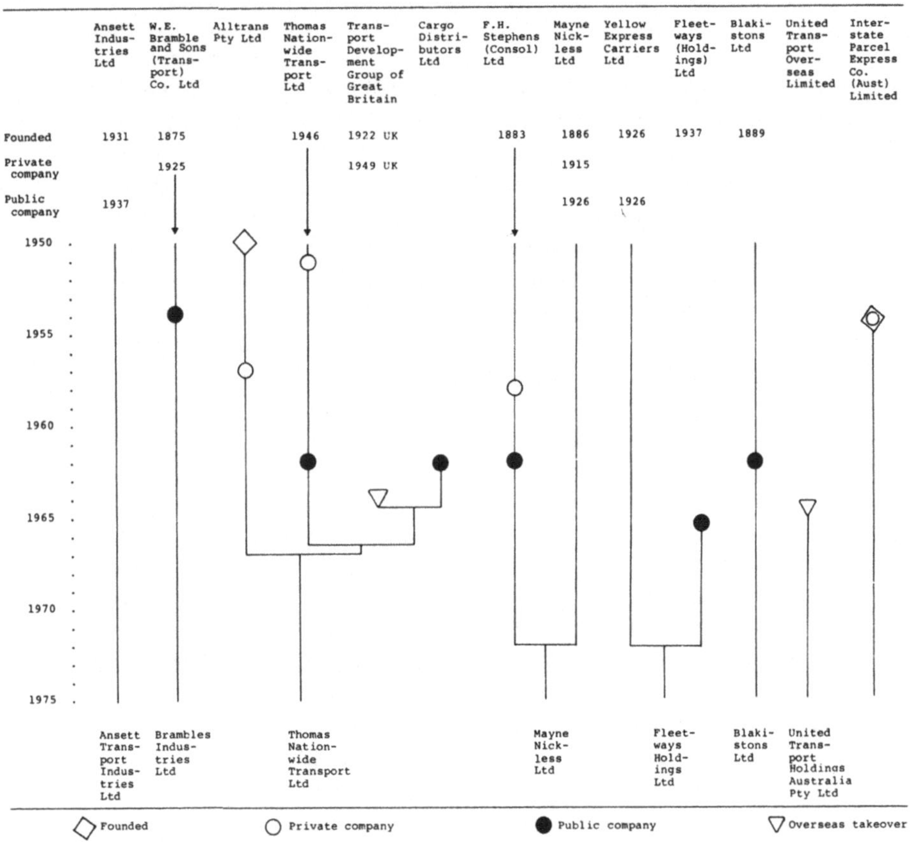

Fig. 6.3 Merger activity among Australian freight forwarding companies between 1950 and 1975.

Notes: Blakistons Ltd is now predominantly an intrastate road haulier after a spell of national freight forwarding. Data on United Transport Co. Ltd., a United Kingdom-based company, and Interstate Parcel Express Co. (Australia) Ltd, an Australian-based private company, were unavailable. Cargo Distributors Ltd was formed from a merger of two old-established transport companies – Green-McCandlish Ltd, a Melbourne-based carrier, and Rudder's Ltd, a customs, shipping and forwarding agent in Sydney.

diverse services.

Table 6.5: Acquisition and Mergers by the Major Freight Forwarding Companies, 1965-75

State	Ansett	Brambles	Mayne Nickless[a]	Thomas Nationwide Transport[b]	Fleetways[c]	Total
Queensland	0	5	6	7	1	19
New South Wales	4	18	18	11	0	51
Victoria	3	9	15	2	1	30
South Australia	0	7	6	0	1	14
Western Australia	1	4	10	1	1	17
Tasmania	0	2	2	1	0	5
All States	1	1	4	9	1	16
Overseas	0	3	7	9	0	19
Total	9	49	68	40	5	171

Notes:
a. Excluded are eight takeovers made by F.H. Stephens Ltd before 1972.
b. Excluded are six takeovers made by Alltrans Pty Ltd before 1967.
c. Excluded are fifteen takeovers made by Yellow Express Carriers Ltd before 1972.
Source: Annual company reports.

The companies taken over have also been selected with regard to the type of transport service offered as reflected in Table 6.6. When the smaller firms built their output volume by offering a wide range of services, the freight forwarders used takeovers to secure a range of multi-modal activities – refrigerated and insulated transport, heavy haulage, car carrying, furniture removals, dry and liquid cartage, armoured car transport and overnight express services. Other pressures behind takeover and mergers have been to prevent freight going to rival firms, to obtain a strong management component from a competitor, and to retain the image of a progressive firm by offering younger executives the prospects of advancement in an expanding company. These factors, however, were of lesser importance than the desire to provide a complete transport services package and balanced loadings between places of unequal freight generation.

Sources of Absolute Cost Advantages

Firms can easily begin freight forwarding on a small scale and expand

Table 6.6: Range of Services Provided by Major Freight Forwarding Companies 1975

Activity	Ansett[a]	Brambles[b]	Mayne Nickless[c]	Thomas Nationwide Transport[d]	Fleetways
General Transport					
Wharf and local	0	x	x	x	x
Customs agents	x	x	x	x	x
Storage (bonded and free)	0	x	x	x	x
Warehousing	0	x	x	x	x
National freight forwarding					
Road	x	x	x	x	x
Rail	x	x	x	x	x
Sea	x	x	x	x	x
Air	x	x	x	x	x
Specialised services					
Courier	0	x	x	x	x
Taxi trucks	0	x	x	x	x
Overnight express	x	x	x	x	x
Armoured car	0	x	x	x	0
Liquid bulk	0	x	x	0	x
Dry bulk	0	x	x	x	x
Refrigerated	0	x	x	x	0
Insulated	0	x	x	x	0
Low density freight	x	x	x	x	0
Furniture removals	x	0	0	0	x
Heavy haulage	0	x	0	0	x
Car carrying	0	0	0	x	x
Earth moving	0	x	x	0	0
Waste removal	0	x	x	x	0
International freight forwarding					
Sea	0	x	x	x	x
Air	x	x	x	x	x
Ancillary services					
Maintenance of equipment	0	x	x	x	0
Materials handling (including pallet pool)	0	x	0	x	0
Stevedoring	0	0	0	x	0
Line haul ownership					
Road	x	x	x	x	x
Rail	0	0	0	0	0
Sea	0	0	0	x	0
Air	x	0	0	0	0
Associated activities					
Travel	x	0	x	x	0
Insurance	x	0	0	0	0

Notes: a. Ansett is also involved in television, general trading, manufacturing and primary production.
b. Brambles is also engaged in industrial plant hire, marine towage, metals reclamation, deep sea diving, supplying boats and logistical support for contractors.
c. Mayne Nickless is also concerned with computer payroll services, civil engineering, helicopters and quarrying.
d. Thomas Nationwide Transport also has property interests and computer payroll services.

Source: Company reports, 1975.

by ploughing profits into the company and only inviting public subscription when the position seems assured. Large-scale entry is a more costly proposition requiring terminals and rolling stock. Although the burden of entry can be lessened by leasing terminals and subcontracting line haul operations, any new large-scale firm would have to compete with the financial advantages, which probably include pecuniary economies, of established rivals. These have accrued from the encouragement of widely held equity through public listing and increased access to cheaper investment funds from institutions and debenture capital.[23] The advantages accruing in the capital market were amply demonstrated in the ability of Thomas Nationwide Transport to make a bid to take over Ansett Transport Industries.[24]

The problem of making a large-scale entry into the freight forwarding industry is also heightened by service differentiation through advertising. Although advertising and promotion costs, comprising salesmen, direct mail advertising via schedules, price lists and pamphlets, and a minimal amount of public advertising aimed at image building, constitutes less than two per cent of total costs, it is a handicap for a new entrant.[25] There is also the cost of countering the mobile advertising (i.e. service brand image) of established companies who obtain the right to paint the pick up and delivery vans and line haul equipment in the company livery that are operated and owned by permanent subcontractors.

A large-scale entrant will also have additional entry costs in supplying the range of specialist services such as overnight express services or refrigerated services on a national network. If the new entrant does not generate the necessary volume to maintain the quality and regularity of these services the firm's standing is quickly sapped by small freight forwarders able to provide a personalised service despite the possibility of off-loading freight onto another freight forwarder's service. The vertical integration of established freight forwarders with line haul modes also works pervasively against the large-scale entrant. While the vertically integrated freight forwarder is reputed not to receive any special freight rate advantages from an associated line haul mode operated as a public utility, there are benefits in deriving extra volume.[26]

There have also been the costs of rivalry conflicts within the industry which are believed to have increased the relative market share of Thomas Nationwide Transport and Mayne Nickless at the expense of Brambles and Ansett Freight Express. Mayne Nickless acquired F.H. Stephens Ltd in 1972, which previously had been a large competitor, because a duopoly situation was thought imminent.

> We [Mayne Nickless] felt that with the development of major transport (that is, of the national network type) – we had one railway system (Railways of Australia), two shipping lines, two airlines – that there should be at least two major network carriers.[27]

As the anticipated duopoly has not eventuated it impels us to examine the effect of the freight forwarding industry's market structure on its conduct and performance. Initially, attention is centred on market conduct because it links the freight forwarding industry's structure with the level of and variations in its performance. Interest in examining market conduct is centred on pricing policy and service quality control because these aspects encapsulate a freight forwarder's policy towards its service market and moves made by rivals in that market.

Market Conduct

The activities of the National Freight Forwarders Association, an independent and autonomous body, provide a useful starting point for discussing pricing behaviour within the freight forwarding industry.[28] Almost all major and some medium-sized freight forwarders are members of this Association. A condition of membership is that the freight forwarder is affiliated with the Australian Road Transport Federation.

Wright provides the only documented evidence of market behaviour within the Australian freight forwarding industry.[29] As such, it is only of historical interest because it describes the activities of freight forwarders *before* the bringing down of the *Trade Practices Act 1974.*

Trade Practices Before 1974

Prior to the Act the National Freight Forwarders Association's committee recommended rate schedules to the state associations' sub-committees. If these were accepted by the state associations the freight forwarders had identical interstate freight rate schedules for full unit load, part load and small consignments. In arriving at these recommended rate schedules the various bodies used a cost-plus-profit basis which, if followed, was intended to yield the larger firms a rate of return on investment (net profit after tax: shareholders funds) of 15 per cent – a rate considered fair by the associations. Wright considers that this fair rate of return approximates to what the economist considers 'normal' for the industry due to ease of small scale entry into it and the limited powers available to the associations in enforcing its rate schedules.[30]

At intervals the state associations announced that freight rate schedules had been increased by a given percentage based on a weighted cost index, prices of new vehicles, fuel, tyres, ancillary equipment and administrative expenses. It is implicitly assumed that all freight forwarders experienced uniform cost (factor price) increases (an assumption that may be acceptable according to Wright).[31]

Whether the agreed rate schedules were used as a basis for pricing in a particular instance depended on the nature of the consignment. Not every parcel and part load consignment could be costed, so that rate schedules up to two tonne consignments were followed reasonably closely. Although intended as minimum rates the schedules were usually the maximum rates obtained and then only for a proportion of the cargoes. A major carrier of small consignments estimated that because of discounting for larger shippers only 60-70 per cent of clients pay scheduled rates.[32] Another forwarder indicated that on average the maximum rate obtained is about 80 per cent of its rate schedule.[33] For consignments above two tonnes the schedules were used as guidelines for making separately costed and special quotes. Discounted scheduled rates, for example, accounted for three-quarters of the revenue of two Mayne Nickless interstate divisions (Mayneroad, a road and rail-road forwarding unit, and Railex, a unit using hired railway equipment).[34] Approximately 64 per cent of the road component revenues and 87 per cent of the railway segment undertakings represented contracts entered into at a discount.

Trade Practices Since 1974

The National Freight Forwarder's role in proposing interstate freight rates was abandoned with the introduction of the *Trade Practices Act 1974.*[35] An application was made for 'authorization'[36] (Registration No.A3019) under the Act by TNT Management Ltd on behalf of itself and seven other companies, all Australian, for the purpose of agreeing on a common rate schedule for maximum rates chargeable by the industry for normal freight transport and disseminating such information to industry and statutory bodies such as the Prices Justification Tribunal.[37]

An authorisation was sought on 17 December 1974 by 'the companies' under Section 88(1) of the *Trade Practices Act 1974* to meet together and discuss rates because the Prices Justification Tribunal:

(a) had granted rates that varied as much as 33 per cent in some areas by carriers;
(b) had created a system of price leadership within the industry because it is not practicable for any carrier to publish a rate schedule which gives another carrier a market advantage;
(c) had forced carriers to discount schedules to prices equivalent or better than their competitors because the Prices Justification Tribunal insisted that increases must be taken up;
(d) may not be averse to a common rate schedule for maximum rates chargeable for normal freight transport.

The interim application was denied by the Commission without prejudice to a further submission.

The second application was filed on 7 May 1975 with a view to satisfying Section 90(5) of the Act. A summary of the main grounds supporting the application were:

1. the highly competitive nature of the market for land transport services justifies the adoption of a uniform maximum price for the provision of these services to prevent 'uninformed and unreasonable competition';
2. the desirability of establishing uniform and controlled rates where a system of exclusive licensing has been adopted (i.e. as in the states);
3. the Inter-State Commission Bill's recognition of the concept that freight rates can be controlled in the public interest;
4. the Prices Justification Tribunal has recognised that the particular circumstances of the market may justify the adoption of a uniform price across a group of companies although it deals basically with individual companies;
5. the need to achieve stability in the industry because historically and economically it is in the public interest;
6. the desire to set maximum price schedules for casual shippers of goods as a ceiling under which real and effective competition could occur between scheduled companies giving lower rates for regular and volume customers and special 'jobbing' rates and, of course, continuous competition by way of service offered.

The Trade Practices Commission view was that 'their agreement would clearly restrict price competition between "the companies", and pricing would be on an industry basis instead of a company basis except to the extent large customers could force prices below the agreed common schedules'.[38] As a result the application failed and was dismissed.

Since the *Trade Practices Act 1974* the National Freight Forwarders Association has, therefore, concentrated on the co-ordination and consolidation of advice to the Government in the legislative and industrial spheres. In addition, the Association liaises with line haul modes on new developments, keeps a watching brief on inter-union disputes affecting transport and leaves rate proposing to the state associations.

Following the introduction of the *Trade Practices Act 1974* the various state associations reassessed their positions and deleted certain sections of agreements such as non-competing for existing clients of another carrier, and penalties for non-adherence to rate schedules. However, all of the state associations, except Tasmania, applied for an authorisation under the *Trade Practices Act 1974* to continue the practice of issuing recommended rate schedules to members for various cartage operations. The applications generally stress that the cartage rate schedules are only recommended, and no sanctions are applied to those carriers not adhering to them.[39]

Prices Justification and Rate Schedules

The practice of each freight forwarder following identical rate schedules drew criticism from the Tribunal established under the *Prices Justification Act 1973* which required all freight forwarding companies with a revenue of more than $A20 million per annum to notify increases in their freight rates.

> We [the Prices Justification Tribunal] believe that the practice of... large operators in the [freight forwarding] industry, of following recommended freight schedules for the industry tends, and has tended in the past, to produce an over recovery of cost increases at the expense of the consumer. Quite apart from the fact that industry recommended schedules appear to be computed without paying regard to the effects on costs of improved productivity, we feel that a company...should pay closer regard to its own circumstances and costs rather than the industry's average in computing general rate increases.[40]

A result of having to notify the Prices Justification Tribunal and satisfy its strictures was that companies prepared their own individual schedules and did not co-ordinate the timing of their submissions to the

Tribunal. Thus the scheduled rates from Melbourne to Adelaide in August 1976 for a 10,000 kg consignment ranged from $442.75 for Brambles, $455.90 for Mayne Nickless to $463.00 for Thomas Nationwide Transport.

As exemplified for movements from Sydney to mainland capitals in Table 6.7 an individual company schedule provides a range of rates for differing mass (weight) and cubic consignment sizes. Irrespective of size, the express transit service, which guarantees delivery not later than noon on a specified day, is most expensive. The difference in the rate between the express transit service and other services increases with size of consignment. Roadfast rates are slightly cheaper than Railfast charges for parcel and part load freight but Railfast is generally cheaper than Roadfast for full load consignments.

Table 6.7: Scheduled Door-to-door Freight Rates for Different Services and Consignment Sizes between Sydney and Mainland Capital Cities effective from 1 February 1976[a]

(dollars)

	Melbourne	Brisbane	Adelaide	Perth
50 kg or $0.2m^3$				
X-press Transit	13.75	14.65	14.75	25.40
Roadfast[2]	11.45	12.00	12.90	20.90
Railfast	11.45	12.10	12.90	21.60
500 kg or $2m^3$				
X-press Transit	64.15	84.40	82.25	172.55
Roadfast[2]	49.70	63.75	66.45	139.75
Railfast	49.70	64.75	66.45	153.90
10,000 kg or $40m^3$				
X-press Transit	691.15	777.90	1022.75	2804.05
Roadfast[b]	426.20	499.75	516.45	2045.75
Railfast	426.20	466.25	516.45	1466.40

Notes:
a. Prices Justification Tribunal Matter N75/7539, N76/62, N76/151.
b. Includes road-rail containers.
Source: TNT Transport System Rate Schedules.

Other inherent differences in freight rates are revealed in Table 8 for Roadfast services on inter-capital routes. The rates between Melbourne and Sydney are almost equally balanced – the Sydney-Melbourne leg is slightly more expensive because New South Wales is not a party to the Five State Award negotiated by the Industrial Relations Committee of the Australian Road Transport Federation and the Transport Workers Union. Other differences reflect unbalanced loadings. For example, rates from Melbourne to Adelaide, Brisbane and Perth are respectively 3 per cent, 7 per cent and 68 per cent more expensive than the inbound leg because of the difficulties of obtaining return loadings.

It must be emphasised that such rates for different services are only guidelines. They do not demonstrate differences in rate schedules between firms for similar services. Competition by rate cutting and client persuasion appears more frequently in the inter-state market than in intra-state and intra-metropolitan work. Special rates may also be available after a consideration of such factors as 6/30/90 days credit payment, nature of commodity, variety of items, type of cartons, value of insurance, distance involved in pick up and delivery, ease of access to client's premises, speed of delivery, idle time, fragility, possibilities of back-loading, special types of service, and amount of handling. These special rates are necessary because on highly competitive routes, such as Melbourne and Sydney, no freight forwarder can raise rates above those of his rivals and survive unless the client involved, such as a distributor of papers and periodicals, is prepared to pay a premium for guaranteed, rather than advertised, delivery.

Performance and Allocative Efficiency

In examining market performance attention is centred on the allocative efficiency of major national freight forwarders – Ansett Transport Industries, Brambles Industries, Mayne Nickless and Thomas Nationwide Transport – and a medium-sized firm, Fleetways. Their market record forms the basis of assessing whether the government should regulate the industry on economic efficiency or welfare grounds. Following Wright's methodology, a measure of the allocative efficiency of these firms is determined by calculating the ratio between long run accounting profit, as measured by net profit before tax, and owners equity, as measured by shareholders funds.[41] This figure is calculated over a fourteen year period, 1962-75, and compared with the market rate of interest, taken as 2 per cent greater than the yield on Commonwealth securities (which may be too narrow a margin at current interest rates given the greater risks of commercial investment). Allocative

Table 6.8: Scheduled Door-to-door Freight Rates between Capital Cities for 1,000kg or 4m³ effective from 1 February 1976[a]
(dollars)

Roadfast[b]	Sydney	Melbourne	Brisbane	Adelaide	Perth
Sydney	–	73.20	89.75	102.45	250.75
Melbourne	69.15	–	120.50	60.40	182.90
Brisbane	71.45	112.30	–	148.95	308.40
Adelaide	88.50	58.65	152.25	–	(170.60)[c]
Perth	120.25	109.05	154.85	87.10	–

Notes:
a. Prices Justification Tribunal Matter N75/7539, N76/62, N76/151.
b. Includes road-rail containers.
c. Railfast service only.
Source: TNT Transport System Rate Schedules.

efficiency can be considered in Table 6.9 by comparing each firm's long run weighted average percentage return with the long run average market rate of interest. The weighted return was calculated for each company by taking total net profits 1962-75 for each freight forwarder (1965-75 for Fleetways) expressed as a percentage of its total shareholders' funds over the period. Although the long run average market rate of interest could be weighted by the amount of funds available in the market each year a straight average is taken as a close approximation. Such a strategy is considered acceptable not only because of the problem of quantifying available annual funds but because the market rates of interest display less variability than returns on shareholders funds. No allowance in calculating these figures is made to mitigate the upward bias to accounting profits imparted by inflation or to allow for a 'real' rate of interest. Accounting for the bias may have only slightly reduced the return on shareholders funds because the effect is largely counteracted by the retention of past profits in shareholders funds and the expansion of assets at current market rates.

Assuming that the variations in returns on shareholders funds do not stem from significant differences in capital turnover rates – a dubious proposition when takeovers and mergers are frequent – Table 6.9 shows that all companies, except Fleetways, have a weighted long run average return above the market rate of interest. The danger of drawing strong inter-group conclusions from such an exercise stems from the marked

Table 6.9: Allocative Efficiency of Australian Companies with Substantial Freight Forwarding Interests 1962-75

Year	Ansett Transport Industries	Brambles Industries	Mayne Nickless	Thomas Nationwide Transport	Fleetways[a]	Market rate of interest[b]
1962	12.3	8.6	9.6	11.6	–	6.93
1963	12.3	9.3	9.6	14.6	–	6.50
1964	12.4	12.0	11.6	15.7	–	6.70
1965	11.7	12.6	8.4	13.6	–	7.25
1966	10.5	10.7	7.2	13.0	7.7	7.25
1967	10.5	11.2	7.3	7.1	12.3	7.25
1968	10.4	11.4	8.8	10.8	9.4	7.25
1969	10.9	12.2	8.4	12.5	11.5	7.48
1970	11.1	11.8	10.3	11.7	7.6	8.60
1971	10.7	13.5	11.3	13.2	6.8	9.00
1972	12.6	11.5	10.1	16.3	2.8	8.00
1973	12.1	8.1	9.6	19.5	-(–7.1)	9.00
1974	12.0	12.0	11.4	18.6	3.0	11.50
1975	14.1	17.3	13.9	16.9	5.2	12.00
Weighted long run average	11.8	12.1	10.5	15.0	5.0	8.2[c]
Percentage point difference from market rate	(+43.9)	(+47.6)	(+28.1)	(+82.9)	(–39.0)	
Mean	11.7	11.6	9.8	13.9	5.9	8.2
Variance	1.1	5.0	3.3	10.8	31.0	2.9
Range	3.7	9.2	6.7	12.4	19.4	5.5
Standard deviation	1.1	2.2	1.8	3.3	5.6	1.7
Coefficient of variation (per cent)	9.4	19.0	18.4	23.7	94.9	20.7

Notes:

a. Fleetways did not become a public company until 1965.

b. Market rate of interest has been calculated by adding 2 per cent on Commonwealth securities. The yield on Commonwealth securities over 1962-5 is for a theoretical fifteen years; a theoretical twenty years for 1965; and a rebatable twenty year bond for 1966-75.

c. This is the mean figure and not the weighted long run average.

Source: Annual company reports and Reserve Bank Statistical Bulletins.

differences in the structure of the output mix of services offered by the firms involved. As Ansett's freight forwarding activities only comprised 7 per cent of gross assets in 1975 much of the consistent performance of Ansett Transport Industries originates from its airline operations. The stronger showing of Mayne Nickless since 1970 is reputed to stem from its security services. While Thomas Nationwide Transport draws its inherent strength from its full unit load traffic services in Australia and overseas, the performance of Brambles is widely coloured by its industrial services. The performance of Fleetways is believed to stem from the non-profitability of its engineering and car carrying services and difficulties experienced in ingesting Yellow Express Carriers Ltd.

The disparate nature of the activities within the major conglomerates highlight the need for a separation of their freight forwarding services from their other activities. As illustrated in Table 6.10 for Mayne Nickless, a breakdown of freight forwarding activities by line haul modes would provide the basis for more penetrating analysis. These figures show that Railex and Seapak were the main contributors to the group's meagre profit of 0.53 per cent. METS barely broke even and JETS and Mayneroad recorded losses. Ideally, such company information should go further and indicate the performance of the different services on varying routes over time. As such data are rarely forthcoming, the government has to base its role as regulator on the general results of allocative efficiency derived from published company data or special enquiries. There may be some justification for the paucity of information however, as the government is a strong competitor in its own right with freight forwarders.

Government as Regulator and Competitor

The Commonwealth Government keeps a watching brief on price rises under the *Prices Justification Act 1973* and a continuing surveillance under the *Trade Practices Act 1974* of business practices, including mergers, that may restrict competition, and of provisions for consumer protection. Mergers are also monitored under the *Foreign Takeovers Act 1975.* Hence the collapse of an oligopoly into a duopoly or monopoly through the intervention of overseas interests would be of immediate ministerial concern because of its widespread implications on line haul modes, the economy and defence capabilities. However, the fears of overseas control over the freight forwarding industry that surfaced with the activity of United Kingdom-based transport firms in the mid-1960s and the economic nationalism of the 1970s may have receded. Indeed, the situation has, in many respects, been reversed

Table 6.10: Profitability of the Mayne Stephens Group based on estimated Divisional and Group Results for the year ending 30 June 1974[a]

(million dollars)

Items	Subdivisions					
	Mayne-road[b]	Seapak[c]	Jets-press[d]	Railex[e]	METS[f]	Group Total
Revenue	14.54	7.33	3.16	11.68	1.01	37.72
Total costs	14.04	6.75	2.94	11.00	0.97	35.70
Margin	0.50	0.58	0.22	0.68	0.04	2.02
Percentage	(3.44)	(7.91)	(6.96)	(5.82)	(3.96)	(5.36)
Less overheads						
Division	0.22	0.19	0.17	0.08	–	0.66
Group	0.07	0.04	0.02	0.06	0.00	0.19
Corporate	0.38	0.19	0.08	0.30	0.03	0.98
Total overheads	0.67	0.41	0.27	0.44	0.03	1.82
Net profit	–0.17	0.17	–0.05	0.24	0.01	0.20
Percentage of total	(–85.00)	(85.00)	(–25.00)	(120.00)	(5.00)	(100.00)

Notes:

a. Estimated group assets are $A16.5 million and the estimated return on group assets is 1.18 per cent.

b. Mayne road is concerned with road and rail-road inter-state movements.

c. Seapak is concerned with coastal shipping and its trade is centred on Bass Strait.

d. Jetspress is concerned with the operation of local metropolitan parcel delivery and taxi-truck activities; it is also being developed with Trans Australia Airlines in the field of domestic cargo consolidation.

e. Railex operates an interstate and intrastate rail network using railway-owned box cars as the line haul medium.

f. METS is an acronym for Maynerail Equipment Transfer System which operates gantry systems in Melbourne and Sydney to facilitate the reciprocal transfer of unit loads between road vehicles and railway flat cars.

Source: Prices Justification Tribunal, *Prices Justification Act 1973: Mayne Nickless Limited Matter No. N74/2532 (Proposed increase of 18 per cent in interstate freight rates) 2 August, 1974 – Report by Prices Justification Tribunal* (Prices Justification Tribunal, Melbourne, 1974) p.35.

because overseas countries are experiencing the penetration of Australian-owned freight forwarding companies into their transport operations.[42]

While these activities proceeded overseas the Commonwealth Government devised legislation to exert control over movements of goods between states through the *Inter-State Commission Act 1975.*

The Act, even though passed, has not (1976) been proclaimed and is of great concern to the freight forwarding industry. It invests the re-established Inter-State Commission with wide powers to prevent undue, unreasonable and unfair preferences and discriminations as to the railways in particular and transport in general.[43]

The freight forwarders anxiety over the Inter-State Commission stems from the fact that it supposedly would have ended 'free enterprise' in long-distance road transport. Control over the road line haul mode would have imposed another indirect influence on the flexibility of freight forwarders as the Commonwealth Government already exerts control over air, sea and the Australian National Railways. However, the freight forwarding industry may experience the relaxation of indirect control within states although this may be countered by consumer protection legislation. Other state governments may follow the example of New South Wales and South Australia and remove their impositions on road movements that aim to protect their railways. Such control, however, may be exerted in another guise because all of the railways in Tasmania and non-metropolitan lines in South Australia have become part of Australian National Railways.

The role of government as regulator, either directly by control over conduct or indirectly through its constraints on line haul modes, is supplemented when government competes as a freight forwarder in its own right. Courier services operated by freight forwarders, for example, compete against the Australian Post Courier without the factor-cost advantages possessed by its rival in obtaining both vehicles and fuel free of tax. Of even greater concern to the freight forwarders, however, has been the decision of the Public Transport Commission in New South Wales to wholesale its containers to clients rather than to freight forwarders who subsequently retailed them to the clients. The freight forwarders claimed that the Public Transport Commission and other state railways contributing to RACE (Railways of Australia Container Express) were undercutting their business by offering a discount schedule to large clients (i.e. acting in some ways like a freight forwarder). Under these wholesaling arrangements the railways have use of capital-intensive facilities supplied by major national forwarders free of charge. It is also argued that the railways, by investing in freight forwarding activities, have lost the opportunity of upgrading conventional passenger and freight facilities that are badly in need of modernisation. There is also a broad consensus, as expressed in the Nimmo Report, that the railways are best at line haul activities involving full loads of such commodities as wheat and coal rather than on general freight involving consolidation, labour, pick up and delivery, and special equipment.[44] The counter argument supporting the move of the railways into freight forwarding is that allocative efficiency will be achieved because freight forwarders will have to reduce their prices and increase their output.[45] Such an argument emphasises that there may be no need for the government to intervene with other control or regulatory measures on efficiency grounds alone.

There may, however, be a case for government intervention on equity grounds because there are particular factor market imperfections in the freight forwarding industry which ought to be removed or alleviated. Much of the attention in this regard has centred on the poor working conditions and remuneration suffered by owner-drivers sub-contracting their services to freight forwarders – a situation that has allegedly resulted in owner-drivers experiencing considerable financial difficulties. These matters have been highlighted by the Transport Regulation Board in Victoria[46] and the Industrial Commission of New South Wales[47] on owner-drivers who comprised about 25 per cent of full time commercial drivers in New South Wales. Evidence given to the Commission suggested that owner-drivers on interstate routes were not receiving returns on their labour and capital commensurate with the opportunities of these two factors of production elsewhere in the economy. As a result of the excessive entry rate of imperfectly informed owner-drivers, the freight forwarders were able to obtain factors of production at less than opportunity cost and produce an output too large relative to those freight forwarders and line haul modes who pay opportunity cost rates.[48] The provision of factors at less than opportunity cost stems from the continuous supply of owner-drivers willing to enter the road haulage industry despite its high absolute number of bankruptcies – a problem essentially of information flows.

Having regard to the poor conditions of owner-drivers in sub-contracting to freight forwarders, the Industrial Commission of New South Wales recommended that an industrial tribunal be established to regulate the conditions of owner-drivers. The report of the Industrial Commission of New South Wales has produced no legislation by the Government of New South Wales.[49] However, greater activity by the Transport Workers Union seems to have ameliorated the difficulties experienced by the owner-drivers. The effect of the union's intervention on efficiency has been desirable to the extent that it has brought freight forwarders' costs into line with opportunity costs. Despite improvements in the operating conditions of owner-drivers the paring of their rates still continues.

Such observations suggest that if the efficiency/welfare goals are to be pursued further, a deeper understanding of the freight forwarding industry is required. This understanding is incumbent on 'performance' data on all sectors of the freight forwarding industry becoming available to ascertain which parts of the industry have above average profits. Above all there is need for better measures of buyer and seller concentration and other key structure variables.

Acknowledgements

In writing a paper of this nature the author has to rely on the help and assistance of many people. Particular mention has to be made of Joe Gouldstone and Roy Heasman of TNT General Freight Services, Ray Phillips, L.E. Marks and Ian Nicol of Brambles, Bob White of Ansett Freight Express, N.A. Olds, Group Commercial Manager, Thomas Nationwide Transport Limited. Bill Levitt of the National Freight Forwarders Association was also most helpful in updating the manuscript. In addition, penetrating comments have been received from K.W. Thomas and encouragement from Sir Peter Abeles. The author is also indebted to Derek Cullen and Brian Pink of the Australian Bureau of Statistics for assisting with information on the transport industry and Peter Cronin and Graham Walker for helping with information on the *Trade Practices Act 1974.* Additional comments have also been received from John Black, University of New South Wales, Howard Dick, University of Newcastle, Stanley Beevor, Public Transport Commission of New South Wales and Charles C. Halton, Department of Transport. Barbara Banks has also been most helpful in proofreading the manuscript and co-ordinating comments on the revised draft.

Notes

1. B.T. Bayliss, *European Transport* (Kenneth Mason, London, 1965); E.J. Taaffe and H.L. Gauthier, *Geography of Transportation* (Prentice-Hall, Englewood Cliffs) 1973, pp.52-72.
2. P.J. Rimmer, *Freight Forwarding in Australia,* Department of Human Geography Publication HG/4(1970), Research School of Pacific Studies, Australian National University Canberra, 1970.
3. See Parliament of the Commonwealth of Australia, *Report from the Standing Committee on Primary and Secondary Industry and Trade on Freight Rates on Australian National Line Shipping Services to and from Tasmania,* Parliamentary Paper No.160, Commonwealth Government Publishing Office, 1971.
4. Bureau of Transport Economics, *An Assessment of Tasmania's Interstate Transport Problems* (Australian Government Publishing Service, Canberra,

1973).

5. Information supplied by W. Levitt (pers. comm.). Figure 1 is based on a discussion with J. Gouldstone, TNT General Freight Services.
6. The case of Hughes & Vale No.1 (Hughes & Vale v. NSW) 93 CLR 1.
7. The standard gauge (1.43m) link between Sydney and Perth was completed in 1970. A connection with Adelaide is also planned. When this link is forged all state capital cities will be connected to the interstate standard gauge network. However, the direct link between Adelaide and Melbourne will still be broad gauge (1.59m).
8. P.J. Rimmer, *Coastal Shipping* (Longmans, Croydon, Melbourne, 1967).
9. Australian shipbuilding policy was designed through the use of import controls to ensure that virtually all domestic requirements for vessels over 204 tonnes gross were supplied by local shipbuilders and a generous subsidy of up to 45 per cent of construction costs was paid on vessels built in Australia for use in Australian waters. A new assistance programme was introduced in 1974 which extended eligibility to vessels of 154.5 tonnes (21.34m for fishing vessels), vessels intended for use by Australian flag operators in international trade and vessel modification in excess of $50,000. However, arrangements were instituted to phase the subsidy of up to 45 per cent down to 25 per cent by 1980. These arrangements did not apply to vessels outside the industry's capacity of 90,000 deadweight tons (91,800 tonnes); such vessels attracted a subsidy of 25 per cent. This policy is currently (1976) under review.
10. K.W. Thomas (pers. comm.).
11. For comments on multi-outlet organisations see K.A. Tucker, 'Performance, Concentration and Structural Features in Australian Retailing'. Chapter 7.
12. No time series data is available to indicate whether the intra-state trade is declining relatively to the interstate trade. K.W. Thomas (pers. comm.) finds such figures misleading. He feels that any comment on freight volume ought to be confined to tonne-kilometres. There is little sense, he argues, in adding a tonne from Sydney to Redfern to a tonne from Sydney to Perth and calling the total two tonnes. Unfortunately, the transport statistics are not available to satisfy Mr. Thomas' expressed needs. His argument is also applicable to Table 2.
13. Commonwealth Bureau of Census and Statistics, *Interstate Freight Movements 1971-2* (Commonwealth Bureau of Census and Statistics, Canberra, 1972).
14. See, for example, the Parliament of the Commonwealth of Australia, *Report from the Senate Select Committee on the Container Method of Handling Cargoes: Part 1 Report; Part 2 Minutes of Evidence,* The Parliament of the Commonwealth of Australia, Parliamentary Paper 46/46A, Government Printer, Canberra. K.W. Thomas (pers. comm.) argues that such technological innovations have not gone far enough. If rail management were further improved and true overnight trains ran between Melbourne and Sydney (leaving 8 pm and arriving 8 am) there would be not only a revolution in modes but there would be a reduction in road deaths and less road damage.
15. Robin Marris and Adrian Wood (eds.), *The Corporate Economy* (Macmillan, London, 1971) Appendix C.
16. Marris and Wood, op. cit.
17. Rimmer, 1970, pp.92-107.
18. The Long Distance Road Transport Association in New South Wales calculated that the top eight freight forwarding firms handled 67.7 per cent of interstate freight, whether it went by rail, road or sea, at 30 June 1967. See J.A. Maddock, 'The Role of Road Transport in the Next Decade', *Australian Transport,* vol.12, 1969, pp.23-52.

19. Unpublished data from Australian Bureau of Statistics. Confidentiality prevents the names of individual firms from being released.
20. Australian Government, *Report of the Commission of Inquiry into Transport To and From Tasmania* (the Nimmo Report) (Australian Government Publishing Service, Canberra, 1976) p.21.
21. See evidence of Mr (now Sir) Peter Abeles in Commonwealth of Australia, *Senate Standing Committee on Primary and Secondary Industry and Trade (Reference: Tasmanian Shipping Freights) 1970-71, (Official Hansard Report)* (Government Printer of the Commonwealth of Australia, Canberra, 1972) pp.545-6.
22. Abeles, *Tasmania Shipping Freights*, pp.539-58.
23. Insurance and Superannuation Funds (over 5,000) held 30.81 per cent of shares on 11 February 1972 in Thomas Nationwide Transport Ltd. Nominees (over 5,000) held 27.80 per cent. Others (under 5,000) 17.80 per cent, Board group 9.31 per cent, Others (over 5,000) 7.34 per cent. Overseas 6.94 per cent (excludes those nominees who represent overseas interests). See *Senate Standing Committee on Industry and Trade (Reference: Proposed takeover of Ansett Transport Industries Ltd by Thomas Nationwide Transport Ltd) Canberra 27 April 1972 (Official Hansard Report)* (Government Printer of the Commonwealth of Australia, Canberra, 1972) p.57.
24. See evidence of Mr (now Sir) Peter Abeles in *Proposed takeover of Ansett Transport*. . .26 April 1974, pp.1-54.
25. R. Wright, Towards a General Theory for the Regulation of Victorian Road and Rail Transport, unpublished M.Com. thesis, University of Melbourne, 1972, p.58.
26. Evidence of Abeles on *Proposed Takeover of Ansett Transport*. . .pp.29-30.
27. Prices Justification Tribunal, *Prices Justification Act 1973: Mayne Nickless Limited Matter No.N74/2532 (Proposed increase of 18 per cent in interstate freight rates) 2 August 1974 – Report by Prices Justification Tribunal* (Prices Justification Tribunal, Melbourne, 1974) p.37.
28. In 1976 the members of the National Freight Forwarders Association were Ansett Freight Express Pty Ltd, Brambles Long Distance Road Transport, Ipec (Interstate Parcel Express Company Pty Ltd), Mayne Nickless Ltd, Tradex Transport, United Transport Holdings Australia Pty Ltd (formerly AUT Holdings Ltd), and Youngs Transport Agency.
29. Wright, pp.25-91.
30. Wright, p.60.
31. Wright, p.61.
32. Wright, pp.60-61.
33. Evidence of Abeles on *Tasmanian Shipping Freights*, p.543.
34. Report by Prices Justification Tribunal concerning Mayne Nickless Ltd, p.28.
35. See J.P. Nieuwenhuysen and N.R. Norman, *Australian Competition and Prices Policy: Trade Practices, Tariffs and Prices Justification* (Croom Helm, London, 1976) pp.43-60.
36. To obtain an authorisation under the Trade Practices Act the applicant is required by Section 90(5) of the Act to satisfy the Trade Practices Commission that the conduct in question results, or is likely to result in a substantial and not otherwise available public benefit which, in all the circumstances, justifies the granting of an authorisation.
37. Trade Practices Commission, 'Commission Determination of 11 June 1975 on Application for Authorisation by TNT Management Ltd on behalf of itself and Seven Other Companies', Registration No.A3019, File No.A74/102, Lodged 17 December 1974. 'The companies' referred to are all members of the National Freight Forwarders Association.

38. Trade Practices Commission, p.5.
39. The list of lodgements from the various State Road Associations and Master Carriers at the Trade Practices Commission include The Master Carriers Association of New South Wales (Ref.No.A3027), Victorian Road Transport Association (Ref. No.A4023), Master Carriers Association of Queensland (Ref. No.A2145), South Australian Road Transport Association (Ref. No.A6040), West Australian Road Transport Association (Ref. No.A7107). There are also lodgements involving rates and conditions of employment of owner-drivers.
40. Report by Prices Justification Tribunal concerning Mayne Nickless Ltd, p.40.
41. The methodology employed in this section follows Wright, pp.77-91.
42. W.D. Breit, 'Australian Multinationals: Growth or Survival', *Journal of World Trade Law,* vol.10, 1976, pp.265-79. Reference is made in the article to Thomas Nationwide Transport Ltd acquisitions.
43. These powers have yet (1976) to be exercised as the Commissioners under the Act brought in by the Whitlam Labor Government have not been appointed by the Fraser Liberal-National Country Coalition Government.
44. The Nimmo Report, p.29.
45. Beevor (pers. comm.), Public Transport Commission of New South Wales, expands this argument by stating that changes in the market place are working persuasively in favour of direct rail-based services from manufacturer to market place. Such changes have included (a) a reduction in the number of manufacturing points which have produced greater volume per pick up, (b) a reduction in the number of market places producing greater volume per delivery, (c) greater awareness of total distribution costs by managements, (d) escalating wages and (e) the performance of the various modes of service and freight rates. Conversely, it is believed that these changes within the market place do not favour the freight forwarding industry which is at its most efficient and profitable where warehousing is involved between manufacturing and consumer.
46. Transport Regulation Board, *Annual Report,* Transport Regulation Board, Melbourne, 1968-69, pp.36-7; 1970-71, pp.9-10.
47. Industrial Commission of New South Wales, *Report to the Hon. E.A. Willis B.A., M.L.A. Minister for Labour and Industry, on Section 88E of the Industrial Arbitration Act, 1940-1968, Vol.II, containing Part C. Lorry-Owner Drivers,* Government Printer, Sydney.
48. Wright, p.130.
49. Industrial Commission, p.739.

Bibliography

Australian Bureau of Statistics, *Freight and Furniture moved Inter-state by major Freight Forwarders and Road Transport Operators between specified Australian Centres, 1974-5* (Australian Bureau of Statistics, Canberra, 1975)

Australian Government, *Report of the Commission of Inquiry into Transport to and from Tasmania,* (The Nimmo Report) (Australian Government Publishing Service, Canberra, 1976)

Brogden, S.M.W., *Australia's Two-Airline Policy* (Melbourne University Press, Melbourne, 1968)

Bureau of Transport Economics, *An Assessment of Tasmania's Interstate Transport Problems* (Australian Government Publishing Service, Canberra, 1973)

Commonwealth Bureau of Roads, *Report on Roads in Australia – 1974* (Commonwealth Bureau of Roads, Melbourne, 1973)

Commonwealth Bureau of Roads, *Report on Roads in Australia – 1975* (Commonwealth Bureau of Roads, 1975)

Commonwealth of Australia, *Senate Standing Committee on Primary and Secondary Industry and Trade (Reference: Tasmanian Shipping Freights) 1970-71, Official Hansard Report* (Government Printer of the Commonwealth of Australia, Canberra, 1972)

Fitzpatrick, M.D. and Taplin, J.H.E., 'A Model to Estimate the Price Elasticity of Demand for Transport of Goods by Road', *Proceedings of the Sixth Conference of the Australian Road Research Board*, Vol.6, no.2, 1972, pp.252-65

Gattorna, J.L., *The Role of Air Cargo in Australia's Domestic and International Distribution Systems, Productivity Promotion Council of Australia* (Melbourne, 1974)

Gilmour, P. (ed.), *Physical Distribution Management in Australia* (Cheshire, Melbourne, 1974).

Gilmour, P., Gattorna, J.L., Oh, Y-L., 'The Subjective Determinants of Transport Mode Selection: A Multivariate Approach', (unpublished paper presented at 46th ANZAAS Conference, Canberra, 1975)

Hensher, D. (ed.), *Urban Transport Economics* (Cambridge University Press, Cambridge and London, forthcoming)

Hirst, R.R., 'The Transport Industry' in A. Hunter (ed.), *The Economics of Australian Industry* (Melbourne University Press, Melbourne, 1963), pp.65-111

Hocking, R., 'The Costs of Domestic Airline Operations' in G.R. Webb and J.C. McMaster (eds.), *Australian Transport Economics: A Reader* (Australia and New Zealand Book Company, Sydney, 1975) pp.37-50

Joy, S., 'Unregulated Road Haulage: The Australian Experience', *Oxford Economic Papers*, vol.16, no.2, 1964, pp.275-285

Kolsen, H.M., 'Structure and Price Determination in the Road Haulage Industry of New South Wales', *Economic Record*, vol.32, no.63, 1956, pp.291-304

Kolsen, H.M., *The Economics and Control of Road-Rail Competition: A Critical Study of Theory and Practice in the United States of America, Great Britain and Australia* (Sydney University Press, Sydney, 1968)

Kolsen, H.M., 'Efficiency and Regulation in Land Transport', *Queensland Papers in Economic Policy*, vol.3, 1974, pp.1-23.

Maddock, J.A., 'The Role of Road Transport in the Next Decade', *Australian Transport*, vol.12, 1969, pp.23-52.

Owens, J.M., 'Economics of Truck Operations in Urban Areas', *Proceedings of the Second Conference of the Australian Road Research Board*, vol.2, 1964, pp.34-55

Pak-Poy and Associates, *Study of the Transport of Goods for Tasmania*, 5 vols (P.G. Pak-Poy and Associates, Adelaide, 1971)

Parliament of the Commonwealth of Australia, *Report from the Standing Committee on Primary and Secondary Industry and Trade on Freight Rates on Australian National Line Shipping Services to and from Tasmania*, Parliamentary Paper No.160 (Commonwealth Government Publishing Office, 1971)

Rimmer, P.J., 'The Australian Freight Transport Industry: Individual Modes, Regulation and Future Prospects' in P. Gilmour (ed.), *Physical Distribution Management in Australia* (Cheshire, Melbourne, 1974) pp.12-33

Rimmer, P.J., *Coastal Shipping* (Longmans, Croydon, Melbourne, 1967)

Rimmer, P.J., *Freight Forwarding in Australia*, Department of Human Geography Publication HG/4(1970), Research School of Pacific Studies, Australian National University, Canberra, 1970

Rimmer, P.J., 'Transport' in D.N. Jeans (ed.), *Australia – A Geography* (Sydney University Press, Sydney forthcoming).

State of South Australia, *Report of the Royal Commission on State Transport Services* (Government Printer, Adelaide, 1968)

State of Victoria, Legislative Assembly, *Report of the Inquiry into the Victorian Land Transport System* (The Bland Report), (Government Printer, Melbourne, 1972)

Taplin, J.H.E., 'Energy and Transport in an Island Continent', *Transportation Research,* vol.8, 1974, pp.259-276

Webb, G.R. and McMaster, J.C. (eds.), *Australian Transport Economics: A Reader* (Australia and New Zealand Book Company, Sydney, 1975)

Wheeler, S.J., 'The Rate and Regulation Structures of the Australian Freight Transport Industry and their Effects on Corporate Freight Movements', Monash University M. Admin thesis, 1974

Wilkes, J. (ed.), *Australia's Transport Crisis* (Angus and Robertson, Sydney, 1956

Wright, R., 'Towards a General Theory for the Regulation of Victorian Road and Rail Transport', Univ. of Melbourne M. Com thesis, 1972

7 PERFORMANCE, CONCENTRATION AND STRUCTURAL FEATURES IN RETAILING

K.A. Tucker

God, how I hate all this, the things in the shop windows, the obtuse face of merchandise, and, above all, the ceremonial of transaction, the exchange of cloying compliments before and after! And those lowered lashes of modest price. . .the nobility of the discount. . .the altruism of advertisements. . .all of this nasty imitation of good, which has a strange way of drawing in good people.

Vladimir Nabokov, *The Gift* (Panther Books, 1966)

Introduction

Retail services are usually subsumed in unrealistic economic abstraction. They are included in the concept of an all-embracing 'goods' market and are thereby theoretically and empirically treated as an undistinguished part of the output of manufacturing processes. The economic services of stockholding, bulk-breaking, distribution, display and providing product information are often either incorrectly assumed to be part of the manufacturing sector or are, alternatively, ignored in the theory of consumer behaviour as if all goods and services were purchased directly by households at the manufacturer's factory gate or somehow arrived as unsolicited mail from overseas (i.e. as cost-less imports). For example, some recent descriptions of performance/structure relationships for manufacturing industries (i.e. Jackson Report[1] and the Industries Assistance Commission enquiry into the motor vehicle industry[2]) have highlighted, by their gross neglect, the often overlooked functions of retail institutions and the costs of distributing products and services, whether manufactured locally or overseas.[3]

Retail and distributive organisations claim a considerable share of resources and contribute importantly towards gross output. They provide a multi-dimensional output that includes value added to tangible goods and the provision of a range of associated services. Their market relationships with manufacturers, importers, transport institutions, advertising agencies and consumers make them capable of affecting the distribution of incomes, expenditure patterns and social welfare. Their operating methods and decisions on resource acquisition affect the efficiency of many areas of the economic system. Retail firms, like those in other sectors, are capable of generating idle capacity, hoarding labour resources and adopting an incorrect scale of plant or organisation.

Much of applied economic analysis has focused on manufacturing industries. Their performance has been investigated and the many structural features of industries have been measured. In addition, some studies have considered the nature of relationships between an index of performance and given structural elements. For example, if manufacturing industries are highly concentrated (i.e. a large share of total supplies is controlled by a few of the largest firms) or protected by tariffs, economic theory and analysis suggests certain implications for prices, cost structure, relative efficiency and welfare. Are there analogous situations in retail markets? For example, what is the effect of regional concentration, restricted trading hours, licensed operation or land use and development zoning? Do the structural features of retail markets moderate or exacerbate the structural conditions present in domestic manufacturing? Is the performance of the retail sector explicable in terms of structural conditions within that sector alone? Are there elements of conduct and methods of regulation that, apart from structural features, influence the achieved performance?

Two particular structural variables have received a good deal of attention in manufacturing. The first is the level of concentration and its influence on profitability or productivity, while the other is the extent to which economies of scale are available and have been achieved. Attention also has been directed to the difference in input coefficients (i.e. labour to capital ratio) of operations and the vintage of capital structure. Cost structure has been analysed by reference to key inputs such as R & D services, advertising expenditure and energy use.

The purpose of this study is to examine some of the arguments advanced by economic theory and previous studies of manufacturing in relation to cross-sectional data on retail activities for the year 1968/9. There are several reasons for undertaking this analysis. First, retail markets have been relatively neglected by government agencies concerned with competition policy and consumer welfare.[4] Secondly, research and teaching programmes have concentrated on macro-economic policy objectives and external trade relations and have thereby overlooked the micro-economic functioning and structural features of internal markets. This undue emphasis on international trade flows has resulted in an almost exclusive consideration of agriculture, mining and manufacturing activities.[5] Thirdly, overseas studies and a growing consumer awareness have revived an interest in distributive and retailing systems. Researchers are now developing a useful analytical framework for empirical investigation.[6] Finally the relative importance of retailing services has grown within the economy by reference to certain key indicators and shares of resources. It appears, therefore, that there is adequate justification for the study of structural conditions and performance in Australian retail markets.

The relative importance of retailing and distributive services within the economic system can be illustrated by reference to some basic statistics on gross product shares, labour force shares and fixed capital expenditure as a percentage of sales for each sector. In the year 1962/3, the gross product share for manufacturing activities was 27.88 per cent at constant (1968/9) prices, while for the wholesale and retail trades it was 16.67 per cent. By contrast, primary and extractive industries contributed a share of 12.05 per cent and community services (i.e. energy utilities, education and health etc.) and recreational and entertainment services generated a share of about 9.12 per cent. Ten years later, in 1972/3, the share for manufacturing was 27.04 per cent (again at constant – 1968/9 – prices), that for wholesale and retail activities was 15.16 per cent and those for primary/extractive activities and the other services mentioned above were 11.31 per cent and 10.83 per cent respectively.[7] If it is accepted that these output shares are measured correctly – and it should also be noticed that they are not net value added estimates – then it can be noted that distributive and retail activities, while providing a substantial share of 'service' output, nevertheless, like primary and manufacturing industries, contributed a smaller proportion of total economy output at the end of the period.

The share of labour inputs is even less easy to measure and interpret than the above crude output shares, due to the lack of adequate standardisation procedures among sectors of the economy to account for differences in hours employed. Taking figures for persons in the workforce, and remembering that the full-time equivalent inputs would differ markedly across activities, manufacturing industries absorbed 26.22 per cent of the workforce in February 1971 while the wholesale and retail trades took 17.55 per cent. In February 1976 the figures were 21.43 per cent and 19.68 per cent respectively. These estimates, based on persons in the workforce, will overestimate the changed share in retail activities where there is an increasing use of part-time employees relative to manufacturing industries or other activities. Apart from this influence, the total labour inputs for the retail sector are very likely seriously understated as a level and may be also biased downwards in terms of changing shares due to the shifting of some service functions towards the use of non-market consumer labour inputs. For example, self-selection, self-service and the private transport and storage of final goods all involve a greater use of consumer time in relation to retail employee time.

Other inputs acquired and used by the economic system are still less adequately measured for all sectors than are labour resources. Census data for 1968/9 makes it possible to estimate the current period levels of fixed capital expenditure in relation to sales for some sectors. The figure for manufacturing is 4.97 per cent while, by contrast, that for mining (excluding services to mining) is 43.20 per cent. Wholesaling and retailing activities have a capital expenditure to sales level of 1.74 per cent and 1.32 per cent respectively.

The above indicators clearly demonstrate that there are wide variations in factor proportions between sectors and that any partial labour productivity (i.e. output per person) measure is of little interpretative value on its own. It is to be expected that factor market conditions may vary within the sectors to a similar extent. Without adequate information on the age of capital stock, its heterogeneity and other inputs, it is difficult to obtain any very firm perspective of the integral and relative roles of separate sectors and activities. The data on output shares could even be misleading when it is noted that many 'public' services are not sold at market prices, that entry is often restricted and that levels of concentration may be high in both public and private sectors. Despite these limitations, retailing services in a highly urbanised society clearly rank high in importance by output volume, in terms of labour force opportunities and by reason of the potential for greater capital inputs. Given Australia's historical growth pattern of predominantly urbanised population settlement it is perhaps difficult to understand why conditions determining the supply of and demand for retail services have been so neglected in the past. Within the framework of priority to consumer welfare, different work-force participation features and conflicting claims for capital resources, it is unlikely that these economic activities can be overlooked in the future.

Concentration and Structural Features

J.S. Mill astutely observed nearly 130 years ago that the structural feature of local and regional monopoly in retail markets was being eroded.

> Competition is making itself felt more and more through the principal branches of retail trade in large towns, and the rapidity and cheapness of transport, by making consumers less dependent on the dealers in their immediate neighbourhood, are tending to assimilate more and more the whole country to a large town. (1848)[8]

By contrast, Alfred Marshall maintained much later that some spatial and competitive advantages were always maintained by retailers, provided they maintained a favourable image with customers.[9]

> A retail dealer when once he has established a good connection has always had a partial and limited local monopoly. If he has used it ill, he has lost it sooner or later. But so long as he has retained it, he has not been under the necessity of adjusting his charge for each particular service to the cost of that service. (undated MS)[10]

These views, despite initial appearances, do not contain any conflict of interpretation about structural change. Mill points to a *trend* for reduced regional concentration and increasing national concentration, while Marshall maintains that there is a level of local concentration that cannot be competed away (i.e. cost and price differences) due to features of distance, convenience and other service elements that make up the competitive reputation of the retailer. Neither economist deals explicitly with the scale, or changes in size, of retail outlets or organisations.

However, the above quotations capture very adequately the conceptual difficulties encountered when applying measures of structural features, such as concentration and economies of scale, in retailing. They point to the role of goods and services supplied by retailers; they refer to the influence of the joint-supply of transport and information in overcoming barriers of distance and utility comparisons (i.e. search, distribution and transaction costs); and they underline the nature of competitive strategy. In the classical economist's world, it was as important to understand the process by which the retailer 'established a good connection' as it was to analyse the resource and welfare implications of that current situation. Business practices and the conduct of decision-making within a bargaining or conflict context were considered to be as crucial as the outcome deriving from a set of structural features. For want of data and space, however, it is the latter which is the primary focus of this chapter.

Despite their facility for realistic appraisal and relevant comment, these early economists were not able to forecast one feature of modern retailing – although perhaps Marx could be said to have implied it. There has emerged, principally during this century, the dominating feature of multiple-outlet ownership and common managerial control in several locations. This aggregation of ownership (or, more correctly, management) and the centralisation of decision-making through merger and urban development or suburban expansion[11] – and made possible by changes in the technology of information storage and retrieval and transport – has augmented the role of the corporate owner and has reduced the influence of the 'independent' single-location proprietor. In some retail and service trades, this higher level of national and regional concentration of ownership and control has policy implications in the fields of pricing behaviour, trade practices, enterprise efficiency and consumer welfare. But these wider repercussions can only be understood when we have available reliable measures of some of the fundamental structural features, such as levels of concentration and the minimum/maximum efficient size of unit, for each kind of retail business.

Ideally, three sets of structural variables should be investigated. First, there are those that generally apply to the retail sector and can be related to each type of activity; for example, concentration, economies of scale, barriers to entry, and diversification. Then there are those which connect the retail sector to structural features of other parts of the production-distribution process. Vertical integration and manufacturer concentration are relevant in this context. Finally, there are structural conditions which apply more particularly to the goods and factor market conditions within which firms in a particular kind of retail business operate. For example, some of the pertinent variables would be measures of factor proportions and prices, capacity utilisation, asset age structure, and the elasticity and rate of growth of demand. Variables from each of these three sets of structural conditions should assist in explaining differences in performance among kinds of retail business.

The primary focus on the concentration variable in manufacturing is suggested by theories of imperfect competition. The basic argument in theories of oligopoly is that the *exercise* of market power by firms in goods or factor markets proceeds from the *existence* of seller or buyer concentration and generates maximum profits in relation to committed resources. Abnormal returns (or 'rents') are not able to be competed away because of restrictions on supply and higher-than-necessary prices for the supply available.[12] Within a dynamic context this may involve setting prices (e.g. resale price maintenance) or engaging in pricing strategies that deter entry. Or it may result in expenditures (e.g. advertising and R & D) or practices (e.g. exclusive dealership contracts) that generate scale economy barriers for new entrants or discriminatory disadvantages for existing smaller competitors (i.e. non-price competition).

The implication of high concentration for performance, as measured by profitability, is that factor rewards to some inputs are higher than their marginal physical product and that this may result in both allocative (i.e. lower incomes to factors and skewed income distributions) and X-inefficiency (i.e. evidence of lower profits and lack of administrative or technical change). The traditional models therefore assume that firms do attempt to maximise profits and not some other corporate objective function (e.g. growth of assets or sales) *and* that the excess factor rewards flow exclusively to owners of capital funds or real assets. But by modifying the assumption about firms' goals and by taking account of institutional changes which separate control over the market for managerial skills from that in the market for real assets and money balances, it is possible to modify the expectation that profitability, as but one measure of performance, will be positively related to concentration. Differences in other 'performance' measures may take over the role of profitability as an effect of the exercise of market power. These anti- or non-competitive characteristics will most likely reveal themselves in 'non-price' areas (e.g. under-utilised capital goods or limited user access, onerous contractual rights or obligations, rivalrous conduct to exclude groups of potential entrants or to reduce product quality etc). Also, the rewards from the exercise of market power may be distributed to different recipients (e.g. executive consumption benefits, pay-offs to militant unionists or preferences for institutional suppliers of capital funds). Should this be the case, constant factor prices cannot be assumed to persist over all ranges of output or between different sized firms.

There are two alternative interpretations of a measure of concentration. First, its existence is not a sufficient condition for its abuse. It may be either an unexercised latent power or matched by the countervailing power of consumers. And the interventionist role of government agencies may deter this anti-competitive conduct and moderate any excessive performance benefit. Secondly, a high level of concentration achieved may be attributable to successful competitive behaviour, certain given technical and spatial features of time lags in adjusting supply to changes in demand. It is either a natural consequence of market features and forces or would be adjusted in time by economic or social processes.[13]

While the level of concentration is the most commonly used measure of market power, it is not possible to obtain a fully satisfactory summary statistic by which to measure this structural feature. Nor is it meaningful to relate it solely to performance indicators. Adequate and appropriate specification of the functional relationships has been of recent concern in studies of manufacturing industries where concentration is but one relative influence along with other market structure variables. Another question has been whether there is a 'critical' level of concentration above which the existence and exercise of market power reveals itself in above-average profitability. Both of these aspects are considered for retail markets in this chapter.

Within the Australian context, the extent of competition in overseas supply from imports or the degree of tariff protection should also be considered. It may be expected that rewards to factor inputs in the retail markets dealing with protected goods would be above average, but that once again this need not be reflected in retail profitability alone. A lack of adequate input/output commodity-mix data by origins and institution of purchase prevent an investigation of this feature.

Performance Measures

In the literature on industrial structure and performance, the concept of 'performance' normally refers to actual profits (before or after tax) as a percentage of capital funds or total assets employed. Additional measures such as labour productivity or 'technological progressiveness' also may be used in some cases. Data constraints often make it necessary to adopt as a profitability index the measure of gross profit to sales margin earned.[14]

The available performance measures each have a number of merits and limitations. The declared rate of return on capital employed is the 'ideal' measure, in that it purportedly represents the factor rewards to accumulated capital resources or financial claims over the use of acquired assets. However, this computation is affected by non-proportionate taxation deductions and rates, explicit subsidies or transfer payments, different methods of depreciation and inventory valuation, and the deduction of amounts for employee consumption (e.g. insurance payments, entertainment allowances, health services, travelling and accommodation expenses and employee discounts) that should properly be classified as household expenditure.[15] The difficulties encountered in standardising both the numerator and denominator of the net profitability measure for kinds of biases that are essentially non-linear are well reported.[16] Furthermore, when firms are highly diversified in output mix, but jointly utilise common resources, the effects of inter-sectoral aggregation and methods of internal transfer pricing may be such as to remove much of the variation in either component of the rate of return index. Ideally, *product* profitability measures that incorporate a full allocation of utilised or available fixed capacity cost should be employed.

The major merit of a labour productivity measure is that it is easy to compute. But such a partial measure overlooks differences in the factor input coefficients (i.e. different factor mix) of activities under comparison. Unless a separate measure can be constructed for non-labour inputs, it is not a measure of 'physical' efficiency (i.e. quantities of labour per unit of output) and even if deducted from the level of profits to obtain a 'residual' attributable to other inputs, would still ignore factor prices and many other input components.

Should it be assumed that the rate of growth of output is a measure of 'technical progressiveness' then it is clearly the case that demand influences must be separated out from this indicator to give the growth performance attributable to changing supply conditions alone. A better measure may be the percentage of R & D expenditure to turnover. But this measure could merely indicate that rivalry patterns of expenditure are only part of an oligopolistic behaviour strategy designed to ease the firm's recruitment of or command over resources or to hasten the exit of competitors. If this is the case, the performance variable becomes a measure of how profits are absorbed by patterns of expenditure to prevent entry or increase the frequency of exit from the industry. Profitability is not being kept high with the likelihood of attracting entry. Similar arguments apply to the advertising to sales ratio.[17]

Gross margins or cost-price margins have serious deficiencies as measures of performance and these defects have been adequately described in the literature on manufacturing industries.[18] There are, however, situations where gross margins may be more instructive than rates of return; especially where product aggregation and different accounting procedures result in biases of unknown directions and magnitude. This is particularly the case in retailing where the composition and vintage of capital assets differ considerably among kinds of business.

First, data on capital employed in retailing is often not an adequate indicator of differences in the opportunity cost of fixed assets where accounting methods record differing vintages of assets at historical cost less depreciation allowable. Where current fixed capital expenditure data are available, provided that they represent the average outlay for each kind of business, they may provide a better measure of current capital/output differences (i.e. replacement cost). Such a variable can be included as a separate explanatory term. Secondly, in retailing, most of the pecuniary economies (i.e. buyer concentration effects) are probably attributable to buying advantages[19] that are implicit in a reduced cost-of-sales (i.e. increased gross margins) figure. Bulk purchase discounts are therefore represented in the size of gross margins net of the deduction of other variable costs and after taking account of fixed costs. Thirdly, the labour market is of particular importance in retailing. Part-time and female employment and different local employment conditions make it necessary to consider the separate role of wage costs as a deduction from gross profitability. Finally, any residual variation in gross margins can be taken as that proportion attributable to unspecified cost influences (e.g. economies of scale for some cost components or excess capacity costs), to variables which mainly affect demand (e.g. advertising and promotional expenditure) or to the 'abnormal' return generated by unspecified structural or conduct variables. The extent of diversification is an important feature of retail markets, and this particular variable can be considered more readily in the context of a gross performance index than in net profitability terms, where the output-mix can be ignored. By contrast, for manufacturing industries the product range is often narrow and the rate of return measure is therefore a better proxy for average performance.

In summary, by making use of a broader concept of profitability and by taking account of a greater number of the determinants of variation in that variable, it may be possible to analyse more adequately the separate, and possibly negating, roles of different factor and goods market conditions affecting retail market performance.

Data Sources and Limitations

Information collected under the 1968/9 Census of Retail Establishments permits a limited and exploratory analysis of the relationship between measures of performance and a given set of structural variables, which includes the level of concentration. The cross-sectional data relates to forty-six kinds of retail and service activity.[20]

The census classification system was revised for the first integrated economic census in 1968/9 and, although the subsequent 1973/4 Census of Retail Establishments was consistent with the ASIC system adopted, it was not a full census. It is therefore not possible to obtain any consistent data *prior to* 1968/9 on, for example, the growth of output, labour productivity or changes in structural conditions. And *after* this date some of the structural variables cannot be estimated (e.g. fixed capital expenditure to sales). As a result alternative measures of performance cannot be generated and variables that represent structural *change* over time, including the growth of demand, cannot be included.

It is possible to employ two performance variants. The gross margin or value added percentage in output can be used in its own right or by deducting wages and salaries from it. This reduces it to a 'net margin' or price-cost margin measure. The structural variables are divided into two groups for the purposes of interpreting the estimated relationships. *General market structure* variables include concentration, diversification or output-mix and the average scale of retail outlet for each kind of business. No comprehensive data is available on entry barriers resulting from advertising expenditure, vertical integration by ownership or contractual obligations (i.e. 'tied' outlets), or manufacturing concentration in terms of a weighted product mix measure.[21] *Retail market structure* variables focus more on the acquisition and use of factor inputs and include the male to female employment ratio, the labour to capital ratio, a capital/output (intensity) index, a measure of labour productivity (i.e. sales per person employed), wages per employee and the stock turnover rate or level. A full description of these variables and their derivation is provided in Appendix 7.1, while the concentration series (CONA) used for most of the performance/structure estimates is shown in Table 7.1.

There are several limitations to these series despite the fact that, where possible, alternative measures have been derived and tested for their different effects. First, no breakdown exists for part/full-time employees or labour inputs on an hourly basis. Retailing activities are characterised by part-time employment and seasonal (i.e. daily and weekly) variations in output. Secondly, without measures of capital stock, its composition and its vintage, it is not possible to isolate new from replacement expenditure; to fully distinguish fixed from working capital; to generate capacity utilisation variables or to express profitability as a rate of return on assets employed. Thirdly, all values are in current terms. Where there are different methods employed among retail activities in valuing inventories or where price changes have differentially affected output or value added measures, the series will be biased and lack strict comparability between activities. Finally, performance data ideally should be based on an averaged series for several periods to eliminate any cyclical element of the variation. The merits and defects of the gross margin to sales measure as against profitability expressed as a rate of return on capital funds were discussed earlier.

Functional Relationships

It is hypothesised, from theoretical constructs of non-competitive market structures, that increased levels of seller or buyer concentration will lead to increased profitability; either directly through control over prices and quantities in goods markets and by deterring entry (i.e. additional supply), or indirectly by influencing demand (i.e. advertising and product differentiation), and the prices at which factor inputs are acquired. In addition, features of conduct (e.g. restrictive practices and resale price maintenance) may be established to reinforce market control and raise profitability. Studies of profitability and concentration in manufacturing have often shown that a positive relationship exists between these two variables.[22] The existence of other structural features (i.e. vertical integration, economies of scale and the extent of diversification) may be complementary to or a substitute for the level of concentration. In addition, there may be conditions of operation or factor market features that are peculiar to retail markets and that should be allowed for in explaining performance. A distinction is therefore made between general market structure variables and those variables which are more characteristic of retail markets.

There are, in effect, two formal propositions to be tested. The first is the nature of relationships among structural variables and the second is the manner in which these jointly, along with features of conduct or regulation – that may be independent – influence performance. These two functional relationships can be expressed as follows:

$$C = f(S, D, I, E, O) \qquad (1)$$

Where, C = concentration, S = economies of scale, D = diversification, I = vertical integration, E = entry barriers, O = other structural features.

$$P = g(X, Y, Z)$$

Where, P = performance indices, X = general market structure variables, Y = retail market structure variables, Z = conduct, regulation and protection variables.

In addition, where time-series are available, the latter relationship could be investigated in the form:

$$\Delta P = g\,(\Delta X, \Delta Y, \Delta Z) \qquad (3)$$

To test for the independence of conduct or regulatory variables from those of the structural context, the following relationship would be further explored

$$\Delta Z = h\,(\Delta X, \Delta Y) \qquad (4)$$

Finally, it may be necessary to examine the nature of the relationship between a particular structural variable (usually concentration) and performance, to establish whether performance is linearly determined by concentration or if there are discontinuities in the relationship. The functional form adopted may be either a test of the slope of the function (i.e. significant differences in the size of the coefficient) or a description of its non-linear features, as follows:

$$P = f'(C, C^2, C^3) \qquad (5)$$

Both the linear discontinuity and the non-linear functional relationships are investigated in the following section.

Empirical Estimates

The empirical findings are derived from the results of estimates based on the functional relationships represented in equations 1, 2 and 5 above. An additional equation was used to assess the underlying determinants of the average wage per person employed.

Equations Estimated

Those equations estimated are listed below, with the variable codes for alternative measures omitted and without predetermining any expected sign for the explanatory variables.

$$\begin{aligned} CON &= a + bDIV + cMES + d && (1') \\ GSM &= a_1 + b_1CON + c_1CON^2 + d_1CON^3 + e_1 && (2') \\ GSM &= a_2 + b_2CON + c_2DIV + d_2MES + \\ &\quad e_3WPE + f_3TPE + g_3\,STK + h_3CAP + i_3 && (3') \\ WPE &= a_4 + b_4LFC + c_4LCA + d_4 && (4') \end{aligned}$$

In addition, further estimates were made to determine the role that 'high' or 'low' levels of concentration played in determining performance in relation to the other structural variables specified.

Where alternative measures of the variables were derived, they were tested for their effects in altering the estimated coefficients significantly. The results reported should also be interpreted in relation to the simple correlation coefficients for all variables generated and employed in the estimation procedures.[23] It should be noted that no suitable measures were available that could account for the effect on retail markets of conduct, regulation and protection. However, any independent influence arising from this source could be noticed in the extent to which sub-sample estimates provide a significantly different coefficient of determination – provided it is accepted that the model is adequately specified.

Concentration and General Market Structure

Several alternative measures of concentration, minimum efficient scale and diversification were constructed, with the objective of obtaining series that represent conditions prevailing in the overall structure of retail activities. The simple correlation coefficients, means and standard deviations for these measures are given in Table 7.2. On theoretical grounds, a *relative* measure of concentration (CONA) is to be preferred. The measure of concentration based on establishments (CONB), would indicate that, in this context, the size and number of establishments do not substantially alter the organisation measure of levels of concentration. An *absolute* measure of scale (MES) is more appropriate for entry barriers in retailing should entry be dependent on capital outlays for assets and goodwill. The diversification indices show a relatively high degree of correlation but with the *range* of commodities offered and the percentage of total sales accounted for by the *primary* commodity being less representative of output-mix concentration than the Herfindahl index (DIVH).

Regression estimates of the association of other general market structure variables with concentration (CONA only) are given below (with T-statistics in brackets):

$$\text{CONA} = \underset{(3.08)}{14.033} + \underset{(2.43)}{.001}\ \text{MES} + \underset{(1.72)}{16.437}\ \text{DIVH}$$

$\bar{R}^2 = 1.56$ and S.E.E. = 14.67. N = 46.

$$\text{CONA} = \underset{(3.84)}{18.454} + \underset{(.26)}{.634}\ \text{MESR} + \underset{(1.75)}{18.215}\ \text{DIVH}$$

$\bar{R}^2 = .026$ and S.E.E. = 15.75. N = 46.

Table 7.1: Concentration of Retail and Service Activities, 1968/9 (calculated as percentage of sales controlled by top 1% of enterprises)

1.	Department Stores	16.4
2.	Variety and General Stores	(66.4)
3.	Supermarkets	(22.6)
4.	Grocers and Tobacconists	(68.6)
5.	Butchers	(25.2)
6.	Fruit and Vegetable Stores	12.8
7.	Liquor Stores	6.1
8.	Confectionery and Soft Drink	9.0
9.	Fish, Chip, Hamburger Stores	11.4
10.	Bread and Cake Shops	14.7
11.	Bread Vendors	18.1
12.	Milk Vendors	(24.6)
13.	Furniture, Floor Coverings	(26.5)
14.	Fabrics, Household Textiles	20.4
15.	Men's and Boys' Wear	(32.7)
16.	Women's and Girls' Wear	(42.5)
17.	Footwear Shops	(33.4)
18.	Shoe Repairers	19.2
19.	Household Appliance	(32.9)
20.	Household Electrical Appliance	(37.5)
21.	China, Glassware, Hardware	(40.2)
22.	Watchmakers and Jewellers	(28.9)
23.	Musical Instrument, Records	(36.2)
24.	New Motor Vehicle Dealers	(45.6)
25.	Used Motor Vehicle Dealers	(21.6)
26.	Tyre and Battery Retailers	(60.2)
27.	Service Stations	9.1
28.	Smash Repair Workshops	11.3
29.	Motor Cycle Dealers	22.4
30.	Boat and Caravan Dealers	18.5
31.	Pharmacies	8.0
32.	Photographic Equipment Stores	14.3
33.	Sporting Goods, Bicycles, Toys	17.4
34.	Newsagents, Stationers	(32.0)
35.	Antique, Second-Hand Dealers	14.4
36.	Nurserymen and Florists	13.8
37.	Retailers N.E.C.	(30.5)
38.	Motion Picture Theatres	(46.2)
39.	Cafes and Restaurants	17.7
40.	Licensed Hotels, Motels etc.	(21.7)
41.	Licensed Bowling Clubs	4.5
42.	Licensed Golf Clubs	5.0
43.	Licensed Clubs N.E.C.	14.1
44.	Laundries, Dry Cleaners	(28.0)
45.	Men's Hairdressing, etc.	3.8
46.	Women's Hairdressing, etc.	16.3

( ) High concentration group. The sample has been divided into equal numbers of observations for the 'high' and 'low' groups.

Table 7.2: Simple Correlation Coefficients for General Structural Variables (N=46)

	CONA	CONB	CONC	MES	MESR	DIVR	DIVP	DIVH	Mean	Standard Deviation	Coefficient of variation
CONA	1.0000	.9324	.5035	.3684	.0000	.3615	–.2499	.2707	25.26	15.96	63.18
CONB		1.0000	.5839	.3268	.0366	.3694	–.3843	.3965	28.94	17.70	61.16
CONC			1.0000	.0637	.4428	–.0955	.1129	–.1024	12.61	11.92	94.53
MES				1.0000	.2975	.1086	–.0356	.0594	68,599.49	71,449.25	104.15
MESR					1.0000	.0115	.1539	–.1473	.5833	1.0273	176.12
DIVR						1.0000	–.7108	.7241	5.24	2.88	54.96
DIVP							1.0000	–.9812	75.25	22.67	30.13
DIVH								1.0000	.3533	.2425	68.64

These findings suggest that both the minimum efficient scale of retail outlets and the extent of product diversification are positively associated with concentration.

Performance and Concentration

Earlier studies of manufacturing industries estimated a simple linear relationship between measures of performance and levels of concentration. More recent studies have examined non-linear relationships and have made allowance for specification biases that may have been introduced by not taking account of other structural features affecting performance. The empirical estimates for equation 2′ are presented below using the relative concentration measure only in relation to the net margin measure of performance. Again, T-statistics are shown in brackets beneath the coefficient values. The results for CONB and CONC were substantially similar to those for CONA and are not reported. The $CONA^2$ and $CONA^3$ terms have not been scaled.

$$\begin{aligned} NMT &= \underset{(9.90)}{.276} - \underset{(-2.25)}{.002}\,CONA \\ &\bar{R}^2 = .083 \text{ and S.E.E.} = .100.\ N = 46. \\ NTM &= \underset{(5.45)}{.403} - \underset{(-2.14)}{.019}\,CONA + \underset{(1.89)}{.006}\,CONA^2 - \underset{(-1.82)}{.000005}\,CONA^3 \\ &\bar{R}^2 = .116 \text{ and S.E.E.} = .099.\ N = 46. \end{aligned}$$

The results obtained are contrary to theoretical expectations in that a negative coefficient is estimated for the linear relationship. The non-linear cubic function provides significant coefficients for all terms but suggests that profitability declines as concentration increases and that there is a range of concentration over which the relationship is positive before assuming a negative sign at the higher levels of concentration.

Several interpretations may be offered as an explanation for this tendency. First, it may be argued that the measure of performance is subject to errors which will systematically bias downwards (possibly non-linearly) the ‘true’ level of profitability. Secondly, it may be the case that the theoretical hypothesis is inappropriate in the case of retail competition, where the growth of sales or the maintenance of a market share of sales is the primary objective and where maximum profitability is a subsidiary aim. Thirdly, the relative freedom of entry and the existence of competitive conditions in both factor and goods markets may result in retail firms being unable to exercise market power to augment profitability. Finally, it is suggested that the low coefficient of determination points to an inadequate specification of other specific retail factor market conditions and methods of operation that are responsible for the variation in profitability.

Before proceeding to the estimates obtained for equations 3′ and 4′, it is possible to elaborate on the competitive mechanisms which may lead to this unexpected finding. The result suggests that if abnormal profits are earned, they accrue to those enterprises in markets where concentration is relatively low. This is not surprising if it represents the short-run market entry gaps that appear before adequate supply (entry) responds to compete away the above-long-run equilibrium returns. But the static theory of the profit-maximising firm also may be inadequate on other grounds.

If large enterprises maximise the rate of growth of sales [24] (or asset accumulation), through internal expansion and by takeover and merger, they may expand costs beyond the rate of growth of revenue and thereby erode current profits in an attempt to achieve a 'satisfactory' long-run rate of return. Using this objective function, it would be expected, therefore, that activities with the greatest increases in concentration would depress their profit performance.[25] Similarly, if advertising and R & D expenditure (e.g. on packaging, new product formulae etc.) is 'excessive' in relation to revenue generated in the short-run, these outlays will depress profit performance.[26] Alternatively, more concentrated activities may make a greater use of taxation advantages for deductible costs (which augment managers' real income through fringe benefits and better working conditions, while maintaining money income relativities) and thereby reduce *declared* profitability.[27] Finally, there may be evidence that administrative costs and 'control loss' are generated when attempting to manage large enterprises or a high share of the market and that these limit potential profitability.[28] These organisational costs are, in effect, dis-economies not represented at the plant size level and seldom measured in empirical studies.[29] Apart from these specific suggestions about the expected sign of the estimated relationship between profitability and performance in retailing, there will be other structural features that may contribute towards explaining some of the variation in performance.

Retail Market Structure and Factor Markets

The simple correlation coefficients of the performance variables with the retail market structure variables are shown in Table 7.3. These estimates suggest that no serious collinearity difficulties should arise that would bias the values of the coefficients in multiple regression

Table 7.3: Simple Correlation Coefficients for Performance and Retail Market Structure (N=46)

	GSM	NTM	WPE	LFC	LCA	TPE	STK	STKL	CAP	Mean	Standard Deviation	Coefficient of variation
GSM	1.0000	.9283	.0828	.0486	.0756	−.6495	−.2071	−.4082	.6779	34.36	13.93	40.54
NTM		1.0000	−.1395	−.0781	.1863	−.6490	−.1574	−.4319	.5948	21.20	8.15	38.44
WPE			1.0000	.5454	−.2428	.5201	.1267	.2615	.1989	1.5772	.5959	37.78
LFC				1.0000	−.1135	.3745	−.2613	.0752	−.0084	2.0572	1.8679	90.80
LCA					1.0000	−.1820	.4618	−.0162	−.3508	6.0314	6.1546	102.04
TPE						1.0000	.1432	−.4582	−.3446	14.4112	8.7046	60.40
STK							1.0000	−.2290	−.4355	.1076	.0841	78.16
STKL								1.0000	−.2797	26376	39733	150.64
CAP									1.0000	.0252	.0294	116.67

Table 7.4: Regression Estimates of Performance and Retail Market Structure (N=46)[a]

Dependent Variable	Constant Term	WPE	TPE	STK	STKL	CAP	CONA	MES	DIVH	$\bar{R}^2$	S.E.E.
GSM	.3262	.0933	–.0118	–.0041		1.6279				.717	.074
	(8.60)	(3.39)	(–6.19)	(–.03)		(2.92)					
NTM	.2326	.0033	–.0049	.1110		1.2791				.544	.055
	(8.25)	(.16)	(–3.42)	(.91)		(3.08)					
GSM	.3250	.0962	–.0113		–.0001	1.5405				.726	.073
	(9.70)	(3.72)	(–5.94)		(–1.08)	(3.19)					
NTM	.2434	.0115	–.0048		–.0001	1.0246				.545	.055
	(9.63)	(.59)	(–3.35)		(–.95)	(2.82)					
GSM	.3124	.0962	–.0105	.0232		1.6447	–.0009	–.0001	.0719	.732	.072
	(7.29)	(3.28)	(–5.14)	(.14)		(2.85)	(–1.07)	(–1.21)	(1.38)		
NTM	.2369	.0068	–.0045	.1351		1.2221	–.0008	–.0001	.0242	.535	.056
	(7.17)	(.30)	(–2.90)	(1.08)		(2.75)	(–1.26)	(–.35)	(.60)		
		LFC	LCA	TPE	STK	CAP					
GSM	.3012	.0236	.0036	–.0088	.2443	2.8971				.735	.072
	(7.47)	(3.34)	(1.55)	(–5.31)	(1.41)	(6.09)					
NTM	.1930	.0066	.0038	–.0044	.0592	1.5599				.623	.050
	(6.87)	(1.33)	(2.37)	(–3.79)	(.49)	(4.70)					

a. t-statistics are shown in brackets beneath the coefficient values.

estimates.

Table 7.4 provides the multiple regression results for equation 3′ using both performance variables. The top section of the table shows the results obtained for the retail market structure variables only, with separate estimates for the alternative inventory variable.

It is to be expected that the coefficient for *wages and salaries per person employed* (WPE) would be a significantly positive determinant of the gross margin performance measure, as wages and salaries are a component of the defined dependent variable. The *labour productivity* (TPE) coefficient is at all times significantly negatively related to both performance variables. This result suggests that lower sales per person is a determinant of higher profitability. Such a finding is attributable to two influences. First, service inputs in retailing are an integral part of the distribution process and this measure of productivity merely reflects the differences in 'service' levels available (but possibly underutilised) among activities.[30] Secondly, this variable reflects the different pricing policies adopted by retail organisations in different branches of activity and shows that, where mark-ups are varied to augment sales in relation to labour inputs, the margins achieved are lowered (as a percentage of sales) but the amount of profit available to meet capital costs and managerial and/or shareholder payments is satisfactory. In summary, the finding for this variable is no more than a reflection of differences in service levels adopted (non-price competition) and the mixture of trading objectives in expanding market shares by price competition.

The two remaining variables depict conditions relating to working capital – as represented by inventories – and fixed capital outlays (i.e. plant and equipment and land and buildings). While both *inventories as a percentage of sales* (STK) and the *level of stockholding* (STKL) are negatively related to performance variables, neither provide significant coefficients. This may be in part due to the diversity of stockholding practices adopted within kinds of business. But even so, high levels of inventories, if associated with fixed costs of storage and display, can be expected to reduce net margins as suggested by the sign for this coefficient.

The capital intensity (CAP) coefficient can be interpreted in two ways. Either a lower index (through the utilisation of capacity) can be expected to leave little of the product revenue available for distribution as profits or a higher capital-output ratio may indicate that higher factor rewards are necessary to keep capital resources in this particular activity independently of their degree of utilisation. Neither interpretation can be tested empirically due to the problems of measuring capital composition and vintage and of being unable to establish the dynamic connections between product pricing and investment behaviour within the context of a cross-sectional study. All that can be concluded is that in Australian retailing activities, capital intensity is positively (and significantly) associated with gross and net margins.[31]

The lower section of Table 7.4 shows the results of (a) combining the general market structure variables with the retail market structure variables and (b) the separate estimation of the *labour/capital ratio* (LCA) and *labour force composition* (LFC) variables implicit in the wage rate (WPE) variable (i.e. equation 4′).

It can be readily seen that the set of general market structure variables adds very little to the overall explanation of variation in performance and that the signs and sizes of the coefficients are stable. This suggests that the particular factor market and cost structure conditions of the retail activities may be of greater significance in determining performance than measures of market power, scale economies or strategies of diversification. But any concluding interpretation of these respective roles is deferred until the discussion of the 'high' and 'low' concentration groups.

Determinants of the Wage Rate

Wages per person employed are in part influenced by labour force composition, the labour/capital ratio and labour productivity. The respective strengths of these determinants of the wage rate, as expressed in equation 4′, are shown below and can be read in conjunction with the lower section of Table 7.4.

$$\begin{aligned} \text{WPE} &= \underset{(5.93)}{1.052} + \underset{(2.99)}{.128}\ \text{LFC} - \underset{(-1.06)}{.013}\ \text{LCA} + \underset{(2.55)}{.024}\ \text{TPE} \\ \bar{R}^2 &= .384 \text{ and S.E.E.} = .467.\ \text{N} = 46. \end{aligned}$$

Under the prevailing conditions of unequal pay for female employees in 1968/9, it is to be expected that the higher the proportion of males in the labour force for a kind of business, the higher would be the wage per person employed. Also, it may be expected that the larger is the labour force in relation to fixed capital expenditure for an activity, the lower would be the factor rewards to labour per person employed. But this result depends in part on the fact that the labour force comprises a greater number of part-time and less skilled operatives. Otherwise, increased capital substitution for labour may require, on balance, higher factor rewards to attract complementary skills. Alternatively, greater capital intensity in any retail activity may also lead to a shift in the function of employment towards administrative and technical personnel rather than 'selling' personnel whose function is superceded by a self-service technology and media (i.e. 'pre-selling') promotion.

High and Low Concentration and Structural Variables

By breaking the total sample of observations into two groups of 'high' and 'low' concentration it is possible to ascertain (a) whether the average level of concentration, in conjunction with other retail market variables, affects performance differently and (b) which retail market variables, if any, largely determine performance variation in the different concentration regimes.

Table 7.5 provides the means, standard deviations and coefficients of variation for the two samples of observations. The average level of concentration for the 'high' groups is almost 36 per cent while for the 'low' group it is below 13 per cent. The average minimum efficient scale of outlet for the former group is over three times that for the 'low' concentration group, but the average degree of diversification does not differ greatly.

In the case of the retail market structure variables, both the means and standard deviations generally differ quite markedly between the two concentration groups. This suggests that the mechanisms explaining differences in performance may operate quite distinctively. Table 7.6 shows regression estimates for both groups according to the general market structure variables by themselves and then along with the retail market structure variables. For the 'high' concentration group, the general market structure variables do play some role. The concentration variable (CONA) is significantly and negatively related to performance. This perhaps confirms that retail activities with relatively high levels of concentration maximise the growth of their market shares rather than current period profitability and that the competitive strategies required for this process result in some cost elements accumulating at a faster rate than marginal revenue.

A consideration of the comparative role of retail market structure variables highlights which particular variables this revenue maximisation process may operate through. Without data on advertising outlays and changes in demand, any such interpretation is limited. The only significant variable in the 'low' concentration group is that depicting labour productivity, while for the high concentration group, those variables

Table 7.5: Means and Standard Deviations for 'High' and 'Low' Concentration Activities

Variable	High concentration (N=23)			Low concentration (N=23)			Total sample (N=46)		
	Mean	St.dev.	Coeff.V.	Mean	St.dev.	Coeff.V.	Mean	St.dev.	Coeff.V.
GSM	32.33	15.25	41.31	40.82	18.39	45.05	34.36	13.93	40.54
NTM	18.93	7.82	47.17	25.66	11.85	46.18	21.20	8.15	38.44
CONA	35.93	13.70	38.14	12.88	5.00	38.87	25.26	15.96	63.18
MES	94272	83784	88.87	28014	30339	108.30	68599	71449	104.15
DIVH	.4071	.2767	67.97	.3668	.2476	67.50	.3533	.2425	68.64
WPE	1.7855	.5336	29.88	1.3601	.5923	43.55	1.5772	.5959	37.78
TPE	16.51	9.11	55.22	11.29	7.67	67.92	14.41	8.70	60.37
STK	12.56	8.67	69.03	7.87	7.21	91.61	10.76	8.41	78.16
STKL	40245	47691	118.50	15496	33751	217.80	26376	39733	150.64
CAP	.0196	.0182	92.86	.0312	.0351	112.50	.0252	.0294	116.67
LFC	2.0671	1.9010	91.96	1.9692	2.0222	102.69	2.0572	1.8679	90.80
LCA	6.1101	7.4449	121.85	6.3720	4.5169	70.89	6.0314	6.1546	102.04

Table 7.6: Regression Estimates for High and Low Concentration Activities (N=23)[a]

Dependent Variable	Concentration Level	Constant Term	CONA	MES	DIVH	WPE	TPE	STK	CAP	$\bar{R}^2$	S.E.E.
GSM		.3743	–.0018	–.0001	.1904					.162	.140
	High	(4.14)	(–.78)	(–1.89)	(1.68)						
NTM		.2313	–.0007	–.0001	.0365					.019	.077
		(4.61)	(–.59)	(–1.60)	(.58)						
GSM		.1994	–.0021	–.0001	.0543	.0774	–.0070	.3882	5.8514	.810	.066
	High	(2.38)	(–1.83)	(–.48)	(.92)	(2.14)	(–2.64)	(1.81)	(4.68)		
NTM		.1381	–.0012	.0001	–.0190	.0051	–.0022	.3923	3.922	.802	.035
		(3.14)	(–2.02)	(.36)	(–.61)	(.27)	(–1.58)	(3.48)	(5.98)		
GSM		.5117	–.0081	–.0001	.0944					–.044	.188
	Low	(3.51)	(–1.00)	(–.83)	(.55)						
NTM		.3667	–.0062	–.0001	–.0058					–.036	.121
		(3.91)	(–1.19)	(–1.09)	(–.05)						
GSM		.4930	.0001	–.0001	.0140	.0077	–.0154	–.3245	1.0564	.425	.139
	Low	(3.50)	(.01)	(–.93)	(.09)	(.84)	(–2.59)	(–.61)	(.66)		
NTM		.3982	–.0024	–.0001	–.0143	–.0180	–.0077	–.008	.8022	.212	.105
		(3.74)	(–.47)	(–.74)	(–.12)	(–.26)	(–1.72)	(–.02)	(.66)		

a. t-statistics are shown in brackets beneath the coefficient values.

depicting outlays for inventory and fixed asset acquisition are of key importance. Table 7.7, showing the retail market structure variables only, with the wage rate variable (WPE) replaced by the labour force composition variable (LFC) and the labour/capital ratio (LCA) provides some interesting contrasts in explaining performance for the two groups. The 'high' concentration group shows that performance is determined through the stock purchasing and asset formation variables. This suggests that bulk purchasing (STK) behaviour and retail outlet location and development (CAP) confer performance advantages to this group. For the 'low' concentration group, performance is determined more by their management of labour resources (LCA) and capital assets (CAP). Therefore, it is possible that where the 'service' component is a larger element of output, profitability depends upon the aspects of non-price competition and quality management, while for predominantly 'goods' activities, competition is reflected through inventory policies and, possibly, advertising outlays.[32]

Conclusions

This study has investigated the determinants of performance and the relationships between performance, concentration and other market structure variables. Contrary to the findings of overseas studies for manufacturing industries, it has found that concentration was not a significantly positive determinant of retail and service activity performance in the period 1968/9 in Australia. Indeed, in the case of 'high' concentration activities, the reverse appeared to be the case. The possible theoretical explanations for this empirical relationship have been discussed and will not be repeated. However, in addition to these reasons, it also may be the case that the level of concentration in retail activities is not yet sufficient high, as a historical trend in this country, to permit the market power effects of seller concentration, as postulated by theory, to hold. Alternatively, it may be argued that it is buyer concentration features, with associated pecuniary economies and X-inefficiency, which operate through factor markets that are of more significance in Australian retailing and service activities. In the product market it is always possible for a diversified product or service mix – that meets demand conditions – to be offered by any potential or existing rival. Therefore, evidence of trade practices or conduct that result in discrimination in factor price negotiation may be of more importance as a measure of anti-competitive behaviour than a measure of the current market share held.[33] The study has several limitations. The omission of a separate demand variable in the estimated relation-

Table 7.7: Retail Market Structure and Levels of Concentration (N=23)[a]

Dependent Variable	Concentration Level	Constant Term	LFC	LCA	TPE	STK	CAP	$\bar{R}^2$	S.E.E.
GSM	High	.1602	.0176	.0037	−.0053	.4073	7.2099	.768	.073
		(2.00)	(1.61)	(1.40)	(−2.00)	(1.55)	(5.46)		
NTM		.0753	.0055	.0028	−.0019	.2959	4.0579	.826	.033
		(2.11)	(1.14)	(2.35)	(−1.58)	(2.54)	(6.91)		
GSM	Low	.1723	.0124	.0254	−.0055	−.0394	3.6966	.727	.096
		(1.76)	(1.07)	(3.40)	(−1.43)	(−.12)	(4.36)		
NTM		.0529	.0070	.0219	−.0016	−.0546	2.3115	.757	.058
		(.89)	(.99)	(4.84)	(−.67)	(−.26)	(4.49)		

a. t-statistics are given in brackets beneath the coefficient values.

ships (even if partly determined by a reaction function to advertising outlays) provides cause for concern, particularly should profitability be dynamically determined by a lagged relationship between market gaps appearing (i.e. at a faster rate than anticipated) and new entrants taking up the supply slack.[34] In addition, a lack of data for variables representing *changes* in structure and the *average* performance record of retail activities over time may have resulted in a failure to adequately specify and measure the underlying economic relationships.[35]

Despite the above findings and their limitations, some further research perspectives and the need for improved data sources are suggested. It would be useful to undertake further analysis of the relevance of various managerial theories of the firm to retailing and service activites. It also would be instructive to focus on the determinants of retail buyer concentration in relation to manufacturing concentration, advertising and promotional expenditures, access to self-service technology and the availability of new retail site developments. Further study of the supply side relationships between factor proportions and prices would also be helpful. Similarly, the conditions governing the extension and use of consumer credit facilities may in part determine demand differences among retail activities.

There are serious data deficiencies in many areas of retail cost structure; namely, packaging, energy, transport, advertising and R & D costs at retail levels. There is no data available on retail capacity (i.e. selling/non-selling areas) or the vintage of capital by kinds of business. The labour force data does not distinguish administrative personnel from sales floor operatives and provides no information that would allow any standardisation for hours worked. It is also to be regretted that data on methods of organisation (e.g. self-service etc.) and form of ownership (e.g. partnership etc.) is not provided by Census authorities. These classifications would allow more detailed tests for what are partially contradictory influences that may be reducing the variation to be explained at an aggregate level of performance or market structure feature.

Appendix 7.1: Derivation and Source of Variables Used

a. Performance variables

GSM - *Gross margin* or value added (percentage) in output, measured as turnover less the cost of sales divided by turnover.

NTM = *Net margin* (percentage), measured as gross margin or value added less wages and salaries divided by turnover.

b. Structural variables

(i) General market structure

CON(A/B/C) = *Concentration* measured as (A) the percentage market share controlled by the top 1 per cent of *enterprises* (by interpolation from largest 4 enterprises group), (B) percentage market share controlled by the top 1 per cent of *establishments* and (C) percentage market share controlled by top four *enterprises.*

MES(R) = *Minimum efficient scale* of establishment measured as the absolute $ size of an establishment accounting for ⩾ 50 per cent of sales or the relative size (R), as above, divided by turnover.

DIV(H/R/P) = *Diversification* index measured as the Herfindahl index (H)[a], range of commodities.

(ii) Retail market structure

LFC = *Labour force composition,* measured as the ratio of male to female employees.

LCA = *Labour to capital ratio,* measured as the ratio of current fixed capital expenditure to total persons employed.

CAP = *Capital intensity index,* measured as current fixed capital expenditure as a percentage of turnover.

TPE = *Labour productivity,* measured as turnover per person employed.

WPE = *Average wage per employee,* measured as the wages and salaries bill divided by total persons employed.

STK(L) = *Stock-turnover and level,* measured as beginning plus end stock levels ÷ 2(L) and expressed as a percentage of turnover.

a. Defined as $1-\sum_{i=1}^{n} P_i^2$, where P_i is the proportion of total retail sales accounted for by the ith commodity traded.

Sources: *Industry Concentration Statistics details by Industry Class.* Australian Bureau of Statistics, Canberra, Reference No.17.14, 1974. *Retail Establishments and Selected Service Establishments: Final Bulletin* Part 2 Australian Bureau of Statistics, Canberra Reference No.11.22 1974 and Part 3 Reference No.11.23.

Notes:

* I thank participants at seminars at the Australian National University and at the University of Adelaide for their comments on earlier drafts of this study. David Round, Fred Gruen and Glenn Withers made a number of useful suggestions that led me to attempt to clarify several aspects of interpretation. Roger Rose and Wayne Naughton assisted with data collection and statistical computation.

1. *Policies for Development of Manufacturing Industry,* Vols. I-IV Canberra, 1975-6.
2. *Passenger Motor Vehicles, etc.* Industries Assistance Commission Report, Canberra, 10 July 1974.
3. Subsequent discussion of the Jackson Report has focused almost exclusively on the possible resource allocation relationships of manufacturing with agriculture or mining and has largely ignored manufacturers' decision-making connections with importers, retailers or transport agencies.
4. Three of the principal government agencies concerned with competition policy are described in John P. Niewenhuysen and Neville R. Norman, *Australian Competition and Prices Policy* (Croom Helm, 1976). Unfortunately, this discussion of the respective policy roles of the Trade Practices Commission, the Industries Assistance Commission (previously the Tariff Board), and the Prices Justification Tribunal, does not provide any analysis of the impact or dynamic effects of public intervention on retail structure or performance. Indeed, the agencies themselves appear to consider their brief as only peripherally related to retail markets insofar as they follow up issues *originating* in manufacturing. Only the Prices Justification Tribunal has considered variations in retail prices, but as a variable to be controlled and not as one to be explained by reference to structural conditions. Specific investigations of trade practices, levels of assistance and prices increasingly require these bodies to remedy their comparative ignorance in this field.
5. For example, the only mention in H.D. Evans, *A General Equilibrium Analysis of Protection: The Effects of Protection in Australia* (North-Holland, 1972) of retail markets is in determining the inventory and consumption relationships over the planning period (p.74). No changes or differences in structure are allowed for. The gains from free trade are surely conditional on the bargaining power and administrative efficiency of large retail groups. Indeed, what do the conventional demand elasticities mean without considering the price-setting conditions in retail markets? Similarly, in P.J. Lloyd, *Non-tariff Distortions of Australian Trade* (Australian National University Press, 1973) there is no recognition of retail structure influencing the nature and impact of distortion costs (pp.135-65). The only published study of the retail sector as a whole for Australia is in F.G. Davidson and B.R. Stewardson, *Economics and Australian Industry* (Longman, 1973) Chapter 6. Here the indebtedness to financial journalists and industry spokesmen is all too apparent. Despite its title, K. Sheridan, *The Firm in Australia* (Nelson, 1974) only deals with growth, size and profitability for manufacturing firms.
6. For a study of manufacturer and retailer structural relationships in the US see M.E. Porter, 'Consumer Behaviour, Retailer Power and Market Performance in Consumer Goods Industries', *The Review of Economics and Statistics,* vol.LVI, no.4 (November, 1974) pp.419-36. F.H. Gruen, 'Food Marketing in the United States – a Review Article', *Review of Marketing and Agricultural Economics,* vol.36, no.2 (June, 1968) pp.55-7 provides an appraisal of the structure/performance relationships of food production-distribution activities as investigated by the National Commission on Food Marketing. For the UK a

study of cost and size relationships is reported in K.A. Tucker, *Economies of Scale in Retailing: an empirical study of plant size and cost structure* (Saxon House/Lexington Books 1975).

7. See Chapter 1 for further information on sectoral shares and growth rates.
8. Reprinted in K.A. Tucker and B.S. Yamey (eds.), *Economics of Retailing* (Penguin, 1973) p.7.
9. For a stimulating article exploring the economic trade-offs involved in the adoption of an appropriate 'image' see W.J. Baumol, 'Calculation of optimal product and retailer characteristics: the abstract product approach', reprinted in K.A. Tucker and B.S. Yamey (eds.), *op.cit.* p.275-88.
10. Ibid. p.20
11. Not only has there been a tendency to expand by acquisition and takeover among retail groups, but this has been reinforced by internal expansion whereby the large retail chains each acquire representation in suburban shopping centres.
12. It is usual for this static analysis to postulate increasing returns to scale over the relevant output range of the demand function.
13. The *effect* of concentration on performance if the resulting market power were not exercised or were effectively counter-balanced would be insignificant in any empirical testing. The interpretation of the *causes* of concentration would probably require a simultaneous equations model that included the determinants of changes in performance. It is not the purpose of this chapter to estimate the determinants of levels of concentration or to forecast the effects of changes in concentration on performance over time.
14. This 'margin' is to be distinguished from the 'mark-up' which is the percentage added to the acquisition cost of final goods at the retail level to determine their selling price.
15. These items of post-tax income equivalents will not bias measures of corporate profitability greatly unless (a) these practices differ markedly between firms or industries and (b) the marginal tax rates for personal income are significantly above company taxation rates.
16. For attempts to account for some of these 'opportunity cost' and centralised administration costs in studies of manufacturing and retailing activities see Daryl N. Winn, *Industrial Market Structure and Performance 1960-1968* (University of Michigan, 1975) Appendix D pp.200-17 and K.A. Tucker, *Economies of Scale in Retailing: an empirical study of plant size and cost structure* (Saxon House/Lexington Books, 1975) Chapter 8 pp.147-71.
17. Rather than profitability being a function of advertising, with $\frac{\partial P}{\partial A} > 0$, the reverse causation applies, with $\frac{\partial P}{\partial A} < 0$. For a full discussion of these possible relationships see K. Cowling *et al*, *Advertising and Economic Behaviour* (Macmillan, 1975) and R. Schmalensee, *The Economics of Advertising* (North-Holland, 1973).
18. For a recent exposition see Stanley I. Ornstein, 'Empirical Uses of the Price-Cost Margin', *Journal of Industrial Economics* (December 1975) pp.105-17.
19. This would be true even where seller concentration was not high but buyer concentration was increasing relative to manufacturing concentration.
20. These kinds of business obviously do not represent *product* markets in a theoretical sense, where the goods are near-substitutes in demand. But a separate variable measuring diversification is included to account for this feature of retail markets. It would be expected that differences in levels of convenience or service supplied will be reflected in variables representing factor market or operating conditions.
21. It is not possible therefore to evaluate the effects on profits of advertising or

to consider directly the countervailing (i.e. relative buyer concentration) power of retail groups in relation to manufacturer or importers.

22. See the survey by B.S. Yamey, 'Do Monopoly and Near-monopoly matter? a survey of empirical studies' in M.H. Peston and B.C. Corry (eds.), *Essays in Honour of Lord Robbins* (Weidenfield, 1972) pp.290-323, L.W. Weiss, 'Quantitative Studies of Industrial Organisation' in M.D. Intriligator (ed.) *Frontiers of Quantitative Economics* (North Holland, 1971) Ch.9, and J.M. Vernon, *Market Structure and Industrial Performance: a review of statistical findings* (Allyn and Bacon, 1972). For a study of US food processing industries using this methodology see Blake Imel, Michael R. Behr and Peter G. Helmberger, *Market Structure and Performance* (Lexington, 1972), and for a review of food marketing activities F.H. Gruen, op.cit.
23. The zero-order correlation matrix for all general market structure variables considered is presented in Table 7.2, while that for performance and retail market structure variables is given in Table 7.3.
24. This formulation of the firm's objective function was first suggested by W.J. Baumol, 'On the Theory of Expansion of the Firm', *American Economic Review* (December, 1962) pp.1078-87, J. Williamson, 'Profit, Growth and Sales Maximisation', *Economica* (February, 1966) pp.1-16 and R. Marris, *The Economic Theory of 'Managerial' Capitalism* (Macmillan, 1964).
25. This hypothesis must be tested in the form $\Delta P=f(\Delta C)$ with the expectation that $\frac{\partial P}{\partial C} < 0$.
26. For studies that relate to advertising expenditure by both manufacturers and retail firms see M.M. Metwally, 'Advertising and Competitive Behaviour of Selected Australian Firms' *Review of Economics and Statistics* (November, 1975) pp.417-27 and 'Profitability of Advertising in Australia: A Case Study', *Journal of Industrial Economics* vol.XXIV, no.3 (March, 1976) pp.221-31.
27. For a study of executive remuneration where the causative influences operate in the reverse direction see Geoffrey Meeks and Geoffrey Whittington, 'Directors' Pay, Growth and Profitability', *The Journal of Industrial Economics,* vol.XXIV, no.1 (September, 1975) pp.1-14.
28. See O.E. Williamson, 'Hierarchical Control and Optimum Firm Size', *Journal of Political Economy,* vol.75 (April, 1967) pp.128-38, for this organisational diseconomy and Harvey Leibenstein, 'Allocative Efficiency vs. "X-Efficiency" ', *American Economic Review* (1966) pp.392-415.
29. For an approach that reallocates centralised cost back to the level of the plant in estimating cost functions see K.A. Tucker, op.cit. Ch.8.
30. Higher levels of labour in relation to sales are a type of fixed cost that must be recovered by higher margins to meet factor payments and to generate a risk premium to cover seasonal or cyclical demand changes.
31. A recent article on manufacturing industries shows that variations in price-cost margins for industries are largely attributable to capital-sales ratios. See Stanley I. Ornstein, op.cit.
32. These findings and tentative interpretations suggest that some method of distinguishing 'convenience', 'shopping' and 'specialty' goods or of obtaining an independent measure of service levels would allow further exploration of the determinants of performance. Should these differing outlet attributes influence demand over time then a single equation approach is probably inadequate.
33. This proposition could only be tested adequately if it were possible to obtain, for example, a measure of the extent to which an activity was subject to resale price maintenance.
34. This process would result in identification problems and the 'supply' coeffi-

cients would be biased.

35. The generally high coefficients of determination cannot be relied upon with any certainty if there are identity relationships between some of the structure measures and the performance variables. For a general comment on some of these problems see Almarin Phillips, 'A Critique of Empirical Studies of Relations Between Market Structure and Profitability' *The Journal of Industrial Economics,* vol.XXIV, no.4 (June, 1976) pp.241-49.

PART THREE: ADVISORY AND FINANCIAL SERVICES

As the division of tasks in an economy becomes more specialised and as transactions are expressed more frequently in monetary units, services proliferate for the provision of technical expertise and welfare consultation. In some cases, services to improve product or process design and organisational efficiency are made available almost exclusively to corporations or government agencies. For other services, the individual or household may require representation, support or facilities to serve a number of social or economic purposes.

Tisdell (chapter 8) provides information about agencies supplying research and development services in relation to sources of funds, types of service and the nature of users. He also considers the ways in which the benefits of this effort may accumulate and some problems of allocating resources to these pursuits. An addendum by McLean and Round provides some preliminary results on the pattern of R & D expenditure by firm size for types of manufacturing activity.

Legal services are available for the settlement of conflicting claims in many economic and community contexts. Vinson, Homel and Bonney (chapter 9) have studied the spatial distribution of access to these services in relation to those supplied by doctors and dentists and by reference to a set of socio-economic variables that contribute towards the existing inequality of this provision.

Rutledge (chapter 10) discusses the types of service provided by banking and insurance organisations and the structure of these activities. He provides estimates of household demand for these services using, as explanatory variables, income, family size and stage in the family life cycle.

8 RESEARCH AND DEVELOPMENT SERVICES

C.A. Tisdell

The level of R & D expenditure in Australia in the 1950s and 1960s as a percentage of GNP was lower than in most industrialised countries [2, 23, 27, 36]. Government dominated R & D activity in the early 60s. It supplied, according to Clark's [21] estimates, 85 per cent of R & D funds and used 70 per cent of national research funds in its performance of R & D. The share of research services (per cent of GERD, gross national expenditure on R & D) supplied by business enterprises was only 13 per cent and the higher education sector accounted for 17 per cent of GERD. Research and development intensities for agricultural activities were higher than those for manufacturing [28] with research for the former being principally supplied by government. Those R & D services undertaken for manufacturing were mostly supplied by business enterprises themselves, and foreign controlled firms and large firms accounted for the lion's share.

Although comparisons of Australian R & D effort between years are hazardous because R & D has been evaluated by altering procedures, statistics for 1973/4 indicate that the pattern of Australian R & D effort has apparently changed in some respects. Relatively, the Australian R & D effort no longer seems so low; the government is undertaking comparatively less R & D and business enterprises more. The proportion of R & D funded by government has also declined. Research intensities for manufacturing industry have risen and have declined for agriculture. The supply of R & D services in manufacturing industry continues to be dominated by foreign-controlled firms and by large firms.

In 1973/4, the latest year for which statistics are available, Australia's gross domestic expenditure on R & D amounted to 1.3 per cent of GNP. This was much the same as in 1968/9, 1.23 per cent, and about 25 per cent higher than for 1964/5. While Australia maintained its ratio of GERD to GDP during the late 60s and early 70s, this ratio declined markedly in many other countries, e.g. USA, UK, France, Canada, so that in 1973/4 the Australian effort appeared relatively more significant than in the early 60s. However, the ratio may have been declining by 1976 in Australia due to the effects of the current recession on business enterprises, the policy of the Australian

Government of curbing the growth of the public sector and restraints on funding for universities.

Table 8.1: GERD as a percentage of GNP in selected OECD Countries 1973/4 (unless otherwise stated)

USA	2.4 (1972/3)	Canada	1.1
UK	2.1 (1972/3)	Norway	1.1 (1972)
Germany	2.0 (1973)	Austria	1.0 (1971)
Netherlands	1.8	Denmark	1.0
France	1.7 (1973)	New Zealand	0.9
Japan	1.7	Finland	0.8
Sweden	1.6 (1973)	Ireland	0.7
Australia	1.3	Portugal	0.3
Belgium	1.2 (1972)	Spain	0.3

Sources: *The OECD Observer* No.80, March-April, 1976, and Department of Science, 'Preliminary Statistics for Project SCORE, 1973-74', Canberra, 1976.

In 1974/4, 53,794 Australians, 0.9 per cent of the workforce, were employed to provide R & D services. Thus almost as many persons were employed in this endeavour as were employed in the Australian chemical industry.

The sources of R & D funds and their allocation in 1968/9 and 1973/4 are summarised in Table 8.2. Because of statistical variations in surveys, comparisons between the years must be treated cautiously but a number of general observations can be made. The apparent position of the Australian Government in generating research services declined sharply between the surveys and that of the business enterprise sector rose considerably. In 1973/4 research undertaken by the business sector exceeded that for the Australian Government – a reversal of the previous position. The Government R & D supply failed to keep pace with the growth of GDP whereas the opposite was the case for business enterprises. It also seems clear that the relative decline in the supply of R & D services was greater for the Australian Government than for State Governments.

However, the decline in the proportion of R & D performed by the Government and the rise in that performed by the business sector may be more apparent than real. The Project SCORE Business Enterprise Survey of 1968/9 was confined to mining and manufacturing enterprises and limited to firms thought likely to perform R & D whereas in 1973/4 an attempt, by sampling was made to obtain an unbiased estimate of R & D for all industries. The business enterprise estimate for 1968/9 would need to be revised upwards, by an unknown amount, to be comparable to that for 1973/4. Furthermore, in 1968/9 the Commonwealth Government results included a number of R & D programmes which would have been excluded by the criteria used in 1973/4. Nevertheless, taking account of such complications, there still seems to have been some decline in the proportion of R & D performed by the Government and a rise in that undertaken by business enterprises.

Table 8.2: Intramural supply of R & D Services in Australia and Sources of Funds for 1968-9 and 1973-4[a]

	Funds Spent on R & D			Funds Provided for R & D		
	1973/4		1968/9	1973/4		1968/9
	$m.	Per cent	Per cent	$m.	Per cent	Per cent
Australian Government	201.6	30.7	42	351.7	53.5	52
State Governments	*73.4*	*11.3*	*13*	*63.7*	*9.7*	*17*
Total Government	275.0	42.0	55	425.4	63.2	69
Private Non-Profit	5.9	0.9	<1	7.3	1.1	1
Business Enterprise	228.2	34.7	25	222.3	33.9	25
Higher Education	148.1	22.5	20	0.3	0.0	2
Overseas	–	–	–	11.8	1.8	3
Total[b]	657.3	100.0	100.0	657.3	100.0	100.0

Notes:
a. Note that the basis of estimates for 1968-9 and 1973-4 differ. See text.
b. Do not sum exactly because of rounding.
Sources: Based on Department of Science, 'Preliminary Tables for Project SCORE 1973-4', Canberra, 1976, and Department of Science, *Project Score: Research and Development in Australia,* Report No.5, Australian Government Publishing Service, Canberra, 1973.

Although the government's role as a provider of R & D services was slightly reduced in 1973/4 compared to 1968/9, the government still provided almost two-thirds of the funds used for R & D in the economy. The proportion of gross R & D funds supplied by business enterprises rose from one-quarter to a little over one-third. Flows of research funds between sectors were not strong, except from the Government to the Higher Education sector.

Let us consider each sector for 1973/4 in more detail, dealing with the business enterprise sector last. The government sector undertook, on an expenditure basis, 42 per cent of R & D in the economy and financed 63 per cent of R & D activity. About one-quarter of total government research was undertaken by the States and three-quarters by the Australian Government. Approximately only 5 per cent of government-supplied research was financed by business enterprises. These funds came mainly from agricultural enterprises compulsorily levied under various agricultural levy schemes.

Table 8.3, which breaks down government research and development services into a classification of main purposes, indicates that the principle objective is economic development. This component received 57.1 per cent of funds used, of which R & D services for the economic development of primary industry (excluding mining) is dominant. At the State Government level, services for the development of primary industry is the main objective. National security (defence) is the goal allocated the second largest share of funds, 28 per cent. This contrasts with the position in countries such as the USA, France and UK where research service inputs for defence purposes received a larger share. Research services for community welfare receive the smallest share of funds, if research for the advancement of science is excluded.

Table 8.3: Government Expenditure on R & D in 1973/4 Classificed by Purpose

Category	Expenditure by Australian Govt.		Expenditure by State Govt.		Total Government Expenditure	
	$'000	Per cent	$'000	Per cent	$'000	Per cent
Primary Industry[a]	39,154	19.4	47,296	64.4	86,450	31.4
Secondary Industry[b]	25,726	12.8	5,768	7.8	31,494	11.5
Economic Services	26,350	13.1	8.990	12.2	35,330	12.8
Other	3,196	1.6	–	–	3,196	1.2
Economic Development	94,426	47	62,054	84.4	156,480	56.9
National Security (Defence)	56,487	28	–	0	56,487	20.5
Community Welfare	22,510	11	10,132	13.8	32,642	11.9
Advancement of Science	28,138	14	1,308	1.8	29,446	10.7
Total	201,561	100	73,494	100	275,055	100

Notes: a. Excludes mining. b. Includes mining.
Sources: Based on Department of Science, 'Preliminary Tables for Project SCORE 1973-4', Canberra, 1976.

In Australia, private non-profit organisations provide a small fraction of total research. Their expenditures are less than 1 per cent of GERD. A significant proportion of their funds are used to fund research by higher educational institutions. Most of their own research is for socio-economic purposes and improvements in health are a prime objective.

Research in the higher education sector was financed 95.1 per cent by the Australian Government, 0.8 per cent by private non-profit organisations, 1.4 per cent by business enterprises and 0.6 per cent from overseas. The business enterprise contribution was small, much of it flowing from agricultural industries under research levy schemes [30]. Little collective research is funded by manufacturing industry, possibly because firms cannot be assured of monopoly-profits from such research [9].

As observed earlier, the relative importance of the business sector as a provider of R & D services has increased and in 1973/4 about one-third of all expenditure on R & D was by business enterprises. Approximately 80 per cent of this research was undertaken by manufacturing firms. Government funding of business research through contracts and subsidies amounted to 8.3 per cent of their total expenditure on R & D. Most of this support was derived from industrial research and development grants, first introduced in 1967 to encourage increased R & D by business firms [26]. Government contracts were of minor importance as a source of business enterprise R & D funds – they amounted to less than 0.07 per cent of the total. The extent to which Government research is contracted out to business enterprises is much less in Australia than in countries like the USA and the UK. Where there are adequate facilities and expertise, there may be spin-off benefits and possibly cost-savings to be derived from increasing the extent to which government research contracts are let to business enterprises and other sectors of the economy, including universities.

Because manufacturing industry takes up such a large share of R & D conducted by business enterprises, its effort should be analysed in some detail. The distribution of R & D effort among various manufacturing industries is indicated in Table 8.4, together with measures of the intensity of the research effort of these industries. R & D expenditure in fabricated metal products and transport equipment amounted to more than half of manufacturers' expenditure on R & D. Together with chemicals and basic metal products, these industries accounted for more than three-quarters (78.1 per cent) of R & D performed by manufacturers.

Just how one should measure the research intensities of industries is

Table 8.4: R & D Expenditure by Australian Manufacturing Industries 1973-4 and Measures of their Research Intensity

Industry	Expenditure on R & D $m.	Percent of Total R & D Expenditure by Manufacturing Industry	R & D Expenditure per Person Employed in the Industry $	Fraction of R & D Expenditure per Person Employed in Industry to Average for Manufacturing	R & D Expenditure of R & D Performing Enterprises on a Percentage of their Turnover[a]	R & D Professional Employees per 1,000 Employees (All Enterprises)	Last Column Divided by R & D Professional Employees per 1,000 Employees in Manufacturing, 3.8
Fabricated Metal Products	55.6	30.4	174.31	1.00	1.5	5.3	1.4
Transport Equipment	53.0	29.0	482.22	2.76	2.3	5.1	1.3
Chemicals	19.5	10.7	348.66	2.00	1.2	17.5	4.6
Other Manufacturing	15.6	8.5	68.46	0.39	0.9	1.9	0.5
Basic Metal Products	14.6	8.0	143.34	0.82	0.6	4.8	1.3
Food, Beverages, Tobacco	9.9	5.4	47.15	0.27	0.2	2.3	0.6
Pharmaceuticals	8.1	4.5	813.80	4.66	4.2	13.0	3.4
Textiles, Clothing & Footwear	3.9	2.1	22.94	0.13	0.6	0.5	0.1
Paper and Printing	2.4	1.3	23.73	0.14	0.4	1.0	0.3
Total Manufacturing	182.7	100	174.61	1.00	1.1	3.8	1.0

a. Turnover as defined in the SCORE Survey includes sales, the imputed value of within enterprise transfers to other industries, plus capital expenditures. It is *not sales turnover.*

Source: Based in part on 'Preliminary Tables for Project SCORE 1973-74', Canberra, 1976.

debatable. In capital-intensive industries for instance the use of employment as a base may inflate calculated research intensities. Aggregation may also conceal important differences between sectors of industries. Indicators of research intensity shown in Table 8.4 are R & D expenditure per person employed in an industry, R & D expenditure of R & D performing enterprises as a percentage of their turnover and R & D professional employees per 1,000 employees in the industry. On the basis of the first indicator the pharmaceutical industry has by far the highest research intensity in manufacturing, followed by transport equipment and chemicals which remain well above the average level for manufacturing industry as a whole. Research intensity in fabricated metal products is average, in basic metal slightly below average and extremely low in other manufacturing industries, including the food, beverages, tobacco category, textiles, clothing and footwear category and paper and printing. An examination of the other indicators does not materially alter this ranking.

Spearman's Rank Correlation Coefficient is 0.908 for industry rankings based on (1) R & D expenditure per person employed in the industry and (2) R & D professional employees per 1,000 employees in the industry. For indicator (1) above and (3), R & D expenditure of R R & D performing firms as a percentage of their turnover, R = 0.858. However, Spearman's R for ranking by characteristics (2) and (3) is only 0.692.

Another feature of the R & D services provided by manufacturing enterprises is the high proportion undertaken by large firms. For instance business enterprises employing more than 1,500 persons generated more than half the R & D undertaken by business enterprises in 1973/4. A skewed distribution of this kind has been observed in most countries. For instance, in the USA, in 1968 the 300 largest companies accounted for 92 per cent of industrial research expenditure and the 40 largest for 70 per cent [16].

Unfortunately, the data available does not enable the relationship between research intensities and size of firms in Australia and inventive output and size of firms to be determined. Studies overseas indicate that research intensities for larger firms tend to be greater up to a point but decline once the size of firms exceeds some bound [4, 10, 14, 15], and marginal returns from R & D may behave likewise [10, 18].

As is the case in Canada, R & D in Australian manufacturing industry is dominated by foreign-controlled firms. At least, 55 per cent of R & D undertaken in manufacturing industry is supplied by foreign-controlled firms and their actual share is probably almost two-thirds

[17, 29].

The share of R & D provided by foreign-controlled firms is significant in most manufacturing industries except in paper, paper products and printing. In its *SCORE Survey* for 1973-4 of enterprises employing more than 150 persons, the Australian Bureau of Statistics acting for the Department of Science found that foreign-controlled firms supplied the percentage of R & D indicated in brackets for the following industries: Chemical, Petroleum, Coal Products including Pharmaceuticals (90.2), Transport Equipment (86.2), Textiles, Clothing and Footwear (61.0), Fabricated Metal Products (58.1), Food Beverages and Tobacco (45), Other Manufacturing (37.7), Basic Metal Products (36), Paper, Paper Products, Printing (8.0).

The greater the proportion of R & D expenditure accounted for by foreign controlled firms in Australian manufacturing industries, the greater the research intensities of firms performing R & D. The nature of the relationship for 1973/4 is indicated in Figure 8.1. For the regression line shown in this Figure, R = 0.7. The observed relationship may arise as Parry's research indicates [17], because foreign-controlled firms account for a larger share of the assets of research intensive industries and foreign-controlled firms within industries have higher research intensities. If Hufbauer's [7] thesis applies to Australia, as Parry suggests it does, we would expect research intensive manufacturing industries to become increasingly dominated by foreign controlled companies even though transnational firms are not on average more profitable than domestically-owned ones.

Of course, other factors also effect research intensities in different industries. Rivalry and potential rivalry in an industry may influence its research intensity [5, 10]. But it is difficult to test for this relationship using existing Australian data or by using surrogates for rivalry such as concentration ratios in industries.

It has been claimed that much Australian R & D in manufacturing industry is of an adaptive development nature in which foreign discoveries are adapted to Australian conditions [8, 11, 13, 17]. A large proportion of R & D funds are indeed used for experimental development as is common in manufacturing industry in all countries. In 1973/4 manufacturing firms employing more than 150 persons allocated 70 per cent of their R & D expenditure to experimental development and firms employing more than 150 persons accounted for 87 per cent of total funds used for R & D in manufacturing industry. Almost 55 per cent of their total R & D expenditure was for experimental development of new products. Basic research accounted

Figure 8.1: Percentage of R & D Expenditure of Australian Industry accounted for by Foreign Controlled Firms.

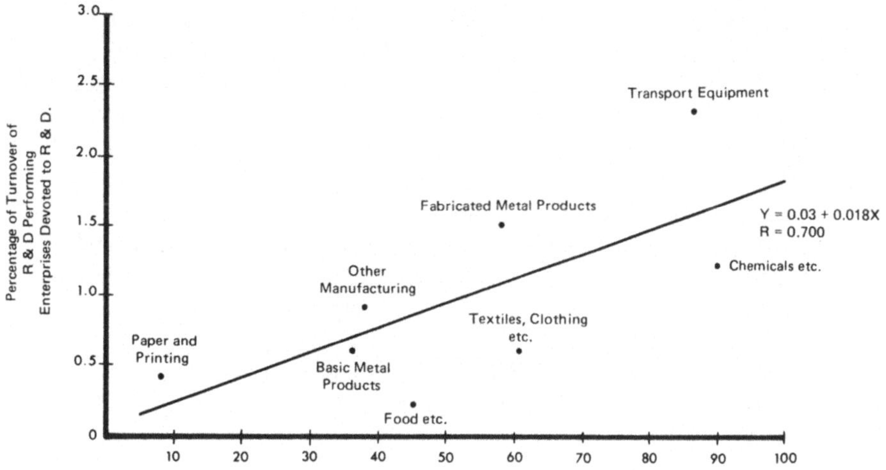

for 10 per cent of their total R & D expenditure and 20 per cent was allocated to applied research. However, the distribution of R & D funds between basic research, applied research and experimental development had a different pattern for foreign-controlled and Australian-controlled firms. The proportion of R & D funds allocated to basic research by foreign-controlled firms was twice the proportion for Australian-controlled firms, a result which differs from a recent claim by McKern [13] that there is little difference in the research pattern of foreign and Australian owned firms in Australia. A slightly higher proportion of their R & D funds is also allocated to experimental development. The reason for the higher basic research ratio of foreign-controlled firms is not clear but basic research tends to be more profitable for larger firms and foreign-controlled firms, besides being large, have possibilities for international transfer of research results. Also, they can minimise aggregate tax payments and maximise the value of claims on grant-giving agencies.

R & D for economic development in the economy as a whole, as shown in Table 8.5, amounted to about $381.3m in 1973/4 or 58 per cent of GERD. About 23 per cent of this was undertaken on behalf of primary industry (excluding mining), 63 per cent on behalf of secondary industry (including mining) and about 14 per cent on behalf of tertiary industry. The ratio of R & D for secondary industry in relation to that for rural industry was about 2.7:1, indicating a slightly higher research intensity (in relation to employment and contribution to GDP) for rural industry, than for secondary industry. The research intensity for tertiary industry was very much lower than for the other two sectors. One must be careful in drawing implications from Table 8.5 because the nominal area of R & D may show little relationship to the incidence of the benefits from R & D. Some rural research, e.g. on vetinary products, benefits manufacturers. Likewise, some research in manufacturing industry, for instance in relation to farm machinery, benefits agriculture and has an incidence elsewhere.

Table 8.5: Estimate of R & D Supplied on behalf of Primary, Secondary and Tertiary Industry in 1973/4 – Gross Expenditure in $'000

Supplier / Nominal Beneficiary	Government	Business Enterprises	Total	Per Cent
Primary Industry	86,450	2,000[a]	88,450	23.2
Secondary Industry	31,494	207,741	239,235	62.7
Tertiary Industry	35,530	18,295[a]	53,625	14.1
Total	153,274	218,036	381,310	100

Note: a. Rough estimate only.
Source: Based in part on 'Preliminary Tables for Project SCORE 1973-74'.

Benefits from Australia's R & D Effort

It is extremely difficult to measure the social and economic benefits from R & D activity. Both the measurement of effective inventive output as well as the evaluation of the benefits from this output present difficulties.

The crudest approach to measuring inventive output is to use inputs as a proxy. Consequently, gross expenditure on R & D is sometimes used as an indicator of scientific and inventive output on the implicit hypothesis that one automatically follows from the other by some fixed linear rule. There is, as far as I am aware, no grounds for the hypothesis.

Patent statistics provide another basis for measuring inventive output and have been used for instance by Scherer and by Schmookler for this purpose [18, 20], even though they too have a number of limitations, as Taylor and Silberston argue forcefully [24]. The value of patents can vary widely, many discoveries cannot be patented, sometimes inventors choose not to patent inventions, for example to preserve secrecy, and sometimes patented inventions are not used or worked. Patent applications may also be influenced by the general level of business activity. Large companies sometimes economise on patent applications in times of recession.

Special difficulties arise in using Australian patent statistics as indicators of Australian inventive output. The Patent Office is hard pressed to examine inventions for novelty or ingenuity and generally the novelty of inventions is checked only with respect to prior Australian patents [6]. Patent applications originating in Australia are sometimes based upon foreign inventions. For instance some inventions patented by Australian subsidiaries of foreign firms are in fact inventions of their parent companies and so patent statistics inflate the degree of apparent Australian inventiveness.

The largest share of Australian patent applications originate from abroad. In 1972, 72 per cent of Australian patent applications were from abroad. Of the 16,460 patent applications lodged in Australia in 1973, 4,651 (28 per cent) were of Australian origin, 5,152 (31 per cent) were from USA, 1,173 (1 per cent) were from UK, 1,084 (1 per cent) from Germany, 958 (16 per cent) from Japan and from other countries 3,352 (20 per cent). These figures may give a rough indication of the relative technological dependence of Australia on various countries.

Encel and Inglis [30] observed a long-term tendency for the ratio of Australian patent applications of foreign origin compared to those of domestic origin to rise and hypothesised its continuance. However, since 1967, this ratio has fallen slightly, principally because the number of patent applications lodged from the rest of the world has fallen [33].

Between 1950 and 1973 the number of patent applications per annum of Australian origin remained fairly steady at around 4,000 on average. Consequently, since resources devoted to R & D rose in this period, productivity of R & D as measured by the output of patented inventions declined. But as mentioned earlier, one must be wary in drawing such implications from these statistics.

Another crude way of measuring at least a part of scientific and inventive output is to use the volume of scientific articles as a guide. This measure has a number of shortcomings. For instance the overall quality and value of publications may vary over a period of time. However, on this basis Australia ranks high by world standards. On a per capita basis, the number of Australian scientific authors publishing in 1973 was relatively high and indeed, using de Solla Price's statistics [22], Australia ranked seventh in the world when compared to other countries. The results are possibly a reflection of the large share of R & D provided by government organisations such as CSIRO and by the universities.

Apart from difficulties involved in measuring the volume of output from R & D activity, considerable problems arise in attempting to evaluate its social benefits. The returns which suppliers of R & D Services receive are not a reliable guide to the social benefits of R & D. Gains may arise from other than profit. For instance, consumers may gain by lower prices or a better quality product, other inventions may stem from an original invention and an invention may have favourable external effects. For example, an invention may reduce pollution as a by-product of its use.[1]

The extent to which suppliers of R & D can appropriate the gains from their research has important implications. If they are able to appropriate all or most of the social gains from R & D at the margin of this activity, this ensures in some circumstances that R & D is conducted at a socially efficient level in the Kaldor-Hicks sense [25]. This is readily seen. If $G(x)$ represents the social net gain from activity x and if $V(x)$ indicates the net gain to the performer of the activity, social optimality is not achieved unless $V(x)$ reaches a maximum for the same value of x as is required to maximise $G(x)$. Acting in his own self-interest the performer of the activity aims only to maximise $V(x)$. If both $G(x)$ and $V(x)$ have a unique maximum, are at least twice differentiable, and if the activity x is worthwhile engaging in from the private and social viewpoint, the maxima of the functions occur for the same value of x if $G'(x) = V'(x)$ in the neighbourhood of the value of x for which $G'(x)$ equals zero and is decreasing. In these circumstances, private action leads to a social optimum in the Kaldor-Hicks sense but research activities are under-supplied from a social viewpoint when $V'(x) < G'(x)$ in this neighbourhood; that is when marginal private gains to the supplier are less than marginal social gains. Several economists claim that as a rule marginal factors imply a social undersupply of R & D services. Particularly in the case of basic research, the extent to which a provider of research services can appropriate the gains from them is likely to be small. In these circumstances, there are efficiency grounds for government intervention in the provision of R & D services.

But 'market' failure at the margin, whether from difficulties of appropriation or problems of uncertainty, is not the only important type of allocation failure which can and possibly does arise in the optimal supply of R & D services. An economy may become trapped in particular R & D patterns favouring established industries. Considerable collective thresholds and entry barriers frequently have to be overcome to establish profitable R & D activities in completely new fields. Individuals acting in isolation may only overcome such thresholds by chance and the thresholds which they do overcome may not be the most profitable ones from society's point of view. In some countries of which Japan is one, the government takes a leading role in ensuring that *selected* new fields of R & D activity are commenced and expanded in the light of potential national gains [22]. The Australian Government has not been active in the same way, although there have been suggestions by the Jackson Committee on manufacturing industry and in the Green Paper on rural industry that it ought to be.

An important issue in Australia is the extent to which R & D activity by foreign-controlled or owned firms should be encouraged. In manufacturing industry, such firms perform the lion's share of R & D. One may ask whether there is a case for subsidising their R & D as has been done in Australia through industrial research and development grants. I have argued elsewhere [17, 8, 23] that there is a case for marginal subsidy in certain circumstances but not all. If a marginal subsidy induces a foreign-controlled firm to perform globally more R & D than it would otherwise undertake and if this results in extra innovations which raise the surpluses of domestic consumers or buyers, the subsidy may be socially justified. Since foreign-controlled firms do not appropriate the surpluses of domestic buyers they may undersupply R & D activities from the social standpoint.

But we should also consider non-marginal possibilities. These pose a dilemma. Barriers to the entry of domestically-owned firms may be increased by improvements in the technical knowledge and skill of foreign-controlled firms in an industry. An early start by foreign-owned firms and their early development in a host country, whether or not supported by subsidisation of their R & D effort, may eventually raise entry preventing barriers to domestic firms. Domestic firms may consequently fail to enter the industry even when economic efficiency could be improved by their entry. The initial presence of technologically and economically superior foreign-controlled firms can prevent infant domestic firms from forming, entering new fields, growing and developing superior skills and efficiency so that in line with Hufbauer's thesis [7] foreign domination of domestic industry increases. This can provide a rational basis for favouring domestically-owned firms in *selected* industries and for restricting the entry of foreign-controlled firms as has been done in Japan. An infant domestically-owned industry argument analagous to the infant industry argument for trade protection applies.

This is not to say that domestic firms ought to have preferred entry conditions in the development of all industries or in many. The empirical possibilities and evidence must be examined in each case. But if a long-term point of view is taken, the early development of an industry by foreign-owned firms in a host country is not *always* economically efficient nor in the national interest. In monopolised or oligopolistic industries, the national costs of such development may be high because monopoly profits (rent) may be transferred abroad, and continue to be transferred for a long period. A host government could in principle appropriate these rents by imposing appropriate levels of discriminatory tax on foreign-owned companies. But in practice this is difficult. The prices at which transnational companies transfer resources between divisions may diverge from market prices so that the profitability of a subsidiary may be distorted. Again, it is the level of discounted profits which needs to be considered and the stream of a company's rents or profits is liable to be uncertain and difficult to assess. Furthermore, discrimination may not be politically acceptable or politically workable, for instance if major parties rely heavily on contribution from transnational companies.

When technology is exchanged directly across national boundaries, for instance a domestic firm may purchase technology from abroad, a country may be able to improve its gains from exchange by interfering in the market as has been done in Japan. Import of technology may be restricted and competition between domestic purchasers for its import may be controlled by government intervention. Forces of monopsony in import of technology or of monopoly in export of technology can be brought into play by a government in appropriate cases to raise national gains. The success of this policy is dependent in part on foreign countries not adopting countervailing measures. Nevertheless, some regulation of Australia's import and export of technology could be in the national interest.

In a non-marginal world, the parochial view gains support that in the national interest, R & D incentives should in selected industries, be restricted to domestically-owned firms. Possibly, some industries should also be reserved for domestically-owned firms and the required technology directly purchased from abroad if necessary. Since there are marginal and non-marginal relationships in the real world, optimal national policy may involve discriminating in favour of foreign-controlled firms in some industries, discriminating against them in others and treating them equally in others.

Another issue worthy of consideration in the Australian context is the extent to which the government should undertake R & D generally or specifically for economic development. Most agricultural R & D is supplied by government in Australia but little is undertaken on behalf of manufacturing industry.

The provision of R & D services by government is advantageous if it utilises economies of scale in R & D, avoids 'excessive' duplication of research and helps ensure community-wide disclosure of results. Possible disadvantages include a failure to evaluate adequately the economic potential of research because of the remoteness of researchers from market and industry conditions and the likelihood of research being motivated more by academic interest than economic potential.

It has been observed that manufacturers are reluctant to engage in or to encourage collective R & D [9, 10] especially when it may result in patentable or economic inventions. This is understandable since many manufacturers believe that collective R & D may deprive them of a profitable invention which could give them a competitive advantage over rivals [5,10]. One expects manufacturers with superior R & D capabilities to strongly oppose collective R & D, for they stand to lose most unless such research is principally basic research.

As observed, little government-sponsored research is contracted out in Australia. Increased contracting out might raise economic benefits but this is not certain to occur. More R & D for defence purposes could for example be contracted out to industry despite the difficulties for national security which this could raise. The benefit could be greater 'spin-off' in commercial application of developments as shown in US space technology activities and in European nuclear research [10]. Research contracts could be used to encourage the growth of new Australian-owned industries. However, in the absence of selective contracting out of R & D in Australia, most contracts for defence or 'big-science' research would possibly tend to go to foreign-controlled firms. Australia and Canada face a similar problem in this regard.

Policies for patenting and licensing the use of government inventions of commercial value are also important. Optimal policy varies but it is generally in the national interest, as recognised by CSIRO, for the government to patent its commercially viable inventions. The policy which the government should adopt in licensing inventions varies. Sometimes it is in the national interest to give an exclusive licence for use of an invention, in others it is not, and often the Government may need to impose a variety of conditions. A number of the factors which need to be taken into account in reaching decisions in this area have been discussed elsewhere [19]. Such factors as the state of competition in the industry using the invention and the export status of the industry need to be taken into account.

The rules which a government should follow in selecting industries to be favoured in the supply of R & D services need further investigation but there is no reason to believe that those industries should be favoured in which a country has a comparative advantage. In some circumstances, R & D for the non-traded goods sector for example brings greater national returns than R & D for the export sector.

Commonalty, Averaging and the Allocation of Scientific Resources

The importance of 'commonalty' and 'averaging'[2] in determining the allocation of R & D resources has been inadequately recognised. Researchers in their search for discoveries are attempting to gather what is conceptually common-property and consequently the allocation of R & D resources may be more influenced by average returns than by marginal returns. If this is so, it has important implications for the efficiency of our R & D effort.

Yoram Barzel [1] seems to have been the first to recognise the common-property element in technical change. Restricting his attention to innovations, Barzel argues that the basic knowledge used by innovators is a free public good and that competition between potential innovators to embody this common-property in innovations, and so obtain priority rights, can result in the premature development and application of technology. The common-property element may cause innovation to proceed at a faster rate than is socially optimal [10]. This argument can be extended.

Prior to discovery, all knowledge is common-property just as fish in international waters are common-property awaiting capture. The situations are analagous and many of the theorems developed by Gordon Scott [21] in the latter context apply *mutatis mutandis* to the allocation of resources for R & D. But the analogy is only accurate when discoverers obtain exclusive rights to their discoveries, for example through the patent system or by *de facto* possession of the discovery such as might occur if the discoverer's exploitation of the invention in an industry makes entry by others unprofitable. These conditions are more likely to be satisfied towards the development end of the spectrum than towards the basic research end.

When these conditions are met in a world without threshold and substantial collective economies of scale, too many R & D resources from a social efficiency standpoint are liable to move into the most profitable areas of R & D and too few are liable to be attracted to less profitable areas of R & D in a competitive situation. Resources move to the area where they obtain the highest expected returns and since no rents are charged for entering different fields of R & D, overcrowding could occur in more productive areas. This is akin to Gordon Scott's example in which the most productive fishing grounds are over-fished relative to the others.

The problem can be illustrated by Figure 8.2. Imagine that the resources which are used in R & D are homogeneous and that they can be allocated between two scientific fields in the economy. The average return in scientific field 1, the field with highest average returns, is indicated by the curve marked A_1 and the average return in field 2 by the curve marked A_2. The corresponding marginal curves are marked M_1 and M_2.

If the cost per unit of scientific resources is r_1 *all* scientific research will be conducted in field 1 and K_1 of resources will be engaged in R & D. On average, resources engaged in field 1 will earn a return of r_1 if each unit has an equal probability of making a discovery in the field. But this allocation of scientific effort does not maximise total returns from research. Total returns are only maximised if scientific resources are allocated in a pattern which equates their marginal returns in all scientific fields. In the case illustrated in Figure 8.2, total returns from K_1 of research resources are only maximised if K_1* of these resources are allocated to field 1 and K_2* to field 2. The correct allocation might be achieved by imposing a per unit tax of $r_1 - r_0$ on resources used for R & D in field 1. But in any case, profit maximisation in circumstances of commonalty, as encountered in scientific research, is likely to result in too many resources being concentrated in research fields offering the highest average level of returns.

Figure 8.2

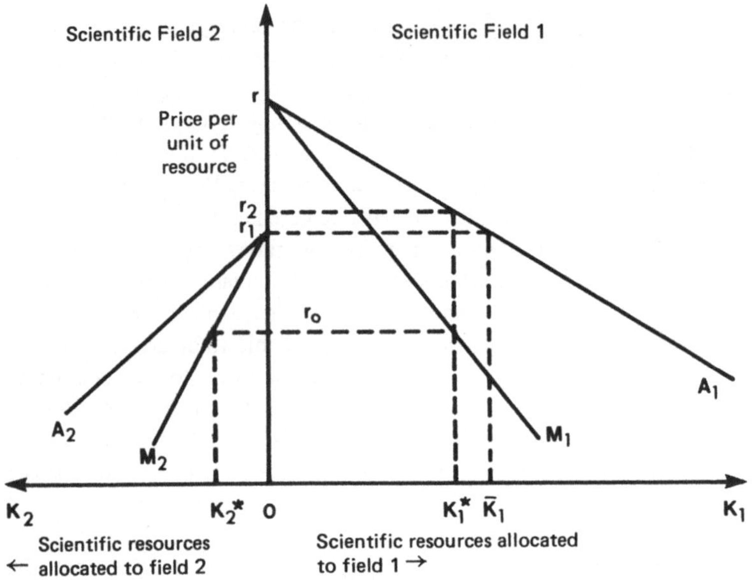

A similar phenomenon may also be present in non-commercial research. The funds for such research may be allocated on an 'average' basis. For example, the amount of funds which a scientists may receive may depend upon his relative number of publications and contributions. Previous contributions per head or per dollar (average concepts) may be a *desideratum.* Consequently, competition between researchers to maximise their share of research funds may lead to over-expansion of their effort in more productive and 'well-fished' fields. As a result, the extent of their overall contribution to the growth of knowledge is not maximised.

Commonalty may also create distortions in international R & D effort. As a result of commonalty too much international research effort may be directed to fields offering the highest expected or average returns. The amount of international competition in some scientific fields, for instance in areas of nuclear research, may be socially excessive from a world point of view. Commonalty may also cause, as in the case of urban populations [32], distortions in the location of scientific effort.

The averaging or commonalty phenomenon implies that if collective economies can be achieved in the supply of R & D services in a field, the resources are liable to be over-supplied once R & D output passes a threshold. Similar problems of misallocation arise to those involved in the growth of cities [20] and in advertising expenditures.[3] Because of commonalty and collective economies, established fields of R & D can become inefficiently overexpanded. No mechanism in existing market and current non-market systems prevents such distortions in the allocation of R & D resources although different methods of funding and granting access to government supplied R & D services may help.

Notes:

1. For example innovation may have repercussions for health services (See Deeble and Scotton, chapter 11) or environmental services (see Harris and Ulph, chapter 3).
2. Commonalty arises when a resource is owned by no identifiable individual and all have free access to it. All are equally free to appropriate the fruits of the resource. Average gains rather than marginal gains determine the allocation of resources to the exploitation of common-property [21].
3. See, for example, chapter 12 by Metwally.

References

1. Barzel, Y., 'Optimal Timing of Innovations', *Review of Economics and Statistics,* vol.50 (1968) pp.348-55
2. Clark, N.F., 'Expenditure on Research and Development in Australia', *The Journal of the Institution of Engineers,* June 1966, pp.N63, N64.
3. Encel, S. and A. Inglis, 'Patents, Inventions and Economic Progress', *The Economic Record,* vol.42, 1966, pp.572-8
4. Grabowski, H.G., 'The Determinants of Industrial Research and Development: A Study of the Chemical, Drug and Petroleum Industries', *Journal of Political Economy,* vol.76, 1968, pp.292-306
5. Grabowski, H.G. and Baxter, N.D., 'Rivalry in Industrial Research and Development', *Journal of Industrial Economics,* vol.21 (1973) pp.209-35
6. Grant, P., 'Patents and the Australian Interest', 1975 ANZAAS Paper, CSIRO, Canberra.
7. Hufbauer, G.C., 'The Multinational Corporation and Direct Investment', International Finance Section, Princeton University, Conference on Research in International Trade and Finance, 30-31 March 1973.
8. Hunter, A., *The Economics of Australian Industry* (Melbourne University Press, Parkville, 1963) Ch.1.
9. Johnson, P.S., *Co-operative Research in Industry* (Martin, Robertson, London, 1973).
10. Kamien, M.I. and Schwartz, N.L., 'Market Structure and Innovation: A Survey', *Journal of Economic Literature, vol.8 (1975) pp.1-37.*
11. *Lamberton, D.M., Science, Technology and the Australian Economy* (Tudor Press, Sydney, 1970).
12. McFetridge, D.G., 'The Distribution of Research Grants: A Comment and an Extension', *The Economic Record* (forthcoming).
13. McKern, R.B., 'The Multinational Enterprise and Technology Transfer in

Australian Manufacturing Industry', *Research Paper No.102*, School of Economic and Financial Studies, Macquarie University (January 1976).
14. Mansfield, E., *Industrial Research and Technological Innovation* (Norton, New York, 1968).
15. The Monopolies Commission *A Report on the Proposed Mergers of Beecham Group Ltd. and Glaxo Group Ltd. and of the Boots Company Ltd. and Glaxo Group Ltd* (HMSO, London, 1972).
16. Norris, K., and Vaizey, J., *The Economics of Research and Technology* (Allen and Unwin, London, 1973).
17. Parry, T.G., 'Technology and the Size of the Multinational Corporation Subsidiary: Evidence from the Australian Manufacturing Sector', *The Journal of Industrial Economics*, vol.23 (1974) pp.125-34.
18. Scherer, F.M., 'Firm Size, Market Structure, Opportunity, and the Output of Patented Inventions', *American Economic Review*, vol.55, 1965, pp.1097-125.
19. Schmied, H., 'A Study of the Economic Utility Resulting from CERN Contracts', CERN, European Organization for Nuclear Research, Geneva, 1975.
20. Schmookler, J., *Invention and Economic Growth* Harvard University Press, Cambridge, Mass., 1966).
21. Scott, G.H., 'The Economic Theory of a Common Property Resource: The Fisher', *Journal of Political Economy*, vol.62 (1954) pp.124-42.
22. De Solla Price, D. and Suha Gursey, 'Some Statistical Results for the Numbers of Authors in the States of the United States and the Nations of the World', Department of History of Science and Medicine, Yale University.
23. Stubbs, P., *Innovation and Research: A Study in Australian Industry* (Cheshire, Melbourne, 1968).
24. Taylor, C.T. and Zilbertson, Z.A., *The Economic Impact of the Patent System: A Study of British Experience* (Cambridge University Press, London, 1974).
25. Tisdell, C., 'On the Theory of Externalities', *The Economic Record*, vol.46, 1970, pp.14-25.
26. —— 'Commonwealth Industrial Research and Development Grants – An Economic Evaluation', *Economic Analysis and Policy*, vol.2 (1971) pp.27-50.
27. —— 'Australian Industrial Research and Development Policies and Some International Comparisons', *Economic Activity*, vol.15 (1972) pp.33-42.
28. —— 'Research and Development in Australia – A Summary of Expenditure and the Allocation of Funds', *Science and Industry Forum Report No.5*, Australian Academy of Science, Canberra, 1972, pp.28-34.
29. —— 'The Australian Research Subsidy to Overseas Firms and Other Aspects of the Distribution of Research Grants', *The Economic Record*, vol.49 (1973) pp.194-210.
30. —— 'Research and Promotional Levies for Australian Rural Products', *Farm Policy*, vol.14 (1974) pp.63-75.
31. —— 'Patenting and Licensing of Government Inventions', *Australian Economic Papers*, vol.13 (1974) pp.188-207.
32. —— 'The Theory of Optimal City-Sizes: Some Elementary Considerations', *Urban Studies*, vol.12 (1975) pp.61-70.
33. —— 'Science Policy and the Flow of Australian Inventions', *Search*, vol.6, 1075, pp.174-8.
34. —— 'An Australian Review of Japanese Science and Energy Policy', *The Australian Quarterly*, vol.47 (1975) pp.44-61.
35. —— 'The Distribution of Research Grants: A Rejoinder', *The Economic Record* (forthcoming).
36. Williams, B.R., *Technology, Investment and Growth* (Chapman and Hall, London, 1967) Ch.8.

ADDENDUM: R & D EXPENDITURE AND FIRM SIZE IN AUSTRALIAN MANUFACTURING, 1971-72

I.W. McLean and D.K. Round[1]

It is the purpose of this short note briefly to summarise some early findings on the relationship between R & D expenditure and firm size in Australian manufacturing industries in 1971-72. The data are drawn from an Australian Department of Manufacturing Industry survey, and cover R & D activity in 996 firms.[2]

A widely canvased question in the literature of the economics of innovation concerns the existence of some relationship between the size of an industrial enterprise and its R & D effort or innovational progressiveness.[3] The general hypothesis is that for cross-sectional analysis larger firms are more likely to undertake more R & D expenditure. It is also postulated that R & D effort is likely to increase more than proportionately with size – at least up to some 'threshold' size of firm. The reasons for expecting non-linear relationships between total R & D expenditure and the size of enterprises have been discussed widely in the literature.[4] Industrial R & D programmes frequently require high set-up costs and are characterised by 'lumpiness' in expansion, both classic sources of scale economies. And as a high level of uncertainty as to commercial success surrounds much R & D activity, risk is spread in larger-scale operations. However, it is not hard to uncover *a priori* grounds for contrary arguments about the R & D/size nexus, or for scepticism as to the postulated relationship. The small-scale, even individual, inventive effort has often been spectacularly successful in the history of technology. It is possible that the scale arguments may apply with greater force to some types of R & D activity than others (say 'basic' as contrasted with 'developmental') or to some types of industry. Also, the existence of specialist R & D producing enterprises, which may be relatively small but obtain work by contract from manufacturing firms (with whom they may or may not bear some loose affiliation), complicates the picture.

Because *a priori* reasoning can argue for the R & D/size relationship to be either positive or negative over a given size range, empirical work on this topic is particularly difficult. What may be loosely labelled

Table 8A.1: Research and Development Intensity : Averages for Sales Size Classes, 1971/2 (as a percentage of sales)

Industry	Size Class[a] 1	2	3	4	5	6	7	8	9	10	11	12	Total observations
1 Food, beverages, tobacco	7.7	1.3	1.1	0.3	0.4	0.6	0.3	0.3	0.2	0.3	0.1	0.3	
	(–)	(11)	(7)	(8)	(10)	(17)	(9)	(5)	(8)	(9)	(5)	(4)	96
2 Textiles	–	21.4	1.4	2.2	0.3	0.2	0.2	0.5	–	2.5	0.1	–	
		(–)	(4)	(–)	(5)	(6)	(–)	(–)		(–)	(–)		24
3 Clothing and footwear	3.5	6.2	1.1	0.6	1.3	0.5	–	–	0.3	–	–	–	
	(–)	(–)	(–)	(7)	(8)	(4)			(–)				29
4 Wood and wood products	12.1	3.2	1.6	0.9	0.8	0.2	0.3	0.6	1.0	–	–	–	
	(8)	(17)	(4)	(7)	(9)	(4)	(–)	(–)	(–)				53
5 Paper, paper products, etc.	2.1	1.4	0.4	2.1	0.5	0.8	0.1	0.6	0.9	–	0.6	0.6	
	(–)	(4)	(–)	(–)	(6)	(6)	(–)	(–)	(–)		(–)	(–)	28
6 Chemicals, petroleum, coal	13.5	4.3	2.0	2.2	1.8	0.9	2.4	1.1	1.9	0.9	0.1	0.6	
	(11)	(28)	(12)	(19)	(31)	(12)	(10)	(6)	(5)	(6)	(–)	(5)	147
7 Glass, clay, other non-metallic products	5.0	1.2	0.9	0.7	0.6	0.4	0.8	–	0.4	0.2	0.9	0.2	
	(–)	(4)	(–)	(4)	(4)	(4)	(–)		(–)	(5)	(–)	(–)	30
8 Basic metal products	5.6	4.0	1.2	1.8	1.0	0.8	0.4	–	0.3	0.3	0.3	0.5	
	(–)	(8)	(7)	(4)	(8)	(6)	(–)		(–)	(–)	(–)	(4)	47
9 Fabricated metal products	16.9	1.6	2.2	1.7	0.8	0.5	1.2	1.6	0.6	5.8	0.3	–	
	(7)	(33)	(13)	(22)	(23)	(20)	(5)	(–)	(5)	(–)	(4)		136
10 Transport equipment	947.7[b]	2.0	1.0	1.1	0.9	1.2	3.8	1.5	–	1.5	1.6	1.5	
	(–)	(–)	(4)	(–)	(9)	(8)	(–)	(5)	–	(–)	(–)	(3)	41
11 Other industrial machinery and household appliances	55.6	8.8	3.3	2.1	1.9	1.5	1.2	1.3	2.1	2.2	0.7	–	
	(36)	(73)	(46)	(50)	(57)	(31)	(11)	(4)	(5)	(4)	(–)		320
12 Leather, rubber, plastic products	9.0	4.1	1.9	1.0	1.2	0.9	0.9	–	–	1.0	0.4	–	
	(–)	(9)	(11)	(5)	(7)	(4)	(–)			(–)	(–)		45

Notes: a. Size classes are as follows: 1 is less than $101,000 in total sales; 2 is $101,000 to $0.5m; 3 is $0.5m to $1m; 4 is $1m to $2m; 5 is $2m to $5m; 6 is $5m to $10m; 7 is $10m to $15m; 8 is $15m to $20m; 9 is $20m to $30m; 10 is $30m to $50m; 11 is $50m to $100m; and 12 is greater than $100m. Numbers in brackets refer to number of observations in the sample falling in this size category. (–) indicates that there are less than 4 observations.

b. This very high mean R & D intensity is due to two firms in this industry and size class reporting for this year R & D expenditure greatly in excess of their total sales.

'theoretical support' can be found for almost any possible outcome, and it is far from satisfactory to conclude that 'the question is an empirical one'.[5] Nonetheless, applied economists have little alternative but to continue with current methods of analysis if they believe further inquiry into the problem is warranted. At the very least, the appearance of suitable Australian data permits a comparison of overseas findings with local experience, and special characteristics of the Australian industrial environment suggest some differences in results might be anticipated.

As an initial description of the data characteristics, it is possible to express the average cost of R & D in relation to firm size by calculating R & D *intensity* for each type of industry within given size classes. The intensity measure chosen is expenditure on R & D as a percentage of the value of sales. This measures for twelve types of industry and expressed as averages across all firms within the industry is shown in Table 8A.1 for twelve size classes.[6] It is to be noted that mean R & D intensity for each industry initially *declines* as size increases, then in most cases remains roughly constant, although the extent of the decline varies considerably between industries. The five industries with the highest average R & D intensity in the larger class sizes are transport equipment, industrial machinery and household appliances, chemicals, and fabricated metal products. At the other extreme, the lowest average values of R & D intensity were recorded by the larger firms in the food, beverages and tobacco, clothing and footwear, glass, clay and other non-metallic mineral products and basic metals industries. The remaining industries lay between these two groups. This pattern is more readily apparent from an inspection of the summary information presented in Table 8A.2.

Two propositions can be explored using this data. First, it is necessary to demonstrate differences in the average elasticity of R & D expenditure with respect to firm size for each industry and test whether any industry increases R & D expenditure more than proportionately to sales. Secondly, it is possible to approximate the shape of the average R & D/size relationship for the each industry by fitting a cubic function to the individual observations.

An estimated log-linear relationship was positive for all twelve industries and was significant at the one per cent level for all industries except textiles. In no case was the elasticity of R & D expenditure with respect to firm size greater than one. The values of this elasticity ranged from 0.907 (paper and paper products) to 0.223 (textiles). Table 8A.3 shows the calculated relationship for each industry.

Table 8A.2: Research and Development Intensity (1971/2) by Industry and Size Class: Summary (unweighted averages, percent)[a]

Industry		Size Classes 1-6	Size Classes 7-12	All Size Classes
1.	Food, beverages, tobacco	1.1	0.3	0.8
2.	Textiles	3.9	0.8	3.4
3.	Clothing and footwear	1.7	0.3	1.6
4.	Wood and wood products	3.5	0.5	3.3
5.	Paper, paper products, etc.	0.9	0.6	0.9
6.	Chemicals, petroleum, coal	3.5	1.4	3.1
7.	Glass, clay, other non-metallic products	1.0	0.4	0.8
8.	Basic metal products	2.1	0.4	1.7
9.	Fabricated metal products	2.3	1.4	2.1
10.	Transport equipment	95.8[b]	1.7	70.6[b]
11.	Other industrial machinery and household appliances	10.4	1.5	9.7
12.	Leather, rubber, plastic products	2.6	0.7	2.4

Notes:
a. Figures are derived from Table 8A.1.
b. See note to Industry 10 in Table 8A.1.

In order to assess whether an inflection point occurs in the relationship between R & D and size, a more appropriate model[7] is of the form $R \& D = \alpha + \beta_1 S + \beta_2 S^2 + \beta_3 S^3 + \epsilon$. Table 8A.4 shows the results obtained from fitting this function to the twelve industries.

Six industries (Group I) exhibited concave or U-shaped functions for R & D intensity, although in only three cases (food, beverages and tobacco, wood and wood products, transport equipment) were all three terms significant and the degree of fit satisfactory.

One industry (Group II, textiles) exhibited a convex or inverted U-shape function for R & D intensity. Five industries (Group III) showed that R & D expenditure increased more than proportionately over part of the sales size range only to reach a threshold. However, except for basic metal products, the fit obtained for this relationship was poor.

In summary, the results, in common with overseas findings, show that considerable variation exists among industries in the pattern of R & D expenditure in relation to firm size. Although absolute R & D

Table 8A.3: Relationship between R & D Expenditure & Firm Size, 1971/2

$$[\ln (\text{R \& D exp.}) = \hat{\alpha} + \hat{\beta} \ \ln (\text{sales})]$$

Industry	Constant	$\hat{\beta}$	R^2
1. Food, beverages, tobacco	–3.103	0.655 (8.166)	0.402
2. Textiles	0.949	0.223 (0.968)	–0.050
3. Clothing and footwear	–1.713	0.526 (3.018)	0.194
4. Wood and wood products	–1.800	0.538 (5.214)	0.322
5. Paper, paper products, etc.	–4.555	0.907 (7.603)	0.665
6. Chemicals, petroleum, coal	–1.708	0.640 (11.980)	0.490
7. Glass, clay, other non-metallic products	–3.039	0.699 (6.324)	0.557
8. Basic metal products	–1.924	0.642 (9.946)	0.672
9. Fabricated metal products	–2.795	0.703 (11.094)	0.471
10. Transport equipment	–2.689	0.773 (6.767)	0.516
11. Other industrial machinery and household appliances	–0.905	0.559 (14.924)	0.408
12. Leather, rubber, plastic products	–3.413	0.779 (5.564)	0.391

Note: Figures in parentheses are t values.
All regressions are significant at the 1% level using a one-tail test, except regression 2 which is significant only at the 20% level.

expenditure increased with firm size, the elasticity of R & D expenditure was less than unity in all twelve industries. However, there is some support for a U-shaped average R & D expenditure function and more-than-proportionate increases in R & D expenditure over some firm size ranges.

Table 8A.4: Cubic Regression of R & D Expenditure on Sales, 1971/2
(R & D = $\hat{\alpha} + \hat{\beta}_1 S + \hat{\beta}_2 S^2 + \hat{\beta}_3 S^3$)

Industry	$\hat{\alpha}$	$\hat{\beta}_1$	$\hat{\beta}_2$	$\hat{\beta}_3$	$\bar{R}^2$	n
Group I						
Food, beverages, tobacco	−13.633	.009 (9.497)	−.220(−06) (11.076)	.137(−11) (13.597)	0.86	96
Clothing and footwear	−2.114	.018 (1.197)	−.204(−05) (0.760)	.631(−10) (0.660)	0.04	29
Wood and Wood products	5.851	.006 (2.497)	−.759(−06) (2.299)	.373(−10) (3.669)	0.81	53
Paper, paper products etc.	−0.746	.008 (2.942)	−.657(−07) (0.881)	.358(−12) (0.923)	0.93	28
Glass, clay, other non-metallic products	−10.209	.008 (1.234)	−.558(−07) (0.419)	.123(−12) (0.217)	0.18	30
Transport Equipment	−37.802	.023 (14.123)	−.114(−06) (9.085)	.256(−12) (11.401)	0.99	41
Group II						
Textiles	63.348	−.024 (6.146)	.216(−05) (13.597)	−.250(−10) (16.068)	0.95	24
Group III						
Chemicals, petroleum, coal	18.913	.012 (3.086)	−.266(−07) (0.569)	−.416(−13) (0.341)	0.26	147
Basic metal products	19.439	.001 (1.033)	.273(−07) (3.079)	−.331(−13) (2.941)	0.96	47
Fabricated metal products	−15.385	.016 (1.880)	.108(−06) (0.334)	−.341(−11) (1.175)	0.17	136
Other industrial machinery and household appliances	22.578	.003 (0.737)	.875(−06) (3.669)	−.116(−10) (4.276)	0.37	320
Leather, rubber, plastic products	11.829	.004 (.971)	.534(−06) (2.186)	−.101(−10) (2.984)	0.64	45

Note: Figures in parentheses beneath each regression are t values.
Figures in parentheses alongside the regression coefficients are the scaling factor employed.
Group I comprises concave functions; Group II comprises convex functions; Group III comprises functions of other forms.

Notes:

1. We would like to thank Terrie Banker and Michael Petty for their computing assistance and the Department of Industry and Commerce for providing us with the data.
2. Some general results of the survey are described in *R & D in Manufacturing Industry 1971-72* (Australian Department of Manufacturing Industry Bulletin No.11, November 1974). Responses to the survey questionnaire were obtained from 2175 firms, on the basis of which it was claimed that 'survey results covered practically all manufacturing firms in Australia undertaking R & D in 1971-72'.' (p.1). A slightly narrower definition of industrial R & D was sought for this study by eliminating respondents classified as research laboratories which were separate organisations, and also those firms operating principally in the gas and coal, the mining, and the residual group 'other manufacturing' industries. Second, some of the survey questions were basic to our inquiries, but only 1118 of the 2175 enterprises stated their total R & D expenditure, 1112 their total R & D employment, 2010 their total employment and 1947 the total value of annual sales. It was decided to restrict the sample to those firms which had supplied information on all these four questions, the final sample thus being 996 firms, and was used throughout the study unless otherwise indicated.
3. For a recent summary of the literature in this area, see M.I. Kamien and N.L. Schwartz. [1].
4. For a survey see Kamien and Schwartz, [1, pp.15-19], and F.M. Scherer, [3, pp.352-62].
5. Scherer, [3, p.354].
6. R & D expenditure is the expenditure on research and development performed within a company for that company, and thus excludes R & D expenditure either undertaken within the company for another company or incurred through payment for research contracts undertaken by other organisations.
7. Scherer [2] suggests a more appropriate specification is of the form

   $R \& D = \alpha + \beta_1 \log S + \beta_2 \log S^2 + \beta_3 \log S^3 + \epsilon$, which has the effect

   of supressing the dominance of really large firms. We fitted this model, but the results were not as good as those shown in Table 4.

Bibliography

1. Kamien, M.I. and N.L. Schwartz, 'Market Structure and Innovation: A Survey', *Journal of Economic Literature*, vol.13 (March 1975) pp.1-37.
2. Scherer, F.M., 'Size of Firm, Oligopoly and Research: A Comment', *Canadian Journal of Economics and Political Science*, vol.31 (May 1965) pp.256-66.
3. Scherer, F.M., *Industrial Market Structure and Economic Performance* (Rand McNally 1970)

9 TERRITORIAL JUSTICE IN ACCESS TO LEGAL SERVICES

T. Vinson, R. Homel and R. Bonney

Introduction

There is a long-standing suspicion in the field of social administration that those segments of the population who could most benefit from social services are among the last to take advantage of them. The fatalism and social conditioning of depressed groups and their suspicion of 'outside' agencies are said to help explain the poor's sluggish response to new social services. The British authority Richard Titmuss (1963) in a general comment on modern social services has said: 'those who have benefited most are those who have needed it least'.[1] This may be due in part to the fact that some professions or agencies supplying social services have cultivated client groups. These groups promise the maximum 'pay-off' for the time and energy invested in their welfare.

While there is evidence to support both these lines of reasoning, there is a danger of overlooking an equally important and somewhat more obvious explanation. Recently, research has drawn attention to regional inequalities in the distribution of social and medical services. A basic assumption of this research has been that policy should be directed toward distributing available services in accordance with need criteria. This focus has been developed in respect of legal services by applying the concept of 'Territorial Justice'. An acknowledged weakness of the research that has so far been undertaken is that the nature and extent of requirements for legal services in different communities have not been adequately charted. In the absence of such information, a policy assumption can be adopted that specifies professional legal services as being readily available to individuals within their residential area.

It must, of course, be acknowledged at the outset that the presence or absence of legal practitioners within a defined geographical area provides only a general indication of the 'accessibility' of legal services. In one sense, a sparsity of professional services merely increases the costs to potential consumers of those activities. Depending on the availability and cost of transport and knowledge concerning the nature and availability of services, the individuals will be affected to varying degrees by their geographic proximity to or distance from practitioners. Ultimately, the study of territorial justice in Australia needs to incorporate a number of indicators of costs incurred in supplying and obtaining legal services. Such data currently are being assembled but an even more basic and hitherto neglected task is the charting of the spatial distribution of legal and other professional services. The present study focuses on this limited but important geographic aspect of the concept of accessibility of services.

A National Committee established to review legal aid services in Australia acknowledged the relationship between poverty and inaccessibility of legal services. The Committee indicated the need not only to expand legal services but also to provide services which 'in structure and administration as well as in principle render legal advice and assistance accessible to the vast number of people presently denied the service'.[2]

Many proposals for extending legal services focus on the personal and social well-being of individuals and families, as well as on the rights of disadvantaged groups. This emphasis was reflected in a submission to the National Poverty Enquiry by the Australian Council of Social Services (1973):

> There is no doubt that the focus of Australian Law, in theory and in practice, must change from concern for propertied interests to active protection of disadvantaged persons in the community.

The Council (ACOSS) provided examples of the types of service needed to 'protect' disadvantaged persons. These included the provision of legal advice to all persons in the community before they actually enter into binding transactions. ACOSS also believed that there was evidence that the privacy and dignity of individual social welfare recipients was threatened by administrative procedures aimed at eliminating dishonest claims. Therefore, it recommended that the legal profession do more to represent the interests of those applying for or receiving social welfare assistance.[3]

These proposals have been the subject of considerable debate within the legal profession and general community. The present study does not seek to join issue with either those favouring or those opposing the extension of particular services. Rather, an attempt is made to examine some structural features of the legal profession which could affect its ability to implement the types of recommendation put forward by ACOSS or to supply new services demanded by the community.

Objectives of Study

The main aim of this study is to assess whether spatial inequalities exist in the distribution of legal services throughout Australia. The two major indicators of the local availability of legal services are the number of solicitors practising in an area and the number of solicitors' offices located there.

The study focuses on two types of information, using mainly data provided by the 1971 census. First, it generates estimates of variations in the number of solicitors and solicitors' offices throughout specified urban and rural areas of Australia. Secondly, it explores the relationship between the distribution of solicitors and solicitors' offices per 100,000 of population in 1973 and a number of economic and social characteristics for each area. These characteristics are a combination of socio-economic indices and variables which have been found important in comparable overseas studies.[4] The variables considered are as follows:

1. percentage of total population 65 years and older,
2. percentage of total population foreign-born.
3. percentage of labour force in 'upper working' category (categories A, B and C of Congalton's (1969) occupational prestige scale),
4. percentage of labour force in 'lower working' category (category D of Congalton's scale),
5. percentage of labour force unemployed,
6. percentage of labour force in primary industry,
7. percentage of labour force in secondary industry,
8. percentage of labour force in tertiary industry,
9. average rent per week for State housing,
10. average rent per week for private housing,
11. income per head of population,
12. number of doctors per 100,000 of population (1972),
13. number of dentists per 100,000 of population (1972),
14. retail sales (1968/9) per head of population.

While it would have been advantageous to have based the above variables on data collected over exactly the same time period this was not possible due to the substantial amount of clerical time and expense involved in assembling data on the distribution of the professions (see below). In each case, the most recent listing which could be verified by clerical checking was used. This unavoidably resulted in the census variables and data on the professions spanning a three year period. Also, changes in statistical boundaries meant that it was not possible to combine information from successive censuses.

Data Sources and Methods Employed

The study is based on a sample of 8,873 solicitors in private practice throughout Australia. Plotting the location of solicitors and their principal office address was more complicated than for either doctors or dentists. There is a directory of legal practitioners published for the whole of Australia but it is not a comprehensive listing. Using a comparable directory to the Australian one, Foster (1973) found a discrepancy of slightly more than 2,000 names when he compared his totals with the number of practising certificates issued to solicitors in private practice in England and Wales. The totals for practising certificates were derived from the English Law Society's independent figures.

In New South Wales, all the data relating to solicitors were obtained from the New South Wales Law Almanac for 1973. In some other states it was necessary to combine information from government law calendars and almanacs with telephone listings to get the complete set of data. In Victoria, the files of the Law Institute were employed as the data source. It is an accurate record of all solicitors in that state with current practising certificates.

The Medical Directory of Australia for 1972 was used to establish the numbers and distribution of doctors across the country. This directory of medical practitioners is recognised as being the most comprehensive listing available. The Dental Board of New South Wales stated that a more reliable listing than their records could be derived from the commercial telephone directories. To standardise the approach to the distribution of dentists, commercial telephone directories were used in all states.

In deciding which practitioners to include in the study much the same approach as that used by Foster was adopted. Only those practitioners employed in private practice were counted. Hence practitioners in government or semi-governmental service and private industry were excluded. Some entries were omitted on the basis of direct inquiry or by inference from the listed information. In South Australia and Western Australia, unlike most other states, it is possible to practise as both a barrister and a solicitor. In these states therefore, barristers have been included although they have been excluded in other states. However, those practitioners in the two states who practise solely as barristers have been excluded. In Victoria, there are a small number of solicitors who also practise as barristers and they have been included in the study.

The analysis divides naturally into two sections: namely, comparisons between indices (expressed as rates per 100,000 population) and the exploration of possible reasons for differences between regions. First, a number of comparisons are made between the numbers of doctors, dentists and solicitors in specific centres and regions within each state. This essentially involves searching for patterns in the geographical distribution of professional services. Because any comparison involves populations of varying sizes, it is necessary in each case to express the number of medical, dental and legal practitioners as a rate per 100,000 population. By this means it is possible to assess whether, on a population basis, major urban areas contain more or fewer doctors, dentists and solicitors than rural areas. Using the same sets of rates for each individual municipality, shire or region, it can be determined whether areas that appear to be poorly serviced in one respect (for example, doctors) are also poorly serviced in respect of dentists and solicitors. The procedure adopted is to rank the geographical units within each state according to the number of solicitors present in relation to the size of population. After repeating the same procedure for doctors and dentists it is a relatively simple matter to identify by inspection those areas which rank consistently high or low. However, the analysis can be taken one step further by computing rank order correlation coefficients. This measures the tendency for high or low concentrations of one profession in a region to be accompanied by high or low concentrations of another profession. Rank order correlation also helps to overcome the problem of the extreme concentration of services in a small number of areas.

The final step in the analysis uses the key demographic and social characteristics of some 311 regions throughout Australia. This information makes it possible to explore reasons for and the implications of variations in the distribution of professional services. In particular, some social factors may be more dominantly connected with the distribution of solicitors throughout the Commonwealth. A statistical procedure known as principal components analysis is employed to test the strength of these associations. It is a form of 'factor analysis' which attempts to reduce the information conveyed by a large set of indices into a smaller number of factors. Principal components analysis involves constructing weighted sums of the indices, the weights being determined automatically on the basis of the magnitude of the correlation between indices. Since principal component weights are usually difficult to interpret, a further transformation (called 'rotation') is often made. There are many different methods of rotation but the varimax criterion employed in this study yields factors which are statistically uncorrelated and relatively easy to interpret.

Differences in the Spatial Distribution of Services

Of primary interest is the geographic accessbility of different professional services. Accordingly, any analysis must focus on the distribution of these services across regions and sub-regions of the states. Nevertheless, it may be instructive to take a brief overview of the number of doctors, dentists and solicitors practising in each state. One way of gauging the relative position of the states and territories is to rank them according to the number of practitioners per 100,000 population. Table 9.1 shows that while there are exceptions, each state generally occupies a consistent position on the separate rankings. New South Wales never drops below second position and Western Australia never rises above sixth. South Australia was ranked fourth on each of the three professional indices and the Australian Capital Territory occupied positions ranging from first (doctors) to third (solicitors). The rank order positions occupied by Victoria and Western Australia were fairly consistent except for the ratio of doctors to population. Victoria ranked comparatively high on solicitors and dentists, but low on doctors. Tasmania's equal second position on doctors contrasted with its comparatively low ranking on the dental index. This was due to a very high concentration of doctors in the state capital, Hobart.

Table 9.1: State Rankings for Medical, Legal and Dental Practitioners per 100,000 Population

Solicitors		Doctors		Dentists	
Rank	Rate per 100,000	Rank	Rate per 100,000	Rank	Rate per 100,000
1. NSW	91	1. ACT	108	1. NSW	34
2. VIC	76	2.= NSW	86	2. ACT	33
3. ACT	74	3.=TAS	86	3. VIC	28
4.= SA	49	4. SA	73	4.= QLD	27
5.= TAS	49	5. VIC	69	5.= SA	27
6. QLD	45	6. QLD	65	6. WA	26
7. WA	31	7. WA	61	7. TAS	15
Australia	67	Australia	71	Australia	28

To the extent that the ratio of solicitors to population is an accurate indicator of spatial access to legal services, there are marked geographic differences in their availability throughout Australia. The same holds true for the distribution of private medical and dental services. In some localities there may be factors which compensate for a comparative shortage of private practitioners. For example, in some areas there are community health centres. However, for the present (1976), these are not common. There would appear to be few analogous public services in the legal field.

The capital city/rest of state comparisons highlight a fundamental contrast in the distribution of health and legal services. The concentration of doctors, dentists and solicitors in the metropolitan areas of the capital cities is between one and a half and two and a half times greater than in other regions of the six states. An examination of Table 9.2 shows that, with the possible exceptions of Victoria and New South Wales, the capital city/rest of state ratios for the three professions were very similar. In New South Wales, solicitors, and to a lesser extent dentists, were concentrated in Sydney but in Victoria it was the dentists who were more prevalent in the capital.

Another method of assessing the geographic concentration of the professions is simply to compare the percentage of doctors, dentists and solicitors who practise in the capital cities and elsewhere. This approach ignores the relative sizes of the populations involved but has the advantage of showing to what extent practitioners are concentrated in a

Table 9.2: Capital City/Rest of State Comparisons (Rates per 100,000)

	Solicitors			Doctors			Dentists		
	Capital	'Rest'	Capital: 'Rest'	Capital	'Rest'	Capital: 'Rest'	Capital	'Rest'	Capital: 'Rest'
NSW	117	51	2.3:1	103	59	1.7:1	43	21	2.0:1
VIC	87	48	1.8:1	76	52	1.5:1	33	14	2.4:1
ACT	74	–	–	108	–	–	33	–	–
TAS	70	36	1.9:1	125	60	2.1:1	22	10	2.2:1
SA	59	24	2.5:1	87	38	2.3:1	31	15	2.1:1
QLD	55	36	1.5:1	81	50	1.6:1	32	22	1.5:1
WA	37	14	2.6:1	76	29	2.6:1	32	14	2.3:1

single location. Simple analyses in terms of the percentage of doctors, dentists and solicitors practising in each capital show that the distribution of the three professions *within* each state is quite similar (Table 9.3). In five cases, the variation in the number of doctors, dentists and solicitors practising in the capital cities is less than 5 per cent. In the remaining state, Victoria, the variation is only slightly greater (7.5 per cent). With reference to the variation between states, Table 9.3 shows that there were basically two patterns of distribution. Between approximately 75 and 85 per cent of doctors, dentists and solicitors in New South Wales, Victoria, Western Australia and South Australia, were located in the capital cities. In Queensland and Tasmania the figure was somewhat lower – between 55 and 60 per cent. However, it should be noted that in these two states there is a more even distribution of population between city and country.[5]

Table 9.3: Percentage of Solicitors, Doctors, Dentists Located in Capital Cities

	Solicitors Capital City %	Doctors Capital City %	Dentists Capital City %
South Australia	86.2	85.1	83.9
Victoria	81.9	78.4	85.9
Western Australia	81.5	85.1	83.7
New South Wales	78.0	73.1	76.4
Queensland	57.9	59.6	56.1
Tasmania	55.9	57.4	56.8

To some extent, the above figures are misleading, at least so far as solicitors are concerned. The high percentages of solicitors in the capital cities reflect an even more marked concentration within the central business districts of the state capitals. Out of the total of 8,873 solicitors in the sample, more than half (56 per cent) practise within the inner city local government areas. In other words, one out of every two solicitors can be found practising within one or two kilometres of the centres of Australian capital cities. An additional 22 per cent practise in the suburbs of the capitals, 8 per cent in urban areas outside capital cities, and the remaining 14 per cent in country areas.

For other than the major population centres it can be noted that some regions have consistently high rates of professional services while others have consistently low numbers of doctors, dentists and solicitors in relation to their population size. A number of statistical devices can be used to explore these relationships, but as a preliminary step it is instructive simply to rank the regions of each state according to their numbers of legal, medical and dental practitioners. In New South Wales for example, Woollahra ranked second out of seventy-two for dentists, was third for doctors, fifth for solicitors and third for solicitors' offices. North Sydney was ninth for doctors, and fourth for dentists and solicitors and second for solicitors' offices. At the other extreme, Kiama – Shellharbour, was 69th for doctors, 71st for dentists, 68th for solicitors, and 69th for solicitors' offices. Wollondilly was similarly placed: last for doctors, 68th for dentists, 69th for solicitors and 67th for solicitors' offices. Lake Macquarie was 66th for doctors, 70th for dentists, and also 70th for solicitors and solicitors' offices.

Within the Sydney metropolitan region there were a number of areas with consistently low rankings. Among these was Blacktown – 65th for doctors, 66th for dentists, 67th for solicitors and 60th for solicitors' offices. The adjoining municipality of Holroyd was only marginally better serviced: 63rd for doctors, 60th for dentists, 71st for solicitors, and 72nd for solicitors' offices. Nearer the centre of the city, South Sydney was 71st for doctors, 58th for dentists, 55th for solicitors and 66th for solicitors' offices. Similar examples of areas with uniformly high or low rates can be detected in the remaining states. Appendix 9.1 contains the five regions in each state with the highest and the five with the lowest rates of provision of legal services.

Another way of determining the similarity of rankings for the three indices of professional service makes use of rank order correlation. The rank order correlation coefficient takes the value of +1.0 whenever the rankings for two variables are in perfect agreement, –1.0 if they are in perfect disagreement and 0.0 if there is no relationship whatsoever. Thus, the closer the coefficient is to unity, the greater the similarity of ranking for the indices. As might be expected from the preceding discussion, the rank order correlation coefficients between the distribution of doctors, dentists and solicitors was generally high. The coefficient between doctors and dentists was .61, between doctors and solicitors .49, and for dentists and solicitors was somewhat lower at .39. Not surprisingly, solicitors' offices and practising solicitors were highly correlated (.80). In later tabulations involving these four indices together with the other social variables mentioned in the introduction, it will become clear that these values are comparatively high. In general, rank order correlation coefficients above .5 can be regarded as indicating a substantial degree of similarity in ranking.

The similarity of rankings of areas for the three types of professional service has already been noted. This raises the question as to whether the pattern of their distribution reflects the operation of a common set of factors. In order to examine this possibility, fifteen economic and social variables gathered for each region throughout Australia are employed. Of course, it must be recognised that there are countless possible influences shaping the geographic distribution of professional services. However, standard census data and some estimates derived from census information for the 311 areas provide a comprehensive set of demographic and socio-economic indices with which to explore the patterning of services.

There are two ways in which the relationship between the fifteen indices (including the three types of professional service) can be examined. The first is simply to examine the rank correlations between pairs of variables. These correlations are presented in Table 9.4. But with this amount of information, it is difficult for the eye and mind to discern the conceptual unity of the data. The most commonly used statistical technique for dealing with this problem is principal components or factor analysis.

Table 9.4 shows the degree of association between the economic and social indices and the distribution of medical, dental and legal services. In only a few instances is there a high rank correlation. There is, however, a positive association between medical and dental services and income per head of population (.45 and .53 respectively). Income in turn is associated with three other indices of status; namely, percentage of population in 'upper' occupations (.59), percentage of work force in tertiary occupations (.57) and the level of private rent paid (.65). It is not surprising, therefore, that two of these three indices (tertiary occupations and private rent) also correlated – although rather more weakly – with the distribution of medical and dental services. Thus one of the implied influences shaping the distribution of medical and dental services is a status/income factor.

Before presenting the results of the principal components analysis some additional correlations may be considered which foreshadow the results of that analysis. Unlike doctors and dentists, there were zero or near zero correlations between the distribution of solicitors on the one hand, and on the other hand, income and rent, as well as the type of industry and the occupational status predominating in an area. With

Table 9.4: Rank Correlations of Indices

		2	3	4	5	6	7	8	9	10	11	12	13	14	15	16
1.	Population 65+	−.03	.14	−.15	.16	−.29	−.10	.39	−.24	.16	.43	.57	.47	.30	.29	.42
2.	Foreign-born		.05	−.06	.18	−.50	.52	.10	.09	.44	.26	.06	.13	−.08	−.08	.00
3.	Upper working			−.99	−.43	−.30	−.15	.70	−.04	.59	.59	.26	.35	−.02	.09	−.16
4.	Lower working				.39	.30	.16	−.71	.04	−.59	−.59	−.27	.36	.02	−.09	.16
5.	Unemployed					.13	−.04	−.07	.00	−.23	−.23	.12	.00	.14	.04	.22
6.	Primary industry						−.56	−.43	.16	−.71	−.46	−.29	−.36	.03	.05	−.15
7.	Secondary industry							−.26	−.03	.23	−.16	−.09	−.03	−.06	−.07	−.03
8.	Tertiary industry								−.06	.60	.57	.40	.43	−.09	.00	−.06
9.	State rent									.03	−.11	−.08	−.07	.07	.14	−.06
10.	Private rent										.65	.30	.43	.02	.03	.09
11.	Income/head											.45	.53	.15	.19	.28
12.	Doctors												.61	.49	.44	.61
13.	Dentists													.39	.41	.44
14.	Solicitors														.80	.61
15.	Solicitors' offices															.47
16.	Retail sales/head															

what other variables then was the distribution of solicitors correlated? The predominant correlation was with retail sales per head of population. It should also be remembered that the same index (number of solicitors practising in each area) correlated, albeit at a lower level, with the distribution of doctors and dentists.

What is implied by the above correlations? They suggest that differences in the spatial density of solicitors are related to differences in the level of retail activity as between areas. That is, where the level of retail business activity per capita in a region is high there is a greater concentration of solicitors. This means something more than just the fact that solicitors' offices tend to be located in central business districts. The correlations indicate a strong association between business activity and legal services on a regional basis. Unlike the doctors and dentists whose relative concentrations appear to be partly a response to the average level of income in an area, the distribution of solicitors is only weakly correlated with the wealth and status of the residents.

As previously mentioned, principal components analysis represents an attempt to go beyond individual correlations and discover

Table 9.5: Principal Components Analysis based on Rank Correlation, Loadings on First Five Principal Components

		1	2	3	4	5
1.	Population 65+	.52	.52	.10	–.37	.08
2.	Foreign born	.27	–.11	–.76	.11	.31
3.	Upper working	.76	–.47	.31	.09	–.05
4.	Lower working	–.77	.45	–.31	–.08	.02
5.	Unemployed	–.21	.52	–.18	–.17	.70
6.	Primary industry	–.64	.09	.62	.16	.11
7.	Secondary industry	–.01	–.10	–.87	.00	–.28
8.	Tertiary industry	.78	–.22	.22	–.15	.37
9.	State rent	–.12	–.08	–.02	.85	.33
10.	Private rent	.80	–.25	–.31	.14	.02
11.	Income/head	.83	.01	.06	.01	–.02
12.	Doctors	.63	.55	.09	.03	.04
13.	Dentists	.70	.38	.01	.08	–.04
14.	Solicitors	.22	.70	.09	.40	–.25
15.	Retail sales/head	.27	.80	–.07	.13	–.20

underlying patterns involving groups of variables or 'factors'. In the present Australia-wide study it was found that most of the information about the intercorrelations between the indices was reproduceable by reference to five mathematical constructs (the first five principal components). The percentage of variance explained was 79.7 per cent.

To aid interpretation of the meaning of principal components it is standard practice to undertake an additional step in the analysis known as 'rotation' of components. The rotated components are referred to as 'factors'. Thus according to the results the pattern of correlations can be explained largely by reference to an area's position on each of five factors (Table 9.6). Factor 1 is termed a general 'status-income' factor. The most important individual indices associated with Factor 1 were the percentage of population in upper status occupations, the percentage of the labour force in tertiary industry, the income per head of population and the level of private rent paid. Doctors and dentists, but not solicitors, were also associated with this factor, although less strongly than the above-mentioned indices. Moreover, solicitors and retail sales per head of population were slightly negatively associated with this factor.

Table 9.6: Varimax Rotation of first five Principal Components

		Factor 1	Factor 2	Factor 3	Factor 4	Factor 5
1.	Population 65+	.29	.55	–.02	.45	.31
2.	Foreign born	.13	–.05	.80	–.20	.29
3.	Upper working	.90	–.02	–.02	–.02	–.29
4.	Lower working	–.91	.01	.02	.02	.25
5.	Unemployed	–.28	.13	.00	–.03	.88
6.	Primary industry	–.38	–.16	–.79	–.24	.04
7.	Secondary industry	–.28	–.05	.86	.05	–.19
8.	Tertiary industry	.89	.03	.01	.11	.24
9.	State rent	.00	.00	–.01	–.92	.05
10.	Private rent	.69	.14	.55	–.07	–.09
11.	Income/head	.72	.37	.17	.11	–.05
12.	Doctors	.36	.73	.02	.10	.19
13.	Dentists	.45	.65	.14	.07	.05
14.	Solicitors	–.11	.84	–.09	–.19	–.10
15.	Retail sales/head	–.14	.86	.06	.07	.07

A second factor might be best entitled 'retail sales/professional-business' because of its association with retail sales per head of population and the percentage of solicitors, dentists and doctors per 100,000 of population. In other words, the earlier observation that there are two distinct factors underlying the distribution of medical, dental and legal services was supported by the factor analysis. A less easily interpreted aspect of Factor 2 was its relatively high association with the percentage of population 65 years and older in each area.

The final three factors were not associated with the distribution of doctors, dentists and solicitors. Factor 3 is called a 'secondary industry/migrant' factor. The percentage of the labour force in secondary industry and the percentage of the population foreign-born were both highly associated with this factor. Factor 4 is called a 'state rent/age' factor. The two indices associated with this factor were negatively correlated. Finally, Factor 5 called 'unemployment' was not associated strongly with any other index.

Some Explanations for Service Variations

This study has focused on certain structural features of the legal profession. Implicit in this analysis has been the question of whether or not the orientation and geographical distribution of the profession's private practitioners would make them appropriate agents for the delivery of services designed to 'protect' the poor. Before reviewing the evidence on this issue, it will help in the interpretation of the findings if three basic social mechanisms through which legal services can be made available are distinguished.

Howard (1969) has called the first of these 'market-like transactions'; meaning transactions in which the medium of exchange is primarily money. Clearly, fees paid (whether subsidised or on a full-cost pricing basis) to solicitors, doctors, dentists and other professional persons fall within this category. As a mechanism for the delivery of desired goods and services the 'market' obviously enjoys both considerable utility and approval in our society. However, as Howard has observed: 'For those without money, a market may be only a mockery'.[6] For this reason, many propose that the types of professional services considered in the present study should be treated as either a 'public good' (like libraries, parks, police and fire services) or a 'social service'. Many of the legal services intended to 'protect' the poor fall into the latter category. In Howard's terms, they are part of a wide range of welfare services which gratuitously offer a mixture of public services. These may be provided by granting free access to services or by making transfer payments to individuals and families who do not have adequate financial resources to supply themselves with the requirements that the community considers they should have.

In terms of their professional orientation and geographic distribution, how well equipped are private solicitors to participate in the development of any new category of legal-social services? Evidence provided by the present study suggests that a great many difficulties would need to be overcome.

First, there is the marked concentration of solicitors within urban areas and especially the capital cities. In four of the six states approximately 80 per cent of all the solicitors are contained within a 25 kilometer radius of the capital city centres. Earlier, many instances of regions poorly serviced by 'fee-for-service' practitioners in the medical, dental and legal fields were documented. However, with the aid of factor analysis an important difference has been identified in the orientations of solicitors on the one hand and doctors and dentists on the other. It was noted that there is a strong tendency for solicitors to concentrate their operations in areas characterised by high levels of commercial activity. The distribution of doctors and dentists is apparently associated more with the personal wealth and status of people living in different regions. Neither orientation, commercial activity nor wealth, is a satisfactory basis for ensuring that important professional legal services are distributed in an equitable manner.

There is strong evidence that the pattern of distribution of lawyers which exists in Australia is not peculiar to this country. A study of English solicitors by Foster (1973) suggests that the location of solicitors is associated principally with economic considerations very similar to those which govern the location of retail distribution outlets. Foster's study did not proceed beyond the stage of examining correlations but he observed a strong association between the distribution of solicitors on the one hand and the amount of retail sales per head and the age structure of regions on the other. The distribution of solicitors and the class structure of regions were unrelated. Similar patterns have been observed by Blaustein and Porter (1954) in the United States, where high agreement has been found between 'lawyer population and the number of manufacturing establishments, the number of corporations, retail sales volume, the number of retail trade establishments, and the size and service of trade units'.[7]

Indirect confirmation of the heavily commercial orientation of lawyers has been provided by Purcell's (1974) study of solicitors in New South Wales. This research, undertaken by the Law Foundation, was designed to investigate the need for continuing legal education. Almost 2,000 practitioners representing 45-50 per cent of the profession, responded to a mail survey. One of the questions in the survey listed 43 separate subjects which were presented as being the type of course which might be offered. The researchers found that those subjects with a commercial flavour were strongly favoured. The preferred course was 'Tax planning' (requested by 61 per cent of respondents). Almost half (45 per cent) requested courses in such subjects as 'Negotiating and drafting commercial agreements', 'How to manage legal work flow', 'Representing the subdivider' and 'Setting up a New South Wales Company'. Little interest was expressed in any course dealing with representation of the individual non-commercial client.

A major policy assumption was stated at the outset of this study: The services of professionals in the legal field should, as far as possible, be readily available to individuals in their residential area. Evidence has been presented which shows marked differences in the standards of provision throughout Australia. The magnitude of these differences is unjustified. The same conclusion as that reached by English researchers must be adopted: adherence to the concept of territorial justice would require at least a reduction of the extremes of disadvantage.

It would be hazardous to rely on the natural growth of the profession to rectify the imbalances reported. It has been shown that it is within commercially buoyant regions that solicitors are to be found. Foster must be agreed with when he says that the relationship between commercial and legal activity must, in some cases, 'be consciously substituted by more equitable criteria of distribution before territorial injustice ceases to be one of the increasing number of criticisms directed against the legal profession'.[8]

Further Research and Policy Implications

Despite the conclusions reached in the foregoing study, the best way to provide legal aid services is likely to remain a contentious issue. Nevertheless, governments and the legal profession are under considerable pressure to extend the scope of legal aid throughout Australia. Putting to one side the question of how the services will be provided, there remains the equally challenging issue of where they should be located. It is not surprising that discussion on this point has tended to be rather vague. In many respects, it is a question beyond the competence of lawyers to answer. It is, however, the type of question that attracts the attention of the social researcher.

Three types of information could help guide decisions about the areas in greatest need of additional legal services. They are: (a) the extent to which defendants are legally represented in different regions of a state, (b) the availability of legal services and (c) the level of social problems in each region. All three measures have in common the fact that they are based on objective data rather than general impressions.

Extent of Legal Representation

Considerable effort is required to establish and maintain a system of court statistics. Once the data is available however, it can be analysed in many different ways to help throw light on a variety of practical issues. Regrettably, this point is poorly understood by lawyers and many administrators who think of 'official statistics' as the sole return on a considerable investment of clerical and professional resources. In 1972 the Bureau of Crime Statistics and Research launched a system of data collection in over 250 Courts of Petty Sessions in New South Wales. Some of the ways in which it has been possible to analyse the information compiled annually on some 100,000 criminal or quasi-criminal cases have been reviewed in a recent publication.[9] Just one type of analysis warrants discussion here.

It is a relatively simple and inexpensive matter to obtain, with the help of the computer, an answer to the following question:

> How many defendants charged with offences A, B and C, and appearing before Courts D, E and F, were legally represented?

The real difficulty is in establishing a system of data collection and storage which contains the ingredients needed to facilitate rapid interrogation of the computer data bank. It is necessary to work within a standard framework of regional boundaries and to be able to relate both courts and where the defendants live to that framework. The system used by the Bureau fulfils these requirements. This enables the status of the individual concerning legal aid services to be referred to information about other known features of the same region.

Availability of Legal Services

This study has demonstrated that it is possible to use indicators, like the number of solicitors and solicitors' offices, to assess the spatial availability of legal services within a region. It has been shown that each locality can be appraised in terms of an absolute standard of legal services (for example, number of practitioners per 100,000 population), as well as its position relative to other regions throughout Australia and in relation to other professional services.

Level of Social Problems

Growing interest in providing legal services to the 'poor' raises a further technical issue. How are 'poor' or 'disadvantaged' areas identified? To help resolve this question an index of disadvantage has been developed based on twenty-five medico-social variables ranging from infectious disease and life expectancy to levels of crime, wealth and education. The index is now (1976) being applied to 72 regions in New South Wales. The same framework could be extended to cover the whole of Australia (Vinson and Homel, 1975). Later it may prove possible to combine the above three types of information in a single index of 'legal need' throughout Australia.

Appendix 9.1: Availability of Legal Services: Best Served and Least Served Areas

(Rates per 100,000 of population in local government areas and statistical subdivisions)

Statistical Region	Population	Solicitors		
		No.	Rate	Rank
New South Wales				
Sydney	62,470	2,398	3,838	1
Southern Tablelands	77,037	85	110	2
Upper Murray Subdivisions	49,567	48	96	3
North Sydney	53,338	49	91	4
Woollahra	59,964	52	86	5
Kiama-Shellharbour	37,905	4	10	68
Wollondilly	12,670	1	7	69
Holroyd	77,317	5	6	70
Lake Macquarie	122,421	8	6	71
Concord	26,104	1	3	72
Victoria				
Melbourne	75,830	1,348	1,777	1
Dandenong	40,883	44	107	2
South Melbourne	26,995	27	100	3
Mornington	14,289	13	90	4

Statistical Region	Population	Solicitors No.	Solicitors Rate	Solicitors Rank
Prahran	56,766	48	84	5
Chelsea	26,372	0	0	60 =
Altona	30,589	0	0	60 =
Cranbourne	12,511	0	0	60 =
Melton	5,974	0	0	60 =
Healesville	5,223	0	0	60 =
Tasmania				
Hobart	52,426	89	169	1
North Central Stat. Division	35,107	38	108	2
Kingborough	9,781	8	81	3
North West Stat. Division	92,220	33	35	4
Midland Stat. Division	9,187	3	32	5
North Midland Stat. Division	27,563	3	10	11
Southern Stat. Division	15,984	1	6	12
Sorell	2,575	0	0	13 =
Western Stat. Division	12,368	0	0	13 =
Brighton	1,336	0	0	13 =
South Australia				
Adelaide	16,313	414	2,537	1
Gawler	5,495	4	72	2
Unley	39,928	17	42	3
Meadows	5,128	2	39	4
St Peters	10,675	4	37	5
Kensington and Norwood	11,081	0	0	25 =
Hindmarsh	10,306	0	0	25 =
Far North Stat. Division	13,977	0	0	25 =
Henley and Grange	16,128	0	0	25 =
Glenelg	15,237	0	0	25 =
Munno Para	20,179	0	0	25 =
Mulda Wirra Gawler	186	0	0	25 =
Mitcham	54,377	0	0	25 =
West Torrens	50,097	0	0	25 =
Thebarton	11,831	0	0	25 =

Statistical Region	Population	Solicitors		
		No.	Rate	Rank
Woodville	72,806	0	0	25 =
Willunga	2,614	0	0	25 =
East Torrens	4,202	0	0	25 =
Enfield	77,435	0	0	25 =
Campbelltown	37,942	0	0	25 =
Colonel Light Gardens	3,369	0	0	25 =
Australian Capital Territory				
North Canberra	52,093	105	201	1
South Canberra	27,687	1	3	2
Woden	33,783	0	0	3 =
Weston Creek	8,724	0	0	3 =
Belconnen	19,508	0	0	3 =
Balance ACT	2,268	0	0	3 =
Queensland				
Brisbane City	9,550	383	4,010	1
Toowong	9,659	6	62	2
Greenslopes	13,063	8	61	3
Moreton Stat. Division	164,944	96	58	4
Cairns Stat. Division	112,177	46	41	5
Mitchelton	15,221	0	0	41 =
Meeandah	1,432	0	0	41 =
Morningside	11,187	0	0	41 =
Moreton	1,592	0	0	41 =
Nudgee	2,517	0	0	41 =
Peninsular Stat. Division	11,738	0	0	41 =
Nundah	15,427	0	0	41 =
North City	20,436	0	0	41 =
Normanby	10,617	0	0	41 =
Newmarket	12,289	0	0	41 =
Murarrie	4,109	0	0	41 =
South Eastern	9,043	0	0	41 =
South Western	8,954	0	0	41 =
The Gap	9,162	0	0	41 =
Tarragindi	14,037	0	0	41 =
Wynnum West	8,842	0	0	41 =
Windsor	13,468	0	0	41 =

Statistical Region	Population	Solicitors No.	Rate	Rank
Western	5,279	0	0	41 =
Yeronga	11,795	0	0	41 =
Fruitgrove	4,997	0	0	41 =
Fernberg	10,476	0	0	41 =
Far Western Stat. Division	4,317	0	0	41 =
Hendra	7,026	0	0	41 =
Graceville	7,812	0	0	41 =
Kenmore	9,980	0	0	41 =
Inala	21,940	0	0	41 =
Ithaca	9,987	0	0	41 =
Chatsworth	14,501	0	0	41 =
Carina	8,200	0	0	41 =
Caboolture	6,682	0	0	41 =
Darra	5,058	0	0	41 =
Eastern	6,102	0	0	41 =
Enoggera	10,543	0	0	41 =
Acherfield	3,000	0	0	41 =
Bald Hills	6,030	0	0	41 =
Aspley	2,822	0	0	41 =
Boondall	5,321	0	0	41 =
Banyo	8,366	0	0	41 =
Balmoral	15,128	0	0	41 =
Western Australia				
Perth	97,546	213	218	1
Fremantle	26,036	14	53	2
South West Stat. Division	77,347	23	29	3
South Agric. Stat. Division	45,281	11	24	4
Central Agric. Division	53,661	10	18	5
Bayswater	34,261	0	0	21 =
Cockburn	25,011	0	0	21 =
Claremont	9,179	0	0	21 =
Central Stat. Division	9,420	0	0	21 =
Bassendean	11,360	0	0	21 =
Armadale Kelmscott	15,644	0	0	21 =
Serpentine Jarrahdale	1,981	0	0	21 =
Rockingham	11,608	0	0	21 =

Statistical Region	Population	Solicitors		
		No.	Rate	Rank
Wanneroo	8,620	0	0	21 =
Kwinana	12,224	0	0	21 =
East Fremantle	7,325	0	0	21 =
Gosnells	22,040	0	0	21 =
Peppermint Grove	1,511	0	0	21 =
Pilbara Stat. Division	28,985	0	0	21 =
Mundaring	12,018	0	0	21 =

Notes:

1. Richard Titmuss, *The Welfare State* (Unwin University Books, 1963), p.229.
2. *Australian Legal Aid Review Report,* Australian Government Publishing Service (Canberra, 1974).
3. Moreover, there is an opportunity for the legal profession to assist in the improvement of many areas of substantive law (for example, legislation governing consumer credit transactions) that at present work to the disadvantage of the poor. Similarly, ACOSS believes that amendments to legislation designed to improve the lot of the tenant of low rental accommodation may require institutional changes to ensure that the tenant's rights are honoured in practice as well as in theory.
4. See K. Foster, 'The Location of Solicitors', *Modern Law Review* vol.36, (1973) pp.153-66.
5. The Brisbane Statistical Division has a lower proportion of the state's population than that of any other capital except Hobart. (Commonwealth Bureau of Census and Statistics, *Queensland Year Book,* no.32, 1971-73, p.71).
6. D. Howard, *Social Welfare: Value, Means and Ends* (University of California, 1969) p.74.
7. A.P. Blaustein and C.O. Porter, *The American Lawyer* (University of Chicago Press, 1954) p.13.
8. K. Foster, op.cit., p.164.
9. New South Wales Bureau of Crime Statistics and Research, Statistical Report No.18, *Minor Offences – city and country,* October 1974.

Bibliography

Abel-Smith, B., M. Zander and R. Brooke, *Legal Problems and the Citizen* (Heinemann, London, 1973).

Australian Council of Social Services, *Poverty – The A.C.O.S.S. Evidence* (Sydney, 1973).

Australian Legal Aid Review Report (Australian Government Publishing Service, Canberra, 1974).

Benham, L., A. Maurizi and M. Reder, 'Migration, Location and Remuneration of Medical Personnel: Physicians and Dentists', *Review of Economics and Statistics,* vol.50, (1968) pp.332-47.

Benjamin, C. and J. Morton, *A Model for Welfare Service Planning and Delivery* (Australian Government Publishing Service, Canberra, 1975).

Bice, T.W., R.L. Eichhorn and P.D. Fox, 'Socioeconomic Status and Physician Services; A Reconsideration', *Medical Care*, vol.10, (1972) pp.261-71.
Blaustein, A.P. and C.O. Porter, *The American Lawyer* (University Press, Chicago, 1954).
Cass, M. and R. Sackville, *Legal Needs of the Poor* (Australian Government Publishing Service, Canberra, 1975).
Congalton, A.A., *Status and Prestige in Australia* (Cheshire, 1969).
Elesh, D. and P.T. Schollaert, 'Race and Urban Medicine: Factors Affecting the Distribution of Physicians in Chicago', *Journal of Health and Social Behaviour*, vol.13, (1972) pp.236-50.
Foster, K., March, 'The Location of Solicitors', *The Modern Law Review*, vol.36 (1973) pp.163-66.
Freestone, R., *Spatial Aspects of Health Care Provision in Sydney*, University of New South Wales, School of Geography Occasional Paper No.8, 1975.
Henderson, R.F., 'Welfare Services', in *Poverty in Australia*, vol.1, (Australian Government Publishing Service, Canberra, 1975).
Howard, D., *Social Welfare: Values, Means and Ends* (University of California, Los Angeles, 1969).
Jeffers, R.J., M.F. Bognanno and J.C. Bartlett, 'On the Demand Versus Need for Medical Services and the Concept of Shortage', *American Journal of Public Health*, vol.61, (1971) pp.46-63.
Joroff, S. and V. Navarro, Medical Manpower: A Multivariate Analysis of the Distribution of Physicians in Urban United States', Medical Care, vol.9, (1971) pp.428-38.
Lankford, P.M., 'Physician Location Factors and Public Policy', *Economic Geography*, vol.50, (1974) p.244-55.
Marden, P.G., 'A Demographic and Ecological Analysis of the Distribution of Physicians in Metropolitan America, 1960', *American Journal of Sociology*, vol.73 (1966) pp.290-300.
Monmonier, M.S., 'Socio-Economic Controls on Spatial Variations in the Physician Population', *Proceedings of the Pennsylvania Academy of Scien*, vol.46 (1972) pp.91-3.
Purcell, T., 'Continuing Legal Education', *Law Society Journal*, vol.12, (1974) pp.103-6.
Reskin, B. and F.L. Campbell, 'Physcian Distribution Across Metropolitan Areas', *American Journal of Sociology*, vol.74, (1974) pp.981-98.
Robin, G., Winter, 'Reaching People', *Social Security Quarterly*, Canberra, 1974.
Sackville, R., *Legal Aid in Australia* (Australian Government Publishing Service, Canberra, 1975).
Titmuss, R.T.. *The Welfare State* (Unwin University Books, London, 1963).
Vinson, T., and R. Homel, 'Indicators of Community Well-being: Problems and Services', *Regional Funding Under the Australian Assistance Plan* (Australian Government Social Welfare Commission, Canberra, 1975).
White, R., 'Lawyers and the Enforcement of Rights', in P. Morris, R. White and P. Lewis, *Social Needs and Legal Action* (Martin Robertson, London, 1973).

10 HOUSEHOLD DEMAND FOR INSURANCE AND BANKING SERVICES

D.J.S. Rutledge*

Introduction

Unlike the majority of activities in the Australian service sector, banking and insurance has received considerable attention from economists. This is doubtless because of the role played by these activities in the capital market and their consequent importance in macro-economic policy. The major contributions to this literature have been made by Arndt and Stammer (trading banks), Lewis and Wallace (savings banks), Grant (life assurance) and Pursell (non-life insurance).[1] Furthermore, the availability of cost data for banks and life assurance firms has provided the basis for empirical estimation of cost functions for banking and insurance services.[2] In this respect these particular service activities have received more attention than most other Australian industries, with the possible exception of primary production activities.

On the other hand relatively little is known about the determinants of demand for these services, particularly at the household level. The present paper addresses itself primarily to the question of household demand for banking and insurance services and examines some evidence from cross-section data on household finances and expenditures.

The plan of this chapter is as follows. The following section consists of a discussion of the nature of the services provided by the banking and insurance industries, together with some background material on industry structure. The next section examines household demand for banking and insurance services from a theoretical viewpoint. Finally, the sources and nature of the available cross-section data are described and a set of empirical results are presented.

The Nature of Banking and Insurance Services

Life Insurance

Life insurance companies provide a range of services, each of which can be characterised as an agreement for the supplier of the service to pay an amount of money (the sum assured) on the death of the insured or on the occurrence of some other specified contingency dependent on human life. In return the policyowner (i.e. service user) undertakes to pay money (the premium) to the life office. In practice this agreement or life policy usually falls into one of five classes.

(a) Whole of life policy, in which the sum assured, together with any bonuses, is payable only on the death of the life assured.
(b) Endowment insurance policy, where the sum assured is payable on the survival of the life assured to a certain age or on his death before attaining that age.
(c) Pure endowment, in which the sum assured is payable only on survival by the life assured to a certain age. No payment is made by the life office in the event of the life assured not surviving to the specified age.
(d) Term or temporary insurance, in which the sum assured is payable only if death occurs during a limited period of time (the term of the policy). If the life assured survives to the end of the specified term no payment is made by the life office.
(e) Life annuity, in which the life office makes regular payments to the annuitant during his life or some other specified period.

Life insurance may be effected for a variety of reasons. The usual ones are the provision of security for the insured's dependents, provision for his retirement, or as a means of personal saving.

In addition to purchasing life insurance contracts of the above form, many households also contribute to superannuation schemes which provide benefits for employees or self employed persons on retirement, death or injury. Life insurance companies provide superannuation facilities but an increasing proportion of superannuation schemes are being managed by separately constituted superannuation funds. In 1975 the assets of private pension funds and public authority pension and superannuation schemes slightly exceeded the superannuation business of life insurance offices. In the following discussion, however, attention will be confined to the business of life insurance companies.[3]

Many of the official statistics relating to the life insurance industry (and the only ones dealing with individual companies) are collected and published by the Life Insurance Commissioner under the Life Insurance Act 1945-73. The Act defines three classes of business undertaken by life insurance companies: superannuation business; industrial business, which relates to policies for which premiums are usually paid to collectors at intervals of less than two months; and ordinary business,

Table 10.1: Life Insurance, Australia. Number of Policies, Sum Insured and Annual Premiums

Year Ended 31 Dec.	Number of Policies			Sum Insured			Annual Premiums		
	New Business	Dis-continued	In Force 31 Dec.	New Business	Dis-continued	In Force 31 Dec.	New Business	Dis-continued	In Force 31 Dec.
	'000	'000	'000	$m	$m	$m	$m	$m	$m
ORDINARY BUSINESS									
1962	318	218	3480	1263.4	491.6	7296.0	a	a	204.58
1965	353	228	3831	1614.9	575.4	10159.7	36.73	14.02	266.25
1968	419	245	4292	2600.0	819.9	14435.3	56.70	17.66	357.69
1971	560	285	5007	4803.3	1537.8	22563.2	90.17	27.99	513.75
1972	568	319	5256	5567.1	1908.1	26222.2	99.18	33.86	579.07
1973	523	255	5524	6275.0	2049.0	30448.2	93.22	34.33	637.76
1974	484	407	5601	6693.6	2688.6	34453.2	90.37	52.05	676.08
1975 b	473	439	5635	7888.9	3127.3	39214.8	97.65	58.13	715.60
SUPERANNUATION BUSINESS									
1962	75	96	597	486.0	172.2	2314.0	a	a	58.06
1965	85	54	641	900.3	421.9	3591.2	19.10	7.80	85.30
1968	88	64	716	1318.9	538.6	5518.1	32.90	14.20	153.53
1971	79	81	654	2794.2	1130.6	9429.5	72.74	29.04	252.70
1972	80	66	668	2919.2	1315.5	11033.2	77.69	32.69	297.70
1973	69	114	623	3792.2	1801.0	13024.4	93.79	43.96	347.53
1974	88	95	616	5428.8	1900.6	16552.6	138.47	48.47	437.53
1975 b	115	71	660	7019.2	2686.2	20885.6	176.76	60.86	553.43
INDUSTRIAL BUSINESS									
1962	156	276	3062	104.4	67.6	742.0	a	a	33.04
1965	131	221	2749	121.4	71.7	872.5	4.81	3.27	36.76
1968	132	173	2557	145.6	86.7	1041.4	5.78	3.69	42.42
1971	136	165	2467	232.8	115.9	1332.1	8.03	4.50	51.92
1972	135	222	2380	257.8	144.0	1445.9	8.83	5.37	55.38
1973	118	198	2300	253.8	160.9	1538.8	8.55	5.50	58.43
1974	86	228	2158	216.8	180.1	1575.5	7.13	6.88	58.68
1975 b	62	209	2011	187.8	165.6	1597.7	6.16	6.10	58.74

Notes: a. Not available

b. Figures for 1975 are provisional only.

Source: Annual Reports of Insurance Commissioner and Life Insurance Commissioner, various issues.

Table 10.2: Life Insurance, Australia. Analysis of New Business

Year	Total New Sum Insured Effected on Basis 1962=100 (1)	Average Sum Insured per New Policy (2) $	Whole Life (3) Per cent	Endowment Insurance (4) Per cent	Term Insurance (5) Per cent	Other Insurance (6) Per cent	Endowment (7) Per cent	Total (8) Per cent
				Ordinary Business				
1962	100	3976	49.1	27.0		23.1	0.8	100.0
1965	128	4570	51.6	23.4		24.0	0.0	100.0
1968	206	6206	54.4	17.3	25.4	1.1	1.8	100.0
1971	380	8577	56.1	10.8	31.5	0.5	1.1	100.0
1972	441	9802	57.7	9.3	31.7	0.2	1.1	100.0
1973	497	12003	55.5	6.5	37.4	0.2	0.4	100.0
1974	530	13830	55.7	5.0	38.8	0.2	0.3	100.0
1975a	624	16680	b	b	b	b	b	b
				Superannuation Business				
1962	100	6454	7.5	47.0		42.0	3.5	100.0
1965	185	10577	6.7	39.6		49.9	3.8	100.0
1968	271	14918	5.5	31.3	26.9	33.6	2.7	100.0
1971	575	35521	3.7	21.2	20.3	52.8	2.0	100.0
1972	601	36500	4.3	19.7	19.5	54.4	2.1	100.0
1973	780	54351	4.5	19.0	21.0	53.7	1.8	100.0
1974	1117	61943	6.1	16.2	21.6	54.5	1.6	100.0
1975a	1444	61088	b	b	b	b	b	b
				Industrial Business				
1962	100	670	6.5	89.7		—	3.8	100.0
1965	116	925	4.9	95.1		—	—	100.0
1968	140	1101	3.9	96.1	—	—	—	100.0
1971	223	1717	5.1	94.0	0.9	—	—	100.0
1972	247	1910	5.6	93.7	0.7	—	—	100.0
1973	243	2144	4.9	94.4	0.7	—	—	100.0
1974	208	2529	4.3	94.9	0.8	—	—	100.0
1975a	180	3012	b	b	b	—	—	100.0

Notes: a. All figures for 1975 are provisional only
b. Not yet available

Source: Annual Reports of Insurance Commissioner and Life Insurance Commissioner, various issues.

which relates to all other policies written by life insurance companies.

An indication of recent trends in life insurance business is provided in Tables 10.1 and Table 10.2. Table 10.1 shows the relative importance of ordinary, superannuation and industrial business while Table 10.2 indicates the market shares and growth rate index for each type of policy. In the period prior to about 1970 the structure of life insurance business was rather stable with ordinary business comprising about 70 per cent of total business, superannuation business about 25 per cent and industrial business playing a small and declining role. In more recent years, industrial business has continued to decline and in 1975 only five life offices issued new industrial policies. Of greater significance however is the increasing importance of superannuation business, which suggests that the community as a whole is placing more reliance on superannuation benefits to provide security for dependents and retirement than on life insurance. A further contributing factor, no doubt, is the compulsory nature of many superannuation schemes.

Whole of life policies have remained the most popular form of ordinary business, but Table 10.2 illustrates clearly the movement away from endowment insurance towards term insurance. The reasons for this will be discussed below. Endowment insurance has also declined in importance for superannuation business, which has come to be dominated by the 'other insurance' category. This is made up of deposit administration and investment-linked insurance in roughly equal proportions.

In purchasing a life insurance policy other than a term policy an individual is doing more than insuring against the specific risk of death or disability, he is also increasing his level of personal saving. Indeed the fact that life insurance may increase a community's level of savings has been advanced as one of its socially desirable aspects. Several studies in the United States and United Kingdom[4] have concluded that personal saving is increased by life insurance premiums and superannuation contributions over and above what it would have been in their absence. This conclusion is based on a comparison of the savings behaviour of households which own life insurance policies with those who do not. Although the mechanism by which this increase in saving is effected is not explicitly identified in these studies, the presumption is that it occurs because the savings component of the premium is not separately distinguished from the charge for risk cover; in other words, it is a form of contractual saving.

At present (1976) taxpayers in Australia may claim tax rebates for up to $1,200 annual expenditure on life insurance premiums and superannuation contributions. This concession has been historically justified on the grounds that it provides the means for low income earners, who may be unable to accumulate capital during their working life, to provide for their dependents. More recently it has been justified also on the grounds mentioned above, that it encourages personal saving.[5] There can be little doubt that this tax relief has had a significant impact on both the level of and changes in the demand for life insurance policies.[6]

Although the emphasis in this paper is on household demand for insurance services, it may be useful to briefly examine industry structure as this has some indirect bearing on household decision making.[7] There are presently some fifty private firms providing various types of life insurance services in Australia although not all of these deal directly with the public; some being primarily involved in reinsurance business.[8] The industry is highly concentrated as can be seen from Table 10.3 which shows four-firm and eight-firm concentration levels for the years 1965, 1970 and 1975.[9]

Under the Life Insurance Act 1945-73 a company must be registered by the Life Insurance Commissioner before undertaking life insurance business. This requirement is primarily designed to protect policyholders by ensuring that, so far as possible, companies will be able to meet future policy liabilities. The extent to which potential entrants are deterred by this restriction is difficult to assess but it is possible that there has been some consequent restrict of supply. The number of registered companies increased from twenty-two to forty-eight between 1946 and 1970 but has since remained virtually unchanged.[10] The possibility that economies of scale may constitute a barrier to entry is not supported by the small amount of empirical work so far undertaken.[11]

A further factor to be considered in examining the structure of the Australian life insurance industry is the nature and extent of overseas control. A detailed study of this question has been carried out by the Australian Bureau of Statistics for the year 1972-3. Using premiums as the measure of industry output this study concluded that in June 1973 the aggregate level of foreign ownership of life insurance business in Australia was 36.8 per cent of which is 18.8 per cent was direct foreign ownership and 18.0 per cent was other identified foreign ownership. The level of foreign control was estimated to be 19.4 per cent while that for Australian control was 80.6 per cent.[12] Additional evidence on the question of overseas control is available from Annual Reports of the Life Insurance Commissioner. Although these figures are not strictly

Table 10.3: Concentration in Australian Life Insurance Industry

Percentage of output attributed to	1965			1970			1975		
	Ordinary Business	Superannuation Business	All Business	Ordinary Business	Superannuation Business	All Business	Ordinary Business	Superannuation Business	All Business
Four largest firms	63.2	77.7	65.9	61.3	79.9	68.2	60.5	80.0	69.0
Eight largest firms	87.7	94.7	89.0	83.7	93.6	87.7	81.3	93.4	86.5

Source: Insurance Commissioner and Life Insurance Commission, Annual Reports various issues.

comparable with those collected by the Australian Bureau of Statistics they strongly suggest that overseas control is greater in respect of ordinary life insurance business than in respect of superannuation business. For example, the Commissioner's figures for 1975 indicate that 36.1 per cent of new sums assured in respect of ordinary business were attributable to overseas controlled companies, while the corresponding figure for superannuation business was 18.3 per cent.[13]

The market structure described above, together with the complexity of the life insurance service itself, has led some commentators to suggest that many policyholders are not in a position to make a rational purchasing decision.[14] The possibility that many consumers act with imperfect information is mentioned also in a recent report of the Commissioner. Noting that the number of enquiries and complaints received by his office increased by more than 70 per cent in the period 1971-74, he states

> The principal cause of enquiry in 1974 has been the amount offered or available for the surrender of the policy. In many cases the surrender value granted has been well in excess of the value specified by the Act but the policyowner has not been aware of or has misunderstood the principles upon which life insurance is based.[15]

Against this must be set the fact that the number of complaints received by the Commissioner represents a very small proportion of policies in force or surrendered. Furthermore the recent trend towards term insurance, in which the savings component is removed and risk cover only is provided, is consistent with a rational reponse to the observed increase in the rate of inflation. In this context it may be of some interest to examine the relationship between educational and other socio-economic characteristics of households and their ownership of life insurance policies.

Non-Life Insurance

Non-life insurance companies supply a wide range of general insurance services, each of which provides financial protection against possible loss. An indication of the extent and composition of general insurance services provided in Australia is given in Table 10.4. In that table 'Houseowners and Householders' insurance relates predominantly to insurance of private dwellings and their contents. Of the other classes of insurance only motor vehicle insurance and compulsory third party insurance reflect direct household demand to any significant degree.

Fire insurance, for example, refers largely to insurance against fire in industrial and commercial premises. It can be seen from these figures that direct household demand for insurance services represents a relatively minor component of total demand.

Unlike most life insurance policies a general insurance policy contains no savings component and is of a relatively short term. Furthermore, finance companies and other lending institutions frequently require that property be insured as a condition on which credit is made available for the purchase of that property. For these reasons it is commonly held that household demand for property insurance is relatively inelastic.[16]

Some observers have suggested that consumer dissatisfaction with general insurance services is increasing, particularly with respect to the harshness of certain policy conditions.[17] At the same time industry spokesman have been voicing some concern that householders' comprehensive policies are perhaps providing coverage against too wide a class of risk.[18]

Prior to 1973, general insurance in Australia was regulated under the Insurance Act 1932-66. Under this Act it was possible for persons to conduct insurance business on payment of a relatively small deposit only. The Insurance Act 1973 established stricter financial conditions which insurers had to satisfy in order to conduct business and also provided for continuous supervision of non-life insurance companies by the Insurance Commissioner.

Unlike the life insurance industry the degree of concentration in the general insurance industry is low. As of June 1975, 264 companies had lodged application for authority to carry on insurance business with the Insurance Commissioner. Market share data for individual firms are not readily available but data collected by Pursell[19] for the year 1971 suggest that the market share of the four largest firms (as measured by premiums written) was approximately twenty per cent and that of the eight largest firms approximately thirty five per cent.

In a market structure such as the one just described, particularly with little regulatory supervision, it is inevitable that firms should fail, with consequent loss to policyholders. As at 30 June 1975, sixteen non-life insurance companies were in liquidation. The provisions of the Insurance Act 1973, outlined above, are designed to increase the level of consumer protection by attempting to ensure the solvency of insurance companies. Statistics collected under the Act, being internally consistent and more comprehensive than those previously available, will eventually provide the basis for a better understanding of the structure

Table 10.4: Non-Life Insurance, Australia. Premium Income by Class of Business, 1973-4 ($ million)[a]

	Fire	Houseowners & Householders	Contractors	Marine	Motor Vehicle	Compulsory Third Party	Employers' Liability	Public Liability	Other	Total
Private Sector	125.3	91.6	6.8	40.4	286.8	61.9	238.0	29.2	112.0	992.1
%	12.6	9.2	0.7	4.1	28.9	6.2	24.0	2.9	11.3	100.0
Public Sector	13.8	16.8	–	2.8	58.2	135.7	110.8	1.7	6.6	346.4
%	4.0	4.8	–	0.8	16.8	39.2	32.0	0.5	1.9	100.0
Total	139.1	108.4	6.8	43.2	345.0	197.6	348.8	30.9	118.6	1338.5
%	10.4	8.1	0.5	3.2	25.8	14.8	26.1	2.3	8.9	100.0

Note: a. Excludes the net effect of inward and outward reinsurance premiums.

Source: *First Annual Report of the Insurance Commissioner* (Canberra, 1975).

of the industry.

Two further aspects of the structure of the non-life insurance industry in Australia deserve comment. The first of these is the extent to which banks and finance companies have in recent years entered the insurance industry. Some government banks have been authorised to insure property which they own or hold as security for loans. Furthermore private banks and finance companies have established insurance subsidiaries and an extensive network of overlapping directorates exists between banks and insurance companies.[20]

The second concerns overseas ownership and control of the industry. For the year 1971, Pursell estimated that forty-one per cent of non-life business written in Australia was by overseas-controlled insurers or brokers for overseas insurers.[21] A detailed survey undertaken by the Australian Bureau of Statistics for the period 1972-73 indicated that the aggregate level of foreign ownership of general insurance business in Australia was 45.7 per cent and that of foreign control was 45.0 per cent. However, when each class of general insurance business is taken separately the extent of foreign control varies considerably. For marine insurance it is 77.7 per cent and for compulsory third party insurance only 16.3 per cent. The figure for householders' comprehensive insurance is 51.0 per cent.[22]

Banking

The Australian banking system provides a wide range of financial services including the traditional banking services of deposit, credit and foreign exchange facilities together with more recent innovations such as credit card facilities and travel agency services. This study focuses on the traditional services, concentrating particularly on household demand for deposit and credit facilities.[23]

Current account or cheque deposit accounts have come to play a dominant role in Australian economic life as they have in all other developed countries. Being payable on demand in cash they are a form of money and are widely used as a means of payment. The rate of growth in the deposit liabilities of the trading banks in recent years may be seen from Table 10.5. Of the current deposits other than those held by Governments and other banks, approximately sixty per cent are business deposits and approximately twenty five per cent are personal deposits. Table 10.6 illustrates the growth in personal loans, overdrafts, personal deposits and numbers of branches and agencies of trading banks in Australia. No official statistics on the number of current deposit accounts are available, but Arndt and Stammer estimated this number to be about 4.5 million in 1971.[24] They also estimated that about one in three adult Australians own a cheque deposit account.[25]

Table 10.5: Australian Trading Banks, Deposits Repayable in Australia ($ million)

Year	Fixed Deposits[a]	%	Current Deposits	%	Total Deposits	%
1955/6	502.2	17.4	2376.8	82.6	2879.0	100.0
1960/1	977.6	27.2	2622.4	72.8	3600.0	100.0
1965/6	2073.0	39.6	3158.7	60.4	5231.7	100.0
1970/1	3188.7	43.4	4151.1	56.6	7339.8	100.0
1975/6	9587.2	57.7	7022.1	42.3	16609.3	100.0

Note: a. Includes certificates of deposit.
Sources: Commonwealth Bureau of Census & Statistics, *Banking & Currency* (various issues); Australian Bureau of Statistics, *Banking Statistics*.

As can be seen from Table 10.5, fixed deposits also comprise a significant and increasing proportion of the liabilities of the Australian trading banks. Personal deposits comprise approximately 40-45 per cent of total fixed deposits while business deposits make up about forty per cent of the total. No estimates are available as to the number of fixed deposit accounts.

At the present time there are thirteen trading banks conducting banking business in Australia, of which four are government banks. The industry is highly concentrated, the market share (measured by deposits) of the six largest trading banks being approximately ninety per cent. The structure of the industry has been fairly stable since 1945 with the only significant changes involving mergers among the private banks. The most recent of these occurred in October 1970 with the merger of Australia and New Zealand Bank Ltd, and the English Scottish and Australian Bank Ltd. The stability of the structure of the industry is largely due to legislative controls over the industry, designed to ensure stability of the monetary system. Economies of scale have been detected for the Australian banking system[26] and it is possible that these have also acted as a barrier to entry.

The primary banking service offered by savings banks is the ordinary deposit account. These cannot be transferred by cheque but are convertible on demand to cash and do earn interest. It is widely

Table 10.6: Australian Trading Banks, Selected Statistics[a]

Year	Personal advances ($ mill)	Personal overdrafts ($ mill)	Personal fixed deposits ($ mill)	Personal current deposits ($ mill)	Number of branches	Number of agencies
1955	322.2	n.a.	n.a.	n.a.	3298	1210
1960	340.3	n.a.	901.8		3769	1668
1965	425.4	n.a.	1425.8		4440	1769
1970	781.1	936.3	1166.4	995.6	4798	1580
1975	2448.4	2795.5	2875.5	1664.0	4906	1303

Note: a. Statistics on advances, overdraft limits and deposits relate to major trading banks only. Those on numbers of branches and agencies relate to all trading banks.

Source: Commonwealth Bureau of Census & Statistics, *Finance Bulletin* (various issues); Commonwealth Bureau of Census & Statistics, *Banking & Currency* (various issues); Australian Bureau of Statistics, *Banking* (various issues).

believed that savings deposit accounts are used by many low income earners as a substitute for cheque deposit accounts.[27] Statistics illustrating the growth in savings bank branches and deposits are contained in Table 10.7.

Table 10.7: Australian Savings Banks, Selected Statistics

Year	Number of operative accounts	Depositors Balances at end of year ($ mill)	Number of branches	Number of agencies
1955/6	7189	2282.0	1960	6468
1960/1	9074	3145.0	2871	10724
1965/6	12469	5253.7	5212	15728
1970/1	16178	7634.5	5465	15248
1974/5	19390	12790.4	5537	14377

Sources: Commonwealth Bureau of Census & Statistics, *Banking & Currency* (various issues); Australian Bureau of Statistics, *Banking* (various issues).

Savings banks are also significant suppliers of credit to households. In July 1976 loans, advances and bills discounted by Australian savings banks amounted to $6744.0 million or 43.3 per cent of their total assets. Of these $6049.7 million or 89.7 per cent were housing loans.

Thirteen savings banks were operating in Australia as at June 1976, of which four are government banks. The largest bank, the Commonwealth Savings Bank of Australia, has a market share of about forty per cent and the three largest savings banks together have a market share of about seventy per cent.

Finally it should be noted that the banking and insurance industries do not provide the totality of financial services to the Australian community. Deposit facilities are of course provided by credit unions and building societies. These institutions, together with finance companies, provide credit facilities.[28]

Determinants of Household Demand

In this section the determinants of household demand for banking and insurance services are examined with particular emphasis on those variables which may be relevant in analysing cross-section data on household demand.

Life Insurance

Economists have turned increasingly to theoretical models of decision making under uncertainty in an attempt to explain individual demand for certain financial assets. For the purposes of this discussion one contribution of particular interest is that by Fortune.[29] Fortune applies the familiar Friedman-Savage[30] exposition of the expected utility hypothesis to a model in which the individual compares his end-of-period wealth under two alternatives, one in which he purchases a life insurance contract and one in which he does not. He purchases the contract only if his expected utility is greater under the first alternative than under the second.

Assuming the individual to be risk-averse in the sense defined by Pratt,[31] the quantity of life insurance demanded is found to depend on three variables.

(a) the rate of interest;
(b) the amount of non-property income (wages and salaries) expected to be received over the period and
(c) the amount of non-human wealth held at the time the decision to purchase insurance is made.

Fortune provides empirical support for his model by regression analysis of aggregate US time series data for the period 1964-71.

The thrust of the present discussion is to develop a framework within which cross-sectional data on household demand can be analysed. If it is assumed that all households face the same interest rate[32] the Fortune model suggests that the primary determinants of household demand are household income and wealth. This analysis does not explicitly recognise that purchase of a life insurance policy also involves an increase in personal saving. No difficulties are created, however, by incorporating this component into the model since income and wealth are also the primary determinants of saving.[33]

There are, however, other variables not mentioned by Fortune which may assume particular importance in cross-sectional analysis. In particular age, household size and the stage of the family life cycle would seem to be potentially important variables in explaining household demand for life insurance. Furthermore, discussion in the earlier section of the possibility of decisions being influenced by imperfect consumer information would seem to suggest that education and perhaps also country of birth should be included as possible explanatory variables.

Non-life Insurance

Non-life insurance can be considered within essentially the same analytic framework as that adopted for life insurance. One such theoretical treatment is developed by Mossin[34] who concludes that the primary determinant of individual demand for property insurance is individual wealth. He also suggests that age and education are likely to play an important role. But this analysis does not take account of the fact, mentioned above, that many households insure property not on the basis of expected utility maximisation but rather as a condition under which credit is obtained. To this extent the wealth effect on insurance demand must be somewhat diminished.

Banking Services

Cheque deposit accounts, savings deposit accounts and fixed deposit accounts are included in almost all definitions of money so that an appropriate point of departure in examining household demand for banking services is the extensive literature on the demand for money. Surveys of this literature may be found elsewhere;[35] there appears to be general agreement, however, that the major determinants of the demand for money are income or wealth (or possibly both), interest rates, prices and expectations concerning future interest rates and prices. Most empirical studies have used aggregate time series data and have accordingly placed considerable emphasis on interest rates, prices and the expectational variables.[36] In view of the fact that the theoretical underpinnings of the demand for money relate to individuals it is surprising that little empirical analysis has been attempted using data disaggregated to the household level. Furthermore, if cross-section data are used, the price and interest rate variables can be ignored and primary attention can be paid to income and wealth effects.[37] In particular, two important questions can be examined. Are household holdings of these money balances determined by household income, wealth or both? Is there any evidence of economies of scale in household holdings of these money balances? Finally, as in the case of demand for life and non-life insurance, cross-section analysis of the demand for bank deposits should allow for the possible effects of socio-economic variables.

Empirical Analysis

Data

The primary sources of data for the analysis reported below are the

Survey of Consumer Expenditures (SCE) and Survey of Consumer Finances (SCF) conducted over the period 1966 to 1968 under the direction of Edwards, Drane and Gates.[38] The surveys were conducted on an Australia-wide basis and comprised two stages. The first stage was a survey of household incomes and expenditures only, while the second stage was a supplementary survey of the same households to obtain data on finances.

For present purposes the relevant data on the SCE file are those on household income and household expenditure on home and other property insurance. Motor vehicle insurance premiums are incorporated into motor vehicle overhead costs and cannot be separately identified.[39] Information on bank accounts and life insurance policies is included in the SCF file. A household may hold more than one bank account and, on occasion, more than one account of the same type (i.e. cheque, saving or fixed deposit). The SCF file contains data on ownership and type of each bank account together with the balance of each type of account as at 30 June 1967.

With respect to life insurance policies a wide range of information is contained in the SCF file. As with bank accounts households may hold more than one policy. For each policy data are held on ownership, type of policy (whole of life, pure endowment, endowment), and other policy details. Data on household contributions to superannuation schemes and the type of benefits offered by the scheme are also available.

The SCF file further includes data on income and an exhaustive analysis of assets and liabilities including calculation of household net worth. As suggested earlier, these variables may be of particular importance in the analysis of life insurance holdings.

Finally, the SCF file includes data on a variety of demographic and other non-financial characteristics of the household. Of particular interest for present purposes are the following: household composition, stage in family life cycle, number of workers in household, age, education and occupation of head of household.

Empirical Results: Insurance

Of the 2,757 households in the SCF file approximately two-thirds owned one or more life insurance policies. Of these, however, only about two hundred households reported information for both premiums paid and sum assured. As it is likely that the data on life insurance are most reliable for these households, the regression analysis which follows was carried out using these observations only.

The earlier theoretical discussion suggests the following formulation,

$$DLI = f(W,Y,X) \quad (1)$$

where DLI denotes household demand for life insurance,
W denotes household wealth,
Y denotes household income and
X denotes a vector of demographic and socio-economic variables such as household size, age, education and occupation of household head and stage in the family life cycle.

Equation (1) was formulated as a linear relationship for purposes of estimation. Most of the X variables were incorporated into the analysis using dummy variables but household size (HS) was measured directly by the number of persons in the household. Stage in the family life cycle (SLFC) was measured on a continuous scale defined in the survey itself.

A number of alternative combinations of these variables for X was considered but the only variables consistently appearing with coefficients significantly different from zero were household size and stage in the family life cycle. A more surprising, but equally persistent, result was the insignificance of the wealth coefficient. Accordingly, in the estimated equations reported here, only income, household size and stage in the family life cycle are included as independent variables.

A further point to be resolved is the way in which DLI is to be defined. In the aggregate time series study by Fortune[40] the dependent variable was measured by 'net life insurance in force', which suggests that the appropriate measure of demand in a cross-section study is the value of sum assured. However, other studies[41] have examined variations in the value of life insurance premiums between households and estimation was also carried out using this as the dependent variable.

When ordinary least squares was applied, an examination of the residuals suggested the presence of heteroscedastic errors, which is of course to be expected in a cross-section analysis of the present kind. Accordingly, weighted least squares was employed, using the reciprocal of the square root of income or wealth as the weighting factor. The results are reported in Tables 10.8 and 10.9.

Several points concerning the results warrant some comment. The insignificance of wealth in all estimated equations is puzzling. A possible explanation is collinearity with income although this appears not to be a real problem. The view held by the author, although this is necessarily speculative, is that the probable source of the problem is a

Table 10.8: Insurance Regression Results – Sum Assured[a]

Class of policy	Whole of life	Endowment	Pure endowment
Mean value of dependent variable ($)	4480.84	4910.29	2665.52
Constant	1887.7 (0.90)	4144.5 (0.78)	2605.3 (3.19)
Y	0.2669 (1.86)	1.077 (2.11)	–0.06490 (–0.99)
HS	1154.2 (2.51)	–2246.7 (–1.45)	311.19 (1.55)
SFLC	–549.5 (–1.43)	3400.7 (2.71)	–125.31 (–0.89)
R^2	0.117	0.353	0.004

Note: a. Numbers in brackets are t-statistics.

Table 10.9: Insurance Regression Results – Premiums Paid[a]

Class of policy	Whole of life	Endowment	Pure endowment
Mean value of dependent variable ($)	155.56	112.36	141.04
Constant	17.01 (0.21)	19.09 (0.10)	126.9 (1.66)
Y	0.025 (2.67)	–0.024 (–1.26)	0.00031 (0.05)
HS	24.52 (1.42)	–32.16 (–0.56)	18.98 (1.01)
SFLC	–12.58 (–0.87)	79.33 (1.70)	–9.20 (–0.70)
R^2	0.153	0.110	0.014

Note: a. Numbers in brackets are t-statistics.

deficiency in the wealth data themselves. Data on net worth, being a linear combination of a number of financial variables, each of which is subject to error, are notoriously erratic[42] and comparatively little experience has been gained in Australia in collecting such information.

These difficulties aside, the results are interesting if not particularly exciting. The R^2 values, while hardly impressive are not atypical of cross-section studies of this kind.[43] In general the results using sum assured as the dependent variable appear to be more satisfactory than those using premiums. In the sum assured regressions income is significant for whole of life and endowment insurance, but not for pure endowment policies. The probable explanation for this is that the pure endowment policy is frequently used as a means for saving for those unable to qualify for other forms of ordinary life insurance.[44] Hence the motives for effecting this type of policy are probably more complex than for whole of life and endowment insurance policies, and these are not adequately reflected in the simple model outlined above. Of the remaining variables household size is significant only for whole of life policies, presumably reflecting the fact that these policies are largely effected as a means of providing for dependents.

With respect to non-life insurance no significant relationships could be detected and hence no statistical results are presented. Several factors have no doubt contributed to this. First, it is not possible from the SCE file to identify the property insured or its value. Nor is it possible to estimate the extent to which the insured property is secured for the purposes of obtaining credit. Finally, the earlier discussion suggests that in any event the demand for non-life insurance is likely to be relatively inelastic with respect to premium paid and hence not likely to exhibit substantial variation from one household to the next.

Empirical Results: Banking

In addition to providing the basis for the regression results to be reported below, the survey data may shed some light on the question of multiple holding of cheque and saving deposit accounts and also on the conventional wisdom that savings accounts are frequently used by lower income households as a substitute for cheque accounts. Table 10.10 contains a frequency distribution of household ownership of bank accounts cross-tabulated against household income. These figures indicate the ubiquity (in terms of income distribution) of the savings deposit account, but also illustrate its particular importance to lower income households.

Turning now to those households in the sample which did own a

Table 10.10: Ownership of Bank Accounts, 1967

Household Income ($)	Cheque Account Only (number of households)	%	Savings Account Only (number of households)	%	Both Cheque and Savings Account (number of households)	%	Neither Cheque nor Savings Account (number of households)	%
0-999	22	9.4	262	22.3	61	7.2	151	30.3
1000-1999	20	8.6	159	13.5	65	7.6	72	14.5
2000-2999	57	24.5	279	23.7	149	17.5	144	28.9
3000-3999	63	7.0	285	24.2	218	25.6	102	20.5
4000-4999	35	15.0	120	10.2	151	17.8	17	3.4
5000-5999	13	5.6	41	3.5	96	11.3	6	1.2
6000-6999	9	3.9	13	1.1	41	4.8	1	0.2
7000-8999	8	3.4	11	0.9	36	4.2	4	0.8
9000-11999	4	1.7	4	0.3	22	2.6	0	0.0
12000 and over	2	0.9	2	0.2	11	1.3	1	0.2
Total	233	100.0	1176	100.0	850	100.0	498	100.0

Source: Macquarie University Data Archive, *Survey of Consumer Finances.*

bank account, the earlier theoretical analysis suggests the following relationship:

$$DB = f(W,Y,X) \qquad (2)$$

where DB is the balance of household bank deposits of a particular kind, cheque deposit, savings deposit or fixed deposit, and where W,Y, and X are as defined above.

As in the case of equation (1), equation (2) was formulated as a linear relationship and estimated using weighted least squares. However, in order to test for the existence of economies of scale in the demand for bank deposits, several alternative functional forms were considered.

As in the case of life insurance, the coefficient of wealth was not significantly different from zero in any of the estimated equations. Furthermore, of the X variables, only household size and stage in the family life cycle again appeared to be significant. The results are reported in Table 10.11. The R^2 statistics are significant in every case, as is the income variable. Household size exerts a significant negative effect for both cheque and savings accounts, but no significant effect for fixed deposit accounts. A possible explanation is that larger households hold more of their money balances as cash, although further examination of the survey data would be required before this view could be held with any conviction.

Table 10.11: Regression Results – Banking[a]

Dependent Variable	Cheque Account Balance	Savings Account Balance	Fixed Deposit Balance
Mean value of dependent variable ($)	496.07	981.08	2906.75
Constant	–15.79 (–0.106)	938.7 (11.19)	710.85 (0.44)
Y	0.1368 (7.49)	0.09262 (2.99)	0.513 (2.74)
HS	–85,98 (–2.81)	–56.39 (–2.24)	–154.0 (–0.49)
SFLC	41.38 (2.06)	–20.78 (–2.10)	98.09 (0.51)
R^2	0.051	0.127	0.038

Note: a. Numbers in brackets are t-statistics.

When alternative functional forms were considered, to test for economies of scale, virtually identical results were obtained. The only case in which markedly different results occurred was for fixed deposits where the linear formulation performed significantly better than the alternatives, suggesting that economies of scale do not exist for this class of account. For cheque and savings accounts no firm conclusion can be drawn on the presence of scale economies.

Concluding Remarks

The empirical analysis described above should to some extent be regarded as exploratory. The analysis of consumer finances data in Australia is very much an unexplored area and a study such as the present one can do little more than highlight some of the difficulties involved.

Nevertheless the results are of some interest in their own right, with household income persistently playing an important role in determining household demand for banking and insurance services. The role of wealth remains an enigma deserving further attention, preferably in the light of additional data on household finances.[45]

Notes

* The author thanks Stephen Clift for programming assistance.

1. See, in particular J. McB. Grant, 'Life Assurance and Superannuation Funds', G. Pursell, 'Non-life Insurance', M.K. Lewis and R.H. Wallace 'The Savings Banks' all of which are contained in R.R. Hirst and R.H. Wallace, *The Australian Capital Market*, 2nd Ed., (Cheshire, Melbourne, 1974). See also H.W. Arndt and D.W. Stammer, *The Australian Trading Banks* 4th Ed., (Cheshire, Melbourne, 1972).
2. See R.J. Edgar, J.H. Hatch and M.K. Lewis, 'Economies of Scale in Australia Banking, 1947-68', *The Economic Record,* vol.47, No.117, (March 1971) pp.17-37 and D.J.S. Rutledge and R.H. Tuckwell, 'Economies of Scale in Australian Life Insurance: An Empirical Note', *The Economic Record,* vol.50, No.131 (September 1974) pp.443-8.
3. Selected data on assets, income and expenditure of superannuation funds are published in Australian Bureau of Statistics, *Survey of Selected Private Pension Funds,* Reference No.5.25 and Australian Bureau of Statistics, *Public Authority Pension and Superannuation Schemes, Reference No.5.23.*
4. For example Philip Cagan, *The Effect of Pension Plans on Aggregate Savings,* National Bureau of Economic Research Occasional Paper 95, Columbia University Press, New York, 1965; J.B. Lansing and H. Lydall, 'An Anglo-American Comparison of Personal Saving', *Bulletin of the Oxford Institute of Statistics,* vol.22, No.3 (August 1960) pp.225-58.
5. This was especially so under the concessional deduction scheme in force until 1975-76 whereby high income earners, with larger marginal propensities to save, benefitted more from tax concessions than did lower income earners.
6. Indirect support for this assertion is provided by the enthusiasm shown by

spokesmen for life insurance companies for a return to the concessional deduction arrangement. For example see E.A. Mayer, 'Letter to the Editor', *The Australian Financial Review*, 8 October 1976, p.3.

7. A more detailed discussion of the structure of the industry may be found in Grant, op.cit.
8. Life insurance business is also carried out by two State government offices, but their market share is very small.
9. For the calculations in that table, premium income is used as a measure of output. Other possible measures are sum assured and number of policies. For a discussion of some of the issues involved and an application to concentration in the UK life insurance industry see K. Richards and D. Colenutt, 'Concentration in the U.K. Ordinary Life Assurance Market', *The Journal of Industrial Economies*, vol.XXIV, No.2 (December 1975) pp.147-59.
10. See Grant op.cit. p.175 for a discussion of the circumstances surrounding the rapid increase in the number of companies in the 1950s and 1960s.
11. See Rutledge and Tuckwell, op.cit.
12. These results are reported in Australian Bureau of Statistics, *Foreign Ownership and Control of Life Insurance Business*, 1972-73, Reference No.5.53, Canberra, April 1975. 'Direct foreign ownership' is defined to relate to ownership by a foreigner of at least twenty five per cent of the ordinary shares of an insurance company. 'Other identified foreign ownership' is the remaining foreign ownership by way of portfolio investment. An insurance enterprise is defined as being 'foreign controlled' if the major foreign investor held at least twenty-five per cent of the equity and an Australian investor did not have a larger holding.
13. *Annual Report of the Life Insurance Commissioner, 1975*, Canberra, p.10.
14. For a discussion of some of the issues see A. Lampe, 'Insurance and the Consumer', *The Insurance and Banking Record*, vol.98, No.3 (March 1974) pp.166-7. Most of these criticisms are rejected by the life insurance companies. See, for example, N.H. McLean, 'Letter to the Editor', *The Insurance and Banking Record*, vol.98, No.5 (May 1974) pp.289-90.
15. *Annual Report of the Life Insurance Commissioner*, 1974, Canberra, p.6.
16. These issues are elaborated upon in G. Pursell, 'Australian Non-Life Insurance since 1909', *The Economic Record*, vol.44, No.108 (December 1968) pp.438-69, especially pp.440-1.
17. See Lampe, op.cit.
18. See P.N. Troy and N.G. Butlin, *The Cost of Collisions*, (Cheshire, Sydney 1975) and the comments by R. Sharland in 'How to Overcome the Insurance Communication Gap', *The Insurance and Banking Record*, vol.98, No.5, (May 1974) pp.297-8.
19. Pursell, op.cit, pp.214-5.
20. Further details of the involvement of banks in the insurance industry are provided in W. Spratt, 'The Insurance Market: Battleground for the Banks', *The Insurance and Banking Record*, vol.98, No.2 (February 1974) pp.95-100.
21. Pursell, op.cit. p.212.
22. These figures are reported in Australian Bureau of Statistics, *Foreign Ownership and Control of General Insurance Business 1972-73*, Reference No.5.52, Canberra, April 1975.
23. Little statistical information is available on the travel and credit card services provided by banks. For some background on credit cards see R.B. Cameron, 'Is Money Becoming an Anachronism?', *The Insurance and Banking Record*, vol.98, No.8, August 1974, pp.465-7 and D.M.T. Gibson, 'The Prospect for the Bank Credit Card in Australia', *Growth 27*, Committee for the Economic Development of Australia, 1974.

24. Arndt and Stammer, op.cit, p.26.
25. Ibid, p.27.
26. The only study of scale economies in Australian banking is that by Edgar, Hatch and Lewis, *op.cit.* For a discussion of some of the methodological issues involved see J.C.H. Jones and L. Laudadio, 'Economies of Scale in Australian Banking: A Comment', *The Economic Record,* vol.48, No.124 (December 1972) pp.570-4 and J.H. Hatch and M.K. Lewis, 'Economies of Scale in Australian Banking: A Reply', *The Economic Record,* vol.49, No.127 (September 1973) pp.481-4.
27. See, for example, Arndt and Stammer, op.cit. p.36.
28. See M.R. Hill, 'Housing Finance Institutions', and G. Mc.L. Scott, 'Instalment Credit Institutions', both in Hirst and Wallace, op.cit.
29. P. Fortune, 'A Theory of Optimal Life Insurance: Development and Tests', *The Journal of Finance,* vol. XXVIII, No.3 (June 1973) pp.587-600.
30. M. Friedman and L.J. Savage, 'The Utility Analysis of Choices Involving Risk', *The Journal of Political Economy,* vol.LVI, No.4 (August 1948) pp.279-304.
31. J.W. Pratt, 'Risk Aversion in the Small and in the Large', *Econometrica,* vol. 32, No.1-2 (January-April 1964) pp.122-36.
32. Strictly speaking, of course, this assumption cannot be fully justified. However, in the absence of any further data it is the most reasonable assumption that can be made.
33. A recent example of cross-sectional analysis of household saving behaviour is I. Friend and C. Lieberman, 'Short-Run Asset Effects on Household Saving and Consumption: The Cross-Section Evidence', *The American Economic Review,* vol.LXV, No.4 (September 1975) pp.624-33.
34. J. Mossin, 'Aspects of Rational Insurance Purchasing', *The Journal of Political Economy,* vol.76, No.4, Part 1 (July/August 1968) pp.553-68.
35. See, for example, D. Laidler, *The Demand for Money, Theories and Evidence* (International Textbook Company, Scranton, 1969).
36. See, for example, T.J. Valentine, 'The Demand for Very Liquid Assets in Australia', *Australian Economic Papers,* vol.12, No.21 (December 1973) pp.196-207.
37. See note 31.
38. A more complete discussion of the methodology underlying the surveys may be found in H.R. Edwards, R.C. Gates and R.A. Layton, *Survey of Consumer Finances,* (University of Sydney and University of New South Wales), Sydney, 1974). For other analyses of the data and a discussion of their deficiencies, see N.R. Podder, 'Patterns of Household Consumption Expenditures in Australia', *The Economic Record,* vol.47, No.119 (September 1971) pp.379-98 and 'Distribution of Household Income in Australia', *The Economic Record,* vol. 48, No.122, (June 1972) pp.181-200.
39. The SCE file also includes data relating to household expenditure on accident insurance premiums, but these are included in one item with medical and hospital insurance premiums and are not examined here.
40. Fortune, op.cit., p.596.
41. M.E. Kreinin, J.B. Lansing and J.N. Morgan, 'Analysis of Life Insurance Premiums', *The Review of Economics and Statistics,* vol.XXXIX, No.1 (February 1957) pp.46-54.
42, R. Ferber, 'The Reliability of Consumer Reports of Financial Assets and Debts', Bureau of Economic and Business Research, University of Illinois, *Studies in Consumer Savings,* No.6 (June 1966).
43. See, for example, Friend and Lieberman, op.cit.
44. See M. Esler and C.A. Parkes, *Introduction to Insurance in Australia and New Zealand* (West Publishing Corporation, Sydney, 1970).

45. The recent survey of household expenditures conducted by the Australian Bureau of Statistics did not collect data on household finances. So far as the author is aware there is no prospect of a consumer finances survey being undertaken in Australia in the near future.

Bibliography

Arndt H.W. and D.W. Stammer, *The Australian Trading Banks.* 4th Ed., (Cheshire, Melbourne, 1972).

Australian Bureau of Statistics, *Public Authority Pension and Superannuation Schemes,* Reference No. 5.23 (Canberra, Irregular).

Australian Bureau of Statistics, *Survey of Selected Private Pension Funds,* Reference No.5.25 (Canberra, irregular).

Australian Bureau of Statistics, *Foreign Ownership and Control of General Insurance Business 1972-73,* Reference No.5.52 (Canberra, April 1975).

Australian Bureau of Statistics, *Foreign Ownership and Control of Life Insurance Business, 1972-73,* Reference No.5.53 (Canberra, April 1975).

Benston G.J., 'Economies of Scale in Financial Institutions', *Journal of Money, Credit and Banking,* vol.IV, No.3 (May 1972).

Borch, K., 'Capital Markets and the Supervision of Insurance Companies', *Journal of Risk and Insurance,* vol.41, No.3 (September 1974).

Brigham, E.F., 'Economies of Scale in the Savings and Loan Industry', *Western Economic Journal,* vol.3, No.1 (1964).

Cagan, P., *The Effect of Pension Plans on Aggregate Savings,* National Bureau of Economic Research, Occasional Paper 95 (Columbia University Press, New York, 1965).

Cummins, J.D., *An Econometric Model of the Life Insurance Sector of the U.S. Economy* (Health, Lexington Massachusetts, 1975).

Denenberg, H.S., and W.C. Scheel, 'Concentration in the U.S. Life Insurance Industry', *Journal of Risk and Insurance,* vol.39, No.2, (June 1972).

Department of Repatriation and Compensation, *Establishment of the Australian Government Insurance Office* (Inter-departmental Committee Report, Canberra, 1975).

Edgar, R.J., J.H. Hatch and M.K. Lewis, 'Economies of Scale in Australian Banking, 1947-68', *The Economic Record,* vol.47, No.117 (March 1971).

Esler M. and C.A. Parkes, *Introduction to Insurance in Australia and New Zealand* (West Publishing Corporation, Sydney, 1970).

Fortune, P., 'A Theory of Optimal Life Insurance: Development and Tests', *The Journal of Finance,* vol.XXVIII, No.3 (June 1973).

Gibson, D.M.T., 'The Prospect for the Bank Credit Card in Australia', *Growth 27* (Committee for the Economic Development of Australia, 1974).

Grant, J. McB., 'Life Assurance and Superannuation Funds', in Hirst R.R. and R.H. Wallace, *The Australian Capital Market* 2nd Ed., (Cheshire, Melbourne, 1974).

Halpern, P.J. and G.F. Mathewson, 'Economies of Scale in Financial Institutions: A General Model Applied to Insurance', *Journal of Monetary Economics,* vol.1, No.2 (April 1975).

Hammond, J.D., E.R. Melander and N. Shilling, 'Economies of Scale in the Property and Liability Insurance Industry', *Journal of Risk and Insurance,* vol.38, No.2 (June 1971).

Hatch, J.H. and M.K. Lewis, 'Economies of Scale in Australian Banking: A Reply', *The Economic Record,* vol.49, No.127 (September 1973).

Hensley, R.J. 'Economies of Scale in Financial Enterprises', *Journal of Political*

Economy, vol.LXVI, No.5 (October 1958).

Hirst, R.R. and R.H. Wallace, *The Australian Capital Market*, 2nd Ed., (Cheshire Melbourne, 1974).

Houston, D.B. and R.B. Simon, 'Economies of Scale in Financial Institutions: A Study in Life Insurance', *Econometricia*, vol.38, No.6 (November 1970).

Insurance Commissioner, *First Annual Report*, Australian Government Publishing Service, Canberra, 1975.

Jones, J.C.H. and Laudadio L., 'Economies of Scale in Australian Banking: A Comment', *The Economic Record*, vol.48, No.124 (December 1972).

Kamerschon, D.R., 'A Note on Economies of Scale in Life Insurance', *Journal of Risk and Insurance*, vol.39, No.3 (September 1972).

Kreinin, M.E., J.B. Lansing and J.N. Morgan, 'Analysis of Life Insurance Premiums', *The Review of Economics and Statistics*, vol.XXXIX, No.1 (February 1957).

Lansing, J.B. and H. Lydall, 'An Anglo-American Comparison of Personal Savings', *Bulletin of the Oxford Institute of Statistics*, vol.22, No.3 (August 1960).

Lewis, M.K. and R.H. Wallace, 'The Savings Banks', in Hirst, R.R. and R.H. Wallace, *The Australian Capital Market*, 2nd Ed., (Cheshire, Melbourne, 1974).

Life Insurance Commissioner, *Annual Report* (Canberra, annual).

Mossin, J., *'Aspects of Rational Insurance Purchasing'*, *The Journal of Political Economy*, vol.76, No.4, Part I (July/August 1968).

Pursell, G., 'Australian Non-Life Insurance since 1909', *The Economic Record*, vol.44, No.108 (December 1968).

'Non-Life Insurance', in Hirst, R.R. and R.H. Wallace, *The Australian Capital Market*, 2nd Ed., (Cheshire, Melbourne, 1974).

Richards, K. and D. Colenutt, 'Concentration in the U.K. Ordinary Life Assurance Market', *The Journal of Industrial Economics*, vol.XXIV, No.2 (June 1975).

Rutledge, D.J.S. and R.H. Tuckwell, 'Economies of Scale in Australia Life Insurance: An Empirical Note', *The Economic Record*, vol.50, No.131, (September 1974).

Troy, P.N., and N.G. Butlin, *The Cost of Collisions* (Cheshire, Sydney, 1975).

Wickens, P.C., *The Law of Life Assurance in Australia*, 4th Ed., (Law Book Co., Sydney; 1969).

PART FOUR: SERVICES OF HEALTH, CONVENIENCE AND LEISURE

Changes in technology and tastes are in part influenced by, and, in part derive from, information sources available to society and avenues for satisfying artistic or recreational motivations. The capacity of a community or individuals to realise consumption objectives are in many cases constrained by risk and uncertainty or other forms of temporary or permanent disadvantage.

Deeble and Scotton (chapter 11) present a study of the institutions and professions which provide health services in the community. They point to the nature of trade-offs between equity and efficiency in achieving a system that does not have disproportionate costs or benefits for any one group in society.

Advertising services transmit messages between parties that influence both consumption decisions and welfare status. Metwally's (chapter 12) study of advertising expenditure indicates how it is possible to evaluate the effectiveness of outlays in achieving a given profit maximisation objective.

The concluding chapters deal with performing arts services. Withers (chapter 13) presents information on the structure of the activity and then, after considering the pattern of demand for these services, critically assesses and tests a model of the determinants of a cost-revenue squeeze in the performing arts. By contrast, Throsby (chapter 14) looks at the production and cost relationships endemic in supplying these services from the viewpoint of a non-profit organisation.

11 HEALTH SERVICES AND THE MEDICAL PROFESSION

J.S. Deeble and R.B. Scotton

Introduction

This chapter is about health services and the system of institutions and professions which produces them. It is not about health, although the obvious rationale for these institutions is that they improve health and in the popular view are largely identified as its major source. We do not attempt to appraise their objective efficacy but treat health services simply as objects of final demand and utility.

There are two reasons for this limited approach. The first is that, at the margin of per capita use in rich countries like Australia, overall health levels are more closely related to consumption habits and life styles than to the use of health services.[1] General models have been formulated – which would be equally applicable to other social activities such as education and recreation – in which households produce 'health' (of their members) from their own resources and from a variety of health-related inputs, some of which, including health services, are positively associated and others of which, such as tobacco and alcohol, are negatively associated with health. [Grossman, 1972] Unfortunately, the data needed to make such models operational are rare in any country, and certainly do not exist at present in Australia.

The second reason is the heterogeneity of the group of products loosely identified as 'health services'. While many have clear cut curative and preventive functions, others have little objective relationship to health improvement at all. Some provide social and domestic support, others provide information and the certification of illness for a variety of non-medical purposes, and, at the extreme, there are some services which contribute only to comfort and amenity – the provision of private rooms in hospital, superior personal services and purely cosmetic surgical procedures are examples. Moreover, there is the practical problem that, in the absence of independent information as to the prevalence of illness and disability in the community, most available evidence comes from the health services themselves. Thus, paradoxically, the more effective these services are in discovering and diagnosing illness, the more prevalent illness will appear to be. To relate such a complex mixture of products to uncertain measures of final health outcomes would require a much more detailed and technical analysis than is possible here.

This does not mean that cost-benefit concepts are irrelevant. However, in practice the problem of evaluating benefits has meant that most studies have been restricted to either the cost-effectiveness of alternative treatment methods in very specific circumstances, or to those public health and research activities where benefits are so widely spread and/or accrue so far into the future that problems of interpersonal comparisons in distribution can be ignored.[2] These distribution problems bedevil all welfare analyses of personal health care. If the normative propositions of the competitive economic model applied, their solution could perhaps be left to the interplay of individual consumers' and producers' interests, but the special features of the health service system make many of the standard approaches to micro-economic analysis unsuitable.

Special Features

Empirically, the main features of the health service system are:

- heterogeneity of output, multiple objectives and a wide substitutability of services, both within the orthodox health care network and for other alternatives, including household care and self help;
- an industry structure embodying ethical norms which are basically anti-competitive, which accepts and encourages monopoly through licensure, which contains a substantial non-profit sector and which is dominated by the medical profession;
- a social consensus about access to care which prohibits any withholding of 'needed' services because of inability to pay, and which frequently prices health services (through public provision, subsidisation, insurance, or a combination of these) at levels well below production costs. Every health service system thus works under varying degrees of chronic excess demand.

These observed features all spring from certain basic properties of health care, of which the two most important – and interrelated – are *uncertainty* and *inequalities in information.* The existence of these properties is, of course, quite obvious, even if their significance is not. The demand for health services is irregular and unpredictable, normally arises only in the event of illness (an abnormal state of affairs) and its satisfaction cannot, because of the size of the possible cost involved, be guaranteed by generalised income transfers in the same way as such regular and standardised needs as food and shelter. Moreover, there is uncertainty as to the nature and the quality of the product, at least in consumers' minds, since they can rarely rely on past experience. Very few people possess the information needed to assess their own needs for health care, or to judge the quality and value of that which they receive. Expert knowledge in these matters is, in fact, a major component of the service sought. There is therefore a premium on the correct choice of both advice and treatment under circumstances where the consumer is singularly ill-placed to make the choice and must, inevitably, enter some form of trust relationship with the supplier.

A number of economists have examined the consequences for market structure of uncertainty and unequal information. The classical statement on uncertainty is by Arrow, [1963] whose conclusion is that its prevalence precludes a competitive optimum and that the special structural and behavioural characteristics of the health service industry – (including licensure, restriction of entry, legalisation of monopoly and discriminatory pricing, but with a presumption against competitive behaviour and overt profit-seeking) – are all explicable, and justified, as efforts to reduce uncertainty by non-market means. He further concludes that private health insurance cannot, because of its inability to distinguish between avoidable and unavoidable risks, provide all the security which the community desires. Satisfaction of this demand requires additional public intervention, including national health insurance.

The consequences of unequal information have been examined most thoroughly by a Canadian, R.G. Evans, [1973] in relation to the single phenomenon which most distinguishes the health service industry from others; namely, the dominant position of the medical profession.[3] Its members are responsible for allocation decision covering some 80 per cent of all health care expenditure, but doctors occupy the almost unique position of being simultaneously entrepreneurs selling services to their patients and agents for these same patients in selecting the services used. Under such conditions, the ordinary market assumption of independent demand and supply schedules, with prices performing an equilibrating function, are quite unrealistic. Supplier-induced demand may indeed make it impossible to reach any market equilibrium at which both prices and levels of output are socially acceptable.[4] We will examine the consequences of this management dilemma later.

Structure

Australian health services currently account for over 7 per cent of gross domestic product. They employ nearly 350,000 people at incomes somewhat higher than the national average, with both the internal proportion of labour costs and the relative level of earnings increasing over recent years. As might be expected, the industry is characterised by a consistent upward trend in activity and a relatively high utilisation of capacity. In common with other developed countries, the share of gross domestic product attributable to health services in Australia has increased steadily for many years.

Summary description of the industry's structure is not easy. For some purposes, a functional classification based on diagnosis, treatment, accommodation, social support, etc., would be appropriate; for others, a more 'industrial' classification into medical practice, hospital service, pharmaceutical production and so on would be relevant, with a division between public and private activity in each case. In fact, all these divisions are blurred by the complex interrelationships between the public and private sectors. In the Australian context, many public outputs are actually inputs to the private medical industry (the treatment of 'private' patients in public hospitals, for example), in return for which the public sector has always depended heavily on private doctors for the medical component of much of its health care [Scotton, 1974, ch.4]. Moreover, the existence of joint products, of which professional education and patient care are the best known examples, makes some service divisions unavoidably arbitrary.

The tables which follow show expenditures and their financing according to a system developed by the World Health Organisation and for which Australian statistics are available for the triennial years 1960/1 to 1972/3.[5] Classification is by a mixture of producer and purpose criteria into *institutional care, other medical care, public health services* (subdivided into personal services to identifiable individuals, and environmental services to the population as a whole) and *teaching and research.* Only services designed to care for the sick and to prevent, diagnose, cure or relieve disease and disability are included. The more basic preventive influences of nutrition, housing and sanitation are all excluded, except for some specific supervisory activities.

Expenditures

The most obvious structural divisions of expenditure are between the various classes of service, particularly between institutional and non-

Table 11.1: Current Expenditure on Health Services in Australia

	1960/1 $m	1966/7 $m	1972/3 $m
Institutional Care			
Public			
General Hospitals	201	334	770
Mental Hospitals	38	68	120
Nursing Homes	11	19	50
Ambulances	7	11	23
Private			
Hospitals	23	30	95
Nursing Homes	19	43	130
Administrative Expenses	5	10	17
TOTAL – Institutional Care	303	507	1,205
Other Medical Care			
Government and Charitable	5	11	26
Private – Medical	102	176	400
Dental and Other Professional	53	85	(157)
Medicaments	154	241	398
Applicances	15	23	31
Administrative Expenses	9	14	25
TOTAL – Other Medical Care	338	550	1,037
Public Health Services			
Personal Services	18	30	
Environmental and Supporting	10	17	89
TOTAL – Public Health	28	47	89
Teaching and Research	12	21	(40)
TOTAL – All Health Services	682	1,125	2,371

Source: See note 5. Figures in parenthesis are preliminary estimates.

institutional care, and between public and private activity. Tables 11.1 and 11.2 show that just over half of all current expenditure in 1972/3 was for institutional care, over 5 per cent more than in 1960/1. Preliminary estimates for later years suggest that the proportion has increased still further. The rate of growth was somewhat higher in the private than in the public sector and within this group, in nursing homes rather than in hospitals. Amongst non-institutional services,

Table 11.2: Current Expenditure on Health Services in Australia
Percentage Composition

	1960/1	1972/3
Public		
General Hospitals	29.6	32.5
Mental Hospitals	5.6	5.0
Nursing Homes	1.5	2.1
Ambulances	1.0	1.0
Private		
Hospitals	3.2	4.0
Nursing Homes	2.9	5.5
Administrative Expenses	0.7	0.7
TOTAL – Institutional Care	44.5	50.8
Other Medical Care		
Government and Charitable	0.7	1.1
Private – Medical	15.0	16.9
Dental and Other Professional	7.8	6.6
Medicaments	22.5	16.8
Appliances	2.3	1.3
Administrative Expenses	1.3	1.1
TOTAL – Other medical Care	49.5	43.8
Public Health	4.2	3.7
Teaching and Research	1.8	1.7
TOTAL – All Health Services	100.0	100.0

Source: Table 11.1.

payments to doctors in private practice for personal medical services increased in relative importance, whereas the share of medicament spending declined. Spending on dental services has also declined relative to others, and both trends have continued since 1973.[6] In the case of dentistry, the reason appears to have been a decline in the ratio of dentists to population, but the relative decline in medicament spending has had other underlying causes. The year 1960/1 corresponded with the end of the therapeutic revolution and represented a peak of spending on drugs in relation to both total health service expenditure and GDP; the proportions have since fallen in all developed countries. But the reduction has been in relative prices, not use. In 1960/1, the average cost per prescription covered by Pharmaceutical Benefits was

$1.94, the average number of prescriptions per head of population was 3.32, and the average cost per head of population $6.44. By 1975/6, average use was 7.43 prescriptions per head – over twice the average in 1961 – but the average cost per precription was only $3.23 and the average expenditure per head of population was only $24.00[7] Since these trends in drug prices are international, Australian drug expenditures have remained amongst the highest, if not the highest, in the world relative to income, and the high distribution costs which are largely responsible for them have continued. This, and the factors underlying trends in hospital and medical expenditures and costs, are examined later.

The division between public and private activity, as measured by the ownership of facilities and the occupational status of practitioners, can be derived from Table 11.2. Apart from public health services (which are by definition provided by governments) and teaching and research (where there is very limited participation by some professional groups), direct public provision is restricted almost entirely to institutional care. In 1972/3, public authorities accounted for about 80 per cent of all spending on institutional care, but only for about 4 per cent of 'other medical care'. Overall, about 53 per cent of all expenditures on health services went to private suppliers, and this proportion had declined by only about 2 per cent since 1960/1. By 1974/5 it had fallen a little further, but the whole basis of this division is somewhat misleading. In the general hospitals, where the greatest cost increase occurred, the proportion of 'private patients' almost doubled over the period, so that the importance of private medicine, in terms of control over resources as distinct from the legal ownership of them, had risen considerably.[8]

Financing

The structure of financing presents an equally complicated picture. Over the last two decades, the Commonwealth government's participation has steadily increased, but in the form of cash benefits, not direct provision, and – at least until Medibank – as a supplement to, rather than a replacement of, traditional State government and private sources. As can be seen from Table 11.3, Commonwealth finance is involved in all the major services, whereas State government finance is virtually restricted to institutional care. Neither the State nor local governments provide any significant cash benefits to the users of health services. By contrast nearly 90 per cent of Commonwealth finance in 1972/3 was in the form of cash benefits to consumers, or payments to

Table 11.3: Current Expenditure on Health Services by Source of Finance 1972/3 ($m)

	Government				Private					
	C/wealth	State	Local	Total	Comp. Ins.	Vol. Ins.	Recipients	Other	Total	All Sources
Institutional Care										
General Hospitals	180	405	2	587	(23)	167	78	10	278	865
Mental Hospitals	7	100		107			12	1	13	120
Nursing Homes	93	20		113		1	64	2	67	180
Other	2	6		8		32	13	2	47	55
Total—Institutional Care	282	531	2	815	(23)	200	167	15	405	1,220
Other Medical Care										
Government and Charitable	16	8		24			1	1	2	26
Medical	206			206	(20)	107	67		194	400
Dental and Other Professional	5	9		14		2	(141)		(143)	(157)
Medicaments	166			166			232		232	398
Other	9			9		18	28		46	55
Total—Other Medical Care	402	17		419	(20)	127	469	1	617	1,036
Public Health	31	37	19	87			1	1	2	89
Teaching and Research	(18)	(16)		(34)			(2)	(4)	(6)	(40)
Total—All Health Services	733	601	21	1,355	(43)	327	639	21	1,030	2,385

Source: See note 5. Figures in parenthesis are preliminary estimates.

the States for the operation of specific services.

Table 11.4 shows that, directly, government outlays provided an estimated 57 per cent of all the finance available for current health service expenditures in 1972/3, and the proportion had almost certainly increased by 1974/5. If the value of taxation concessions on private insurance contributions and residual personal expenditures were added to direct outlays, the overall government share would have exceeded two-thirds. The increased public share was almost entirely due to a very large increase in Commonwealth medical benefits, the government share of institutional funding having actually fallen since 1960/1. On the private side, direct payments by recipients fell and the share of voluntary insurance rose. Though important for the particular services covered (fee-charging hospitals and private medical practitioners) private insurance remained a relatively minor source of finance overall. Its real significance lay in its support of a particular system of health care delivery rather than the finance which it actually raised.[9]

Developments Since 1973

No detailed statistics of health expenditures have been published since 1972/3. However, later figures are available for general hospitals, private medical services, and some medicaments (covering nearly 60 per cent of all health expenditures), and preliminary estimates can be made for other items. Comparison with aggregate statistics published by the Commonwealth Bureau of Census and Statistics suggests that, in total at least, these estimates are reliable.[10]

For 1974/5, total current expenditure is estimated at $3,800 million of which general hospitals accounted for $1,500 million (40 per cent), total institutional care about $2,120 million (56 per cent), private medical services about $570 million (15 per cent) and medicaments nearly $600 million (16 per cent). In 1975/6, the figure for general hospitals had increased to some $2,000 million (50 per cent), and for medical services to nearly $850 million (18 per cent) in a total of about $4,900 million.[11] These very large increases were due mainly to inflation, but there were also some technical factors, particularly with respect to payments for private medical care, which require careful interpretation.

On the financing side, the share of direct government funding rose to 62 per cent in 1974/5, and to about 73 per cent in 1975/6. The change in 1975/6 was mainly because of the replacement of voluntary medical insurance by Medibank. Hospital fees paid by patients and voluntary insurance funds also decreased but by a lower proportion,

Table 11.4: Current Expenditure on Health Services by Source of Finance 1960/1 and 1972/3, Percentage Composition

	Government				Private				
	C/wealth	State	Local	Total	Comp. Ins.	Vol.Ins.	Recipients	Other	Total
1960/1									
Institutional Care	26.4	44.3	0.2	70.9	1.9	11.3	14.3	1.7	29.2
Other Medical Care	27.3	0.5		27.8	2.9	10.2	59.0	0.1	72.2
Public Health	42.5	32.1	23.2	97.8			2.1	0.1	2.2
Teaching and Research	33.9	43.1		77.0			6.7	16.3	23.0
All Services	27.6	22.2	1.1	50.9	2.3	10.1	35.6	1.1	49.1
1972/3									
Institutional Care	23.1	43.5	0.2	66.9	1.9	16.4	13.7	1.2	33.1
Other Medical Care	38.8	1.6		40.4	1.9	12.3	45.3	0.1	59.6
Public Health	34.8	41.6	21.4	97.8			2.0	0.2	2.2
Teachine and Research	45.0	40.0		85.0			5.0	10.0	15.0
All Services	30.7	25.1	0.9	56.8	1.8	13.7	26.8	0.9	43.2

Source: Table 11.3.

because many people retained private hospital insurance. The main change in hospital financing was within the public sector, the Commonwealth government's share having increased and that of the State governments declined.

Total Expenditure and Gross Domestic Product

Table 11.5 shows Australian current and capital expenditures as a percentage of gross domestic product. Capital expenditures are limited to the construction of purpose-built health facilities, and so slightly understate total investment in the private sector (in private doctors' surgeries in particular). However, this is unlikely to significantly affect the trend which is steadily rising as in all comparable countries. Table 11.6 shows statistics for Australia, USA, Canada and Britain from 1960 to 1973. The movements were not all regular, but the variations were due as much to irregularities in the growth of the national economies as to fluctuations in the rate of growth in health service expenditures. In all the countries, institutional care contributed the major part of the increase, followed by out-of-hospital medical expenses; public health and other components lagged behind. Through the period shown, the Australian percentage was in the middle of the range; above the British figure but well below the two North American countries. However, the rapid increase in Australian costs since 1973 – to about 6.3 per cent of

Table 11.5: Total Expenditures on Health Services 1960/1 to 1972/3 ($m)

	1960/1	1966/7	1972/3
Current expenditure	682	1,125	2,371
Capital expenditure:			
Public	40	73	117
Private	8	14	48
Total expenditure	730	1,211	2,536
Capital as percentage of current expenditure	7.0	7.7	7.0
Total as percentage of GDP[a]	5.0	5.3	6.0

Note: a. GNP prior to 1972/3

Sources: 1. Deeble (1967, 1974) and unpublished material supplied by hospital authorities.

2. Australian Bureau of Census and Statistics, *Social Indicators*, No.1 (1976).

Table 11.6: Current Health Service Expenditures as a Percentage of GDP: Australia, USA, Canada and Britain 1960-73

	1960			1965			1970			1973		
	Inst.	Med.	Total	Inst.	Med.	Total	Inst.	Med.	Total	Inst.	Med.	Total
Australia[a]	2.1	0.7	4.7	2.2	0.7	4.9	2.5	0.8	5.2	3.2	1.0	5.7
USA	1.9	1.1	5.1	2.2	1.3	5.6	3.3	1.5	7.2	3.5	1.4	7.4
Canada	2.5	0.9	5.0	3.0	1.0	5.6	3.7	1.2	6.7	3.6	1.2	6.6
Britain[b]			3.9			4.3			4.9			5.3

Notes: a. Years ending in June, except for 1960 for which 1960/1 data are used.
b. England and Wales.

Sources:
Australia: Tables 11.1, 11.2, 11.5. Figures for 1964/5 interpolated from data in *Report from the Senate Select Committee on Hospital and Medical Costs*, 1969.
USA and Canada: *National Health Expenditures in Canada 1960-1973 (with Comparative Data for the United States)*, Department of National Health and Welfare, Ottawa, 1975.
Britain: Maxwell, R., *Health Care: The Growing Dilemma* (McKinsey and Co, London, 1974).

gross domestic product in 1974/5, and perhaps as high as 7.1 per cent in 1975/6 – means that they are now much closer to the North American levels and their containment is likely to be just as important a public policy issue as in those countries.

Capacity, Output and Cost

It is obvious that any economic analysis is very limited in the absence of a measure of the output of the activity studied. At the very least, expenditure changes have to be dissected into real output changes and variations in unit costs and prices before criteria of resource use (such as factor productivity and capacity utilisation) are applied. The interpretation of both consumer and producer behaviour, and the relevance of various theoretical constructs to them, necessitates a similar disaggregation.

Unfortunately, there is no generally agreed unit of measurement nor is one likely to emerge if only because the need varies with the purpose of the analysis. For social purposes it would obviously be desirable to measure performance in terms of health outcomes, since the case for diverting resources to health services is, in the public sector at least, based largely on their supposed positive contribution.[12] Discussions of such issues as excess surgery, and overuse of hospital and other services clearly assume some assessment of outcomes. But apart from the conceptual and practical difficulties of compiling such measures, their operational significance is in many circumstances doubtful. Consumers will continue to demand, and use, services which make only a marginal contribution to health, and producers will continue to supply them. To consumers, they may contribute to comfort and amenity or perform a caring, rather than a curing, function which may be equally desirable: to producers, they simply represent a source of livelihood. Moreover, the unit prices which consumers pay and producers receive may not be the same. Finally, there are some practical problems concerned with levels of aggregation and allowances for quality change which have led economists like Scitovsky to adopt the 'episode of illness' as the unit of measurement (instead of the 'bundle of services' approach generally used in, say, consumer price indexes). Others like Reder advocate the use of a constant-coverage health insurance package as a generalised unit for measuring price changes (and thus imputing output changes) on the ground that this is the price which most consumers actually face [Scitovsky, 1967, 1974; Reder, 1969]. Such measures may assist in analysing consumer conduct, but neither is particularly useful for assessing the behaviour of producer units.[13]

The output and capacity measures used in this chapter are of the most basic and traditional kind, representing, in most cases, not final products but intermediate products which are themselves inputs into the 'treatment' process. This means, amongst other things, that health outcomes are pushed into the rather vague concept of 'quality', and that interpretation of both output and cost changes requires a good deal of 'outside' information about variations in service/case mix and the input composition of the units used. The following discussion concentrates on the three major categories of general hospitals, private medical services and the supply and distribution of drugs.

Hospitals

Table 11.7 shows statistics of capacity and output in Australian general hospitals from 1960/1 to 1975/6. Table 11.8 shows some operating cost ratios and some indicators of underlying wage inflation, the most important single source of cost increase.

As can be seen, capacity and utilisation as measured by beds available and occupied have barely kept pace with population growth. In terms of bed occupancy, there was an almost constant use of available capacity, the peak bed occupancy ratio being in 1970 with a slight fall thereafter. At an average of about 70 per cent, the figure may not seem high, but it conceals considerable differences between city and country institutions, average occupancy being around 80 per cent in city hospitals, and as low as 60 per cent or less in some country areas.[14] On a population basis, bed occupancy changed very little over the period, the only significant increase being in private hospitals after 1970 when the government raised its subsidisation of health insurance considerably.[15] It is interesting to note that, despite predictions to the contrary, the use of private hospitals did not fall in the Medibank year of 1975/6. Indeed, the only major increase was in that sector.

Hospital cost changes were dominated by wage and salary increases, particularly in the last triennium. Apart from the general movements affecting all service industries, which might be represented by changes in average weekly earnings, the hospitals have been especially vulnerable to the 'catch up' in female earnings. The index of average minimum female award wages probably understates the actual changes which the hospitals have faced, since it is in the professional and semi-professional groups that wage equality has had most impact. Changes in wage rates were not, however, the only factor. All the available staffing statistics confirm a substantial real increase in labour input per occupied bed-day. Application of the wage indices in Table 11.8 to daily average bed costs,

Table 11.7: Australia: Public and Private General Hospitals Capacity and Output Statistics, 1960/1 to 1975/6

	No. of beds (30 June)					Occupied Bed-days per 1000 pop.			Admissions per 1000 pop.		
	Public		Private		Total	Public	Private	Total	Public	Private	Total
	No. (000's)	per 1000 pop.	No. (000's)	Per 1000 pop.	per 1000 pop.						
1961	54.2	5.25	11.7	1.1	6.34	1,290	260	1,550	120	n.a.	n.a.
1964	58.1	5.26	12.0	1.1	6.35	1,295	265	1,560	123	n.a.	n.a.
1967	61.3	5.23	12.4	1.1	6.29	1,291	259	1,550	126	32	158
1970	62.4	5.03	13.0	1.1	6.08	1,300	256	1,556	137	35	172
1973	65.5	5.00	15.1	1.2	6.16	1,310	274	1,584	143	n.a.	n.a.
1976	69.5	5.10	17.4	1.3	6.38	1,310	326	1,626	147	42	190

Sources:
1. Annual Reports of State Hospital authorities and Commonwealth Director-General of Health; Commonwealth Year Books, 1964, 1967, 1969.
2. Commonwealth Department of Health, Research Section, 'Public Hospitals in Australia', 1967; R.B. Rofe, 'Hospital Beds and Finance', *Health,* 1967, 17(2).
3. Commonwealth Department of Health, *Public and Private Hospitals: Statistical Summary 1970-71;* Australian Department of Social Security, *Public and Private Hospitals: Statistical Summary 1971-72 and 1972-73.*
4. Health Insurance Commission, *Annual Report,* 1975-76.

Table 11.8: Public Hospital Operating Costs

	Average Cost Per Occupied Bed-day		Salary Costs		Average Weekly Earnings	Av. Min. Female Award Wages
	$	(Index 1963/4 = 100)	(Index 1963/4 = 100)	% of Total Costs	(Index 1963/4 = 100)	(Index 1963/4 = 100)
1960/1	12.7	84	83	63.8	90	94
1963/4	15.2	100	100	64.0	100	100
1966/7	19.2	126	129	65.5	120	116
1969/70	25.5	168	180	68.5	148	142
1972/3	41.4	272	304	71.4	197	199
1975/6	88.0[a]	579[a]	660[a]	75.0[a]	329	380

Note: a. Estimated.

Sources: See Table 11.7. Also Hospital and Allied Services Advisory Council, Uniform Costing Committee, *Uniform Statements of Cost, Sources of Funds of Hospitals and Nursing Homes, and Government Assistance to Allied Services in Australia*, 1970-71, 1971-72 and 1972-73 issues.

and its salary component, would indicate a rise of around 70 per cent in real wage cost per occupied bed over the period.

Some of this increase may have been due to improved employee conditions – reduced hours, longer leave, etc. – which would mean that recorded staffing ratios overstate the actual growth in labour inputs. However, another reason is that the measurement of output (and capacity) in terms of bed usage and availability seriously understates the actual rise in productivity. As can be seen from Table 11.7, the number of patients treated per thousand of population rose more rapidly than bed occupancy through a fall in the average length of patient stay. In 1960/1, the average stay in public general hospitals was 11.2 days, equivalent to a 'bed turnover rate' of 32.7 patients per bed per annum. In 1975/6, the estimated figure was just under 9 days, giving a throughput of nearly 40 patients per bed per annum and a 25 per cent output increase over the period. Such an increase is not costless, however. It means, amongst other things, that, with a costant case-mix, a higher proportion of patients are, at any point of time, in the acute phase of illness when the intensity and cost of care is greatest, with a proportionate increase in both the operating and the facilities costs of those hospital diagnostic and 'treatment' services whose activity depends on patient throughput rather than bed occupancy.

Indeed, if the reduction in stay is achieved, not by a 'costless' improvement in medical techniques but by more expensive techniques or the more intensive application of existing methods, some costs may actually rise more than proportionately. Although some Australian research suggests that, at the margin, about 80 per cent of hospital costs vary with throughput rather than bed occupancy, the data are very scanty and it is impossible to be precise in the absence of information on possible changes in case-mix. All that can be said is that some part – up to perhaps one-third – of the increase in real cost per hospital bed day over the past fifteen years *may* have been due to greater quantitative output. The remainder can only be attributed to the use of more expensive techniques resulting in a qualitative improvement of some kind.[16]

Medicaments

Of all the health services, the manufacture and distribution of drugs has most in common with manufacturing and retailing generally. Though the methods of promotion and marketing are obviously influenced by the way in which demand for these products arises, the business behaviour of their producers and distributors is not much affected by the uses to which they are put. Medicaments are, of course, divided into the two distinct categories of (a) specific remedies which are available only on medical prescription, are promoted by their manufacturers only to doctors and must be dispensed by qualified pharmacists; and (b) non-specific 'proprietary' lines which are advertised directly to the public and may be sold without restriction through normal commercial channels. The two categories rarely compete directly since they meet quite different types of demand.[17] Whereas price competition is evident in the proprietary group, it is very rare in the prescribed drug market since even without government intervention in the form of the Australian pharmaceutical benefits scheme, a very low elasticity of demand would make price advantages unimportant [Steel, 1964, 1971]. Under Austrialian conditions, the volume of 'ethical' drugs rests entirely on the prescribing habits of physicians and the amounts paid for them on the prices negotiated by the Commonwealth government with manufacturers. Retail chemists play no part in the latter process, being simply contractors to the Commonwealth in the distribution of prepared, and often pre-packaged medicines for a remuneration linked with both the volume and the value of dispensing.[18]

We shall not be concerned here with proprietary medicines – which account for about one-third of all medicament expenditures – or with the manufacture of drugs, except to the extent that manufacturers' prices vary. All of the main prescription drug manufacturers operate internationally, and their pricing policies in Australia simply reflect international market conditions. As was pointed out earlier, drug prices have steadily declined relative to other prices since 1960-1 and while some of this reduction may have been due to the Commonwealth government's use of its monopsonistic position (negotiated price 'concessions' are regularly included in the reports of the Director-General of Health), it is doubtful if this has had much overall influence. Patent protection is the basis for all pharmaceutical pricing, new drugs being invariably introduced at higher prices than those which they replace and which may well be subject to competition on the expiry of the patent period. The average price level is thus more likely to be directly related to the rate at which new drugs are introduced, and this has slowed down considerably in recent years.

The distribution of drugs through retail chemists is, on the other hand, a wholly Australian activity. The obvious unit of capacity is the chemist shop and that of output the prescription dispensed. Table 16.9 shows estimated total expenditures and average expenditure per pharmacy for all prescription drugs, including those not included in the two major government schemes (pharmaceutical benefits and repatriation). The chemists' gross remuneration is derived from a mark up on the wholesale price of ingredients and containers, plus a fixed dispensing fee. For government financed drugs the mark up is 33⅓ per cent on the list price negotiated with manufacturers (for which the chemist is reimbursed), and the fee is currently 90 cents per prescription. For private prescriptions, both mark up and dispensing fee are higher, to give an overall margin of at least 90 per cent on wholesale price.

The most obvious feature of the table is the very high proportion of total drug cost which is absorbed in distribution: 45 per cent in the early years and slightly more at present. The Australian chemists' share is very similar to that in North America, but the conditions of drug marketing are quite different in the two countries. One would expect costs to be much lower when at least 80 per cent of the market is guaranteed by government subsidisation, and a similar proportion of prescriptions involves no more than the merchandising of ready prepared products. In fact, distribution costs are very much less in the UK and Sweden, where drugs are similarly financed. Though their remuneration formulae differ, both achieve distribution at a cost of

Table 11.9: Prescribed Medicaments (Excluding Hospital Dispensing) Estimated Expenditures and Use 1960/1 to 1975/6

		1960/1	1966/7	1972/3	1975/6
Aggregate					
Expenditures	($mill)	99	156	260	445
Prescriptions	(mill)	41	60	111	116
Pharmacies	(No.)	4,838	5,638	5,817	5,504
Average Per Pharmacy					
Receipts	($000s)	20.4	27.7	44.7	80.8
Prescriptions	(No.)	8,536	12,185	19,082	21,075
Gross remuneration	($)	9,180	12,470	20,150	37,420
Remuneration as % of receipts	(%)	45	45	46	47

Sources: Commonwealth Department of Health, *Annual Reports,* Repatriation Commission, *Annual Reports,* data supplied by manufacturers and distributors.

between 25 per cent and 30 per cent of retail price. The difference of at least 15 per cent amounts to nearly $70 million per annum under current Australian conditions, yet the government has found itself under pressure for many years to increase the chemists' dispensing fee.

One explanation is that high chemist charges have supported a considerable excess capacity in dispensing, the liquidation of which has proved to be a slow and painful process. The assured aggregate market for pharmaceutical benefits encouraged a rapid increase in the number of chemist shops in its earlier years, an entirely predictable response in an industry which is an almost perfect example of monopolistic competition with rigid price maintenance. By 1966-7, the 12,185 prescriptions dispensed by the average chemist shop represented only 41 prescriptions per shop over a working year of 300 days, which was only about 60 per cent of the daily dispensing capacity of a single pharmacist, working under commercial conditions.[19] Since many shops employed more than one pharmacist, the average shop probably operated at less than one-half of its dispensing capacity. By 1975-6, the inevitable rationalisation had lifted capacity utilisation considerably (though not proportionately, because the number of practising pharmacists was not necessarily reduced), but the profitability of pharmacy had not improved. Relatively static wholesale prices meant that the chemists' remuneration per prescription hardly varied; indeed it had increased by only 61 per cent over the whole 15 year period (from $1.07 to $1.77). At a time when the prices of other health services – medical services in particular – more than trebled and the real incomes of their providers soared, the chemists performed more professional work and incurred higher professional costs for a net professional income which almost certainly failed to keep pace with incomes generally. Yet this is the unavoidable result of an essentially correct policy; increased remuneration, based on appeals to equity, would simply preserve excess capacity and maintain the disproportionate share of distribution costs in total expenditure. It is, therefore, of some concern that the Government has recently agreed to a mechanism for determining fees through arbitration that threatens to have precisely that effect.[20]

Medical Services

Despite the apparent ease of measurement in a fee-for-service medical system, the output measures for medical services are less satisfactory than those for hospital treatment. Whereas hospitals record both the number of episodes of illness treated, the units of service (bed-days) provided and the diagnostic category of each patient, there is no such linkage in the statistics for medical care. The capacity of medical services is also more difficult to measure. The numbers of doctors in private practice is quite difficult to determine at any point of time, and their ability to vary working hours makes the concept of capacity somewhat vague. Capacity is also a function of specialisation, which has as much to do with the way in which the profession wishes to organise itself as with technology or the objective needs of patients. Finally, the statistics of services provided and payments for them are all derived from secondary sources, mainly the health insurance system, whereas those for hospitals are collected directly. Medical data are thus more subject to lags and to variations in coverage than those for the other major services.

Table 11.10 shows the estimated numbers of doctors in Australia from 1961 to 1976, the number of graduates from Australian medical schools, and projection of both statistics to 1991. As can be seen, the ratio of doctors to population has been steadily increasing, as has the rate of local additions to the stock. The growth in the doctor-population ratio has been about 1.5 per cent per annum and a similar improvement is projected for the next 15 years. Because the number of doctors employed in education, medical administration and other non-clinical activities has increased, the number of 'practising' doctors has not risen as rapidly, and increased specialisation has meant an even slower growth in general practitioner numbers. Nevertheless, the projections provide for a considerable increase in the output of services over the next 15 years.

Table 11.10: Numbers of Doctors and Medical Graduations 1954 to 1991

Date June 30	Number of Doctors	Per Million Population	Number of Medical Graduates (Year to 30 June)	Per Million Population
1954	9,180	1,022	482	54
1961	12,320	1,168	481	46
1966	14,440	1,245	709	61
1971	17,243	1,352	892	70
1976(est.)	20,429	1,478	1,117	81
1981(proj.)	23,957	1,602	1,385	90
1991(proj.)	31,309	1,762	1,620	94

Sources: *Expansion of Medical Education* (Report of the Committee on Medical Schools to the Australian University Commission, July 1973), AGPS, Canberra (1973), Tables 8.4 and 8.5.
R.R. Andrew, 'Medical Manpower – The Australian Scene', *Medical Journal of Australia,* vol.1, No.23 (June 1976).

Reliable information on the per capita utilisation of different services is difficult to obtain. Apart from the problem of partial coverage through secondary sources, official statistics up to 1974/5 provided only a division between general practitioner visits and other services, although unpublished survey results exist. Table 11.11 shows data compiled from a number of sources. The years do not exactly correspond with those in other tables, but they are indicative of trends. For 1962/3, 1967/8 and 1974/5, the method used was to combine statistics from the voluntary insurance scheme and the Pensioner Medical Service to give a weighted average for the total proportion of the population covered by these schemes. No information was available for the remainder of the population. The estimates for 1975/6 are derived from data in the Second Annual Report of the Health Insurance Commission on Medibank operations, and represent the estimated rate at which services were actually provided during that year. In other words, lags in claiming and payment have been taken into account. No such adjustment was made for other years, but under on-going systems such lags are less significant.

Table 11.11: Private Medical Services Estimated Use per Head of Population 1962/3 to 1975/6

Service	1962/3[a]	1967/8[b]	1974/5[c]	1975/6[d]
General practitioner visits	2.92	2.96	3.09	3.32
Specialist Consultations	.29	.43		.72
Obstetric services	.03	.03		.03
Operations and anaesthetics	.16	.23		.32
Diagnostic services			(2.39)	
Pathology	.17	.33		.90
Radiology	.12	.15		.26
Total	.29	.48		1.16
Other Services	.05	.08		.10
All Services	3.80	4.21	5.48	5.65

Notes: a. Coverage = 77.6% of population.
b. Coverage = 83.3% of population.
c. Coverage = 87.9% of population.
d. Coverage = 100% of population.

Sources: Derived from data in Scotton (1974), Commonwealth Department of Health, *Annual Reports,* Australian Department of Social Security, *Annual Report 1974-75,* Health Insurance Commission, *Annual Report 1975-76.*

The important feature of the table is the relatively slow growth in usage of general practitioner services compared with specialist services and particularly with the diagnostic services of radiology and pathology. To some extent, this was the product of the growing differentiation of services within the fee schedule on which the statistics are based. General practitioner visits are not generally capable of further sub-division, whereas in the procedural specialities, especially the diagnostic ones, proliferation of items within the fee schedule is a feature of all fee-for-service systems in this and other countries. However, the broad division does have a greater significance. By and large the use of general practitioner services is patient-initiated whereas specialist work is internally-generated, particularly under a system like Australia's where referral is at least a formal rule. The diagnostic services are, indeed, almost entirely doctor-generated, since doctors are the only direct users of the results. Patient demand thus appears to have had less influence on utilisation and costs than factors on the supply side such as increasing specialisation and a much greater prescription of diagnostic procedures.

The other major influence on medical expenditures is, of course, fee levels. Table 11.12 shows provisional indexes of medical fees from 1963/4 to 1975/6. Over most of the period fees tended to rise at a slightly lower rate than average weekly earnings, mainly because some of the components of the index used to adjust AMA recommended fees follow CPI movements [Scotton, 1974, ch.6]. The greatest lag between fees and average earnings occurred in 1972/3 and 1973/4, following government pressure to confine a proposed across-the-board increase to general practitioner fees, and delays pending the determination of a formal fees tribunal. Since 1973/4 considerable increases in 'scheduled' fees have taken the total rise since 1969/70 to an almost exact parity with the rise in average weekly earnings. However, from May 1973 onwards the index understates the actual increase in charges; since that date the AMA has recommended – and a significant proportion of doctors have charged – fees which are substantially higher than those on which our figures are based. The benefits of increased medical productivity have thus accrued entirely to doctors, and they have probably made further income gains as well.

These trends in utilisation and fees have produced large increases in payments for private medical services. The best global measure of these payments is in the official taxation statistics, where the total business incomes of doctors in private practice are presented for individuals and partners. Table 11.13 shows the aggregate gross income of doctors subject to provisional tax from 1966/7 to 1973/4, the last year for which statistics are available. The corresponding income figures for 1963/4 and 1974/5 have been estimated from expenditure statistics derived from insurance and other sources.[21]

In Table 11.14, the composite fee index is applied to these payment statistics to provide an indirect measure of overall changes in the volume of doctors' services since 1969/70. Over the period to 1974/5, the volume of medical services apparently increased by over 40 per cent, which is double the estimated growth in doctor numbers. There are, however, good reasons to believe that this significantly

Table 11.12: Provisional Index of Medical Fees 1963/4 to 1975/6[a]

	GP Visits			Other Services	All Services		Average Weekly Earnings	
	Private	PMS	Total			% inc.		% inc.
1963/4	73	65	72	n.a.	n.a.		68	
1966/7	83	86	84	n.a.	n.a.		81	
1969/70	100	100	100	100	100		100	
1970/1	106	100	104	126	117	17%	111	11.1%
1071/2	115	135	122	126	124	6%	122	9.7%
1972/3	121	135	124	126	125	1%	133	9.1%
1973/4	138	162	143	132	136	9%	155	17.7%
1974/5	164	203	171	162	166	22%	194	25.4%
1975/6	214[b]	302[c]	230	219	223	34%	222	14.9%

Notes: a. To 1970/1, private fees for GP visits are those recommended for office visits by State branches of the AMA. To 1974/5, PMS fees are office visit fees actually paid in respect of services to eligible pensioners by the Commonwealth Government. All other indices (except as noted below) relate to a weighted mix of 'most common' or 'scheduled' fees on which Commonwealth medical benefits were based.

b. Average fee for patient-billed services.

c. Average direct-billed fee.

Source: Scotton (1974) and further calculations based on data supplied by the Commonwealth Department of Health. The system of weighting the groups of services is tentative and subject to revision.

over-estimates the actual rise in doctor productivity, simply because the change in 'list' prices almost certainly under-states the effective price rise over the period. The higher fees recommended by the AMA since 1973 have already been mentioned. Extended insurance coverage, culminating in the introduction of Medibank, has been even more important in that the proportion of services rendered for no fee or at reduced fees has steadily declined. After the 1969 and 1970 amendments to the voluntary insurance scheme, fewer patients were treated in hospital as 'public' (non-fee-paying) patients, more pensioners and low-income sick held private medical insurance, less bad debts were incurred and a number of services – such as minor procedures performed during a consultation and the issue of repeat prescriptions – were billed for the first time. The real volume increases were therefore less, and the effective price rises more than is suggested in Table 11.13, but it is

Table 11.13: Gross Incomes of Doctors in Fee Practice

	$m.
1963/64	133[a]
1966/67	182
1969/70	240
1972/73	388
1973/74	430
1974/75	560[a]

Note: a. Estimated.
Sources: 1. For 1966/7 to 1973/4, total business incomes of medical practitioners, individuals and partners, *Taxation Statistics* (Supplement to Annual Report of the Commissioner of Taxation), various issues.
2. For 1963/4 and 1974/5, derived as follows:

	1963/4 $m.	1974/5 $m.
Payments by insured persons	91	428
Payments by pensioner medical service	9	48
Payments by repatriation department	5	14
Sub Total	105	490
Other (estimated)	28	70
Total	133	560

Cost-of-service statistics from Director-General of Health, *Annual Report* 1963-4; Repatriation Commission, *Annual Report,* 1963-64, 1974-75; Department of Social Security, *Annual Report,* 1974-75. The category 'other' is a residual figure which includes income from services to uninsured persons, workers compensation and motor car third party cases, and other sources.

difficult to quantify these errors.

We have deliberately omitted the data for 1975/6 from the preceding analysis because of a number of complexities in interpretation which will be solved only when more information is available. The first impression is that expenditures on medical services, and doctors' incomes, increased enormously in 1975/6. Medibank benefits were paid for services valued at about $680 million in the year and, in addition, benefits were paid under the preceding voluntary arrangements for services worth over $166 million rendered before July 1975, but for which claims for benefit had not then been submitted. There is no clear evidence of whether payment had, in fact, been made for these but if it had not, the total receipts of doctors would have increased to nearly $850 million in 1975/6, a 52 per cent increase on 1974/5. After allowing for the 34 per cent increase in fees in the same year, the 'volume' increase would thus appear to have been about 13 per cent.

Table 11.14: Factors in Doctors' Gross Income Movements: Price and Apparent Volume Changes 1969/70 to 1974/75
(Index 1969/70 = 100)

	Expenditures on Doctors' Service		Fee Index		Apparent Volume of Doctors' Services	
	Index	Annual Change %	Index	Annual Change %	Index	Annual Change %
1970/1	119.9	17.8	117	17.0	102.5	2.5
1971/2	141.2	17.8	124	6.0	113.9	11.1
1972/3	161.7	14.5	125	0.8	129.4	2.8
1973/4	179.3	10.8	136	8.8	131.8	1.9
1974/5	(233.3)	(30.2)	166	22.1	140.5	6.6

Sources: Tables 11.12, 11.13.

Such an enormous increase does not accord with any of the other indicators. The real explanation appears to be a purely financial phenomenon – namely, a large reduction in service to payment lags, or expressed in another way, a reduction in the credit terms allowed by doctors. There is clear evidence of this in the lags from service to benefit payment reported by Medibank and evidenced in the carry-over of medical benefit claims from 1974/5. The overall service to payment lag in 1975/6 was 53.5 days, but because the more expensive items are those for which the delays in payment (by the patient) and submission of claims for benefit are greatest, the lag in value terms is longer – approximating 80 days. By contrast, the carry-over in July 1975 was equivalent to 135 days at the claiming rate of the preceding year. Medical incomes in 1975/6 thus included a once-and-for-all boost of nearly two months' receipts, for which no additional services were rendered. This certainly accords with a number of popular impressions, and it is not difficult to see how it could come about. Medibank paid most claims more quickly than before and the medical profession itself contributed through an increase in the number of doctors who insisted on cash payment at the time of service. It is, however, important to appreciate the temporary and purely financial nature of the change, and the fact that its inevitable reversal in 1976/7 will have had nothing at all to do with real costs under the modified insurance arrangements.[22]

Some Economic Issues

The size of health expenditures, and the need to provide interpretations of their behaviour in terms useful to policy-makers, has led to two separate strands of research effort for which there is now a growing literature. The first approach attempts, as we have done, to isolate the separate influences of output variations, whether in purely quantitative terms, or in changes in product mix or product 'quality', from those of changes in production costs. The second, and more fundamental, interest is in the nature of demand and supply functions, the institutional context in which they operate, and their significance for policy. Very little of this research has been carried out in Australia, and the present availability of data here is such that little is possible.[23] We must, therefore, rely a good deal on overseas studies, fo which those in North America are the most numerous and relevant.

Demand

A number of multivariate analyses of demand have been carried out in North America. In general, they have sought to explain demand in terms of underlying medical 'need' (represented by age, sex and assessments of existing health status), 'tastes' (perceptions of illness, attitudes to the seeking of care and acceptance of medical advice, etc.), and the normal economic factors of prices, incomes and health insurance cover. A new wave of demand studies, following Grossman's seminal work, subsumes need and tastes in household utility and production functions, into which medical services enter as inputs. Examples are Newhouse and Phelps [1974] and Grossman and Benham [1974].

Because of the range of analytical methods and data used, the results show great differences in the estimated values of the parameters of central importance to economists, namely, price and income elasticities. Substantially different income elasticities are derived according to whether the measure of utilisation is expenditures or numbers of services and whether the measure of income is actual or permanent income.[24] Since medical consumers do not face a choice of services at different prices in the same market, the estimation of price elasticities is indirect and complicated by other factors. Moreover, the overall demand for health services is the sum of the demands for a variety of services with quite different individual characteristics. The use of hospital services is explained much more by 'need' and much less by such economic factors as income and insurance coverage than, say, dental services [Andersen, 1964]. Characteristics are not uniform even within broad categories: for example, United States data show that the large additional consumption of dental care by upper-income groups consists of quite different services to the basic emergency care used by low-income patients [Scotton, 1974, ch.9]. Similarly, Australian data indicate that the additional hospital expenditures of high-income patients are on more amenities, not more admissions [Deeble and Scotton, 1971].

Most studies have found income elasticities to be significant and less than unity, ranging between 0.2 and 0.7.[25] The only Australian study by one of the authors, using Melbourne data, gave a value of 0.53 for all expenditures [Scotton, 1974, ch.4]. Price elasticities have also been found to be low, the most recent large-scale study yielding values below –0.1 [Newhouse and Phelps, 1974, Feldstein, 1970].[26] There is some evidence that the opportunity costs of waiting time and travelling time weigh more heavily with consumers than money prices. One of the consequences of universal health insurance (and systems like the British National Health Service) is a redistribution of service towards those who are 'dollar-poor and time-rich' and away from those for whom the price of time is high. Empirical evidence of this effect exists in data from the sudden introduction of universal insurance to the previously low-insured Canadian province of Quebec in 1970/1 [Enterline *et al.*, 1973].

With the existing evidence, there remains a considerable difference of opinion amongst economists about the relative importance of demand pressure compared with influences on the supply side. Evans [1975] maintains that, under Canadian conditions, demand has played little part in expenditure growth and that the manipulation of supply, particularly in the pursuit of target incomes by doctors, has been of greatest importance. However, US economists, of whom Professor M.S. Feldstein is the most notable, generally ascribe the major influence to demand pressures resulting from the spread of insurance and public subsidisation [Feldstein, 1971].

Both approaches may well be correct since they are really discussing different situations. Both have been concerned with the very large increase in hospital expenditures in their respective countries. The crucial link in Feldstein's model is the feedback from increased demand from doctors and the community to the (independent) hospitals' decisions to expand capacity; capacity is thus an endogenous variable. In Canada, on the other hand, hospital funding is almost entirely public, and capacity decisions are mainly functions of the constraints on public budgets. They are clearly exogenous under the particular institutional circumstances of that country. Australia, with hospital systems which are partly public and partly private, is likely to experience elements of both; the dominant public sector can be expected to restrain capacity growth more than in the United States, but evidence of the quite rapid growth in private hospitals since 1970 suggests that, overall, the system is rather more responsive to demand pressures than the Canadian model.

Supply

The main issues on the supply side involve the extent to which the demand for services is influenced by the suppliers in response to financial and other incentives. It has long been observed, for example, that any increase in hospital bed capacity is rapidly used, because of the interest of both doctors and hospital management in filling beds to optimum occupancy levels [Roemer and Shain, 1959]. In his econometric study of hospital costs, Feldstein [1971] found a highly significant 'pure availability' effect which was distinct from any influences on the demand side. Most studies attribute it to the much higher revenues which hospital-based procedures yield to doctors – particularly under a fee-for-service system – and to the methods of paying for hospital care.

There is also evidence of an availability effect for doctors' services, but the relationships are complicated by the varying extent to which doctors can raise prices as well as influence demand. In the United States, where there are few restraints on doctors' pricing, Newhouse and Phelps [1975] found that the ratio of doctors to population had a much greater effect on fee levels (an elasticity of 0.40) than on the number of medical services per head (elasticities of 0.11 – 0.13). Where, as in Canada and Australia, the capacity of doctors to vary their charges is constrained by public programmes, a greater proportion of the income-adjustment burden appears to be borne by variations in utilisation. Data from both countries show that high regional doctor-population ratios are associated with both higher than average fees and higher than average per capita utilisation to yield the doctors similar incomes to those in areas less well supplied [Scotton, 1974, ch.6; Evans, 1975]. Since such regional differentials can and do persist for many years, one product of the doctors' capacity to influence demand is a considerable autonomy for them to choose their speciality and practice location.[27] Evans has argued from Canadian experience that an increased supply of doctors will achieve a redistribution to less favoured areas only when the possibilities of demand induction in their chosen localities have been exhausted, and that this is an exceedingly expensive process.

This empirical evidence of doctor behaviour is consistent with monopoly pricing [Newhouse, 1970] and with the target income hypothesis of which Evans is a leading proponent. Under this hypothesis, doctors have target incomes which are largely determined exogenously and have the power to vary fees and influence their patients' demands for service so as to obtain those incomes. The model implies that within a range which cannot easily be tested there is no independent demand curve for medical services at all. Total expenditures are a function of the number of doctors in practice and their target incomes at the time.[28]

The strongest support for this contention is found in comparative studies of surgical operation rates. The use of these services is almost entirely determined by medical advice and decision, and there are a number of operations for which the clinical indications are by no means clear cut. One American study found that between 50 and 70 per cent of variations in the incidence of such operations could be explained simply by the number of surgeons available and the number of hospital beds per head of population. [Lewis, 1969] Table 11.15 shows comparative operation rates for certain elective operations from studies by Bunker [1970], Vayda [1973] and Lugg [1975]. It indicates considerable differences between surgical rates in England and Wales (where doctors are salaried and the supply of hospital beds is severely restricted) compared with the United States, Canada and Western Australia, where more hospital beds are available and most doctors are in private, fee-for-service practice.

The very low surgical rates in the UK are certainly related to resource constraints (and are associated with much longer than average waiting lists), but they are also a function of the way in which doctors are paid. A number of studies in the United States have showed very large differences in hospitalisation and surgical procedure rates – of the general order of 2:1 – between patients of fee-for-service doctors and those of health maintenance organisations where the cost of hospitalisation falls on the suppliers rather than on patients or third party insurers [Donabedian, 1969; Monsma, 1970]. The latest of these, involving closely matched Medicaid populations, highlights the method of doctor payment as a key factor, since health maintenance organisations in which doctors were not organised in prepaid groups did not show comparable reductions in use [Gaus, Cooper and Hirschman, 1976].

Conclusions

Several conclusions flow from the preceding analysis. First, all the

Table 11.15: Comparative Operation Rates for Certain Elective Surgery: England and Wales, Canada, United States and Western Australia

	Bunker		Vayda		Lugg		
	E & W 1966	USA 1965	E & W 1967	Canada 1968	E & W 1971	USA 1971	WA 1971
	Rates per 100,000 population						
Males							
Tonsillectomy	323	637	351	934	ns	ns	ns
Appendectomy	221	217	243	240	196	173	361
Cholecystectomy	32	95	27	135	33	78	60
Haemorrhoidectomy	61	162	54	104	ns	ns	ns
All operations	ns	ns	ns	ns	3653	6106	7579
Females							
Tonsillectomy	322	641	345	1002	ns	ns	ns
Appendectomy	224	180	250	214	206	151	471
Cholecystectomy	90	273	70	487	86	286	222
Hysterectomy	213	516	213	472	294	524	354
All operations	ns	ns	ns	ns	4250	7918	9103
Beds per thousand pop.	ns	ns	3.7	5.4	4.1	4.7	6.4[b]
Discharges per thousand pop.	ns	ns	90	151	99	129	175
Doctors per thousand pop.	0.18[a]	0.39[a]	0.18[a]	0.27[a]	1.23	1.58	1.22

Notes: a. Surgeons only.
b. Official statistics.
ns = not stated

evidence shows that, to the extent that pricing systems and financial incentives do influence behaviour, they have a much greater effect on producers than consumers. It is for this reason that attempts to restrict utilisation and expenditures by such devices as 'deterrent' charges rarely produce all the results expected of them: producer reactions may well run counter to the consumers' response. Much depends on the way in which doctors are paid, and this is the crucial factor. The Medibank approach was to increase the salaried component of medical care, at least so far as the public hospitals were concerned, in line with similar developments in other countries. The privately-managed alternative (Health Maintenance Organisations) has been strongly urged as a policy objective in Australia [Sax, 1972] and the government has recently shown some signs of response. However, the Australian medical profession holds to fee-for-service as an article of faith and will bitterly resist any attempt to reduce its dominance.

The second conclusion is that a stable market equilibrium is highly unlikely, if not impossible. The visible signs of demand pressure cannot be taken as evidence of real 'shortages' which could be overcome; they are the inevitable consequences of the existing financing and delivery arrangements. To extend supply at current prices would simply invite higher and higher total expenditures, but to use prices as a market clearing mechanism would be neither politically nor socially acceptable. Thus any effective management of the health service system has to work directly on the supply side. If, as seems obvious, the immediate aim of government policy is to minimise expenditures, the only practical strategy must involve both budget constraints and direct administrative controls. For the latter, the prime targets are the growth of hospital capacity, in the private as well as public sector, the size of medical schools and, perhaps, the licensing of pharmacies.

Finally, there is the integration of allocative and distributional goals. The presence of 'need' and the basic human emotion of fear which always surrounds illness make the underlying conditions of demand extremely inelastic, and the massive information gaps which separate consumers and producers render the whole concept of choice somewhat vague. This is particularly so when insurance and other collective financing systems result in package prices rather than separate units. Yet there is ample evidence that risk, uncertainty and the social demand for equality of access make such packages eminently marketable, to the point where many people are, by any objective criteria, prepared to over-insure. These private mechanisms are, however, quite indifferent to resource allocation; indeed, survival in a competitive climate will generally lead them to the development of more and more options of the amenities kind and even further away from such non-marketable services as preventive medicine and the 'uninsurable' but nonetheless essential treatment of the chronically ill. To the authors, the search for private options which will somehow solve both allocative and distributional problems is rather like the search for the philosopher's stone. Public operation of health service systems is not essential, or even necessarily desirable, but public management is and its problems are not going to diminish with the passage of time.

Notes

1. This has probably been true at all times except for the period from the mid-

1930s to the early 1960s, when the suplhonamide/antibiotic revolution was in progress. See McKeown and Record (1961), Fuchs 1974(a) and 1974(b). Some writers – for example, Illich (1975) – go a great deal further and argue that additional resources going to medical care cause more illness than they cure.

2. Although the first cost-benefit calculations go back to Edwin Chadwick and the Report of the Poor Law Commissioners of 1842, the origin of most recent work is Weisbrod (1961). For an attempt to throw some light on the valuation of personal care see Hauser (1972) and Morley's comments in the same volume. A survey of cost-benefit studies is in Dowie (1970).
3. A less technical summary is in Evans' contribution to Mark Perlman (ed.), *The Economics of Health and Medical Care* (London, 1974).
4. These are not, of course, the only reasons why non-market provision may be preferred. One is the possibility of interdependent individual utility functions underlying the concept of a 'merit want'. See Lindsay (1969) and Musgrave (1969).
5. For triennial years from 1961 to 1967, and for 1972/3, see Deeble (1967, 1974). Figures for 1969/70 were published in Australian Department of Health, *Annual Report,* 1972/3, pp.265-275, together with alternative but very similar figures for 1966/7.
6. Although expenditures on dental services are combined with those on 'other professional services' in the estimates, the figure is mainly dental. The data for other professional services are scanty and it is probable that their costs are understated.
7. By comparison, the average use of general hospitals remained almost constant over the 15 year period, but daily costs – in public hospitals at least – had risen from $12.70 per day in 1960/1 to about $88 per day in 1975/6.
8. Between 1960/1 and 1974/5, the proportions of private patient bed-days in the public hospitals of the two major states, New South Wales and Victoria, increased as follows. Data for admissions are also shown for Victoria but similar statistics are not available for New South Wales.

	NSW	VICTORIA	
Year	% Days	% Days	% Patients
1960/1	33.8	32.3	47.3
1966/7	36.5	33.1	49.3
1974/5	54.3	52.0	67.0

Source: Annual Reports of New South Wales and Victorian Health and Hospitals Commissions.

9. This is not, however, quite so true of 'private' (compulsory) insurance under the revised Medibank scheme, which is specifically designed to maximise the role of private funding as well as preserve the market share of private medical practice. See Scotton [1974], ch.7.
10. See Australian Bureau of Census and Statistics, *Social Indicators,* No.1 (1976).
11. The total for 1974/5 corresponds almost exactly with the figures in *Social Indicators.* The 1975/6 estimates are by the authors. No official statistics are yet available.
12. For a relatively optimistic assessment of the possibilities of measurement, see Culyer, Lavers and Williams (1972).
13. They may also be criticised on theoretical grounds. See Barzel (1968) and the discussion of Reder (1969) by M.S. Feldstein and Klarman.

14. This does not have as much significance for average cost as might be imagined, since many of the apparently 'available' beds in country hospitals are not fully staffed.
15. Specifically, by lifting hospital benefits under 'special account' (a device by which the Commonwealth government subsidised the private health insurance funds for bad-risk members) to the full amount for which the patient chose to insure, even at private room rates. Acceptance of such patients by private hospitals thus became much more feasible. A concurrent revision of medical benefits to give higher, differential benefits for private specialist treatment also contributed.
16. Qualitative improvement in the sense of improved health outcomes cannot be assumed, however. Several US studies have pointed out that hospitals tend to maximise amenity, provide the maximum of equipment and facilities (often unused) to doctors, and prefer high-cost rather than low-cost techniques as evidence of a commitment to patient care. [Newhouse 1970, Feldstein 1971] Abelson (1976) found a similar propensity to choose high-cost methods in a study of Sydney public hospitals.
17. Generally, because of differences in specificity. The consumption of non-prescribed medicaments is in fact very similar to many other health-directed activities internal to households which we have omitted.
18. For a detailed analysis of the pricing of prescription drugs in Australia, see Harvey (1974).
19. In 1966/7, an average of between 60 and 70 prescriptions per day was estimated as a full workload for a single pharmacist under commercial conditions. In hospitals, where the patient flow is more organised, a figure of 90 scripts per day could be expected. With the increasing proportion of pre-packaged medicaments, both figures have probably increased since 1967.
20. The system proposed would involve the determination of Chemists' remuneration by a tribunal consisting of a Judge of the Arbitration and Conciliation Commission, with four members nominated by the Pharmacy Guild and four by the Government.
21. For a number of reasons, these differ from those of estimated payments to the same doctors for medical services in the same year. Lags inherent in the process of paying accounts and having claims for benefit assessed and paid affect one of the sets of figures; in the other, the existence of late returns results in a general, but variable, understatement in the taxation statistics of up to 5 per cent.
22. Although in fact only a temporal redistribution of cash flows, this phenomenon may well have a considerable influence on future costs. For the doctors, it became income in that year and will undoubtedly influence future target incomes. This, and the problems created by the impact of provisional tax on a reduced cash flow in 1977, suggest a considerable pressure for fee increases in 1978.
23. Australia has no equivalent to the US Health Interview Survey, or comprehensive data of the kind published in, say, the US Department of Health, Education and Welfare, *Medical Care Costs and Prices: Background Book,* or the Canadian Department of National Health and Welfare's periodic review of *Sources of Increases in Budget Review Hospital Expenditures.* One of the major by-products of universal insurance under the original Medibank scheme was the flow of statistics which it generated, but its division into public and private sectors now makes collation much more difficult.
24. A survey of elasticity results appeared in Lave, Lave and Leinhardt (1975).
25. P.J. Feldstein, (1964) found a value of 0.56 for expenditures. Anderson and Benham (1974) calculated elasticities of 0.41 with respect to permanent

income. Grossman (1972) found an average income elasticity of 0.7. However, Newhouse and Phelps (1974) using the same data, produced a much lower figure of 0.15 to 0.2. The authors account for this by Grossman's omission of insurance (which is positively related to income) as a factor.

26. Newhouse and Phelps (1974) calculated price elasticities of –0.02 to –0.06 for doctor visits and –0.03 to –0.10 for hospital days. Feldstein (1971) calculated a short-run elasticity for hospital days of –0.27 and a long-run elasticity (after the bed supply had time to adjust) of –0.55.
27. Public provision does not necessarily solve this problem. See Cooper and Culyer (1970).
28. A similar conclusion as to the strength of supplier influence on demand was reached by Feldstein (1970).

Bibliography

Abel-Smith, B., *An International Study of Health Expenditures,* World Health Organisation, Public Health Papers, No.32, (Geneva, 1969).

Abelson, P.W., 'An Analysis of Rising Hospital Costs in Sydney', unpublished paper, School of Economic and Financial Studies, Macquarie University, Sydney, 1976.

Andersen, R., *A Behavioural Model of Families' Use of Health Services,* Center for Health Administration Studies (Research Series No.25), Chicago, 1968.

Andersen, R., and Benham, L., 'Factors Affecting the Relationship between Family Income and Medical Care Consumption', in H.E. Klarman (Ed.), *Empirical Studies in Health Economics* (Johns Hopkins Press, Baltimore and London, 1970).

Arrow, K.J., 'Uncertainty and the Welfare Economics of Medical Care', *American Economic Review,* vol.LIII (1963).

Bailey, R.M., 'Philosophy, Faith, Fact and Fiction in the Production of Medical Series', *Inquiry,* vol.7, No.1 (March 1970).

Barzel, Y., 'Costs of Medical Treatment: A Comment', *American Economic Review,* vol.LVIII, No.4 (September 1968).

Barzel, Y., 'Productivity and the Price of Medical Services', *Journal of Political Economy,* vol.77 (1969).

Beck, R.G., 'Economic Class and Access to Physician Services under Public Medical Care Insurance', *International Journal of Health Services,* vol.3, No.3 (1973).

Bunker, J.P., 'Surgical Manpower: A comparison of operations and surgeons in the United States and in England and Wales'. *New England Journal of Medicine,* vol.2821, (1970), pp.135-44.

Cooper, M.H. and Culyer, A.J., 'An Economic Assessment of Some Aspects of the Operation of the National Health Service', in *Health Services Financing,* (BMA London, 1970).

Culyer, A.J., Lavers, R.J., and Williams, Alan, 'Health Indicators', in A. Schonfield and S. Shaw (eds.), *Social Indicators and Social Policy* (Heinemann, London, 1972).

Davis, Karen, 'Rising Hospital Costs: Possible Causes and Cures', *Bulletin of the New York Academy of Medicine,* vol.48, No.11 (December 1972).

Davis, Karen, *National Health Insurance: Benefits, Costs and Consequences* (Brookings Institution, Washington, 1975).

Deeble, J.S., 'An Economic Analysis of Hospital Costs', *Medical Care,* vol.3, No.3 (1965).

Deeble, J.S., 'The Costs and Sources of Finance of Australian Health Services', *The Economic Record,* vol.43, No.104 (1967).

Deeble, J.S., and Scotton, R.B., *Health Care under Voluntary Insurance: Report of a Survey* (Institute of Applied Economic Research, University of Melbourne

Technical Paper No.1, 1968).

Deeble, J.S., and Scotton, R.B., 'Health Insurance Cover and the Use of Hospital and Medical Services', in J. Krupinski and A. Stoller (eds.), *The Health of a Metropolis* (Heinemann Educational, Melbourne, 1971).

Deeble, J.S., 'The Health of the Nation – Who Pays?', in J. Birman (ed.), *The Health Problems of the Nation* (University of Western Australia Press, 1974).

Dewdney, J.C.H., *Australian Health Services* (John Wiley and Sons, Sydney, 1972).

Donabedian, A., 'An Evaluation of Prepaid Group Practice', *Inquiry*, vol.VI, No.3 (September 1969).

Dowie, J.A., 'Valuing the Benefits of Health Improvement', *Australian Economic Papers*, vol.9, No.14 (June 1970).

Dowie, J., 'The Portfolio Approach to Health Behaviour', *Social Science and Medicine*, vol.9 (1975).

Enterline, P.E., *et al.*, 'The Distribution of Medical Services before and after "Free" Medical Care – The Quebec Experience', *New England Journal of Medicine*, vol.289, No.22 (November 1973).

Evans, R.G., *Price Formation in the Market for Physicians Services in Canada, 1957-69*, Study prepared for the Prices and Incomes Commission (Queens Printer, Ottawa, 1973).

Evans, R.G., 'Supplier Induced Demand: Some Empirical Evidence and Implications', in Mark Perlman (ed.). *The Economics of Health and Medical Care* (Macmillan, London, 1974).

Evans, R.G., 'Beyond the Medical Market Place: Expenditure, Utilisation and Pricing of Insured Health in Canada', in S. Andreopoulos (ed.), *National Health Insurance: Can We Learn from Canada?* (J. Wiley & Sons, New York, 1975).

Fein, R., *The Doctor Shortage* (Brookings Institution, Washington, 1967).

Feldstein, M.S., *Economic Analysis for Health Service Efficiency* (North Holland, Amsterdam 1967).

Feldstein. M.S., 'The Rising Price of Physicians' Services, *Review of Economics and Statistics*, vol.52, No.2 (1970).

Feldstein, M.S., 'Hospital Cost Inflation: A Study of Non-profit Price Dynamics', *American Economic Review*, vol.61, No.5 (1971).

Feldstein, M.S., 'The Welfare Costs of Excess Health Insurance', *Journal of Political Economy*, vol.81, No.2 (1973).

Feldstein, P.J., 'The Demand for Medical Care', in Commission on the Cost of Medical Care. *General Report*, vol.1 (American Medical Association, Chicago, 1964).

Fuchs, V.R., 'The Growing Demand for Medical Care', in V.R. Fuchs (ed.), *Essays in the Economics of Health and Medical Care* (National Bureau of Economic Research, New York, 1972).

Fuchs, V.R., and Kramer, M.J. *Determinants of Expenditures for Physicians' Services in the United States 1948-68*, (Department of Health, Education and Welfare Publication No.73-3013, Washington, 1973).

Fuchs, V.R., *Who Shall Live?: Health, Economics and Social Choice* (Basic Books, New York, 1974 (a))

Fuchs, V.R. 'Some Economic Aspects of Mortality in Developed Countries', in Mark Perlman (ed.), *The Economics of Health and Medical Care* (Macmillan, London, 1974 (b)).

Gaus, C.R., Cooper, B.S., and Hirschman, C.G., 'Contrasts in HMO and Fee-for-Service Performance, *Social Security Bulletin*, vol.39, No.5 (May 1976).

Grossman, M. *The Demand for Health: A Theoretical and Empirical Investigation*, National Bureau of Economic Research, Occasional Paper No.117 (Columbia

University Press, New York, 1972).

Grossman, M., and Benham, L., 'Health, Hours and Wages' in Mark Perlman (ed.), *The Economics of Health and Medical Care* (Macmillan, London, 1974).

Harvey, D.R., *The Economics of Pharmaceutical Drug Manufacture in Australia*, Unpublished M.Ec. thesis, Monash University, 1974.

Illich, Ivan, *Medical Nemesis* (Calder and Boyars, London, 1975).

Joseph, H., 'Empirical Research on the Demand for Health Care, *Inquiry*, vol.8, No.1 (March 1971).

Lave, J.R., Lave, L.B., and Leinhardt, S., 'Medical Manpower Models: Need, Demand and Supply, *Inquiry*, vol.12, No.2 (June 1975).

Lavers, R.J., 'The Implicit Valuation of Forms of Hospital Treatment', in M.M. Hauser (ed.), *The Economics of Medical Care* (Allen and Unwin, London, 1972).

Lewis, C.E., 'Variations in the Incidence of Surgery', *New England Journal of Medicine*, vol.281, No.16 (October 1969).

Lindsay, Cotton. M., 'Medical Care and the Economics of Sharing', *Economica*, No.144 (1969).

Lloyd, C., *The Demand for Medical Care: A Selective Review of the Literature*, University of Iowa Working Paper Series, No.71-79 (1971).

Lugg, M.M. *A Comparison of Hospital Utilization under Three Health Insurance Schemes: Australia, United States, Scotland and England and Wales.* Paper presented to the 103rd Annual Meeting of the American Public Health Association, Chicago 1975.

McKeown, T. and Record, R.G., 'Reasons for the Decline of Mortality in England and Wales in the Nineteenth Century', *Population Studies*, vol.XVI (1961).

Marmor, T., and Thomas, D., 'The Politics of Paying Physicians: The Determinants of Government Payment Methods in England, Sweden, and the United States', *International Journal of Health Services*, vol.1, No.1 (1971).

Monsma, G.N., 'Marginal Revenue and the Demand for Physicians' Services', in H.E. Klarman (ed.), *Empirical Studies in Health Economics* (Johns Hopkins Press, Baltimore and London, 1970).

Musgrave, R.A., 'Provision of Social Goods' in J. Margolis and H. Gieitton (eds.), *Public Economics*, (London, 1969).

Newhouse, J.P., 'Toward a Theory of Non-profit Institutions: An Economic Model of a Hospital', *American Economic Review*, vol.LX (1970 (a)).

Newhouse, J.P., 'A Model of Physician's Pricing', *Southern Economic Journal*, vol.37 (1970 (b)).

Newhouse, J.P., and Phelps, C.E., 'Price and Income Elasticities for Medical Care Services', in Mark Perlman (ed.), *The Economics of Health and Medical Care* (Macmillan, London, 1974).

Newhouse, J.P., Phelps, C.E., and Schwartz, W.B., 'Policy Options and the impact of National Health Insurance', *New England Journal of Medicine*, vol.290 (June 1974).

Reder, M.W., 'Some Problems in the Measurement of Productivity of the Medical Care Industry', in V.R. Fuchs (ed.), *Production and Productivity in the Service Industries*, National Bureau of Economic Research: Studies in Income and Wealth No.34 (New York, 1969).

Reinhardt, U.E., 'A Product Function for Physician Services', *Review of Economics and Statistics*, vol.LIV, No.1 (February 1972).

Rice, Dorothy P., and Wilson, Douglas, The American Medical Economy: Problems and Perspectives, in T.E.H.-wei-HU (ed.), *International Health Costs and Expenditures*, U.S. Department of Health Education and Welfare. Publication No. (NIH) 76-1067, Washington 1976.

Roemer, M.I., and Shain, M., *Hospital Utilization Under Insurance* (American Hospital Association, Chicago, 1959).

Roemer, M.I., and Shonick, W., 'H.M.O. Performance: The Recent Evidence', *Milbank Memorial Fund Quarterly – Health and Society* (Summer 1973).

Sax, S., *Medical Care in the Melting Pot* (Angus & Robertson, Sydney, 1972).

Scitovsky, A.A., 'An Index of the Cost of Medical Care – A Proposed New Approach' in S.J. Axelrod (ed.), *The Economics of Medical Care* (University of Michigan, Ann Arbor, 1964).

Scitovsky, A.A., 'Changes in the Costs of Treatment of Selected Illnesses, 1951-65', *American Economic Review*, vol.LVII, No.5 (December 1967).

Scitovsky, A.A., and Snyder, N.M., 'Effect of Coinsurance on the Use of Physician Services'. *Social Security Bulletin*, vol.35 (1972).

Scotton, R.B., *Medical Care in Australia: An Economic Diagnosis* (Sun Books, Melbourne, 1974).

Scotton, R.B., and Grounds, D.A., 'Survey of General Practice in Victoria', *The Medical Journal of Australia*, vol.1 (1969, Supplement).

Steel, H., 'Patent Restrictions and Price Competition in the Ethical Drugs Industry', *Journal of Industrial Economics*, No.3 (June 1964).

Steel, H., 'Prices and Profits in the Drug Industry', *The New Physician* (March 1971).

Stevens, C.M., 'Hospital Market Efficiency: The Anatomy of the Supply Response' in H.E. Klarman (Ed.), *Empirical Studies in Health Economics* (Johns Hopkins Press, Baltimore and London, 1970).

Vayda, E. 'A comparison of surgical rates in Canada and England and Wales'. *New England Journal of Medicine*, vol.289, (1973), pp.1224-9.

Weisbrod, B.A., *The Economics of Public Health: Measuring the Economic Impact of Diseases* (University of Pennsylvania Press, Philadelphia, 1961).

12 OPTIMAL EXPENDITURE ON ADVERTISING SERVICES

M.M. Metwally

Introduction

A picture of society's commitment to the supply of advertising services, both absolute and relative, is a minimum requirement for any enquiry into the contribution of advertising to the effective operation of the economy. Also, an investigation of the alleged 'excessiveness' of advertising based on defined criteria of optimality should contribute towards the development of a 'marketing theory' which is very much lacking in the general theories of corporate behaviour or consumer welfare.

Advertising may be defined as a service rendered by some agent or media (the Press; TV; the cinema, etc.) to enable one party (a seller; an organisation; a government, etc.), who pays directly for the service, to transmit a particular message to a second party (a buyer; a client; a member; a nation, etc.).

In this chapter we are concerned with one particular type of advertising expenditure: the advertisements by manufacturers and retailers to consumers.[1] In Australia, these firms spent approximately 500 million dollars in 1974 on advertising. Since 1960, these advertising expenditures have been increased steadily. Table 12.1 provides data that demonstrates this feature. A time trend has also been fitted to the data by regression methods.[2]

Three main conclusions can be derived from the data given in Table 12.1 and the regression results. First, total advertising expenditures by business firms increased by approximately $30m. every year between 1960 and 1974. Secondly, although total advertising expenditures have increased in Australia in the past 15 years, the proportion of national income devoted to advertising shows a slight decrease in the same period; this decrease is, however, statistically not significant. Thirdly, there has been a significant change in the role played by the different advertising media in Australia in the past 15 years. The role of Press has been reduced and that of TV enhanced, while that of radio and outdoor media have remained, more or less, constant. The cinema seems to have lost popularity as a means of communication between advertisers and

Table 12.1: Advertising Expenditures by Main Media in Australia, 1960-74

	Media of Advertising					Total advertising expenditures	Advertising expenditures as % of national income
	Press	T.V.	Radio	Outdoor	Cinema		
Year	%	%	%	%	%	($)	(%)
1960	61.4	14.8	10.1	10.0	3.7	180	1.64
1961	59.1	17.3	11.3	8.9	3.4	170	1.45
1962	58.2	18.9	10.8	8.8	3.3	186	1.54
1963	58.3	19.8	10.5	8.6	2.8	192	1.50
1964	56.9	22.5	9.7	8.3	2.6	216	1.49
1965	55.5	24.5	9.4	8.1	2.5	235	1.48
1966	53.3	26.3	9.4	8.5	2.5	254	1.54
1967	53.1	25.0	10.6	8.8	2.5	276	1.52
1968	53.0	25.5	10.0	9.1	2.4	302	1.58
1969	53.2	25.1	110.3	9.0	2.4	328	1.52
1970	52.1	26.7	9.8	9.0	2.4	364	1.50
1971	52.4	25.8	10.2	9.1	2.5	398	1.51
1972	51.0	27.1	10.3	9.1	2.5	442	1.50
1973	50.2	28.0	10.1	9.2	2.5	476	1.53
1974	50.2	27.7	10.2	9.3	2.6	496	1.55

Sources: Data on advertising were provided by Marketing and advertising consultants. Data on national income were extracted from Australian National Accounts, National Income and Expenditure.

consumers.

Using the chi-square test we accept the hypothesis that there is a significant difference in the distribution of advertising expenditures between different media at the 1 per cent level of significance. Although the percentage of total advertising expenditures allocated to different media has changed, the relative ranking of these media did not change. The Press is still the first, followed by TV, while the cinema comes last.

The information given in Table 12.2 seems to support the view that 'advertising expenditure is. . .very unevenly distributed between industries. . . In particular, the use of advertising vis-a-vis other methods of competition depends to a considerable extent on the nature of the product and its market'[3].

Two main conclusions can be derived from the information given in Table 12.2. First, it is to be noted that the most heavily advertised products are consumed by most of the population. This does not mean that everyone buys every product or buys it to the extent they can. Some of these products are substitutes for other products. For example, it is readily recognised that cereals provide only one of many alternatives among breakfast foods. In some instances, heavily advertised products compete with each other as, for example, soft drinks and beer [2]. It has also been pointed out that some of the products are '. . .subject to taste and style changes' and that consumers become restive with existing brands and are prepared to try new varieties'. Illustrations include cereals, soups, clothing and motion pictures [51].

Secondly, the ranking of the products with respect to their advertising expenditures has changed very radically in some cases in the past 15 years. These include smoking accessories (which ranked as eighth in 1960; third in 1974); travel and tours (thirteenth in 1960; fifth in 1974); household cleaners (twelfth in 1960; sixth in 1974); household equipment (tenth in 1960, seventh in 1974) and aspirin types (twentyfifth in 1960; eighteenth in 1974). In some cases (e.g. household cleaners and household equipment), the consumer was offered a wide variety of brands from which to choose. Product improvements usually breed competitive product improvements and the advertising of these improvements may result in an increase in total advertising for the class of products. In other cases (e.g. smoking accessories), when a company embarks on an intensified advertising campaign, its competitors must step up their advertising (or other sales promotion efforts) to avoid the possible loss of market share.

Table 12.2: Ranking of Product Groups According to the Intensity of their Advertising Expenditures

Product Group	Percentage of Total advertising Expenditure				Product Ranking			
	1960	1965	1970	1974	1960	1965	1970	1974
Draper's Supply	6.3	5.3	5.0	4.6	5	7	8	10
Men's Wear	5.1	4.8	3.2	1.9	6	10	14	15
Women's Toiletries	4.75	6.1	4.9	4.9	7	4	9	8
Toilet Soaps	1.1	1.32	0.92	1.2	22	17	20	17
Dental	1.2	1.30	0.9	1.1	21	18	21	19
Household Cleaners	3.9	4.6	5.3	6.1	12	11	7	6
Household equipment	4.4	5.1	5.32	5.8	10	8	6	7
Electrical Goods	6.9	5.55	4.4	3.3	4	5	10	13
Gas Accessories	0.66	0.56	0.43	0.34	27	27	28	28
Refrigeration	2.1	0.93	0.7	0.6	17	22	23	23
Radio and T.V.	2.9	1.0	0.8	0.53	15	21	22	24
Proprietary Medicine	1.9	1.8	1.7	1.6	18	16	15	16
Internal Correctives	0.8	1.1	0.5	0.5	24	20	27	25
Tonics	0.5	0.4	0.26	0.18	28	28	29	29
Tonic Foods	0.67	0.28	0.21	0.15	26	29	31	31
Ointments	0.3	0.1	0.05	0.01	30	30	32	32
Coughs & Colds	1.25	0.9	0.65	0.45	20	23	25	26
Aspirin types	0.7	1.2	1.1	1.15	25	19	17	18
Cars & Trucks	7.0	7.6	10.9	12.4	3	3	2	2
Car accessories	0.86	0.7	0.6	0.4	23	26	26	27
Tyres	1.3	0.8	1.0	0.9	19	24	18	20
Motor Cycles and Bicycles	0.2	0.09	0.23	0.16	31	31	30	30
Petrol and Oils	4.6	5.5	4.3	4.65	9	6	11	9
Building Materials & Industrial Machinery	4.1	1.9	3.73	3.43	11	13	12	12
Paints and accessories	2.6	1.87	0.97	0.61	16	15	19	22
Liquor	3.2	3.1	3.7	3.9	14	14	13	11
Smoking Accessories	4.7	9.9	7.2	8.7	8	2	3	3
Foodstuffs	16.0	19.7	22.0	25.2	1	1	1	1
Pet Foods	n.a.	n.a.	1.6	1.96	n.a.	n.a.	16	14
Travel and Tours	3.6	4.2	6.6	8.3	13	12	4	5
Finance and Insurance	10.2	4.85	6.3	8.4	2	9	5	4
Office Equipment	0.4	0.74	0.68	0.70	29	25	24	21

Then again potential markets (e.g. travel and tour) expand as incomes rise and consumers are able to purchase products they previously could not afford. Continuous large-scale advertising provides information to attract some of these new customers.

The reverse trend characterises such products as men's wear, electrical goods, refrigeration, radio and TV. In these industries other forms of promotion such as personal selling, publicity and larger distribution margins seems to be playing an important role.

Table 12.3 shows the association between the type of product and the advertising media in Australia over the period 1960-74. The table also shows the trend in the relative importance of the different media for the different product groups over the same period.

Two conclusions can readily be derived from the information given in Table 12.3. First, there is a clear association between the type of product and the means of communication. Some products, particularly those related to home consumption (e.g. soaps, dental goods, household cleaners) are TV-oriented. Others, particularly durable goods, transport equipment and related products and industrial machinery, are Press-oriented. Secondly, the relative importance of the different advertising media has changed significantly during the period 1960-1974, with TV attracting a larger proportion of total advertising expenditures for almost every product.

This introduction concludes by mentioning that it is not easy to know with precision how much advertising is informational in Australia. Classified advertising and local advertising, which are considered overwhelmingly informational in nature, averaged approximately 21 per cent of total advertising expenditure in Australia during the period studied. It must, however, be realised that a significant part of national advertising is for promotion of new products for which the informational role is vital. Also, some part of advertising that does not seem to have a clear informational content may perform a valuable marketing task in some trades by contributing to economies of scale in production and efficiency in distribution.

Optimal Advertising under Static Conditions

A study of the marketing behaviour of the individual firms with respect to their advertising policy should throw some light on the question of 'excessiveness' of advertising which is often raised.

It is reasonable to assume that firms producing and selling the advertised products have as their main objective the maximisation of their profits. Hence, on this basis, advertising would be considered

Table 12.3: Association between type of Product Advertising Media in Australia

Product Group	Percentage of Total Advertising Expenditure allocated to: Press			Metrop. TV			Country TV		Metrop. Radio	
	1960	1967	1974	1960	1967	1974	1967	1974	1967	1974
Draper's Supply	83	65	54	17	24	31	5	7	6	8
Men's Wear	61	43	40	39	40	41	9	10	8	9
Women's toiletries	70	40	38	30	53	51	4	6	3	5
Toilet Soaps	34	10	6	66	70	71	18	20	2	3
Dental	27	10	9	73	70	71	19	19	1	1
Household Cleaners	29	5	4	71	75	70	18	23	4	3
Household Equipment	73	42	35	27	46	50	6	7	6	8
Electrical	66	50	57	34	40	30	7	5	3	8
Gas accessories	80	63	68	20	14	16	7	7	16	9
Refrigeration	85	70	72	15	26	21	3	4	3	3
Radio and TV	93	60	65	7	32	12	5	3	3	20
Proprietary Medicines	72	44	50	18	40	30	6	7	10	13
Internal correctives	23	18	30	77	70	53	9	10	3	7
Tonics	65	40	30	35	45	52	10	16	5	2
Tonic Foods	42	13	18	58	65	72	5	5	17	5
Ointments	65	50	52	35	25	28	2	3	23	15
Coughs & Colds	37	19	15	63	65	60	8	12	8	13
Aspirin Types	40	20	10	60	42	24	12	31	26	35
Cars & Trucks	89	62	56	11	26	35	6	4	6	5
Car accessories	85	60	47	15	23	27	2	1	15	25
Tyres	99	85	80	1	2	4	1	1	12	15
Petrol & Oils	–	21	12	63	56	57	12	14	11	17
Motor Cycles & Bicycles	89	86	80	11	6	12	1	3	7	5
Building Materials	87	81	80	13	13	13	3	3	3	4
Paints and Accessories	65	31	26	35	45	51	14	17	10	6
Liquor	64	47	44	36	36	37	4	6	13	13
Smoking Accessories	38	9	6	62	64	63	16	19	11	12
Foodstuffs	37	18	17	63	59	58	12	15	11	10
Pet Foods	na	na	13	na	na	73	na	10	na	4
Travel and Tours	88	74	65	12	17	26	2	2	7	7
Finance and Insurance	88	67	64	12	21	23	5	6	7	7
Office Equipment	95	88	94	5	11	5	–	–	1	1

'excessive' if the sums spent exceed those warranted by the object of profit maximisation or if advertising has a negative return. However, in this analysis both static and dynamic conditions of optimisation are considered within the profit maximisation framework.

To establish the static conditions of optimisation, let the basic demand equation for the product of the given firm be given by:

$$q = q\,(p, s, v) \qquad (1)$$

where, q = quantities sold of the particular brand
p = price charged
s = advertising expenditure of the particular brand
v = advertising expenditure of all competitive brands

The function (1) has the following properties:

$$\frac{\partial q}{\partial p} < o, \frac{\partial q}{\partial s} > o, \frac{\partial^2 q}{\partial s^2} < o, \frac{\partial q}{\partial v} < o$$

Also, v is assumed to depend on the decision variable s, in the frame of an oligopolistic interdependence: hence the reaction function:

$$v = v(s), \text{with } \frac{dv}{ds} > o$$

The firm's profit will be given by

$$\pi = (p - c)\,q - s \qquad (2)$$

or

$$\pi = pq\,[p,s,v(s)] - cq\,[p,s,v(s)] - s \qquad (3)$$

where cq = total production costs.

To maximise profits, the following first order conditions apply

$$\frac{\partial \pi}{\partial p} = o, \text{ or } (p - c) = \frac{-p}{\eta} \qquad (4)$$

$$\frac{\partial \pi}{\partial s} = o, \text{ or } (p - c) = \frac{s}{\epsilon q} \qquad (5)$$

where η = the price elasticity of demand, or

$$\eta = \frac{p}{q}\frac{\partial q}{\partial p} \tag{6}$$

ϵ = the (weighted) advertising elasticity of demand or

$$\epsilon = \frac{s}{q}\frac{dq}{ds} \tag{7}$$

Solving (4) and (6) simultaneously, gives

$$\theta = \frac{\epsilon}{-\eta} \tag{8}$$

where $\theta = s/pq$, is the *static* optimal advertising sales ratio. It is directly proportional to the numerical value of the weighted advertising-elasticity of demand and inversely proportional to the numerical value of the price elasticity of demand. The result is similar to that achieved by Dorfman-Steiner [8].

A Simple-Lagged Model of Advertising

Equation (8) provides an operative criterion that can be applied to test whether advertising expenditures on the product concerned are 'too excessive'. This is done by comparing the actual ratios of current advertising expenditure with the optimal ratios given by (8). To estimate the elasticities coefficients as well as the marginal productivity of advertising, the following two models were applied to data for three products. These products are purported to be advertised heavily in Australia[4]:

Model 1:

$$q_{it} = a_o + a_1 q_{i,t-1} + a_2 p_{it} + a_3 s_{it} + a_4 v_{it} + \mu_t \tag{9}$$

Model 2:

$$v_{it} = a_o + a_1 v_{i,t-1} + a_2 s_{it} + \mu_t \tag{10}$$

where q_{it} = quantities sold of the ith brand in period t
$q_{i,t-1}$ = quantities sold of the ith brand in period t-1
p_{it} = price charged per unit sold of the ith brand in period t
s_{it} = advertising expenditure of the ith brand in period t

v_{it} = advertising expenditure of all competitive brands in period t

$v_{i,t-1}$ = advertising expenditure of all competitive brands in period t-1.

μt = error term.

Model 1 is comparable to those found in studies by Telser [52], Palda [39], Frank and Massy [13], Lambin [29] and Simon [45]. The introduction into the model of the lagged dependent variable q_{t-1}, here called 'good will', makes it possibly to evaluate the cumulative effects of advertising.[5] As shown by Kyock [26] this model can be based on the assumption that the effect of each variable dies away to zero according to a decreasing geometric progression with parameter (λ) for periods beyond the maximum lag that is explicitly considered in this model. The regression coefficient of q_{t-1} (i.e. a_1) constitutes an estimate of the advertising retention rate (λ), in a given period, provided the estimate of λ is included between zero and one. Model 2 is not a demand model but an advertising reaction model.

The two models were estimated using the least squares method of estimation. The estimation procedure was carried out in three stages. In the first stage, parameters of the model are estimated consistently by Liviatan's instrumental variable approach. In the second stage results of the first stage are employed in order to produce consistent estimates of the residuals in the model under consideration by ordinary least squares. Finally, using the results of the preceding stage, ordinary least squares is again applied to a transformed regression model to yield estimates of the parameters. The resulting estimates are consistent and asymptotically efficient.

The statistical analysis is applied to the two 'biggest selling' brands (Brands A and B) of cigarettes, toothpaste and washing powder. The total market share of these brands is well above 70 per cent. The data (supplied by the mentioned Marketing and Advertising Consultants) cover the total advertising expenditure by manufacturers on all media, the (wholesale) price and the total sales during the period 1960-70. The data obtained were annual and were deflated, whenever necessary, using the consumer price index.

The regression results for the two models are shown in Table 12.4.[6] These results show that all coefficients have the expected signs. All the regression coefficients are significant at the 5 per cent level and most of them at the 1 per cent level.

The following interpretation can be made of the findings

Table 12.4: Regression Results for Models 1 and 2

	Cigarettes		Washing Powder		Toothpaste	
	Brand A	Brand B	Brand A	Brand B	Brand A	Brand B
Model 1: $q_{it} = \alpha_0 + \alpha_1 q_{i,t-1} + \alpha_2 p_{it} + \alpha_3 s_{it} + \alpha_4 v_{it} + \mu_t$						
α_0	1.3132	0.8814	1.5214	−0.2013	1.7609	1.3123
α_1	0.8213	0.8339	0.7399	0.7769	0.7992	0.7311
	(0.3446)	(0.3010)	(0.2310)	(0.2710)	(0.2879)	(0.2514)
α_2	−1.2989	−1.3169	−2.0100	−2.2314	−1.8671	−1.9912
	(−0.5042)	(−0.4704)	(−0.6016)	(−0.6714)	(−0.6711)	(−0.6545)
$\alpha_3 = (\partial_q/\partial_s)$	0.0122	0.0126	0.0162	0.0161	0.0122	0.0153
	(0.0036)	(0.0034)	(0.0049)	(0.0049)	(0.0032)	(0.0036)
$\alpha_4 = (\partial_q/\partial_v)$	−0.0128	−0.0129	−0.0193	−0.0199	−0.0134	−0.0136
	(−0.0039)	(−0.0044)	(−0.0062)	(−0.0058)	(−0.0061)	(−0.0069)
$\bar{R}^2$	0.8897	0.8736	0.8511	0.9012	0.9115	0.8684
Durbin's "h"	1.8468	1.8099	2.0099	1.9919	2.0407	2.1141
Model 2: $v_{it} = a_0 + a_1 v_{i,t-1} + a_2 s_{it} + \mu_t$						
a_0	0.4601	0.8303	0.7812	0.7101	0.9270	0.8787
a_1	0.6030	0.6304	0.5921	0.6612	0.5832	0.6412
	(0.2018)	(0.1899)	(0.1677)	(0.2125)	(0.2001)	(0.2423)
$a_2 = \partial_v/\partial_s$	0.2902	0.3248	0.4663	0.1608	0.3134	0.7205
	(0.0792)	(0.1006)	(0.1467)	(0.0515)	(0.1044)	(0.2199)
$\bar{R}^2$	0.9274	0.9399	0.9090	0.9666	0.9595	0.9172
Durbin's "h"	1.8354	1.9009	2.0441	1.8461	2.0910	1.9315

presented in Table 12.4. First, since ($\partial q/\partial v$) is negative, the net marginal sales effect must be smaller than its partial effect. To explain this in some detail, under conditions of non-price competition it is assumed that:

$$v = v(s) \tag{11}$$

thus

$$\frac{dq}{ds} = \frac{\partial q}{\partial s} + \frac{\partial q}{\partial v}\frac{dv}{ds} \tag{12}$$

and the necessary condition for profit maximisation becomes

$$\frac{\partial q}{\partial s} + \left(\frac{\partial q}{\partial v}\frac{dv}{ds}\right) = 1/(p\text{-}c') \tag{13}$$

where c' is marginal cost of the particular firm.

Thus equation (13) states that the change in sales per unit change in the firm's advertising outlay depends both on the partial effect of its advertising ($\partial q/\partial s$) and on the indirect effect via changes in advertising outlays of the other firms in the industry ($\partial q/\partial v$), induced by a change in the firms advertising outlay ($\partial v/\partial s$). If total industry sales are stable, it is plausible to expect the following:

$$\partial q/\partial s > o \text{ and } \partial q/\partial v < o \tag{14}$$

Thus the net marginal sales effect of advertising should be less than its partial effect [52].

Secondly, the partial marginal sales effect ($\partial q/\partial s$) is approximately of the same order of magnitude for the two competitive brands in each industry.

Thirdly, a substantial part of advertising is self-cancelling even if the net marginal sales effect remains positive for each brand. This 'cancellation effect' is reflected in the closeness of the estimates of $\partial q/\partial s$ and $\partial q/\partial v$ for the two brands in each industry. This conclusion implies that firms use their advertising expenditure to protect their market position. They react and adjust their own advertising outlays continuously to avoid a loss in the market shares. As long as this escalation goes on, advertising expenditure will increase in the market without reducing the reciprocal cancellation effect. One may object that reciprocal cancellation is the essence of competition, for example, in price reduction or in quality improvements. However, the claim that cancellation in advertising is wasteful rests upon the point that firms competing on price or quality benefit the consumer, whereas a mere increase in advertising confers no additional benefit to consumers.

Applying equations (6), (7) and (8) to the results of Models 1 and 2, the findings in Table 12.5 were obtained. This table gives, for each brand in each case, the price-elasticity of demand, the advertising elasticity of demand and the optimal advertising-sales ratios. Included in Table 12.5 also are the actual advertising-sales ratios for each brand.

It is clear from the information shown in Table 12.5 that the actual advertising-sales ratios of all brands studied exceed the optimal short-run ratios. The short-run analysis, therefore, seems to suggest that advertising expenditure by the industries studied is 'too excessive'. The short-run regression results indicate that advertising in the three industries studied extends beyond the point at which marginal cost of advertising equals its marginal revenue.

This conclusion is also supported by the (rough) estimates made available to us about the ratio of production costs (advertising not included) to net price. These ratios (to be denoted hereafter by the K's ratios) were 0.70, 0.68 and 0.67 for cigarettes, washing powder and toothpaste respectively.

Since at maximum

$$c' = p(1 + \frac{1}{\eta}) \qquad (15)$$

It follows that:

$$\eta = p/(c''\text{-}p) \qquad (16)$$

where $p/(p-c')$ is the reciprocal of the gross margin expressed as a percentage of price. Thus if it is assumed that marginal cost is constant and is approximated by unit variable cost, then a 30 per cent gross margin would give an optimal value of η equivalent to approximately -3.333. It can be seen from Table 12.5, that the elasticity figures of a profit-maximising firm in the three industries differ significantly from the price elasticities observed in the regressions.

However, Table 12.5 also shows that the actual advertising-sales ratios of the two brands of cigarettes, Brand B of washing powder and Brand A of toothpaste do not differ too much from the long run optimal ratios (the ratios which take into account the retention rate of

Table 12.5: Actual and Optimal Advertising — Sales Ratios

Variables	Cigarettes		Washing Powder		Toothpaste	
	Brand A	Brand B	Brand A	Brand B	Brand A	Brand B
Price Elasticities	−2.087	−2.136	−2.311	−2.424	−2.178	−2.190
Advertising Elasticities:						
Short-run	0.038	0.033	0.033	0.036	0.041	0.039
Long-run	0.090	0.101	0.083	0.113	0.112	0.086
Optimal Advertising Ratios:						
Short-run	0.018	0.016	0.014	0.015	0.019	0.018
Long-run	0.043	0.047	0.037	0.047	0.051	0.040
Actual Advertising—Sales Ratios	0.048	0.052	0.056	0.050	0.059	0.057

Note: Long-run elasticities are given by $\frac{\epsilon}{(1-\lambda)}$ and long-run advertising sales ratios are given by $\theta/(1-\lambda)$ where λ is the retention rate of advertising given by α_1.

advertising).

This indicates that these firms associate a positive shadow price with the stock of goodwill. For if $\lambda(t) > o$, equation (5) gives

$$p\,\frac{dq}{ds} < c\,\frac{dq}{ds} + 1$$

which implies that the current marginal revenue generated by advertising is less than the marginal cost equally generated by advertising. Hence, long-run optimal analysis does not seem to support the view that advertising expenditure of the firms producing the three commodities studied is too excessive.

Also, the same view does not seem to be supported by an evaluation of the advertising investment profitability. This evaluation was carried out using the rough estimates of the K's and the following necessary condition of profit-maximisation (which can easily be derived from equation (3), since p is assumed to be independent of s)

$$\frac{dq}{ds} = 1/(p\text{-}c') \tag{17}$$

Let us designate (p-c′) dq/ds, the advertising marginal profit contribution by Ω and recalling that the underlying Kyock model assumes that a one dollar increment in advertising at the beginning of the period generates a revenue stream approximated by a decreasing geometric progression with parameter ω, we have

$$\Omega_t = \Omega_1 \ \omega^{t-1} \tag{18}$$

and the long-run optimisation rule becomes

$$\Omega = 1 - \frac{\omega}{1+\delta} \tag{19}$$

where Ω = marginal profit contribution of advertising
δ = rate of return
ω = retention rate of advertising

Equation (19) can be written as

$$\delta = \frac{\Omega - 1 + \omega}{1 - \Omega} \tag{20}$$

Using the estimates of Ω given in Table 12.6, a positive δ requires ω to exceed the values given by ω^* in the same table. It appears that the available estimates of ω are superior to their critical values for all brands except Brand A of washing powder and Brand B of toothpaste.

It may be concluded, therefore, that although all the brands considered do not seem to meet the 'short-run' conditions of optimality, advertising on the majority of those brands would seem to have positive return. Also the available evidence would seem to suggest that the firms follow a long-run profit maximisation policy as far as their advertising expenditure is concerned.

Optimal Advertising under Dynamic Conditions

Dynamic analysis would have to take into account the stock of good will of the firm, summarising the effect of past advertising outlays.[7]

Let the stock of goodwill be expressed by A. The demand function (1) may then be generalised as

Table 12.6: Advertising Investment Profitability

Variables	Cigarettes		Washing Powder		Toothpaste	
	Brand A	Brand B	Brand A	Brand B	Brand A	Brand B
$\frac{\partial q}{\partial v}\frac{\partial v}{\partial s}$	−0.0032	−0.0038	−0.0090	−0.0032	−0.0042	−0.0098
dq/ds	0.0090	0.0088	0.0072	0.0129	0.0080	0.0055
Ω	0.1898	0.1693	0.2434	0.2231	0.2339	0.2341
ω^*	0.8102	0.8307	0.7566	0.7693	0.7761	0.7659
ω	0.8213	0.8339	0.7399	0.7769	0.7992	0.7311

$$q = q\,(p, s, v, A, t) \tag{21}$$

with $\frac{\partial q}{\partial A} < o, \frac{\partial^2 q}{\partial A^2} < o, \frac{\partial^2 q}{\partial A \partial s} = o$

A is assumed to depreciate over time or

$$\frac{dA}{dt} = \phi\,(s, A, t) \tag{22}$$

with $\frac{\partial \phi}{\partial s} > o$ and $\frac{\partial \phi}{\partial A} < o$

If we assume that A depreciates over time at a constant rate a, we can note

$$\frac{dA}{dt} = s - a\,A \tag{23}$$

with $a > o$

The firm's profit function (3) can be generalised as

$$\pi(t) = pq\;[p,s,v(s),A,t] - cq\;[p,s,v(s),A,t] - s \tag{24}$$

The problem becomes one of maximising the present value of the stream of profits:

$$v = \int_o^{\infty} e^{-rt}\;\pi(p, s, A, t)\,dt \tag{25}$$

with respect to p and s, subject to [23].

Using the Pontryagin maximum principles, the Hamiltonian is obtained

$$H = e^{-rt}\,[pq(p,s,v(s),A,t) - cq(p,s,v(s),A,t) - s + \lambda(t)(s - \alpha A)] \quad (26)$$

The first order conditions for maximising H(t) require that:

$$\text{(i)}\ \frac{\partial H}{\partial p} = 0, \text{ or } (p-c) = \frac{-p}{\eta} \quad (27)$$

$$\text{(ii)}\ \frac{\partial H}{\partial s} = 0, \text{ or } (p-c) = \frac{s[-\lambda(t)]}{\epsilon q} \quad (28)$$

$$\text{(iii)}\ \frac{\partial H}{\partial A} = -\frac{d(e^{-rt}\lambda)}{dt} \quad (29)$$

Solving (28) and (29) simultaneously gives

$$\gamma = \frac{-\epsilon}{\eta(1-\lambda)} \quad (30)$$

where γ is the dynamic optimal advertising-sales ratio which is the dynamic counterpart of θ given by (8) above. The result may be compared with that of the Nerlove-Arrow theorem [37].

Exponentially Lagged-Variables Model with Different Weights

Equation (30) provides an operative criterion that could be applied to test whether the firms follow a dynamic (long-run) profit maximisation policy with respect to their advertising expenditure. To empirically perform this test, however, a more complicated version of Model 1 is required. Model 3 employs exponentially lagged variables with different weights as follows:

$$q_{it} = \gamma_0 + \gamma_1 q_{i,t-1} + \gamma_2 q_{i,t-2} + \gamma_3 p_{it} + \gamma_4 p_{i,t-1} + \gamma_5 s_{it} + \gamma_6 s_{i,t-1} + \gamma_7 v_{it} + \gamma_8 v_{i,t-1} + \mu_t \quad (31)$$

where $q_{i,t-2}$ = quantities sold of the ith brand in period t-2
$P_{i,t-1}$ = price charged per unit sold of the ith brand in period t-1
$s_{i,t-1}$ = advertising expenditure of the ith brand in period t-1
Other variables are defined as in Models 1 and 2

Testing Model 3 requires more observations than used before. To this purpose information on the three 'biggest selling' brands (A, B and C) in washing powder for the period 1956-72 was employed. The market share of these brands is well above 77 per cent. The same method of estimation as for Models 1 and 2 was used and is subject to the same comments on 'serial correlation' and 'heteroscedasticity'. Regression results of Model 3 are presented in Table 12.7.

Table 12.7: Regression Results for Model 3

	Washing Powder		
	Brand A	Brand B	Brand C
Constant	2.319	1.805	2.933
$q_{i,t-1}$	1.004	0.952	1.056
	(0.334)	(0.360)	(0.405)
$q_{i,t-2}$	−0.261	−0.284	0.277
	(−0.079)	(−0.084)	(0.091)
p_{it}	−0.645	−0.814	−0.804
	(−0.245)	(−0.292)	(−0.269)
$p_{i,t-1}$	−0.213	−0.215	−0.204
	(−0.060)	(−0.086)	(−0.068)
s_{it}	0.041	0.042	0.044
	(0.016)	(0.014)	(0.015)
$s_{i,t-1}$	0.029	0.031	0.033
	(0.010)	(0.011)	(0.010)
v_{it}	−0.030	−0.033	−0.034
	(−0.010)	(−0.011)	(−0.012)
$v_{i,t-1}$	−0.022	−0.020	−0.018
	(−0.006)	(−0.005)	(−0.007)
$\bar{R}^2$	0.956	0.964	0.966
Durbin's "h" statistic	2.043	1.969	2.176

Again, the results in Table 12.7 show that all coefficients have the expected signs and all regression coefficients are significant at the 5 per cent level (and most of them at the 1 per cent level). Model 3, however, gives higher values of retention rates of advertising (λ) than Model 1. The values of (λ) given by Model 3 could be calculated by dividing the coefficient of $s_{i,t-1}$ by that of s_{it}.

Applying the advertising reaction model 2 to the three brands of washing powder the following results are obtained:

Brand A

$$v_t = 0.741 + \underset{(0.239)}{0.622}\, v_{t-1} + \underset{(0.205)}{0.508}\, s_t$$

$$\bar{R}^2 = 0.914; \text{“h”} = 2.043$$

Brand B

$$v_t = 0.699 + \underset{(0.245)}{0.567}\, v_{t-1} + \underset{(0.088)}{0.268}\, s_t$$

$$\bar{R}^2 = 0.911; \text{“h”} = 1.969$$

Brand C

$$v_t = 0.786 + \underset{(0.208)}{0.613}\, v_{t-1} + \underset{(0.031)}{0.111}\, s_t$$

$$\bar{R}^2 = 0.926; \text{“h”} = 2.176$$

Using these results, together with the data in Table 12.7, the optimal advertising sales ratios can be derived. They are presented in Table 12.8.

Table 12.8: Optimal Advertising Sales Ratios under Dynamic Conditions

Variables	Brand A	Brand B	Brand C
Price-elasticities of demand	−2.533	−2.493	−2.886
Advertising elasticities:			
Long-term	0.137	0.133	0.158
Short-term	0.041	0.036	0.038
Optimal Advertising-sales ratios:			
Long-term	0.054	0.053	0.055
Short-term	0.014	0.014	0.013
Actual Advertising-sales ratios	0.053	0.048	0.043

Two main points emerge from comparing Table 12.8 with Table 12.5. First, both tables reveal that the actual advertising sales ratios of all brands of washing powder exceed the optimal (short-term) ratios. Secondly, according to the evidence in Table 12.5, the actual advertising sales ratio of Brand B does not differ too much from the long-run optimal (static) ratio, while the actual advertising sales ratio of Brand A is much higher than the long-run optimal static ratio.

The evidence in Table 12.8, however, would seem to suggest that the actual advertising-sales ratios of *all* brands do not differ too much from the long-run optimal ratios, when a two exponentially lagged variables with different weights model is used. In fact, the evidence would seem to suggest that the actual ratios of all three brands are smaller than the optimal long-run ratios.

This last conclusion would also seem to be supported by examination of the marginal sales revenue and profit contribution of advertising using the two exponentially lagged variables model. The results are shown in Table 12.9.

Table 12.9: Marginal Sales Revenue and Profit Contribution of Advertising (Model 3)

Variables	Brand A	Brand B	Brand C
Partial sales effect of brands advertising	0.041	0.042	0.044
Partial sales effect of competitive advertising	–0.030	–0.033	–0.034
Reaction effect of advertising (Model 2)	0.508	0.268	0.111
Net marginal sales effect of advertising	0.026	0.033	0.040
Marginal profit contribution of advertising	0.304	0.363	0.448
Rate of return of advertising	0.006	0.146	0.377

It is to be noted that the net marginal sales effect differs significantly between the three brands. The large differences are caused mainly by the different intensity of competitors' reactions to each brand's advertising efforts. The low reaction effect of advertising for Brand C merely reflects the dynamic role played by this brand and/or the passivity of the other competing brands. Also, the use of the more complicated lag structure given by Model 3 gives a positive rate of return for the three brands (this should be compared with the results of Table 12.6, where one brand shows a negative return).

Conclusions

The above analysis, despite its limitations, has some important findings. First, the total amount of resources allocated to advertising in Australia has increased steadily during the period 1960-1974. The ratio of advertising expenditures to national income, however, has remained practically constant. By contrast, the relative importance of the different advertising media in Australia has changed during the period considered (i.e. the media shares have *not* remained constant). Also, there is a significant association between the type of product and the media of advertising in Australia; but the advertisers, in general, seem to be making more use of TV (particularly in country areas).

Secondly, short-term optimal analysis seems to suggest that the actual advertising-sales ratios of firms selling cigarettes, washing powder and toothpaste, in Australia, are much higher than the optimal ratios. Firms selling the above-mentioned products seem to follow a *long-run* profit maximisation policy with respect to their advertising expenditure. The sellers seem to give a positive shadow price to the stock of goodwill. This implies that the current marginal revenue generated by advertising is less than the marginal cost equally generated by it.

Thirdly, advertising on many products shows a positive return if a long-term optimisation rule is followed and if there is no downward bias in estimating the true rate of return. In addition, it can be stressed that in dealing with advertising effects it is necessary to have a model with at least two-exponentially lagged variables with different weights to avoid downward biased estimates of the true rate of return.

Finally, it can be concluded that a substantial part of advertising in some industries in Australia is self-cancelling. But while the net marginal sales effect of advertising in some Australian industries is smaller than its partial effect, the latter is approximately of the same order of magnitude for the two dominant competitive brands in industries studied.

Appendix 12.1

Regression analysis was carried out on the data given in Table 12.1. The results (with figures in brackets referring to standard errors) were as follows:

$$V^* = 9.83 + 30.95t^*$$
$$(1.343)$$
$$r = 0.989;\ t = 23.09$$
$$\text{d.w.} = 1.781,\ r'_{e.x} = 0.136$$
$$V/Y = 1.528 - 0.0057t$$
$$(0.0042)$$
$$r = -0.0568;\ |t| = 0.205$$
$$\text{d.w.} = 1.19,\ r'_{e.x} = -0.221$$

V = advertising expenditures in all media
Y = National Income
t = time

An application of Durbin-Watson test to the original data revealed a significant positive correlation. In order to solve the problem e_t was regressed on e_{t-1} and the following result was obtained.

$$\hat{e}_t = 0.673\ e_{t-1}$$
$$(0.124)$$

Using the estimate $\hat{p} = 0.673$, the transformed variables (where X stands for time in the regression) were obtained.

$$V^*_t = V_t - 0.673\ V_{t-1}$$
$$X^*_t = X_t - 0.673\ X_{t-1}$$

The statistic $r'_{e.x}$ is the Spearman rank correlation test for homoscedasticity. The results suggest the absence of heteroscedasticity.

Notes

* I am grateful to Garnsey Clemenger Pty. Ltd, Marketing and Advertising Consultants, Brisbane, for supplying the data required for this study. I am also indebted to Professor K.S. Palda of Queen's University for valuable comments and suggestions. Any (remaining) errors are, of course, my own responsibility.

1. Government and other non-business organisations expenditures on advertising were estimated at 13% of total advertising expenditure in 1974.
2. See the Appendix for this analysis.
3. P. Doyle, 'Economic Aspects of Advertising: A Survey', *Economic Journal* vol. LXXVIII (September, 1968).
4. A long debate on the 'excessiveness' of advertising by producers of washing powder in Australia took place in the Australian Federal Parliament in August

1974.

5. Model 1 implies that an increase in advertising expenditure(s) generates a series of increments in sales (q) such that the increment in period t is a fraction a_1 of the increment in the preceding period. Thus the coefficient of lagged sales in this regression estimates the rate of depreciation of the advertising capital; see [52], p.481.
6. A test for serial correlation by means of Durbin-Watson statistics is inapropriate for those models in which one of the independent variables is the lagged value of the dependent variable. A test, called Durbin's 'h' statistic for serial correlation when lagged-dependent variables are present, has recently been developed by J. Durbin [11]. This test is unfortunately applicable only to large samples (say n>30). The Durbin's 'h' statistics estimated in this study must, therefore, be interpreted accordingly. Also the residuals observed over time for each brand, when plotted graphically, suggest a satisfactory behaviour in all cases. The small number of observations rules out more sophisticated tests for heteroscedasticity.
7. The model used here assumed certainty and equilibrium. For discussion on optimal advertising policy under dynamic conditions and uncertainty, see Jacquemin and Dehez [19].

References

[1] Aitchison, J. and J.A.C. Brown, *The Lognormal Distribution with Special Reference to Its Uses in Economics,* Department of Applied Economics, Monograph 5 (University of Cambridge, 1957).

[2] Backman, J., 'Is Advertising Wasteful?' *Journal of Marketing,* 32 (1968), 2-8.

[3] Bain, J., *Industrial Organisation* (Wiley, New York, 1969) pp.390-1.

[4] Baumol, W.J., 'Models of Economic Competition' in P. Langhoff (ed.), *Models Measurement and Marketing* (Englewood Cliffs, NJ, Prentice Hall, 1965).

[5] Comanor, W.S., and T.A. Wilson, 'Advertising, Marketing Structure, and Performance', *The Review of Economics and Statistics* (November 1967) pp.423-40.

[6] Cowling, K., *Market Structure and Economic Behaviour* (Gray-Mills, London, 1973).

[7] *et al., Advertising and Economic Behaviour* (Holmes and Meier, New York, 1975).

[8] Dorfman, R., and P.O. Steiner, 'Optimal Advertising and Optimal Quality', in F.M. Bass *et al.* (ed.), *Mathematical Models and Methods in Marketing,* (Homewood, Illinois, Irwin, 1961).

[9] Doyle, P., 'Economic Aspects of Advertising: A Survey', *Economic Journal,* vol.LXXVIII (September 1968).

[10] Durbin, J., and G.S. Watson, 'Testing for Serial Correlation in Least Squares Regression', *Biometrica,* 38 (1951), pp.159-77.

[11] Durbin, J., 'Testing for Serial Correlation in Least Squares Regression When Some Regressors are Lagged Dependent Variables', *Econometrica,* 38 (1970), pp.410-21.

[12] Edwards, C.D., 'Advertising and Competition: An Evaluation of Exhorative Programs', *Business Horizons,* (1) (1968), pp.65-72.

[13] Frank, R.E., and Massey, W.F., 'Short Term Price and Dealing Effects in Selected Market Segments', *Journal of Marketing Research,* 2 (May 1965), pp.171-85.

[14] Friedman, L., 'Game Theory Models in the Allocation of Advertising

Expenditure', *Operations Research,* 5(5) (1958).
[15] Greer, D., 'Advertising and Market Concentration', *The Southern Economic Journal* (July 1971).
[16] Gupta, J.K., and K.S. Krishnan, 'Mathematical Models in Marketing', *Operations Research,* 15 (1967) pp.1040-50.
[17] Holbert, M., *The Meaning and Sources of Marketing Theory* (McGraw Hill, New York, 1965).
[18] Jacquemin, A.P., 'Optimal Control and Advertising Policy', *Metroeconomica,* 25 (May-August 1973). Fasc. II, pp.200-7.
[19] Jacquemin, A.P., and P. Dehez, 'A Note on Optimal Advertising Policy Under Dynamic Conditions and Uncertainty', *C.O.R.E. Discussion Paper No. 7344* (1973).
[20] Jastram, T., 'A Treatment of Distributed Lags in the Theory of Advertising Expenditure', *Journal of Marketing,* 20 (July 1955), pp.36-46.
[21] Johnston, J., *Econometric Methods,* 2nd ed., (McGraw-Hill Book Company, New York, 1972).
[22] Kaldor, N., and R. Silverman, *A Statistical Analysis of Advertising Expenditure and the Revenue of the Press,* (Cambridge University Press, Cambridge, 1948).
[23] Kaldor, N. 'The Economic Aspects of Advertising', *Review of Economic Studies,* XVIII (1950) 1-27.
[24] Kotke, F.J., 'Market Entry and the Character of Competition', *Western Economic Journal* (December 1960).
[25] Kotler, P., 'Competitive Strategies for New Product Marketing over the Life Cycle', *Management Science,* 12 (4) (1965), 104-19.
[26] Kyock, J.M., *Distributed Lags and Investment Analysis* (North-Holland Publishing Company, Amsterdam, 1954).
[27] Krishnan, K.S., and S.K. Gupta, 'Mathematical Models for a Duopolist Market', *Management Science,* 13 (7) (1967), 569-83.
[28] *Labour Party Report of a Commission of Enquiry into Advertising* (London, 1966) p.42.
[29] Lambin, J.J., 'Measuring the Profitability of Advertising: An Empirical Study', *Journal of Industrial Economics,* 17 (2) (1969), 86-102.
[30] Lambin, J.J., *Advertising, Competition and Market Conduct in Oligopoly Over Time: An Economic Investigation in Western European Countries* (North-Holland, Amsterdam, 1976).
[31] Mann, H.M., J.A. Henning and J.W. Meehan, 'Advertising and Concentration: An Empirical Investigation', *The Journal of Industrial Economics,* (November 1967) pp.34-5.
[32] Metwally, M.M., 'Australian Advertising Expenditure and its Relation to Demand', *The Economic Record* (June 1973) pp.290-2.
[33] 'Economic Strategies of Firms Facing Asymptotic Demand: A Case Study', *Applied Economics,* 5 (4) (1973) pp.271-80.
[34] 'Advertising and Competitive Behaviour of Selected Australian Firms', *The Review of Economics and Statistics,* vol.LVII, No.4 (November 1975) pp.417-26.
[35] 'Profitability of Advertising in Australia: A Case Study', *The Journal of Industrial Economics* (March 1976) pp.221-31.
[36] 'Market Concentration and Advertising: The Australian Experience', *Management Science* (forthcoming).
[37] Nerlove, M., and Arrow, K.J., 'Optimal Advertising Policy Under Dynamic Conditions', *Economica,* XXIV (May 1962) pp.129-42.
[38] Ozga, S.A., 'Imperfect Markets through Lack of Knowledge', *Quarterly Journal of Economics* LXXIV (1960) pp.29-52.
[39] Palda, K.S., *The Measurement and Cumulative Advertising Effects* (Engle-

wood Cliffs, NJ, Prentice Hall, 1964).

[40] Peles, Y., 'Rates of Amortization of Advertising Expenditures', *Journal of Political Economy,* 79 (1971) pp.1032-58.

[41] Reekie, W.D., 'Advertising and Market Structure: Another Approach', *Economic Journal,* 85 (337) (1975) pp.156-64.

[42] Reekie, W.D., 'Advertising and Market Share Mobility', *Scottish Journal of Political Economy,* 21 (2) (June 1974) pp.143-58.

[43] Rees, K.D., 'Advertising, Concentration and Competition: A Comment and Further Results', *The Economic Journal* 85 (337) (1975) pp.165-72.

[44] Schmalensee, *The Economics of Advertising,* vol.80, Contributions to Economic Analysis (North-Holland Publishing Company).

[45] Simon, J.L., 'The Effect of Advertising on Liquor Brand Sales', *Journal of Marketing Research* 6 (August 1969) pp.301-31.

[46] Stigler, G.L., *Introduction to Business Concentration and Price Policy* (Princeton University Press, Princeton, 1955).

[47] 'The Economies of Scale' *Journal of Law and Economics* (1 Oct. 1958), pp.63-6.

[48] 'The Economics of Information', *Journal of Political Economy,* LXIV (1961), pp.312-25.

[49] Sutton, C.J., 'Advertising, Concentration and Competition', *Economic Journal,* 84 (333), (1974) pp.56-69.

[50] 'Advertising, Concentration and Competition: A Reply and Some Further Comments', *Economic Journal* 85 (337) (1975), pp.173-76.

[51] Telser, L., 'How Much Does It Pay Whom to Advertise?' *American Economic,* LI (1961) pp.194-205.

[52] 'Advertising and Cigarettes' *Journal of Political Economy,* 70 (5) (Oct. 1962), pp.471-499.

[53] 'The Demand for Branded Goods as Estimated From Consumer Panel Data', *Review of Economics and Statistics* (Aug.1962), pp.300-24.

[54] 'Another Look at Advertising and Concentration' *Journal of Industrial Economics* (Nov. 1969) pp.85-94.

[55] 'Advertising and Competition' *Journal of Political Economy,* /2 (6) (1964), pp.537-62.

[56] Urban, G.L. 'A Mathematical Modeling Approach to Product Line Decisions' *Journal of Marketing Research,* 6 (Feb. 1969), pp.40-47.

[57] Vernon, J.N., and R.E.M. Nourse, 'Profit Rates and Market Structure of Advertising Intensive Firms' *Journal of Industrial Economics,* XXII (Sept. 1973), pp.1-20.

[58] Vernon, J.N. and N.B. McElvoy 'A Note on Estimation in Market Structure Performance Studies' *American Economic Review* (Sept. 1973), pp.763-67.

[59] Weiss, D.L. 'Determinants of Market Structure' *Journal of Marketing Research,* 5 (1968), pp.290-5.

[60] Zellner, A., and D.S. Huang, 'Further Properties of Efficient Estimators for Seemingly Unrelated Regression Equations' *International Economic Review,* 3 (1962), pp.300-13.

13 DEMAND FOR PERFORMING ARTS SERVICES[1]

Glenn A. Withers

Introduction

The performing arts as public entertainment, arbiter of cultural standards and unpredictable social critic are invariably of interest. Their frequent resort to the public purse sharpens this interest and also prompts investigation of the performing arts from an economic perspective.

This paper focuses on the demand side in the economists' inexorable application of Marshall's scissors to industry analysis. We look first at the economic definition of the performing arts which emphasises the role of demand, and then examine the pattern and the level of this demand for performing arts services. The pattern represents a cross-section view and the level a time-series view of demand. The cross-section perspective highlights audience composition, a matter of great relevance to the equity issues involved in support for the arts, and the time-series perspective considers the problem of cost-revenue squeeze in the performing arts and how this may affect the financing options available.

While many of the questions examined in the paper do bear directly on the matter of justification for assistance to the performing arts, there is no pretence here of producing conclusions on this matter. Our aim is the more selective one of examining market demand for performing arts services so as to improve understanding of this particular aspect of arts activity.[2] The integration of this information with other matters relevant to analysing the industry and assessing the case for government support is, for want of space, among other reasons, left to others or to another occasion.[3]

Economic Definition of the Performing Arts

Definition of an industry is a problem for economists since all resources and outputs are ultimately substitutes for one another. Delimitation is further complicated in the case of the performing arts because the term 'art', like 'culture', carries normative connotations, and many activities would like to see themselves described as a performing art because of this.

In this paper we advance an economic definition of the performing arts industry which corresponds to popular use and which provides some reasons for that usage. No judgement on the merits of activities consequently excluded is intended by the author.

Supply Features of the Industry

In this industry the key feature of production techniques is the live public presentation of an artistic performance. A venue is required, normally an indoor seated facility, in which a live audience can listen and watch the live performer(s), the latter usually on a stage.

The main component of the performance experienced by the audience is the artistic skill of the performer in presenting a created work of art. The artist may make use of equipment such as musical instruments, costumes, scenery, lighting and props.

The emphasis then is on liveness, joint audience-performer presence, and concern for the skilled presentation of created works of art, with the performed labour contribution being the essential feature of the final product as experienced by the consumer audience. Other labour inputs and materials not observed by the audience may also be integral to a performance (from playwrite to stagehand), but the distinctive element remains the direct perception by the audience of the performing artist's presentation.

As is implied by the word 'art', the skills of performance are stressed. These skills will include innate ability (talent), experience and training. The performing arts are nominated to be arts because of the demands they make on talent and skills which only a small proportion of the population possesses or feels able to develop and present. In this case any skill supplied is the effective communication of the ideas and impressions of the created work of art being presented to the audience.

With these production (supply) characteristics we are able to exclude from performing arts, performances which do not operate through live performer-audience contact. We also exclude entertainments which do not present an already created work of art or which do not involve skill and training. Film, radio and television are excluded since they are not live. Also not included are sports, which do not involve presenting a created work of art, much popular music, dancing and amateur performance which do not require a sufficiently high level of skills, training and experience.

Demand Features of the Industry

Demand characteristics are less easy to define than production characteristics because there is no clear gap in the chain of substitutes for the performing arts, because of diversity in preferences. For some individuals live opera (say) will be a close substitute for live orchestral music. For others recorded orchestral music will be a closer substitute for live opera. Again, for some, pop music may be a close substitute for classical music, but not for others who abhor one or the other or both.

If we propose a 'characteristics' model of demand, as in the approaches developed by Lancaster and Becker,[4] we come closer to the industry delimitation suggested by supply analysis. The characteristic of liveness would again be emphasised, in this case because of the reasons for which it is demanded. The audience here demands to see the skill and effort of the performers at each individual performance in order to experience the unpredictability and uncertainty of that, and to experience the empathy and interaction that is possible with the live performers.

The audience may also demand an interaction among those attending as one facet of the performing arts. The group reaction to the performance is not just the sum of each isolated individual reaction. The audience attends partly for the group experience and that group experience in turn may affect the performance.

But what distinguishes this demand for group empathy and interaction from other situations such as popular entertainment or spectator sports? Here resort must be had to a demand for aesthetic quality, of the sort provided by the created art work and by the skill in its presentation by performers, (as also emphasised by our supply discussion). Exactly what constitutes aesthetic quality (beauty in sound, movement and form) is not easy to define for it is ultimately a value judgement, in which opinions may differ and are necessarily subjective. However it can be claimed that what constitutes a demand for aesthetic quality *in this area* as opposed to others is aesthetic judgement based on acquired taste and not simple opinion. The taste here is itself felt to be a product of certain abilities, skills and experiences which, just as with performance skills, are found only in a small proportion of the population. Part of the 'art' in the performing arts then may also be said to lie in the appreciative skills of the audience.

The demand characteristics to be emphasised then are liveness, as for supply, and skill in artistic appreciation. These characteristics basically affirm the delimitations made on the basis of our discussion of supply. Thus we exclude film, television and radio, sports, most pop music, and amateur performance, either because it does not involve live attendance at the performance or it does not require significant skills of aesthetic appreciation.

A Synoptic View of the Industry

In Australia there is a considerable paucity of industry data on the performing arts. The 1971 Census found some 8,286 persons who classified themselves as musicians, actors, dancers or related workers. This figure represented only 0.22 per cent of the total employed population in 1971 and even then included media and teaching work as well as part-time employment.[5]

The industry is thus not a large one. In 1975 the Industries Assistance Commission Inquiry into Assistance for the Performing Arts identified 93 performing arts companies in Australia. Of these, 53 were professional and 27, in turn, provided statistical information. These data are presented in Table 13.1 where it is seen that in 1973/4 the 27 companies, including all major professional performance groups, employed a little over 1000 artists to produce almost 7000 performances for almost 3 million attendances. Total box-office receipts were $11.6 million and $11.5 million in public financial assistance was provided to these companies.

The Pattern of Demand

In examining the pattern of demand we shall look at the characteristics of the consumers of performing arts services and at their rate of performing art consumption, i.e. audience composition and attendance frequency. This focus is clearly important from a policy perspective because of the significance of determining the size and nature of the population that attend art performances. It is commonly assumed that the performing arts cater only to a small proportion of the population and that this group is highly advantaged in terms of income and education. We examine the evidence for these propositions.

Audience Composition

There is some evidence available on audience composition from surveys of *subscribers* to opera, concerts and theatre. This information is summarised in Table 13.2 by the percentage distributions for sex, age, education, occupation and income. Comparative characteristics of the overall population are also provided so that any divergences are readily observable. While several subscriber samples are quite small, the pattern displayed is generally quite consistent and shows that the subscribing audience for performing arts is highly skewed toward older, better-

Table 13.1: Summary of some Features of the Performing Arts Industry, Australia 1973/4

		Output		Employment		Costs		Revenues	
	No. of Companies included in sample	Performances	Admissions	Employment of Artists [a]	Salaries of Artists	Total Salaries	Total Expenditure	Assistance	Box Office Receipts
	No.	No.	No.	No.	$	$	$	$	$
Opera	3	235	287,567	97	1,084,622	2,016,449	3,722,657	1,290,980	2,059,120
Ballet	4	358	253,910	79	439,116[b]	808,941[b]	2,154,222	1,038,206	1,123,598
Drama	15	4,839	902,955	257	1,106,371	2,254,653	3,930,100	2,071,610	2,135,148
Music	4	750	1,040,000	558	4,712,424[c]	5,796,804[c]	8,821,501[c]	7,101,445	1,720,166
Commercial Theatre	1	695	486,224	84	1,232,828[c]	1,578,394[c]	5,747,394[c]	30,000	4,518,972
Total	27	6,877	2,940,656	1,068	8,575,361	12,454,933	24,375,874	11,532,131	11,557,004

Notes: a. Figures represent averages for the calendar year 1974 over all productions.
b. Australian Ballet Company only.
c. Includes fees for visiting overseas artists.

Sources: Compiled from public evidence submitted by the companies to Industries Assistance Commission, Inquiry into Assistance to the Performing Arts, 1975; and Australian Broadcasting Commission, *Forty-Second Annual Report,* for year 1973-74.

Table 13.2: Characteristics of Performing Arts Subscription Audiences in Australia

Survey	ABC Concerts	Australian Opera	Theatre Survey	SATC & Adelaide Film Festival	ABC Radio	Population
Survey Year	(1967)	(1973)	(1975)	(1971)	(1967)	(1971)
Sample Size	(173)	(277)	(781)	(186)	(184)	
	Characteristics (Percentage Distributions)					
Sex						
Male	44.4	47.0	43.0	52.4	–	50.2
Female	55.6	53.0	57.0	47.6	–	49.8
	100.0	100.0	100.0	100.0		100.0
Age						
15-25	2.8	6.8	22.0	21.3	6.8	24.2
26-45	40.5	46.4	48.0	42.7	44.8	36.4
46+	56.7	46.8	30.0	36.0	48.4	39.4
	100.0	100.0	100.0	100.0	100.0	100.0
Education [a]						
Primary	2.3	3.6	1.0	1.1	4.3	31.7
Secondary	47.4	31.1	29.0	28.3	41.8	59.0
Tertiary	50.3	55.1	71.0	70.6	53.3	9.3
	100.0	100.0	100.0	100.0	100.0	100.0
Occupation [b]						
Prof. & Manag.	63.0	74.8	78.4	–	67.3	33.0
Cler., Sales & Techns.	30.6	23.2	11.4	–	24.0	34.0
Skilled, Semi-, Unsk.	6.4	2.0	10.2	–	8.7	33.0
	100.0	100.0	100.0		100.0	100.0
Income [c]						
$0-3,000	–	12.5	8.0	–	–	51.0 (28.0)[d]
$3,001-6,000	–	31.4	11.0	–	–	40.0 (50.9)
$6,000-10,000	–	32.3	27.0	–	–	7.0 (18.0)
$10,001+	–	23.8	54.0	–	–	2.0 (8.1)
		100.0	100.0			100.0

Notes: a. Highest level attained. Those still in primary or secondary school excluded.
b. Students and housewives excluded.
c. Includes those not employed.
d. Figures in parentheses give percentages for taxpayers, 1972/3.

Sources: Australian Broadcasting Commission, *Serious Music Survey*, mimeographed, 1967; E. Cleland and R Stimson, *A Survey of Entertainment Needs and Habits in Adelaide*, mimeograph, 1972; A.W. Meadows, *Audience of the Australian Opera*, Australia Council, 1973; A.W. Meadows & A. Warnock, *Subsidised Theatre in Australia*, Australia Council, 1975; Australian Bureau of Statistics, *Summary of Population – Australia*, 1971 Census; Commissioner for Taxation, *Annual Report*, 1972-73.

educated and higher income groups. There are differences between art forms: for instance, theatre seems to attract a younger but more highly educated group of subscribers than concerts and opera, but in all cases the lack of participation by limited education, low-income, blue-collar groups is striking.

Of course these figures relate only to subscribers and do not include casual attenders, but for many performance seasons most seats are sold on a subscription basis anyway (e.g. ABC Concerts), and subscribers by their frequent attendance do constitute the greater part of total admissions to most performances.

It might be thought that the general level of ticket-prices and the need for large lump-sum payments for subscriptions are sufficient reasons for the observed subscriber characteristics. But other activities such as pop concerts, and spectator sports with similar ticket price levels attract audiences with quite different social characteristics.[6]

Further, in Table 13.2 we include a survey of subscribers to the ABC *Radio Guide.* This guide represents a nominal charge only and radios are found in all homes. Despite this low cost and absence of a need for large lump-sum payments this group of subscribers is also quite typical of the population, conforming instead to the pattern of characteristics observed for live arts performances. It would seem to be lack of sustained interest rather than high cost which constrains the less advantaged from participating in performing arts attendance.

Attendance Frequency

Further light can be thrown on demand for the performing arts by looking at patterns of leisure time activity chosen by the population. Table 13.3. summarises the findings of two studies of this aspect. Unfortunately frequency distribution figures were not given for each type of performing art so that the comparison we have is of live theatre only with cinema and all spectator sports.

Around two-thirds of the population do not go to live theatre, whereas half of the population does not go to a spectator sporting event. It seems likely that the inclusion of other performing arts would decrease the non-attendance proportion for arts to spectator sport levels or even less. For cinemas the proportion falls to about one-third of the population not attending in the capital cities. The Albury-Wodonga results indicate more spectator sports attendance and less cinema. This is also reflected in the average frequency of attendance.

There is one other survey which provides average frequency data affirming the pattern and levels indicated in Table 13.3 but adding that attendance at other performing arts averages 4.5 attendances per year. This gives overall average attendance at 6.5 attendances for performing arts, 7.9 for spectator sports and 6.6 for cinema. These figures relate to a sample of 781 drawn from the Australian capital cities, and are detailed in the note accompanying Table 13.3. The average attendance figure of 6.5 for all the performing arts, even when applied to the 2.94 million total attendances figure given in Table 13.1, indicates the average annual number of individuals who attend arts performances as a minimum of 452,408 for 1973-4. This is undoubtedly an underestimate since the total attendance figure refers only to the 27 major professional companies, but even so this is quite a substantial minority of the adult population. If we look further at the dispersion around the average and recall the likelihood that non-attendance at some arts performance is probably half the population, this means that around half of the population are at least occasional attenders at performing arts activities. On either of the figures for average or total individuals attending, the numbers involved would seem much higher than is often assumed. However, it is still true that regular and frequent attendance is confined to a smaller proportion of the population and that this minority is a demonstrably advantaged group in the community, having a higher income and being more highly educated than average and being drawn primarily from the managerial and professional occupational groups.

Hypotheses on Trends in Demand

It might reasonably be assumed that with such a wealthy and advantaged audience as patrons the financial position of the performing arts would be sound. But in fact the arts are notorious for experiencing financial difficulty; and, as seen in Table 13.1, the Australian arts are no different for the 27 professional companies in that sample. Assistance provided in 1973-4, was almost equal to box-office receipts and represented an almost 50 per cent direct subsidy of total production expenditure. The pattern varied across art forms with ballet and theatre roughly balancing box receipts and assistance, whereas opera earned proportionately more box office receipts and commercial theatre received little subsidy at all. In music, assistance was well in excess of box office receipts, indeed in a ratio of four dollars of assistance for each dollar of box office receipt.

How is it that the performing arts seem unable to sustain their present level of activity through market demand without resort to substantial financial assistance?

Table 13.3: Frequency of Attendance at Theatre, Sports and Cinema

Frequency of Attendance	(Annual No. of Attendances)	Melbourne Live Theatre	Melbourne Spectator Sports	Melbourne Cinema	Adelaide Live Theatre	Adelaide Cinema	Albury-Wodonga Live Theatre	Albury-Wodonga Spectator Sports	Albury-Wodonga Cinema
		Percentage Distribution							
Never	(0)	66	50	37	68	31	64	48	48
Occasional	(1–6)	26	16	38	27	35	29	15	38
Moderate	(7–18)	6	12	15	4	16	6	11	10
Frequent	(19+)	2	22	10	1	18	1	26	4
Total percentage points		100	100	100	100	100	100	100	100
Survey Year (sample size)		1974 (1314)			1970 (750)		1974 (180)		
Average frequency of attendance[a]		1.9	10.4	5.2	1.3	12.1	1.5	11.9	3.4

Note: a. A 1975 survey (N = 781) of Australian capital cities found annual average frequency of attendance for live theatre = 2.0, spectator sports = 7.9, and cinema = 6.6; other performing arts = 4.5. See A.W. Meadows and A. Warnock, *Subsidised Theatre in Australia,* Australia Council, 1975.

Sources: Cities Commission, *Australians Use of Time: Albury-Wodonga and Melbourne, March-September 1974,* Mimeograph, 1974; E. Cleland and R. Stimson, *A Survey of Entertainment Needs and Habits in Adelaide,* mimeograph, 1972.

The Baumol-Bowen Argument

The most influential economic study of the performing arts, that by Baumol and Bowen,[7] sees the financial difficulties of the performing arts as arising from unbalanced sectoral growth. Unlike manufacturing where greater capital intensity, economies of scale and technical progress can enhance labour productivity, labour in the performing arts is itself essentially the final output. Opportunities to increase productivity in live performance are thereby limited. Thus, if wages rise in the manufacturing sector in accordance with productivity there is continuing pressure on wages in the performing arts, which are faced with labour being attracted into manufacturing and with strong demands for the maintenance of wage relativities. Performance production costs will therefore tend to rise and a dilemma of the familiar cost-revenue squeeze kind is the outcome. Consequently, say Baumol and Bowen, 'there are fundamental reasons to expect the financial strains which beset the performing arts organisations to increase, chronically, with the passage of time'.[8]

How valid is this scenario? Are mountebanks and mummers bound to go the way of butlers and blacksmiths, unless massive government subvention is provided?

There are, in fact, several questions which one might wish to ask with respect to the Baumol-Bowen argument:

1. What of the opportunities for arts productivity increase provided by substitution within the arts and by the use of the media (records, television, film, radio)?
2. What of the possibility of increased revenue if prices are being deliberately kept below profit-maximising levels?
3. What of the prospects of increasing affluence and leisure shifting people's expenditure more toward the arts?

We will discuss the potential applicability of each of these questions in general and then turn to the empirical evidence available to evaluate their consequences for the financial position for the performing arts in Australia.

Labour Productivity in the Arts

Should we really expect limited productivity increase in the performing arts? It does seem evident that there are clear constraints on productivity increase in the performance of the pre-existing stock of classical compositions. We could play *Hamlet* without the prince or halve the chorus in *Aida* but only by producing a product of very different quality, with inevitable effects upon demand.

Nevertheless there can be substitution within the arts toward less labour-intensive art forms – say, away from opera and symphonies toward theatre and chamber orchestras. Similarly there can emerge new compositions and new art forms which have adjusted more to changing economic circumstances. Pinter, Beckett and Buzo can write for small casts and Peter Maxwell Davies can compose for smaller ensembles. Also, through media reproduction of performances, a given performance can reach a much larger audience than before, so raising productivity in terms of audience reached per performing arts worker.

Whether these factors can alleviate the financial problem of the performing arts predicted by Baumol-Bowen is not clear. The adaptations within the live arts would seem only to moderate, not offset, the growing cost disadvantages of live performances, since the adaptations do not alter the basic fact that labour remains the end product in the performing arts, rather than being an instrument for the attainment of a final product as in many other industries.

Further the media potential does not alter the productivity of live performer to live audience, whatever the implications for media audiences. What is relevant to the level of activity in the live performing arts is the effect of media performance availability on the demand for live performances. Thus the media itself may even directly reduce demand since it needs to record one live performance only to reach a large media audience, whereas many live performances would be needed to reach the same audience live. To the extent that individuals are satisfied with such media performances they may substitute away from live performance so reducing live attendance and performances required.

By this line of argument the higher media productivity of the arts may diminish the amount of artistic activity, however much it enriches the revenue prospects of those few performing companies chosen for media performance. The offsets to this apparent reinforcement of Baumol-Bowen's dismal forecast for live performance are, first, that the media audience may demand more productions even though having less performances per production; secondly, that the increased exposure given the performing arts through the media may actually encourage live audiences who now wish to see the 'real thing' and come to appreciate it, but would not otherwise have attended; thirdly that the live performing arts can actively use the media as an advertising and promotional vehicle for their own activities; and finally, that for existing live audiences the property of liveness is so important that media performing arts are not an adequate substitute, but represent rather a complement to enjoyment of arts performance.

Pricing Behaviour

As not-for-profit enterprises, most performing arts companies are more concerned with maximising (some combination of) the quantity and quality of their output than they are with maximising profit. This motivating social purpose when it weights the level of output, say in terms of widely disseminating output to large audiences, will lead to prices below the profit-maximising level.[9]

Of course this prediction in turn is compromised to the extent quality is incompatible with quantity and by the need to cover costs. In both of these respects however the optimal avenue for obtaining revenue to cover costs and to finance quality production is not by raising prices but by pursuing a patronage strategy. And, as Geoffrey Brennan has pointed out, an efficient way of doing this is to present potential suppliers of patronage with all-or-nothing choice, for which purposes financial extremity is an essential ingredient.[10] This is the 'if we don't get more money, the show can't go on' syndrome. And through such strategy it is possible for the industry to derive full consumer surplus from donors, including governments.

What this line of reasoning provides, incidentally, is another explanation of why arts organisations have their tradition of financial crisis. It is useful for inducing subvention. Such an explanation is not contradictory to Baumol-Bowen. What Baumol-Bowen suggest is that real financial strains may increase chronically with the passage of time.

There may be some opportunities to increase market revenue by requiring increased attendance prices at performances. Certainly the industry definition given and the earlier evidence on the pattern of demand implied that performing arts are an acquired taste possessed by the higher income groups. Accordingly an hypothesis of relative price inelasticity of demand is reasonable, in which case it may be possible to increase prices without causing much fall in attendance. However, this too, as a once-only gain, will not offset the basic trend propositions of the Baumol-Bowen argument. The same applies for other gains in revenue which may be gained by improved management performance in the performing arts – an area in which trained professional management is notably absent.

Increasing Affluence and Leisure

Of more direct concern to the basic Baumol-Bowen position is the possibility that rising incomes and leisure time will lead people to consume more arts. Sir John Crawford, for instance, has argued that the 'possibility of a "few strong shoots of art" does grow as average personal incomes progress beyond the needs of food, clothing, shelter, education, medical care and preparing for old age'.[11]

This is saying that there is a high income elasticity of demand for the performing arts. And again the cross-section evidence does affirm that arts attendance increases with the higher income groups. However, as always, we must be careful about drawing inter-temporal conclusions from cross-section patterns. A cross-section response describes the effect of differences in a variable, rather than the response to changes in that variable. It is the latter that is relevant for analysing future financial prospects in the arts as community incomes rise.

The need for care here is particularly emphasised by the way in which income effects may be offset by leisure-price effects. This is a good application of Becker's theory of time-allocation.[12] We observe that increases in labour productivity have reduced the price of manufactured goods relative to the price of labour. Since activities require the input of a person's time as labour costs rise relative to other costs so the value of a person's time, including their leisure time, increases. This means that there is an incentive for the individual to shift the pattern of activities more towards those that incorporate a larger amount of manufactured goods and a smaller amount of time. In this way the individual can increase the 'productivity' of his leisure time. The implication for the performing arts arises from their relative labour-intensity and time-intensity and the few prospects they offer for the use of additional goods to enhance enjoyment. When the cost of an individual's time is considered in this way it could even be that consumption of the performing arts will decline as income increases and hence the measured income elasticity of demand for the arts be low or negative. Also, if consumption time includes travelling time, this effect will be augmented. Then only very strong successive increases in total consumption time or changes in tastes will increase live cultural consumption.

Thus it is possible that rising incomes may lead to a shift to the reproduced arts (film, recordings etc.) and to other non-arts leisure pursuits where increased goods-intensity and home-based consumption location can improve the yield on time. In modern society the performing arts have the camera, speed-boat, caravan, trail bike, holiday house and colour TV to compete with. De Tocqueville long ago predicted that 'wealthy democratic societies will cultivate the arts which make life easy, in preference to the arts whose object is to adorn it'.[13] Time allocation analysis might wish to quality this to the extent that the performing arts also have visual art to compete with, since this is a form of cultural consumption which can require little consumption time and a large income.

Empirical Evidence on Demand Trends

Productivity, Wage and Price Movements

The next step is to test the relevance of the Baumol-Bowen argument, and the further considerations we have raised, to the performing arts in Australia.

There are several elements in the discussion that can be tentatively validated from the available evidence in Australia. Some of this evidence is presented in Table 13.4 which covers the dominant professional companies in the major art forms. Comparative figures for the whole economy are also presented.

It is seen that the assumption of limited live productivity increase seems supported for the given performing companies, and because of their dominance, over-all productivity increase cannot be much greater for the industry as a whole. The performing arts seem to have fallen well behind the general trend in productivity in the economy. Of course this says nothing of media effects that will show up in revenue, which will be examined separately below. Suffice it to say here that little revenue currently is received in payment for media reproduction of performances by these companies, so that any present media effect must come through its encouragement (or otherwise) of live attendances.

A second element that can be illustrated empirically is the extent to which labour costs have risen over time in the performing arts. It is seen that award wages have increased, though a little behind average award increases for the economy. Most of the organisations have a high and increasing share of expenditure in artists' wages costs, though the Old Tote has kept this share down.

Relatively constant labour productivity, rising award wages and an inability to reduce wage shares significantly have meant that unit costs of production have risen in the performing arts over time relative to other sectors. The Baumol-Bowen hypothesis that this would result in a rise in the price of the performing arts relative to other goods also is confirmed for the companies in Table 13.4. The price increases have been greatest in opera and ballet, though both music and theatre have

Table 13.4: Productivity, Wage and Price Movements (1964 = 100)

1. Productivity	1964	1969	1974
Australian Opera (paid admissions per artist)	100	82	75
Australian Ballet (paid admissions per artist)	100	114	111
ABC concerts (paid admissions per artist)	100	25	29
GDP per unit labour force	100	113	136
2. Award Wages	1964	1970	1975
Actor and Dancer	100	113	249
Musician	100	123	235
Average Award (all industries)	100	131	267
3. Share of Wages in Expenditure	1964	1969	1974
Australian Opera	.374	n.a.	.523
Australian Ballet	.207	n.a.	.378
Old Tote Theatre	.496	n.a.	.379
ABC Concerts	.661	.670	.713
4. Attendance Prices	1965	1970	1975
Australian Opera	100	243	557
Australian Ballet	100	166	265
Old Tote Theatre	100	185	186
ABC Concerts	100	136	208
Consumer Price Index	100	109	167

Sources: Compiled from: public evidence submitted by the Australian Opera, Australian Ballet, Old Tote Theatre, J.C. Williamson and Australian Musicians Union to IAC, Inquiry into Assistance for the Performing Arts, 1975; Australian Elizabethan Trust, *Annual Report,* 1964 to 1969; Australian Broadcasting Commission, *Annual Report,* 1963/4 to 1973/4; Australian Bureau of Statistics, *Quarterly Summary of Australian Statistics.*

also increased prices by more than the rise in the general price level. Thus it has been necessary and possible for performing arts companies to raise their prices, in some cases quite dramatically.

The Demand Function for Performing Arts Services

The remaining question is 'What effect do these price rises have on the level of attendance?' Before turning to the actual outcome over the period a prediction here could be arrived at by looking directly at the demand function for arts services in Australia. Such a demand function would give us both the price elasticity of demand and the income elasticity of demand, so indicating the extent to which price increases would reduce attendance rates and the extent to which this effect might be offset by increasing income levels.

The results of an attempt to estimate such a demand function are given in Table 13.5. Since economic theory postulates that demand is a function of relative prices and of the level and distribution of income, the basic estimating form was taken as:

$$A/POP = \beta_0 + \beta_1 PA + \beta_2 I + \beta_3 PS + \beta_4 D + u$$

where A = number of paid attendances
POP = adult population
PA = price of admission
I = per capita income
PS = price of substitutes
D = income distribution (wage share).

This equation was estimated in logarithms of the variables by ordinary least squares techniques for annual data provided as public evidence to the IAC Inquiry into Assistance for the Performing Arts by six major professional performance companies for the years 1964-74. Equations 1 and 3 give the results for the basic estimating form, the difference between the two being that equation 1 uses data aggregated over the six companies and includes variables for the price of substitutes and income distribution; equation 3 drops the latter variables and runs the regression with individual constant terms for the performance companies, by substituting the company attendance rates for the aggregate attendance as the dependent variable.

Equations 2 and 4 are the same as equations 1 and 3 respectively except that an attempt is made to break the income effect into a 'pure income' effect and a 'price of leisure' effect, following a technique proposed by J.D. Owen[14]. This is an attempt to test the time allocation argument and involves the following re-specification:

$$A/POP = \beta_0 + \beta_1 PA + \beta_2 FI + \beta_3 PL + \beta_4 PS + \beta_5 D + u$$

where PL is price of leisure
FI is full-income

Table 13.5: Demand Function Estimates: Australian Performing Arts 1964-74

Equation [a]	Constant	Attendance Price	Income	(Full Income)	(Leisure Price)	Price of Substitutes	Income Distribution	Opera d.v.	Ballet d.v.	Old Tote	Ensemble d.v.	JCW d.v.	R^b R^b	Durbin-Watson Statistic
1	−8.07	−1.00 [b]	.51			2.38	−4.53 [b]						.24	1.99
2	3.10	−1.16 [b]		3.19	−4.50	5.39	−4.95 [b]						.25	1.80
3	−2.05 [b]	−.61 [c]	.33					.41 [c]	.39 [c]	.31 [c]	.24 [c]	.53 [c]	.93	1.72
4	2.00	−.60 [c]		1.44	−.42			.41 [c]	.39 [c]	.31 [c]	.24 [c]	.53 [c]	.94	1.73

Notes: a. The dependent variable is attendances at six major companies' performances as a proportion of adult population.
b. t-statistic significant at the 5 per cent level.
c. t-statistic significant at the 1 per cent level.

Sources: Attendance and Attendance Price figures: public evidence by six major professional companies to IAC Inquiry into Assistance for the Performing Arts, 1975; Australian Elizabethan Theatre Trust, *Annual Report 1964 to 1974.* Other series: Australian Bureau of Statistics (ABS), *Estimated Age Distribution of the Population;* ABS, *Quarterly Summary of Australian Statistics;* ABS, *Weekly Earnings and Hours*; ABS, *Australian National Accounts.*

and we specify:

$$PL = W(1\text{-}UR)$$
$$FI = T_c PL + T_w W$$

and we use as the full price index:

$$FPI = b(CPI) + (1\text{-}b)PL$$

where W = average wage
UR = unemployment rate
T_w = hours of work
T_c = hours of consumption
FPI = full price index
b = weight of non-leisure income in full-income

This approach represents the application of Becker's concept of time allocation to the problem of consumption choices and attempts to test for bias in the income coefficient of the conventional demand model that results from the suppression of leisure-price as a variable. As well as breaking up income into a full-income and leisure-price effect, this adaptation involves applying the full-price index rather than the consumer price index in obtaining real values of other monetary variables.[15]

Single equation estimation was used since this market seems recursive in structure so that no simultaneity bias ensues. The belief was that price of attendance in one period influences attendance in that same period, but the effect on the supply of new performances does not show up until the next period. This is because of the advance planning and announcement of productions, seasons and prices that is typical in the performing arts.

Single equation estimation is unlikely to be biased by capacity constraints on attendance. Figures on capacity were available for 1972-74 only, but those were the years of greatest government support and interest, and over that period only in one year and for one company did attendances exceed an average of 90 per cent of seating available for the year.

Table 12.5 shows that most of the variation in attendance rates for the companies indicated is explained by features particular to those companies – their art form, location and facilities, quality of production etc. This is seen in the high coefficient of determination for the regressions with individual constant terms representing the companies.

As for the non company-specific variables they are seen to be of the expected sign in the case of attendance price, price of substitutes and income distribution. Of these however only attendance price and income distribution are significantly different from zero, indicating that attendance price increases do lead to attendance decreases and that increases in the share of wages in GDP are associated with a falling attendance rate. The price of substitutes as measured (by the implicit GDP deflator for all recreation services) has little discernable effect on arts attendance for these companies.

The attendance price elasticity seems to lie in the range .60 to 1.16 affirming, for these constant elasticity specifications, a relative inelasticity of demand for performing arts services for the price changes experienced by these companies over the period of analysis. Remember that this is increase in price above the general level of prices that is measured i.e. a *real* price increase for theatre tickets.

By contrast, no significant effect is discerned for income, either in the conventional or time allocation specifications. We do notice however that the time-allocation approach gives a large positive pure-income effect offset by an even larger negative leisure-price effect. The signs are as predicted by time-allocation theory and their net effect and general lack of significance indicates that growth of income has contributed little if anything to growth of attendance rates for these arts companies over the period.

To return to our original question we wished to know what effect rising prices for performing arts services would have on attendance over time. The implication of the demand function estimates would be that for the 1964-74 period price increases themselves would not reduce attendance rates or revenues significantly since price elasticity seems equal to or less than unity. At the same time no great increase in attendance rates due to rising incomes was likely because of an income elasticity estimate not significantly different from zero

Cost and Revenue Outcomes: The 'Income Gap'

Bringing the discussion of wage, productivity, and price trends together with the analysis of price and income elasticity enables us to examine the cost-revenue outcome for the performing arts. This outcome defines the financial position of the performing arts, and any divergence between cost and revenue with cost increasing faster will lead to an 'income gap'.

To show this income gap, trend coefficients were estimated for real total expenditure per admission and real box-office receipts per admission for each performance company for which data was available. The coefficients are given in Table 13.6 and show the slope of the 'best fit' linear trend line for the receipts and expenditure observations, 1964-75.

Table 13.6: Box Office and Expenditure Trends

Performance Company	Real Box Office Coefficient	Real Expenditure Coefficient
Australian Ballet	.0014	.0028
Australian Opera	.0133	.0182
Old Tote Theatre	.0097	.0306
Ensemble Theatre	.0023	.0273
Astra Chamber Orchestra	.0052	.0137
ABC Concerts	.0006	.0034
J.C. Williamson	.0021	.0063

Source: As for Tables 13.4 and 13.5.

In each case we obtain positive trend coefficients, and observe that the coefficients are uniformly higher for expenditure than box office receipts, indicating an increasing absolute real income gap. This applies for J.C. Williamson's which is a useful control since, as the only major commercial performance company, its financial difficulties over the period indicate that increased expenditure may not be a simple response to provision of subsidies, by which means the income gap is made up for the other companies. There would seem to be a real structural problem for the performing arts as indicated by the Baumol-Bowen argument and this structural effect is not being offset by rising incomes being spent more on arts performances or by the media encouraging increased attendance rates. This structural problem is additional to any financial difficulties associated with patronage strategy through which arts companies may seek to generate increasing subsidies.

Conclusion

The performing arts were defined by the live public presentation of a created work of art where skill in both presentation and appreciation was required. As such, the performing arts were felt to cover primarily such areas as ballet, opera, theatre, and orchestral music.

It was seen that attendance at such activities came largely from well-educated audiences from managerial and professional households. The associated high incomes however, did not guarantee an absence of financial difficulties for the performing arts.

In particular it was argued that the labour-intensity of production for the performing arts, with the labour itself as an essential component of the final product, would mean increasing costs for live presentation. To cover these costs by increasing attendance prices might in turn inhibit attendance. Only if media presentation of the arts or rising incomes and leisure time or changing tastes also turned people more to live performance was this cost-revenue squeeze likely to be mitigated.

The Australian evidence was that costs and prices were rising and while demand was relatively price inelastic there was still a tendency for costs and expenditure to increase faster than box-office revenues. Neither media nor income-induced increases in attendance were sufficiently strong to offset this effect.[16]

The resultant 'income gap' implied that if the present level of performing arts activity was to be maintained or increased, further support from private sources or public subvention would be required. More professional management including further price increases, greater use of complementary facilities (e.g. bars) and attention to media opportunities might improve the market position somewhat. But such once-and-for-all gains would not remove the longer-run structural problem.

For those employed in or attending the performing arts the desire to see increasing public assistance is understandable. But it must be recognised that there are many other activities in the economy similarly affected by cost structure or demand deficiency problems and these activities must find ways to increase productivity, increase revenue from sales or else they decline so that resources can be freed for other uses for which demand is effective. For public support, special reasons must be advanced for insulating this particular activity from the consequences of economic change and from the market verdict of private consumers. Certainly the economic prospects of the performing arts do not seem favourable in Australia. Their future will depend greatly upon their ability to make a valid case for public assistance and support.

Appendix B.1: Mathematics

This appendix presents the formal structure of the Baumel-Bowen argument, indicates its lack of analysis of income effects and shows the re-interpretation required by time-allocation considerations.

1. The Baumol-Bowen Model[17]

Assume

1. separability of activities into two production activities, arts and manufacturing where arts (sector 1) has constant labour productivity and manufacturing (sector 2) has labour productivity growing at rate g.
2. unit wage is equal in the two sectors at the level of labour productivity in manufacturing.
3. all outlays other than labour costs are ignored.

Of these 2 and 3 are expositional.

We specify the associated production system by the following output and wage equations for sector i and time t:

$$Q_{1t} = aL_{1t} \quad (1)$$
$$Q_{2t} = b(1+g)^t L_{2t} \quad (2)$$
$$r_t = r_0(1+g)^t \quad (3)$$

where Q is quantity of output
L is quantity of labour input
r is wage
g is growth rate of labour productivity

Pertinent properties of this system can be stated as:

Property 1: cost per unit of output in arts will rise without limit while unit cost in manufacturing remains constant.

Proof:

$$C_{1t} = r_t L_{1t}/Q_{1t} = r_o(1+g)^t/a \quad (4)$$
$$C_{2t} = r_t L_{2t}/Q_{2t} = r_o/b \quad (5)$$

where C is labour cost per unit of ouput.

Property 2: arts output tends to zero over time, given unitary elasticities of demand.

Proof:

$$\frac{C_{1t}Q_{1t}}{C_{2t}Q_{2t}} = \frac{r_tL_{1t}}{r_2L_{2t}} = A \text{ (constant)} \tag{6}$$

Hence the output ratio is:

$$\begin{aligned} Q_{1t}/Q_{2t} &= aL_{1t}/bL_{2t}(1+g)^t \\ &= aA/b(1+g)^t \\ &\to 0 \text{ as } t \to \infty \end{aligned} \tag{7}$$

Property 3: If there is a fixed output ratio (through policy or appropriate demand elasticity), labour in manufacturing will approach zero in the limit.
Proof:

$$Q_{1t}/Q_{2t} = aL_{1t}/bL_{2t}(1+g)^t = K \tag{8}$$

i.e. $$L_{1t}/L_{2t} = K(1+g)^t \to \infty \text{ as } t \to \infty \tag{9}$$

2. Time Allocation Theory and the Income Effect[18]

The rising wage level which, given differential productivity increase, produces a relative price increase for the arts, could offset the effects of those price changes on arts output if arts demand is sufficiently income elastic. i.e. the implications of the Baumol-Bowen model's property 3 would be more appropriate than property 2.

We examine this. View the individual as a producer of two consumption activities: 'arts' and 'other recreation'. Assume that two industries exist, arts and manufacturing, and that the arts industry provides a service for which arts consumption time, Tc_1, and manufactures Q_1 are used as inputs for producing arts consumption. Other recreation is produced by the individual from recreation consumption time, Tc_2, and manufactures, Q_2.

The individual utility function is thus

$$\begin{aligned} U &= U(Z_1, Z_2) \qquad (10) \\ &= U(T_{c1}, T_{c2}, Q_1, Q_2) \qquad (11) \end{aligned}$$

where Z_i is the quantity of consumption activity i.

We wish to consider the allocation of a fixed amount of total consumption time between the two consumption activities. The constraints in this allocation are the income constraint:

$$P_1Q_1 + P_2Q_2 = I \tag{12}$$

where I is money income

P_i is price of product i

and the time constraint:

$$Tc_1 + Tc_2 = Tc \tag{13}$$

with money income given by

$$I = r(T - Tc) \tag{14}$$
$$= rTw. \tag{15}$$

where Tw is work time

r is a productivity index measuring consumption goods earned per work hour.

Substitution of (15) into (12) leaves two constraints.

To determine time allocation we wish to maximise the utility function (11) subject to the two remaining constraints. We therefore form the following Lagrangian function:

$$L = f(Tc_1, Tc_2, Q_1, Q_2) + \lambda(P_1Q_1 + P_2Q_2 - rTw) + \mu(Tc_1 + Tc_2 - Tc) \tag{16}$$

and differentiate the Lagrangian with respect to the variables Tc_1, Tc_2, Q_1 and Q_2. Set the resulting expressions equal to zero to obtain the first-order conditions for a maximum. Assuming second-order conditions met, we differentiate the first-order conditions with respect to w. Using Cramer's rule to solve the resulting system gives the following solution for dTc_1/dr:

$$\frac{dTc_1}{dr} = \frac{1}{D} p_2 \overline{Tw}(f'_{23} - f_{13}) \tag{17}$$

Since the determinant is negative, the expression is negative if $f_{23} > f_{13}$. The condition stipulates that if utility is more enhanced in recreation than in arts by an increase in the use of manufactured goods, higher real wages will produce a decrease in the amount of consumption time devoted to the arts.

This is a necessary but not sufficient condition. The formal theorem derived was based upon a two-sector model which gave us gross substitutes in consumption. As in most economics, for more than two sectors there is little that we can say *a priori.* There is also the question of the explicit assumption of fixed total consumption time. Just as with conventional work/leisure choice analysis, time allocation theory does not predict *a priori* the effect of wage increases upon total consumption time. A need for empirical analysis is indicated.

Appendix 13.2: Data

1. Arts Company Time Series used for Performing Arts Demand Regressions

	Aust. Ballet		Aust. Opera		Old Tote		Ensemble Theatre		J.C. Williamsons		Aust. Chamber Music Society		ABC Symphony Concerts	
	PA	BR	PA	BR	PA	BR	PA	BR	PA	BR	PA	BR	PA	BR
1964	159389	541122	184679	362644	77767	145366	(37919)	49764	(1162878)	2558332	(5000)	5000	421204	574874
1965	126266	267189	22314	30008	33068	59722	(26290)	37070	(915714)	2014570	(4318)	4318	488094	783154
1966	230899	471577	121472	230719	49415	63422	(40471)	61112	(788134)	1789065	(5115)	5115	473810	743834
1967	72945	156877	189119	422054	39587	67436	(37107)	56032	(1221659)	3115230	(5142)	6427	375284	701482
1968	273296	475787	160553	553218	43454	68957	(40991)	65996	(1236437)	3214735	(2974)	3717	442920	799478
1969	313360	557559	254543	813715	100033	149470	31150	53114	(1292226)	3359787	(3898)	4872	467876	770790
1970	262661	925778	255593	833286	78534	175173	34457	66840	(925699)	3101094	(2086)	3129	431655	971781
1971	175900	825800	302267	1028635	88065	181793	41921	84198	(538429)	2046031	(7266)	14531	425103	837506
1972	237300	1005300	265927	1211506	100840	243162	40712	83958	(835692)	3342767	(2408)	4816	435641	1067601
1973	181300	875500	223255	1274249	215213	660446	39690	89361	(957668)	4117971	(4344)	10425	608428	1688622
1974	235000	1319800	331162	2476999	260707	854442	38671	92676	(1027039)	4518972	(3206)	7694	553030	1713095

PA = Total Paid Attendances
BR = Total Box Office Receipts ($)
Parentheses indicate attendances calculated by dividing box receipts by median ticket price

Source: Public evidence submitted to Industries Assistance Commission, Inquiry into Assistance for Performing Arts, 1976.

2. General Economic Time Series used for Performing Arts Demand Regressions

Year	W ($)	PDY ($'000)	TW (hrs)	D	U ('000)	CPI (1970=100)	POP ('000)	LF ('000)	PSI (1970=100)
1964	2683	12450	42.8	.55	63.3	82.8	6653	4496	71.8
1965	2886	13498	42.9	.56	60.7	85.9	6783	4628	75.5
1966	3016	14072	43.0	.58	71.5	89.0	6913	4761	79.6
1967	3219	15490	43.1	.57	79.1	91.4	7078	4880	83.6
1968	3406	16167	43.3	.59	77.8	94.4	7237	5001	89.0
1969	3661	18006	43.6	.57	80.0	96.9	7423	5151	93.7
1970	3968	19664	43.5	.58	74.7	100.0	7592	5329	100.0
1971	4410	22155	43.2	.60	87.6	104.8	7734	5425	108.8
1972	4826	24712	42.8	.61	105.7	111.9	7876	5467	119.5
1973	5278	28552	43.0	.60	82.9	118.6	8001	5618	132.5
1974	6136	34399	42.8	.61	134.0	134.0	8126	5733	147.4

W = average annual earnings per employed male unit.
TW = average weekly hours worked in October.
U = total unemployed registered with the Commonwealth Employment Service.
POP = population of persons aged 18-70 years, as at June 30.
PSI = implicit GDP deflator for all recreation services.
PDY = household disposable income.
D = share of wages, salaries and supplements in gross domestic product at factor cost.
CPI = consumer price index.
LF = labour force.

Source: Australian Bureau of Statistics: *Australian National Accounts; Quarterly Summary of Australian Statistics; Survey of Weekly Earnings and Hours; Estimated Age Distribution of the Population.*

Notes

1. Parts of this chapter draw upon work done in collaboration with Susan Bethune and David Throsby. Any merit in the chapter is likely to reflect their important contribution, though the present author accepts full responsibility for the contents. The chapter was completed prior to the publication of the IAC Draft Report and Final Report on Assistance for the Performing Arts.
2. See the companion chapter by David Throsby in this volume for discussion of the supply side of performing arts services.
3. Examples of more broad-ranging discussions are: H.C. Coombs, 'The Economics of the Performing Arts', *Economic papers,* (35), September 1970: 32-47; L. Robbins 'Art and the State' in *Politics and Economics: Papers in Political Economy* (London, Macmillan, 1963), pp.53-72.
4. Gary S. Becker, 'A Theory of the Allocation of Time' *Economic Journal,* 75 (3), September 1965: 493-517; Kelvin J. Lancaster, *Consumer Demand: A New Approach* (New York, Colombia University Press, 1971).
5. Australian Bureau of Statistics (ABS) unpublished data from 1971 Census of Population, May 1975. Comprises ABS occupational groups 067 and 068.
6. See, for instance, Cities Commission, 'Australians Use of Time: Albury-Wodonga and Melbourne, March-September 1974', mimeograph, 1974. This study gives attendance at different activities cross-classified by household income. More information will be forthcoming from the 1974-75 Household Expenditure Survey undertaken by the Australian Bureau of Statistics.
7. W.J. Baumol and W.G. Bowen, *Performing Arts: The Economic Dilemma* (New York, The Twentieth Century Fund, 1966).
8. Baumol and Bowen, *loc cit.,* p.499.
9. This is discussed further in the paper by Throsby in this volume.
10. G. Brennan, 'The Performing Arts: A Diagnosis', unpublished manuscript, Australian National University, 1970, pp.25-27.
11. J.G. Crawford, 'Opening Address' in UNESCO-ANU, *Proceedings of the UNESCO-ANU Seminar on Public Support for the Performing Arts,* Canberra ANU, 1969, p.17.
12. G.S. Becker, *op cit.*
13. Alexis De Tocqueville, *Democracy in America* (New York, Knopf edition, 1953), p.63.
14. J. Owen, *The Price of Leisure* (Rotterdam, Rotterdam University Press, 1969).
15. See Appendix 2 (Data Appendix) for details of statistics and sources used for the performing arts demand regression.
16. Increases in total population may assist aggregate arts attendances even if participation rates do not increase. The 1975 National Population Inquiry, however, predicted a slowing of the rate of population increase in Australia. At the same time there is an increasing average age of the population, associated with the echo effect of the post-war 'baby boom' and with the more recent declines in immigration and rate of natural increase. This may improve aggregate attendances for that majority of arts forms which the cross-section evidence indicated were attended by older age groups. See First Report of the National Population Inquiry, *Population and Australia A Demographic Analysis and Projection,* 2 vols. (Australian Government Publishing service, Canberra, 1975).

17. This presentation is based on Baumol & Bowen, *op cit.*, and W.J. Baumol *Economic Dynamics*, (New York, Macmillan, 1970, 3rd edition), pp.425-434.
18. This section draws on Becker, *op. cit.*, And Staffan B. Linder, *The Harried Leisure Class*, (New York, Columbia University Press, 1970), pp.147-155.

Select Bibliography

Australian Studies

Brennan H.G. 'The Performing Arts: A Diagnosis' unpublished manuscript, Australian National University, 1970.

Coombs, H.C. 'The Economics of the Performing Arts', *Economic Papers*, (35), September 1970, pp.32-47.

Muller, R. 'The Economics of the Australian Opera', unpublished honours thesis, Melbourne University, 1975.

Throsby, C.D. 'Public Policy and the Performing Arts', *Economic Paper*, No.52, (June 1976), pp.1-15.

Tucker, K.A. 'Assistance to the Arts in Australia: An Economic Appraisal', *Economic Analysis and Policy*, New Series, 6 (2), September 1975, pp.42-58.

UNESCO-ANU, *Proceedings of the UNESCO-ANU Seminar on Public Support for the Performing Arts*, (Canberra, Australian National University, 1969, 2 volumes).

Williams, P.L. 'Government Subsidies to the Arts', unpublished M.Ec. thesis, Monash University, 1974.

Overseas Studies

Baumol, W.J. and W.G. Bowen, *Performing Arts – The Economic Dilemma*, (New York, Twentieth Century Fund, 1966).

Blaug, M. (ed.) *Economics of the Arts*, (London, Martin-Robertson, 1976).

Galbraith, J.K. 'Economics and Art' in *The Liberal Hour*, (Harmondsworth: Penguin, 1963, pp.52-69.

Globerman, S. and S.H. Book, 'Statistical Cost Functions for Performing Arts Organisations', *Southern Economic Journal*, 40 (2), April, 1974, pp.668-671.

Hilton, A. 'The Economics of the Theatre', *Lloyds Bank Review*, (101) July, pp.26-38.

Moore, T.G. *The Economics of the American Theater*, (Durham, N.C., Duke University Press, 1968).

Peacock, A.T. 'Welfare Economics and Public Subsidies to the Arts', *Manchester School*, 37 (4), December 1969, pp.323-335.

Peacock, A.T. and R. Weir, *The Composer in the Market Place*, (London, Faber, 1975).

Robbins, L. 'Art and the State', in *Politics and Economics: Papers in Political Economy*, London, Macmillan, 1963), pp.53-72.

Scitovsky, T. 'What's wrong with the Arts is What's wrong with Society', *American Economic Review*, 62 (2), May 1972, pp.62-69.

14 PRODUCTION AND COST RELATIONSHIPS IN THE SUPPLY OF PERFORMING ARTS SERVICES

C.D. Throsby*

Recent literature in the theory of the firm has paid attention to the role of nonprofit enterprises such as libraries, schools, hospitals, theatres, museums and welfare organisations. The distinguising features of such firms, which typically occur in the service sector of the economy, are firstly, that their objective functions do not primarily comprise profit maximisation, and secondly that they purport to fulfil some social purpose. The significance of the latter characteristic may simply be that they produce outputs, which have some public-good or merit-good component.

It has been suggested (e.g. Hurd, 1973) that such firms may be regarded essentially as constrained output maximisers, with quality-of-services-provided playing a significant role either as a constraint (Long, 1964) or as an explicit choice variable (Newhouse, 1970). It has also been shown (Goddard, 1973; Globerman and Book, 1974) that the output and cost relationships of such firms may be amenable to analysis with the familiar techniques of neoclassical production theory.

This paper examines the nature of the performing arts industry[1] from the standpoint of the theory of the nonprofit firm. The structure and conduct of the industry in Australia are briefly surveyed first. A model of a performing arts organisation as a nonprofit enterprise is then proposed and an attempt is made to quantify the relationships involved using Australian data.

Structural Features of the Performing Arts Industry in Australia

Estimates of concentration for the performing arts industry are difficult to make because of a lack of data on the size distribution of firms in the industry, and because of the ephemeral nature of some firms, particularly in the smaller size groups. However, public evidence to the Industries Assistance Commission's 1975 Enquiry into the Performing Arts may be used to construct a reasonably accurate picture of industry concentration.

Across all art forms in the whole of Australia, there is a wide spread in the size of firms, where size is measured in terms of output, as annual paid admissions. The industry appears to contain somewhere between 70 and 100 firms, not including wholly amateur groups. The majority of firms (about 70 per cent) are comparatively small, with attendances of less than 10 thousand per annum, yet the four largest firms account for almost 60 per cent of total output, and the six largest firms account for almost three-quarters of total industry output. Thus by conventional criteria the Australian performing arts industry as a whole must be regarded as reasonably highly concentrated.

However, the degrees of concentration in the sub-markets represented by the several art-forms (music, theatre, opera, ballet) differ from this overall picture. The markets for opera, ballet and symphonic music are each dominated by single firms: the Australian Opera, the Australian Ballet, and the ABC respectively. Drama is much less concentrated, the largest firm in this sector accounting for only about one quarter of theatre output. The reasons for this difference are three-fold. Firstly, there is no national drama company, as there are national companies in the other art forms. Secondly, the degree of monopolisation in opera, ballet and music can be largely explained by the larger minimum efficient scale of investment and working capital required for these three art forms as compared to the more modest resources required for straight drama. Finally, there is a perceived need to maintain variety in the output of drama, a need which to a large extent can only be met by a proliferation of small firms. There appears to be less demand for such variety in opera and ballet, and in the extreme case of symphonic music a single organisation should be capable of providing all the variety sought by consumers.

Other structural characteristics commonly examined in industry analysis are also relevant to the performing arts, though their significance is somewhat different. The extent of product differentiation for example, is very marked in the performing arts, with differentiation on the basis of art-form, geographical location, ancillary services provided, level of sophistication, etc. being so great in many cases that the cross-elasticities between a number of commodities produced within the industry are likely to be close to zero. Likewise, entry barriers are important, as observed above, particularly in opera, ballet and music. However, the difference between the arts and most other industries in respect of these characteristics lies in the fact that performing companies are less likely to use these traditional weapons of non-price competition to secure competitive or profit advantage over rival firms, for reasons which are discussed further in the next section.

Firm Conduct

The behaviour of firms in supplying performing arts services differs from that of other types of business unit in a number of ways. Firstly, given that the goals of performing groups involve maximisation of output rather than profit, their pricing and output decisions are likely to differ from those which would be predicted by the conventional theory of the firm. This difference is magnified by the fact that public subsidies form at least some proportion of the total revenues of most performing arts organisations in Australia. Secondly, it might be further suggested that some part of the utility functions of managers in the performing arts industry relates to the fostering and advancement of the live arts in general. To the extent that this is so, it implies a cooperative rather than a competitive relationship between firms. Of course in the narrow sense companies in a given location at a given time do compete directly with each other for the consumers' dollar. But in addition to this there is ample evidence that firms are aware of the social-good characteristics of their collective output, and this, together with the non-profit goal, suggests a moderation of ordinary competitive behaviour in the conduct of the industry.

Finally, the influence of technology on the performing arts, discussed above by Withers[2], is seen in the inability of firms to recover rising costs from increased admission prices. The implication of this for industry conduct is essentially a dynamic one: that is a widening gap over time between costs and earned revenue, which must be met from donations, grants, subsidies or patronage of some other sort.

A Model of a Performing Arts Firm

To study in more detail the supply of performing arts services, we now propose a model of an opera/ballet/music/theatre company which embodies the sorts of cost and output relationships typical of such firms.

(a) Utility function

Suppose there are n firms in the performing arts industry. Then we assume that the managers of the i-th firm aim to maximise the utility function:

$$U_i = U(y_i, Q_i, \sum_{k=1}^{n} y_k)\ (k \neq i) \qquad (1)$$

subject to

$$AR_{bi} + AR_{gi} \geq AC_i \qquad (2)$$

where
y = total attendances per firm per time period at performances mounted by that firm;
Q = quality variable (see below);
AR_b = average revenue per attendance from box office sales;
AR_g = average revenue per attendance from grants (subsidies, donations, etc.), or from other sources (royalties from reproduction, etc.)
AC = average cost per attendance.

In the utility function (1), output and quality are direct choice variables. The inclusion of the aggregate attendances of all other firms as an argument of (1) reflects the cooperative view of market behaviour mentioned above, that is, it is assumed that the i-th firm's utility is positively related to Σy. This variable can be influenced by the individual firm, though only weakly and indirectly, through such activities as, for example, participating in promotional ventures aimed at stimulating interest in the live arts in general.

The assessment of quality is, of course, essentially a subjective matter, though in the first instance it may be regarded as broadly related to the volume of resources, particularly financial resources, available to the firm. This establishes what might be defined as a vertical measure of quality. Horizontal variation in quality might then be supposed to exist in the range of options open to the firm at a given resource supply, for example in the choice of a repertoire from amongst a range of works all involving much the same total commitment of resources.

The firm's decision problem as posed above could in principle be resolved using information on the management's indifference pattern between the three components of its utility function (that is, on the precise nature of (1)) and on the parameters of the budget constraint. However, to simplify the problem we may disregard the least important variable in (1), namely Σy. Further, we may define Q as a discrete variable, and assume that utility is a monotonically increasing function of output. It is then possible to specify the firm's decision problem as the maximisation of output at given quality levels, subject to the constraint in (2). In this form the empirical problem can be solved using estimates of a given firm's production and cost functions and of the demand function for its service.

(b) Short-Run Production, Cost and Revenue Functions

Define the short run as the length of run of a single production. For a play or an opera the run may vary from a few days to many months, whereas for most musical recitals and symphony concerts only one or two performances are usually given in any one location. We may regard factors such as sets, costumes, rehearsal labour and facilities, designs, etc. as fixed in the short run in the sense that they have to be committed before any output takes place. Their costs are the traditional 'set-up costs' involved in mounting a production.

Variable factors in the short run include materials and services used in the course of each performance, programmes, the labour of actors, musicians, technical and house staff, and so on. These factors are variable in the sense that they are directly related to the number of performances given, which in turn may be able to be increased as a means of raising output. It is thus possible to interpret the number of performances of a particular production (i.e. the length of season) as directly measuring the input of variable factors. Hence we may specify the short-run production function of the firm as:

$$y_s = f(P_s, Q_s) \tag{3}$$

where P = number of performances;
and the subscript s indicates the short run as defined above. Postulating a Cobb-Douglas function, we may write, for a given quality of production:

$$y_s = a_0 P_s^{a_1} \tag{4}$$

As the number of performances of a particular production is expanded, we would expect eventually to find that attendances at the margin would decline, that is, we would expect $a_1 < 1$.

It should be noted that in some cases the season length may be predetermined and all the resources required for the run may be contracted for in advance, as for example, in the case of most musical programmes involving only a small number of performances. In such a case all factors used by the firm may be regarded as fixed in the short run, and the short-run production function does not exist.

The short-run cost functions of the firm may be derived from (4), assuming constant factor prices. It is reasonable to assume that the aggregate cost of variable factors per performance is constant as the number of performances increases.[3] If the variable costs per performance, aggregated over all variable factors, is denoted by w, then it is easily shown from (4) that:

$$MC_s = w(a_0 a_1)^{-1/a_1} y_s^{(1-a_1)/a_1} \tag{5}$$

$$AVC = w\, a_0^{-1/a_1} y_s^{(1-a_1)/a_1} \tag{6}$$

It is clear that if the exponent in (4) is unity, the firm's marginal cost and average variable cost will be constant at w/a_0, and average total cost will therefore decline with output. If, as hypothesised above, $a_1 < 1$, MC and AVC will be upward sloping as output increases. Nevertheless, if set-up costs are high relative to operating costs, as is commonly the case, average total costs are still likely to decline for a substantial range of output. In the case mentioned above where all factors are fixed in the short run, unit costs will of course decline throughout.

We turn now to the firm's short-run demand function. It may be hypothesised that short-run demand, measured as attendance per performance, is a function of the average price per seat, quality variables, and possibly influences such as advertising, critical reaction, etc. Neglecting the latter factors, we may write:

$$y_s/p_s = f(p_s, Q_s) \tag{7}$$

where $p_s = TR_{bs} / y_s$ = average price paid per seat over the length of run of the production.

Since the cost functions are measured on a total output basis over the full season of the production, we may rewrite (7) for a given season length and quality, assuming a constant elasticity of demand as follows:

$$y_s = c_0\, p_s^{c_1} \tag{8}$$

which implies marginal and average revenue functions as follows (the subscript b again denoting box office receipts):

$$MR_{bs} = (1 + c_1)(c_0 c_1)^{-1} v_s^{1/c_1} \tag{9}$$

$$AR_{bs} = c_0^{-1} y_s^{1/c_1} \tag{10}$$

Of course we expect $c_1 < 0$; that is, we expect performing arts services to be a normal good and hence (10) to be downward sloping.

In fact it may be reasonable to suggest that the demand elasticity varies between groups of actual or potential consumers. Specifically we might hypothesise that demand is relatively price inelastic for established consumers of the performing arts who are knowledgeable about music or drama and whose income levels are such that higher admission prices are not a serious deterrent to attendance. Demand might, on the other hand, be more elastic with respect to price amongst groups of consumers who are less familiar with the performing arts and for whom other forms of entertainment are more significant; for such consumers, admission prices for the performing arts (particularly relative to prices of substitute forms of entertainment) are likely to be more important in determining their demand. If such differentials do in fact exist, and the firm is able to separate these two sub-groups, price discrimination may be possible. A certain amount of price discrimination is in fact already practiced by some firms, for example in the form of student discounts etc.

(c) Long-Run Production, Cost and Revenue Functions

The long run may be regarded as a period over which the number of different productions mounted by the firm can be varied. The capacity of venues may also be varied over this period, either by extensions to existing facilities, or more probably by the use of a variety of venues of different capacities to suit particular productions or programmes or to meet the spatial or temporal demands of consumers (e.g. lunch-time or shopping precinct performances). The time span of the long run thus defined might be conveniently taken as one year; this is also likely to correspond to the firm's accounting period.

The long-run production function may be expressed as follows:

$$y_l = f(P_l, m, K, Q_l) \tag{11}$$

where m = number of separate productions mounted in the period;
K = venue capacity;

and the subscript l refers to the long run as defined above. Again, to accord with traditional theory, we might suggest a Cobb-Douglas form for (11).

Long-run cost functions cannot easily be derived from (11) because of difficulties in maintaining the validity of an assumption that factor prices are constant over time and are in equilibrium. Instead we may specify a total cost function directly as follows:

$$TC_l = f(y_l, Q_l) \tag{12}$$

In this case, the variation in output is caused by variations in season length, number of productions and capacity, as expected from the production function. Hence equation (12) represents a long-run cost function insofar as it is generated from simultaneous expansion in all factors of production. To admit of the possibility of increasing, constant and/or decreasing returns to scale, it is appropriate to specify TC in (12) as a cubic function of output as follows:

$$TC_l = d_0 + d_1 y_l + d_2 y_l^2 + d_3 y_l^3 \tag{13}$$

at a given quality level, where $d_1 > 0, d_2 < 0, d_3 > 0$.

The demand function may be specified in a similar fashion to (7), except that in the long run capacity is also variable. Hence quantity demanded should be measured as attendance per performance expressed as a proportion of available capacity. Borrowing a piece of terminology from the airline industry we may call this measure the 'load factor'[4], L, given as y/PK. The demand function may then be written:

$$L = f(p_l, Q_l) \tag{14}$$

where $p_l = TR_{bl} / y_l$ = average price paid per attendance over all productions in the time period considered. Although a price elasticity of demand should be estimable from (14) by imposing on it, for example, a logarithmic form, it should also be possible to establish average revenue as a function of long-run output by setting up:

$$TR_{bl} = f(y_l, Q_l) \tag{15}$$

and deriving the corresponding AR function from the resulting estimate. For instance the function

$$TR_{bl} = e_0 + e_1 y_l + e_2 y_l^2 \tag{16}$$

for a given quality will clearly yield a linear downward-sloping average revenue function if $e_0 = 0, e_1 > 0, e_2 < 0$.

A model such as this establishes the production and cost structure of the firm, and with reasonable *a priori* expectations about the nature of its parameters, can be used to predict the firm's pricing and output behaviour. The precise relationships involved, and hence specific predictions, must ultimately be determined empirically for particular firms or groups of firms. In the meantime, however, some general observations can be made.

Firstly, consider the short-run case where the length of season is fixed. Short-run average costs are downward sloping, marginal costs are zero and a capacity constraint exists (see Figure 14.1). The model suggests that price will be set so as to maximise attendances subject to average revenue being equal to or greater than average cost. No solution exists if AR is everywhere less than AC, though in this case the firm is still likely to produce (for instance, at the point where MR = 0), and incur short-run losses (Figure 14.1A). If AR exceeds AC at capacity output, the firm will price at this level of AR and enjoy short-run profits (Figure 14.1B). If the AR curve cuts the AC curve from above at a point below the capacity constraint, this point will indicate the optimum price and output combination (Figure 14.1C). Under most expected conditions, this point would involve a lower price and higher output level than the firm would set if it were a profit-maximiser.

Secondly, let us turn to the short-run case where the length of season is not fixed, so that the choice of the constrained maximum output level implies a choice of number of performances, via the production function (4). If AC > AR at all output levels the length of run will be as short as possible and short-run losses will be incurred – some Broadway shows, for example, close after only one or two nights if their reception is so poor that unit costs would be expected to rise rapidly if the season were continued. In general 'successful' productions will be marked by AC < AR up to high levels of output implying long runs, the reverse being true of 'unsuccessful' productions. In some cases, average costs might remain below average revenue indefinitely as output is expanded; in such a situation, either the production will 'run and run' as the jargon has it (for example, Agatha Christie's 'The Mousetrap' in the West End), or, if the season has to be terminated for exogenous reasons (availability of artists, venues, etc.), the management will simply make short-run profits.

In the long run, the model suggests again that in most circumstances, the firm will set lower prices and achieve higher output levels than would a profit-maximising enterprise. Quality considerations, which could be side-stepped in the above short-run discussion, assume a

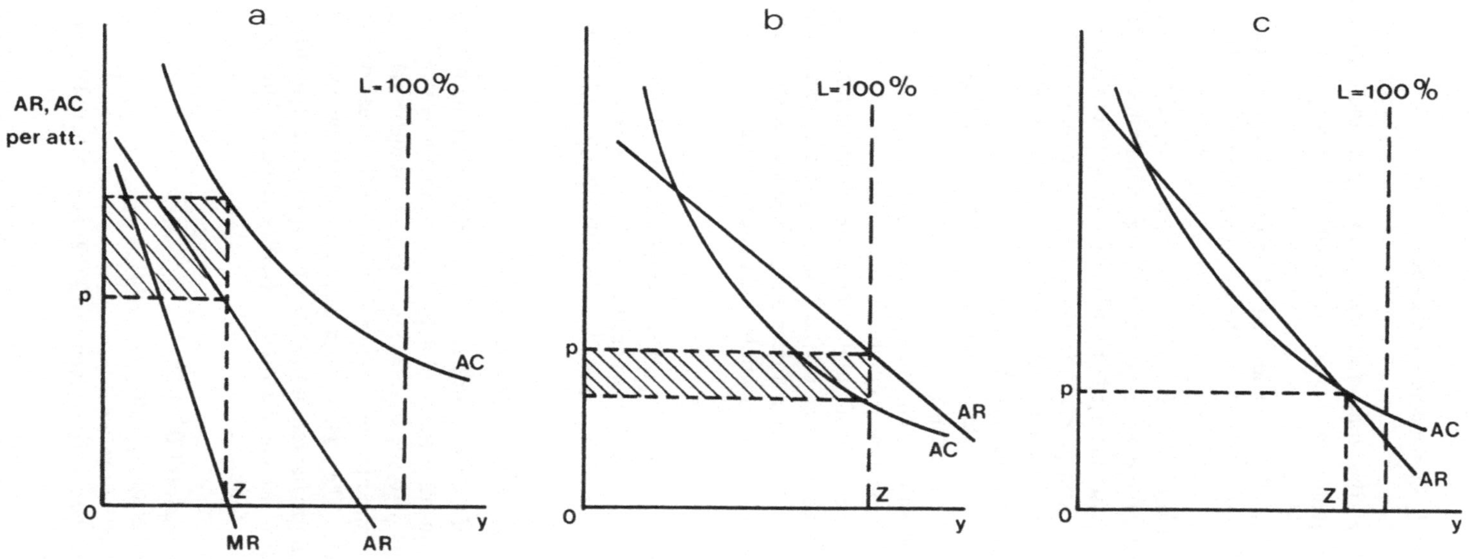

Figure 14.1

Notes: (a) A capacity constraint exists at the aggregate output for which the load factor L = 100%.
(b) The predicted price-output combination in each case is indicated by P,Z.
(c) Shaded areas in Figures 1A and 1B represent short-run losses and profits respectively.

greater importance in the long run. Not only must the direct relationship between quality factors and attendances be considered, a relationship which could as well be negative as positive depending on the interpretation of 'quality', but also the link between quality and costs must be brought into account. In the long term, too, the budget constraint is more significant than in the short run. In the latter situation profits or losses may be willingly accepted by the firm, contrary to the spirit of the basic model, in the anticipation of their being offset by future losses incurred or profits earned by other productions in the firm's long-run programme. Over the long term, however, the firm is under greater pressure to ensure that the net outcome of its operations meets the overall budget constraint.

It should be mentioned finally that we do not discuss here the role of grants in influencing the pricing and output decisions of firms in the performing arts.[5] Depending on whether such grants are paid to consumers as subsidies on ticket purchases or to firms as lump sum payments or subsidies per unit of output, their effects will be reflected in the cost and/or revenue curves of the firm. In general, grants are likely to lead to lower admission prices and, if demand is less than capacity, greater output levels then would otherwise be the case.

Empirical Results

In this section we attempt to quantify some of the relationships postulated above using pooled cross-section and time-series data for Australian firms submitted to the IAC's public enquiry into the performing arts.

(a) Short-run functions

Given our definition of the short run, data are required on an individual production basis to quantify the production, cost and revenue relationships discussed in the previous section. Such data are available relating to local productions mounted by a single firm over a four-year period 1971/2 to 1974/5. The basic data comprise the number of performances of each production in various venues of known capacities, the total paid attendances and the total box-office receipts. The units of measurement are as follows:

y = attendances ('000)
P = number of performances (no.)
K = capacity of venue (no.)
TR_b = total box office revenue ($'000 at constant 1973/4

prices)

The productions covered include straight drama, musicals and concerts, put on in all capital cities of Australia.

In estimating the short-run production function in equation (3), account needs to be taken of the varying capacities of venues in which a particular production is performed. Accordingly, capacity was included as an explanatory variable in (3), and the regression coefficients on log P in the equations reported in Table 14.1 may be interpreted as estimates of the parameter a_1 in equation (4) with the effects of capacity removed. Quality has been handled in this instance by estimating separate equations for different types of production, though it is apparent that there is little difference between them.

Table 14.1: Short-run production functions

Group	Dep. Var.	Explanatory Variables Const.	log P	log K	$\bar{R}^2$	n
Drama + Musicals	log y	−11.0727	1.0552	1.4575	0.8857	62
		(−9.54)	(15.14)	(8.37)		
Concerts	log y	−5.3669	0.9722	0.7359	0.6965	129
		(−7.88)	(14.67)	(8.01)		
Drama + Musicals + Concerts	log y	−6.9286	0.9273	0,9457	0.9077	191
		(−11.59)	(43.23)	(11.75)		

Notes: (a) Logarithms in this and subsequent tables are taken to the base *e*.
(b) Figures in parentheses are *t*-statistics.

The estimated value of a_1 is close to 1 in all cases, contrary to the hypothesis that $a_1 < 1$ as advanced earlier. However, these data do not provide a proper test of this hypothesis, since, for good commercial reasons, no productions appear to have run for long enough for diminishing marginal attendances to appear.

The marginal and average cost equations from (5) and (6) may be quantified if an estimate of w can be made. Looking only at the last equation in Table 14.1, and using data on production costs for this firm submitted to the enquiry, we may isolate the costs per performance which might be reasonably regarded as variable according to the above definitions. The costs of theatre house-staff. direct production costs, and artists' and musicians' fees amount to \$2-3,000 per performance at 1973-4 prices, the range depending on size of cast, whether or not an orchestra is used, etc. The constant term in (4) is calculated for mean capacity as 0.99. Hence we may substitute $w = 2.5$, $a_0 = 1$, $a_1 = 1$ into (5) and (6), to obtain

$$MC = AVC = 2.5 \qquad (17)$$

as our estimates of marginal and average costs.

Total fixed costs as defined above may be roughly estimated from the same data at close to \$100,000 per production, aggregated over all the venues at which a particular production plays, or about \$25,000 on average for a single venue. It is the latter figure which is appropriate to our production function estimates; hence we may combine this with (17) and write:

$$ATC = 2.5 + 25/y \qquad (18)$$

No satisfactory estimates could be made of the demand and revenue function in equations (7) and (10); total box office revenue was found overall to have a strong linear relationship with attendances, indicating constant marginal revenue and an infinitely elastic demand curve. However, some progress was made in testing the hypothesis of a different demand relationship for different types of consumers. The productions mounted by the firm were classified into two categories. In the first group were placed musicals, light drama and pop concerts, whilst the second group comprised serious drama and concerts to classical music. Separate quadratic total revenue functions were estimated for each group (following the argument surrounding equation (16)) with the constant term constrained to zero, as shown in Table 14.2. From these results we derive:

$$\text{Popular:} \quad AR_b = 3.8485 + 0.0030y \qquad (19)$$
$$\text{Serious:} \quad AR_b = 9.0244 - 0.0996y \qquad (20)$$

The demand curve in equation (19) is virtually horizontal, whereas that in (20) is negatively sloped. If we assume that the audiences for these two types of performances are more or less separate, we may conclude that these results lend support to the hypothesis that consumers of

Table 14.2: Short-run revenue functions

Group	Dep. Var.	Explanatory Variables y	y^2	$\bar{R}^2$	n
Popular entertainments	TR	3.8485 (4.00)	0.0030 (1.19)	0.8621	32
Serious drama and music	TR	9.0244 (6.19)	−0.0996 (−3.06)	0.8632	12

serious music and drama are willing to pay higher prices and are less responsive to variations in price than are consumers of more popular entertainments.

Figure 14.2

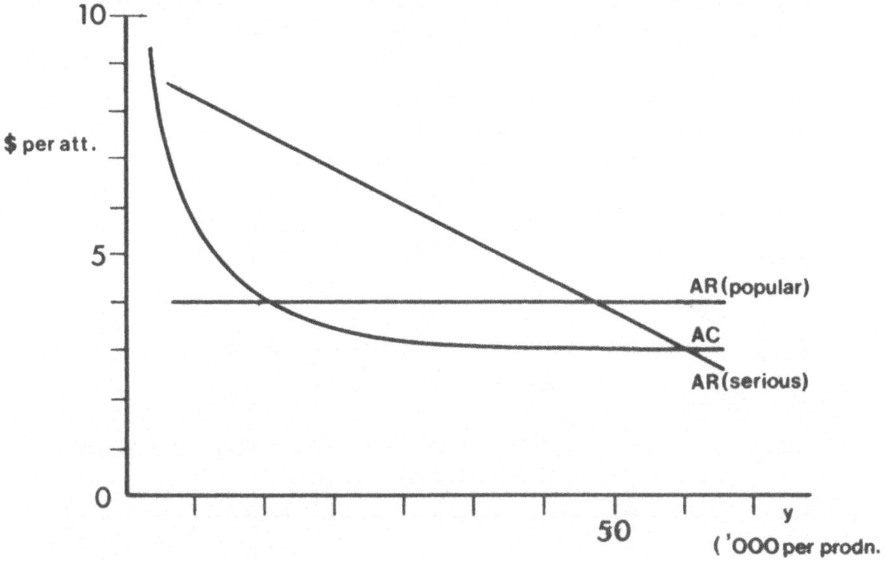

The cost and revenue functions in equations (18) to (20) are graphed in Figure 14.2. In interpreting these results in comparison with Figure 14.1 it must be remembered that they relate to a considerable variety of types of production, the quality differences between which have not been able to be adequately captured in our analysis. The determination of optimal pricing and output strategies by the firm in the case of a specific production depends on the firm's assessment of the cost and revenue relationships expected on the basis of the particular qualitative characteristics of that product.

(b) Long-run functions

Annual data on the operations of performing arts firms covering the period 1971/2 to 1974/5 are brought together to estimate the long-run production, cost and revenue relationships discussed earlier. Attendances and number of performances for each year are available for a wide variety of drama, opera, ballet and music companies operating in many locations of known capacity around Australia. Altogether about 155 observations are available for the estimation of production relationships, although data on the variable m in equation (11) (the number of productions) are not given. Financial data are available only by company, not by separate venues; hence the estimation of cost and revenue relationships had to be carried out from a restricted set of data – about 35 observations for theatre companies and 16 for opera, ballet and music companies combined.

Table 14.3: Long-run production functions

Group	Dep. Var.	Explanatory Variables			$\bar{R}^2$	n
		Const.	log P	log K		
Theatre	log y	−7.2090	1.0681	0.9370	0.9053	79
		(−18.02)	(26.21)	(13.72)		
Opera	log y	−8.0321	1.0830	1.0779	0.9297	45
		(−10.17)	(21.42)	(9.74)		
Ballet	log y	−9.0353	0.9669	1.2644	0.9230	31
		(−7.83)	(13.78)	(7.59)		

The only quality differentiation possible in considering production functions was by art form. Table 14.3 shows estimates of equation (11) for theatre, opera and ballet companies. The sum of elasticities is about 2 for the theatre group and about 2.2 for opera and ballet, indicating markedly increasing returns to the simultaneous expansion of season length and venue capacity.

In estimating the total cost function (13), further allowance was made for quality differences in output. The more significant subsidy is in the revenue structure of a firm, the more costly can be the productions it undertakes. Hence the ratio between grants and box-office revenue was included in (13) as an explanatory variable, with the expectation that the higher this ratio, the greater would be the level of total costs at all levels of output. The results are shown in Table 14.4, where it is apparent that the latter hypothesis is upheld for theatre but not for the opera/ballet/music group.

Table 14.4: Long-run cost functions

Group	Dep. Var.	Explanatory Variables Const.	y	y^2	y^3	TR_g/TR_b	$\bar{R}^2$	n
Theatre	TC	−41.2050	4.5224	−0.0206	0.0001	42.6646	0.8952	34
		(−0.75)	(1.67)	(−0.62)	(1.22)	(2.16)		
Op. + Bal. + Mus.	TC	−108.3859	26.0128	−0.1153	0.0002	5.6950	0.9345	16
		(−0.64)	(1.77)	(−1.07)	(1.13)	(0.33)		

Average cost functions derived from the equations in Table 14.4 are shown below. It is assumed that non-significant coefficients are nevertheless the best estimates of the corresponding true parameters, and may therefore be retained in the long-run average cost functions. The ratio of grants to box-office revenue is taken as 1.5 for the theatre group (i.e. representing companies where subsidy comprises about 60 per cent of total receipts). For the opera group TR_g/TR_b is set at its mean value of 1.76. We have:

Theatre:

$$AC = 4.5224 - 0.0206y + 0.000127y^2 + \frac{6.1416}{y} \tag{21}$$

Op.+Bal.+Mus.:

$$AC = 26.0128 - 0.1153y + 0.00022y^2 - \frac{98.3496}{y} \tag{22}$$

These functions are graphed in Figure 14.3 up to the limits of the sample range in each case.[6] Scale economies are apparent for theatre companies up to an annual attendance of just less than 100 thousand.

In the case of opera/ballet/music companies economies of scale are much more pronounced over a wide range of firm sizes; according to this analysis long-run average costs are not minimised until an annual output of about 260 thousand attendances is reached. The existence of substantial scale economies for opera and ballet emphasises the difficulties posed by the capacity constraint facing large companies using inadequate sized facilities, such as those in the Sydney Opera House.

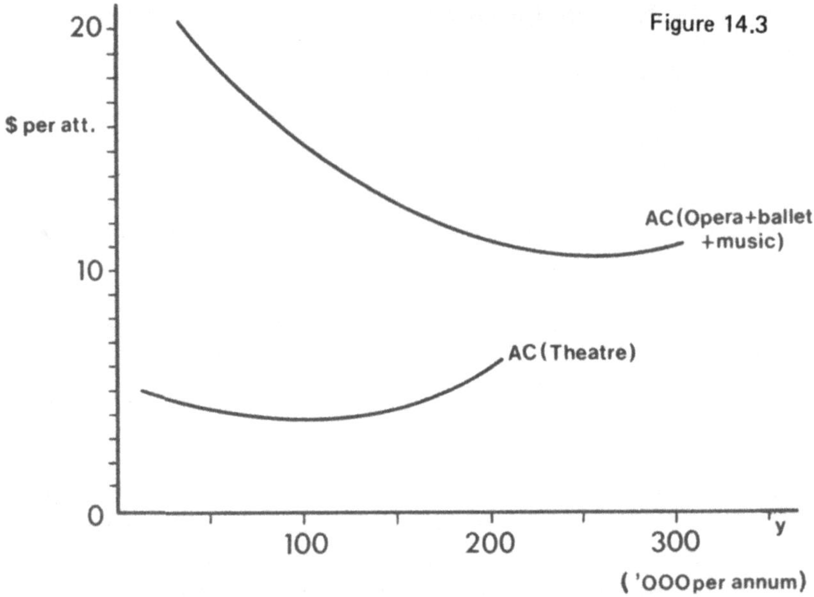

Figure 14.3

The estimation of demand functions presented some difficulties. Demand effects could not be adequately isolated using the approach suggested by equations (15) and (16); however, reasonable estimates were obtained of the model proposed in (14), with total grant revenue used as a proxy for quality along the lines discussed earlier. The results are shown in Table 14.5 for a linear specification of this model. Despite the low overall explanatory power of the theatre equation, we may calculate demand elasticities at the means of the variables from these functions. The price elasticities of demand estimated in this way are found to be –0.31 for theatre and –0.37 for opera/ballet/music. These elasticity estimates are not likely to be as accurate as those obtained from audience studies where, amongst other things, the influences of incomes and substitute prices can be accounted for. Nevertheless, they do confirm the inelasticity of demand with respect to price amongst established audiences which has been noticed elsewhere.[7]

Table 14.5: Long-run demand functions

Group	Dep. Var.	Explanatory Variables			$\bar{R}^2$	n
		Const.	log P	TR_g		
Theatre	L	60.0256	−8.3115	0.0651	0.2237	28
		(7.19)	(−1.98)	(2.74)		
Op. + Bal. + Mus	L	55.1804	−4.0438	0.0408	0.7678	16
		(8.17)	(−3.22)	(7.10)		

Conclusion

In this paper a model of a performing arts firm as a constrained output maximiser has been proposed which leads to certain theoretical predictions about the behaviour of such firms. In quantifying the model with Australian data, we have shown that the production, cost and revenue relationships proposed in the model are broadly consistent with empirical conditions. In particular, a short-run production function implying constant marginal and average variable cost was estimated, with decreasing average total costs resulting from a relatively high level of fixed costs in the short run. In the long-run analysis, production functions indicating substantial scale economies with respect to season length and venue capacity were obtained and these results were largely confirmed by our analysis of costs. As expected, economies of scale were found to be more pronounced for opera, ballet and music firms than for drama companies. On the revenue side, results confirmed the inelasticity of demand with respect to price amongst established consumers of the 'serious' performing arts.

Notes

* Some of the research on which this chapter is based was carried out by the author, in conjunction with Sue Bethune and Glenn Withers, for the Industries Assistance Commission's Inquiry into the Performing Arts (1975-76). The views expressed in this paper are solely those of the author and do not necessarily reflect those of the IAC. The assistance of Kim Sweeny and James Warner is also gratefully acknowledged.

1. As defined in Glenn Withers' chapter in this volume. No adequate data for advertising or promotional expenditure, and its effects on demand and costs,

were available for the industry or firms.

2. Ibid.
3. In the short run an assumption of constant real factor prices is tenable, and the nature of the operation indicates that the input mix will not change over this period; in the long run an assumption of constant real factor prices is more difficult to maintain (see further below).
4. Analogous with 'occupancy rate' as defined for hotels, hospitals, etc.
5. See further in Throsby (1976).
6. The largest aggregate annual attendance in the theatre sample was just over 200 thousand for the Melbourne Theatre Company in both 1973/4 and 1974/5; in the opera/ballet/music group, the largest attendance was almost 340 thousand for the Australian Opera in 1973/4.
7. See further in Withers, op. cit., and in Throsby, op.cit., p.4.

References

Steven Globerman and S.H. Book, 'Statistical Cost Functions for Performing Arts Organisations', *Southern Economic Journal,* vol.40, no.4 (April 1974) pp.668-71.

H.C. Goddard, 'Analysis of Social Production Functions: the Public Library', *Public Finance Quarterly,* vol.1, no.2 (April 1973) pp.191-204.

R.W. Hurd, 'Equilibrium Vacancies in a Labour Market Dominated by Non-profit firms: the "Shortage of Nurses", *Review of Economics and Statistics,* vol.55, no.2 (May 1973) pp.234-40.

M.F. Long, 'Efficient Use of Hospitals' in S.J. Axelrod (ed.), *The Economics of Health and Medical Care* (Ann Arbor, Michigan, 1964) pp.211-26.

Joseph P. Newhouse, 'Toward a Theory of Non-profit Institutions: an Economic Model of a Hospital', *American Economic Review,* vol.60, no.1 (March 1970) pp.64-74.

C.D. Throsby, 'Public Policy and the Performing Arts', *Economic Papers,* No.52 (June 1976) pp.1-15.

Glenn A. Withers, 'The Demand for Performing Arts Services', Chapter 13 of this volume.

FURTHER READING

General

Lewis, Russell, *The New Service Society* (Longman, London, 1973).
Forward, Roy (ed).), *Public Policy in Australia* (Melbourne, Cheshire, 1974).
Hughes, J.T. 'The Service Sector', *Scottish Journal of Political Economy,* vol.21 (1974).
Chez, G.R. and Becker, G.S., *The Allocation of Time and Goods over the Life Cycle,* Human Behaviour and Institutions No.6 New York, NBER(1975).
Haggerty, Patrick E., *The Productive Society* (Colombia University Press, 1974).
Weiss, Thomas, 'Urbanisation and the Growth of the Service Workforce', *Explorations in Economic History,* vol.8 (1971).
Wilson, Paul R., *Australian Social Issues of the 70's* (Butterworths, 1972).
Berg, Stanford V. and Dalton, Thomas R., 'Labour Force Participation in Goods and Services: 1958-1971' *Review of Economics and Statistics,* vol.57 (1975).

Housing Services

Australian Studies:

Bentick, B.L. and Fischer, A.J., 'To have and to hold – some aspects of the economics of urban land subdivision', *Australian Economic Papers* vol.14 (1975).
Bromilow, F.J., 'The Supply of Land for Urban Purposes', *The Developer* (August 1975).
Indicative Planning Council for the Housing Industry, *Report for 1976-7 to 1978-9, Working Papers* (AGPS, Canberra 1976).
Neutze, M., 'The Cost of Housing', *Economic Record,* vol.48 (1972).
Priorities Review Staff, *Report on Housing* (AGPS, Canberra, 1975).

Overseas Studies:

Evans, A.W., *The Economics of Residential Location* (Macmillan, 1973)
de Leeuw, Frank and Ekanen, N.F., 'The Supply of Rental Housing', *American Economic Review* vol.61 (1971).
Muth, Richard, *Cities and Housing* (University of Chicago Press, 1969).
Stegman, M.A., *Housing Investment in the Inner City: The Dynamics of Decline* (MIT Press, 1972).
Stone, P.A., *Urban Development in Britain: Standards Costs and Resources 1964-2004: Vol.1 Population Trends and Housing* (Cambridge University Press, 1970).
Sweeny James, L., 'Housing Unit Maintenance and the Mode of Tenure' *Journal of Economic Theory,* vol.8 (1974).

Defence Services

Australian Studies:

Bellamy, I. and J. Richardson, 'Australian Defence Procurement', in H.G. Gelber

(ed.). *Problems of Australian Defence* (Oxford University Press, Melbourne, 1970).
Brogan, B., 'Economics and Defence', in Max Teichman (ed.), *Aspects of Australian Defence* (Political Studies Association, Monash University, 1966).
Downing, R.I., 'The Cost of Defence' in John Wilkes (ed.), *Australia's Defence and Foreign Policy* (Australian Institute of Political Science, Sydney, 1964).
Edwards, H.R., 'Defence and the Australian Economy', *Economic Papers,* No. 29 (November 1968).
Hunter, A., 'Oil and Defence', in H.G. Gelber (ed.), *Problems of Australian Defence* (Oxford University Press, Melbourne, 1970).
Withers, G.A., 'The Wage Costs of an All-Volunteer Army', *Economic* Record, 48 (September 1972).
——, 'The Welfare Cost of Conscription', *Australian Economic Papers,* 15 (December 1976).
Australian Government, *Australian Defence,* (White Paper), Canberra AGPS, 1976).

Overseas Studies:

Bolton, R.E., *Defense and Disarmament: The Economics of the Transition,* (New Jersey, 1966).
Cooper, R.V.L. (ed.), *Military Manpower Without the Draft,* Proceedings of the RAND Conference on Defense Manpower, Santa Monica (1976).
Hitch, C.J., and R.N. McKean, *Economics of Defence in the Nuclear Age* (Cambridge, Mass., 1967).
Kennedy, G., *The Economics of Defence* (London, 1975).
Peck, M.J., and Scherer, F.M., *The Weapons Acquisition Process: An Economic Analysis* (Boston, 1962).
Weidenbaum, M.L., *The Economics of Peacetime Defense* (New York, 1974).

Crime Prevention Services

Australian Studies:

Bullard, C. and A. Kononewsky, 'Toward a Working Hypothesis for Costing Crime in Australia', unpublished manuscript, Australian Institute of Criminology, (March 1975).
Jacobi, S.N., 'The Economics of Crime', Paper delivered to 47th ANZAAS Congress (Hobart, May 1976).
Rural Bank of NWS, 'The Cost of Crime', *Social Survey* (September 1968).

Overseas Studies:

Becker, G.S., 'Crime and Punishment: An Economic Approach', *Journal of Political Economy,* 76 (March/April 1968).
Becker, G.S. and W.M. Landes (eds.), *Essays in the Economics of Crime and Punishment* (Columbia University Press, New York, 1974).
Carr-Hill, R.A. and N.H. Stern, 'An Econometric Model of the Supply and Control of Recorded Offences in England and Wales'. *Journal of Public Economics,* 2 (November 1973).
Rottenberg, S. (ed.), *The Economics of Crime and Punishment* (American Institute of Public Policy Research, New York, 1973).
Chappell, D. and P. Wilson, *The Australian Criminal Justice System* (Butterworths, Sydney, 1972).

Public Administration and Expenditure

Australian Studies:

Caiden, G.E. *The Commonwealth Bureaucracy* (Melbourne University Melbourne, 1967).

Royal Commission on Australian Government Administration, *Report* and *Appendix Volume 1-4* (AGPS Canberra, 1976).

Spann, R.N. *Public Administration in Australia*, 2nd edn. (Government Printer, Sydney, 1973).

Weller, Patrick and Cutt, James, *Treasury Control in Australia: A Study in Bureaucratic Politics* (Novak, Sydney, 1976).

Overseas Studies:

Baker, R.J.S. *Administrative Theory and Public Administration* (Hutchinson University Library, London, 1972).

Burns, Tom & Stalker, G.M. *The Management of Innovation* (Tavistock, London, 1961).

Diamond, Lord, *Public Expenditure in Practice* (Allen & Unwin, London, 1975).

Downs, Anthony, *Inside Bureaucracy* (Little Brown, Boston, 1966).

Garrett, John, *The Management of Government* (Penguin, Harmondsworth, 1972).

Heclo, Hugh & Wildavsky, Aaron, *The Private Government of Public Money: Community and Policy Inside British Politics* (Macmillan, London, 1974).

Wildavsky, Aaron, *The Politics of the Budgetary Process*, 2nd Edn. (Little Brown, Boston, 1974).

Social Welfare Services

Australian Studies:

Australian Council of Social Service, *ACOSS Report on Accessibility of the Health Services* (Australian Council of Social Service, Sydney 1973).

Benjamin C. & Morton J, *A Model for Welfare Service Planning and Delivery* (Research Report for the Commonwealth Commission of Inquiry into Poverty, Canberra, AGPS, 1975).

Department of Social Security, *Longitudinal Cost-Benefit Survey of Persons Placed in Employment Following Rehabilitation through the Australian Government Rehabilitation Service – A Final Report* (mimeo 1975)..

——, *Rehabilitation Research and Development Digest* (Developments and Special Projects Section, Canberra, 1975 and 1976).

Donald, O.D. *Medical Services in Melbourne: A Geographical Analysis*, Monash Publications in Geography, No.12, (Department of Geograph, Monash University, Melbourne, 1975).

Henderson, R.F., Alison Harcourt and R.J.A. Harper, *People in Poverty: a Melbourne Survey, with supplement* (Melbourne, Cheshire, 1975).

Lawrence, R.J. 'Social Welfare and Urban Growth' in Parker, R.S. and Troy, P.N. (eds.), *The Politics of Urban Growth* (Canberra, ANUP, 1972).

Luntz, H., *Compensation and Rehabilitation* (Butterworths, 1973).

Manning, I., *Municipal Finance & Income Redistribution* (Urban Research Unit, Australian National University, Canberra, 1973).

Troy, P.M., and N.G. Butlin, *The Cost of Collisions* (Melbourne, Cheshire, 1971).

Overseas Studies:

Acton, Jean Paul, 'Non-monetary Factors in the Demand for Medical Services: some Empirical Evidence', *Journal of Political Economy,* vol.83, 1975).

Aday, L.V. 'Economic and Non-Economic Barriers to the Use of Needed Medical Services', *Medical Care,* vol.13, (1975).

Bradshaw, J. 'The Concept of Social Need', *New Society,* vol.19, (1972).

Buttimer, A. 'Spatial Organisation of Health and Welfare Facilities' in Forbes, J. (Ed.), *Studies in Social Science and Planning* (Scottish Academic Press, Edinburgh, 1974).

Conley, Ronald W., *The Economics of Mental Retardation* (Johns Hopkins University Press, London, 1973).

Donabedian, A., 'Models for Organizing the Delivery of Personal Health Services and Criteria for Evaluating Them', *Milbank Memorial Fund Quarterly,* vol.50, Part 2 (1972).

Gross, P.E., 'Urban Health Disorders, Spatial Analysis and Economics of Health Family Location', *International Journal of Health Services,* vol.2 (1972).

Margolis, J., 'The Demand for Urban Public Services' in Perloff, H.S., and Wingo, L. (eds.), *Issues in Urban Economics,* (John Hopkins Press, Baltimore, 1968).

Newman, E., and Demone, H.W., 'Policy Paper: Public Planning for Human Services', *Journal of Health and Social Behaviour,* vol.10 (1969).

Salter, H.C., 'Public Expenditures and the Health and Welfare Services' in Hanser, M.M. (ed.), *The Economics of Medical Care* (Allen and Unwin, London, 1972).

Recreation Services

Australian Studies

Braham Dabscheck, 'The Wage Determination Process for Sportmen', *Economic Record,* vol.51 (1975).

Department of Tourism and Recreation, *Leisure – a new perspective,* (AGPS Canberra, 1975).

V. Ramasamy and J.A. Sinden, 'Allocation of Time to Leisure and to Leisure Activities', *Economic Analysis and Policy,* vol.6 (1975).

R.L. Ranken and J.A. Sinden, 'Causal Factors in the Demand for Outdoor Recreation', *Economic Record,* vol.47 (1971).

R.A. Williams, 'Changes in Trading Hours: Ten O'Clock Closing and Consumption of Alcohol in Victoria', *Economic Record,* vol.48 (1972).

Overseas Studies:

Jack Dowie, 'On the Efficiency and Equity of Betting Markets', *Economica,* vol.43 (1976).

W.C. Neale, 'The Peculiar Economics of Professional Sports: A Contribution to the Theory of the Firm in Sporting Competition and in Market Competition', *Quarterly Journal of Economics,* vol.48 (1974).

J.A. Sinden, 'A Utility Approach to the Valuation of Recreational and Aesthetic Experiences', *American Journal of Agriculture Economics,* vol.56 (1974).

P.J. Sloane, 'The Economics of Professional Football: The Football Club as a Utility Maximiser', *Scottish Journal of Political Economy,* vol.18 (1971).

R.W. Vickerman, *The Economics of Leisure and Recreation,* (Macmillan, London, 1975).

INDEX